SYMBOLIC COMPUTATION

Artificial Intelligence

Springer Series
SYMBOLIC COMPUTATION – *Artificial Intelligence*

N.J. Nilsson: Principles of Artificial Intelligence. XV, 476 pages, 139 figs., 1982.

J.H. Siekmann, G. Wrightson (Eds): Automation of Reasoning 1. Classical Papers on Computational Logic 1957–1966. XXII, 525 pages, 1983.

J.H. Siekmann, G. Wrightson (Eds): Automation of Reasoning 2. Classical Papers on Computational Logic 1967–1970. XXII, 638 pages, 1983.

L. Bolc (Ed.): The Design of Interpreters, Compilers, and Editors for Augmented Transition Networks. XI, 214 pages, 72 figs., 1983.

R.S. Michalski, J.G. Carbonell, T.M. Mitchell (Eds.): Machine Learning. An Artificial Intelligence Approach. 572 pages, 1984.

L. Bolc (Ed.): Natural Language Communication with Pictorial Information Systems. VII, 327 pages, 67 figs., 1984.

J.W. Lloyd: Foundations of Logic Programming. X, 124 pages, 1984.

A. Bundy (Ed.): Catalogue of Artificial Intelligence Tools. XXV, 150 pages, 1984. Second, revised edition, IV, 168 pages, 1986.

M.M. Botvinnik: Computers in Chess. Solving Inexact Problems. With contributions by A.I. Reznitsky, B.M. Stilman, M.A. Tsfasman, A.D. Yudin. Translated from the Russian by A.A. Brown. XIV, 158 pages, 48 figs., 1984.

C. Blume, W. Jakob: Programming Languages for Industrial Robots. XIII, 376 pages, 145 figs., 1986.

L. Bolc (Ed.): Natural Language Parsing Systems. XVIII, 367 pages, 155 figs., 1987.

L. Bolc (Ed.): Computational Models of Learning. IX, 208 pages, 34 figs., 1987.

N. Cercone, G. McCalla (Eds.): The Knowledge Frontier. Essays in the Representation of Knowledge. 552 pages, 93 figs., 1987.

G. Rayna: REDUCE. Software for Algebraic Computation. 344 pages, 1987.

D. McDonald, L. Bolc (Eds.): Natural Language Generation Systems. 400 pages, 84 figs., 1988.

David D. McDonald   Leonard Bolc
Editors

Natural Language
Generation Systems

With 84 Illustrations

Springer-Verlag
New York Berlin Heidelberg
London Paris Tokyo

David D. McDonald
Brattle Research Corporation
Cambridge, MA 02138
USA

Leonard Bolc
Institute of Informatics, Warsaw
Warsaw University
PKin, pok. 850
PL.00.901 Warszawa
Poland

Library of Congress Cataloging-in-Publication Data
Natural language generation systems.
   (Symbolic computation. Artificial intelligence)
   Includes bibliographies.
   1. Linguistics—Data processing. I. McDonald,
David D. II. Bolc, Leonard. III. Series.
P98.N295 1988   410'.28'5   87-35649

Camera-ready copy provided by the authors.
Printed and bound by R.R. Donnelley & Sons, Harrisonburg, Virginia.
Printed in the United States of America.

9 8 7 6 5 4 3 2 1

ISBN 0-387-96691-9 Springer-Verlag New York Berlin Heidelberg
ISBN 3-540-96691-9 Springer-Verlag Berlin Heidelberg New York

Contents

Introduction

There was a time when nearly every paper on generation started out by saying that "research into natural language generation by computers is in its infancy." That time is not all that far behind us, and there is not much awareness in the community at large of what generation really is as a field: What are its issues? What has been accomplished? The ten papers of this book are a step towards changing this.

The purpose of this collection has been to give its authors an opportunity to present their work at much greater length than is available in the usual conference paper or journal article. As a result, these papers contain details of grammatical treatments and processing details seldom seen outside of book length monographs. Their topics range from discourse theory, through mechanical translation, to deliberate writing and revision. The authors are also wide ranging internationally, with contributions from Japan, West Germany, and Austria as well as the United States.

Natural language generation, as a field, is part of artificial intelligence. It is not concerned simply with making computers able to print out fluent texts – that is better done today with simple techniques based on pre-stored text and uncomplicated substitutions. Instead, it looks ahead to the time when machines will think complex thoughts and need to communicate them to their human users in a natural way (natural, at least, for the people who use them). As an engineering matter then, generation systems supply the sophisticated knowledge about natural languages that must come into play when one needs to use wordings that will overpower techniques based only on symbolic string manipulation techniques: intricate patterns of tense and modality, clauses embedded inside complex verbs like *believe* or *persuade*, complex adjuncts, extended texts that use pronouns and other reduced forms, and so on. Many of these phenomena can be coped with by special case techniques for a single application; but when a system needs to express the same idea from multiple perspectives, or to present it to people with varying backgrounds or goals, a full-fledged generation system, with its grammar and planning components, must be used.

But like much of artificial intelligence research generally, research on generation is often aimed at purely scientific concerns about the nature of language and language use in people. As such, it is an unusual cognitive science, since its methods are "synthetic" rather than "analytical." In AI studies of generation, one experiments by constructing artifacts—computer programs, observing their behavior, and comparing it to the behavior of the natural system under study. This approach has both strengths and weaknesses. Since the computer is the premier medium for the definition and modeling of processes, we can be much more concrete than other disciplines in modeling psychological phenomena as interacting processes. We also have a safeguard on the internal coherence of our theories that many other disciplines lack since we are forced to have complete, executable, models before our computer programs will run.

At the same time, however, there is the weakness that we are continually taking a leap into the unknown: In order to give our programs something interesting to work from we are forced to speculate about the nature of thought and intention—the underpinnings of language, and must set our speculations down in a usable notation. In this respect our problems in generation are quite different from those of our sister area in AI, natural language understanding, a difference that is worth looking at.

When the task is understanding language it is very clear what one is starting from. Utterances are directly observable, and there is a great body of careful experimental data from psychology that we can draw on that has characterized the behavioral characteristics of at least the surface levels of the understanding process. Note the hedge, "surface levels," however. Today a person working on understanding is often seen to make a contribution just by developing a better parser and stopping with a structural description of a text's syntax. Yet in generation a processing theory that started at as "late" a stage as a structural description would be considered to have missed the point. In generation one has to come to grips with a deeper set of questions or one will not be doing serious work. For instance: How does the form of the conceptual representation that the process starts with effect the final text and the intermediate processing? Why will one text be effective and another not be, even though they are very similar in form? And of course the deepest question: How do we achieve our goals through the use of language? Just as AI research on generation must venture into the unknown to posit the representational structures from which its process starts, understanding research must ultimately do the same to determine the representation of "meaning" with which it presumably must end. It is only because it has been acceptable to stop at an earlier point that people ever imagine understanding research to be on any firmer ground.

The first paper in this volume, by Richard Gabriel, addresses the problem of what Gabriel calls "deliberate writing": writing that is "careful and considered" in contrast with what can happen with spontaneous writing or speech. This task may well be the ultimate problem for artificial intelligence, since it requires the strongest imaginable capabilities in planning, knowledge representation, problem solving, world and person modeling, creativity, and judgement. Gabriel talks about the qualities of good writing, and of an author's relation to it as originator and reader/reviewer. He lays out the structure and the theory behind his program, YH, which talks about the algorithms of simple lisp programs. He emphasises generation as planning, and the revision of plans as an incremental process driven by critics. The text YH produces (simple descriptions) is strikingly natural, so much so that the major example has been inserted transparently into the body of the article and it will be an unusual reader who notices it before they are told.

Generation has always been concerned with the "discourse structure" that lies above the individual sentences in isolation that so much of linguistics has focused on in the past. William Mann, along with his colleague Sandra Thompson, has for some time been developing what they call "Rhetorical Structure Theory." RST is a structural account of the nature of discourse, characterizing the kind of units that can make up an extended text and the relationships between them. At the same time, RST is a functional theory, with structural units characterized according to the role they play in the forwarding of a speaker's goals. In his paper for this volume, Mann contrasts RST with the other strong treatment of extended texts (specifically paragraph-length monologues) that has been put forward, Kathleen McKeown's "schemas."

Doug Appelt's paper, reprinted from the journal Artificial Intelligence, is the summary of his 1981 dissertation. It presents a logical formalization of the fundamental notions underlying planning to communicate: goals, intentions, actions to recruit a listener's aid, actions to indicate a reference, and so on. This formalization is then used to drive a non-linear, critic-based planner, KAMP, to produce complex sentences that are tailored to what the listener does and doesn't know. KAMP can plan physical actions (e.g., pointing) in coordination with its references, and has a model of how to achieve multiple goals with a single action.

Stephan Busemann's SUTRA system is the subject of the next paper. Working in German, SUTRA is designed as a reusable module that works within a larger generation system. Not specific to any one domain, it has syntactic knowledge of constituent placement and multi-clause structure, and morphological knowledge of case and inflection. As a module, SUTRA is driven from a "verbalized structure" that encodes lexical and case-frame information determined by an earlier verbalization phase within some companion module. SUTRA was originally developed as part of the HAM-ANS system, but has since been widely used in German generation efforts. Its strengths lie in a system of transformations that introduce fluency and naturalness into the form of the surface text without burdening the meaning-centered, earlier generation phases.

VIE-GEN, by Ernst Buchberger and Helmut Horacek, is also a German system. It is the output "half" of the system VIE-LANG developed at the University of Vienna, and shows this through a concern for representing its linguistic (particularly lexical) knowledge in a way that allows it to be used for both parsing and generation. VIE-GEN starts with information given in a structured inheritance network of semantic primitives, and works in two phases: verbalization and realization. Words are determined by using discrimination networks to notice the particular relationships between units, and an intermediate representation containing word roots and unordered, case-marked constituents mediates between the phases. The system has the capacity to form paraphrasing references as a variation on using a pronoun, determines the breakdown of a text into individual sentences deliberately, and has an extensive set of transformations.

Our third paper centered on the German language, by Heinz-Dirk Luckardt, discusses generation as part of mechanical translation. In this particular design, part of the Saarbrucken SUSY translation system, the generator is given the bulk of the responsibility for language specific knowledge and operations. Generation is directed by a language-neutral interlingua structure (used as part of the EUROTRA european MT project), which is essentially a deep syntactic structure. The generation procedure is identical for all target languages, with specific linguistic facts introduced by parameters. Luckardt discusses the differences in issues and focus between generation in AI and in MT, and provides an extensive discussion of the theoretical issues surrounding analyses based on case. The system uses a dependency grammar and a body of local mapping rules that are sensitive to a small set of simple semantic features.

The system developed by Shun Ishizaki and described in the next paper could in some sense be regarded as an MT system, since it is generating stories whose content is given by parsing English originals. However, it is working from a completely conceptual representation, the first generator of Japanese to do so. Ishizaki has dealt with a number of features in the Japanese language that have no direct counter-parts in English, the language most explored in generation; these include empty subjects marked by particles, strict temporal ordering of events with coordinated tenses, head-final ordering within phrases, and omission of NPs that are modified by subject-relative clauses. The source representation is conceptual dependency with MOPs and causal chains organizing larger-scale events.

Karen Kukich's system ANA produces exceptionally facile, paragraph-length summaries of the day's stock activity on Wall Street; its output is not noticeably different from what a human news commentator would say. ANA handles the entire generation process and the conceptualizations underlying it, to the point of starting from the raw statistics of the day's stock transactions, noticing their patterns, and determining the appropriate conventional phrases for describing them. Architecturally, the system consists of a set of production rules that organize a large phrasal lexicon. Kukich always works with large phrasal units, never assembling NPs or PPs from smaller concepts, and includes an extensive discussion of this notion of a "clause-combining," rather than "sentence building" grammar. The name of the system, ANA, comes from the psychological term "anacoluthia," which is the phenomena of starting an utterance with a phrase that establishes a syntactic context that can only be finished in a certain way, only to be unable to complete the utterance because one cannot come up with a continuing phrase of the right kind; the system exhibited this behavior early on when its lexicon was incomplete.

Paul Jacob's PHRED, like ANA, is also a system centered on the use of pre-formed, productive phrases. PHRED was developed at Berkeley as part of the Unix Consultant System, and designed in such a way that its knowledge of the language could be directly shared with the parsing system PHRAN. Jacobs breaks down the generation process into a sequence of "fetching," "restricting," and "interpreting" stages, whereby phrases are first noticed as applicable, then specialized to the particulars of the concepts involved, and finally read out as a text. Much of the effort in the design of PHRED went into how to enable the fetching stage to take into account context and intention. The pattern language for defining and manipulating phrases is presented at length, as are the particulars of the three stages, and a long example of the system in operation is included. Swapping the sets of phrases allows PHRED to generate in languages other than English as shown with an example from Spanish.

Hovy's paper, the last in this volume, focuses on the form that a generator's linguistic knowledge should take. Applying a generation perspective to the customary breakdown into morphology, syntax, lexicon, and semantics, Hovy finds no sharp demarcations between them. He argues instead for a characterization along functional lines according to how the knowledge is perceived by the generator as it tries to determine how some set of concepts is to be realized as a text, a process he takes to be broken down into three kinds of operations: "inclusion," "ordering," and "casting." Hovy presents a model where all linguistic knowledge, grammatical and lexical, is formalized as variations on the common notion of "phrases" that have been frozen (fixed in form and noncompositional in meaning) to a greater or lesser degree. This uniform system of linguistic resources is formalized as a set of specialist procedures, which determine the applicability of each phrase in context.

David D. McDonald

Deliberate Writing

Richard P. Gabriel

1. Introduction

Deliberate writing: When I sit down to write several paragraphs of English text for an audience which I cannot see and which cannot ask me questions, and if I care that the audience understands me perfectly the first time, I am engaged in 'deliberate writing.' Such writing is careful and considered, and for a computer to write deliberately many of the outstanding problems of artificial intelligence must be solved, at least partially.

I want to contrast deliberate writing with spontaneous writing and with speech. For the remainder of this presentation I will use the term 'writing' to refer to deliberate writing, and I will use the term 'speech' to refer to both casual writing and speech.

2. Vivid and Continuous Images

Whether you are writing fiction or non-fiction, good and careful writing has two important qualities: it must be *vivid* and it must be *continuous*. I have borrowed these terms from John Gardner [Gardner 1984], who wrote of them in the context of fiction writing, but I think they are appropriate in non-fiction writing as well.

In a vivid piece of writing the mental images that the writer presents are clear and unambiguous; what the writer writes about should appear in our 'mental dream' exactly as if we ourselves were thinking the thoughts he is describing. When the writing produces this clear image we can absorb what he writes with little effort.

In a continuous piece of writing there are no gaps or jumps from one topic to another. The image that is produced by the writing does not skip around. In non-fiction, especially in technical writing, the problems and questions we have about the subject are answered as soon as we formulate them in our minds. That is, as we read a piece of technical writing we are constantly imagining the details of the subject matter. Sometimes our image is confused because we are not sure how some newly presented detail fits in, or we are uncertain of the best consistent interpretation. At this point the writer is obligated to jump in and settle the matter or provide a clarification. This way we do not have to stop and think, or go back to re-read a passage or some passages.

Insofar as our image must be vivid, it must also be continuous. If our image is discontinuous it cannot be vivid—it is blurred or muddy at the point of discontinuity. Similarly, if our image is not vivid it must be discontinuous—we are apt to stop and wonder about the source of blurriness, and at that point our image stops being continuous.

3. Computers and Writing

I believe that writing is the ultimate problem for artificial intelligence research. Among the problems that must be solved for a computer to write well are: problem-solving, knowledge representation, language understanding, world-modeling, human-modeling, creativity, sensitivity, and judgment.

Problem-solving is important because some aspects of writing require the writer to place in a linear order facts or other statements which describe an object or an action that is inherently 'multi-dimensional.' The order of the facts and the techniques that prevent reader-worry about yet-unpresented facts is as difficult a planning task as any robot planning problem.

Knowledge representation is important for being able to find and refer to facts about a topic rapidly and accurately. The interconnections in the writer's mind between facts must be such that connections that the reader will see are apparent to the writer. If a detailed and complex search must be undertaken by the writer to discover relevant connections, it may be that they will be missed, and the vivid and continuous image will be lost.

Language understanding is important because a human writer will re-read his writing in order to test its effectiveness. Later in this presentation I will talk about this more thoroughly and speculatively.

World-modeling is important because a writer must understand the consequences of his statements; if he talks about some aspect of the world or chooses to use a metaphor or an analogy, he must think carefully whether the correspondence between his subject and the metaphor or analogy is accurate, and whether consequences of his metaphorical or analogical situation are impossible or ridiculous.

Creativity, sensitivity, and judgment fall into the category of things that artificial intelligence has never really looked at seriously. To write with good taste, and, hence, effectively, requires the writer to write in new and interesting ways, to be sensitive to the sore spots that his reader might have, and to judge what is important and useful for his readers.

4. Aspects of Good Non-Fiction Writing

If I expect you to understand my non-fiction writing without problems, I must do two things: I must anticipate what you know about the topic of discussion, and I must anticipate the problems you will have comprehending how my sentences and paragraphs are constructed. As you read from left-to-right, every word must fit in properly; you must never be forced to re-read parts already seen, and you must never have to reflect on my sentences. The text must be transparent.

These two aspects form the ends of a spectrum of concerns that a writer who cares about good writing must consider each time he writes. At one end is the correct decision about what is shared information, and at the other end is the effortless transmission of new information and relationships between facts. I will illustrate these two aspects with an example.

Consider writing the directions on how to get from one place to another in a car. When I tell you how to get to my house, I must know how much you know about the area; I must be certain you know where the Locust Street Eisner's is. If you do not live in the area, then perhaps the specific landmarks I use will be impossible for you to recognize. But if you do live in the area, I can use phrases like, "go to the stadium on Welch Road, and then...." In short, I must carefully reason about what shared information we have about the area and also about what information you will learn while you are traveling through the area following my directions.

If I have tried to explain the directions to you in the past, then I can refer to that conversation or to that document. In short, there can be some common context and shared information about my explanation. My writing of the directions to you must accurately refer to the knowledge I am sure you have. If I refer to something that you don't know or to something that you could find out with some difficulty as if it were something you knew, then my directions would be bad.

At the other end of the spectrum, I must anticipate where along the trip you will become uncertain that you are on the right track. If there is a long stretch of road to traverse after several tricky turns, I must tell you sights that will alert you that all is well. If I say to turn right at the third stop sign, and it is behind a bush, I must warn you of that, or else you will likely have to re-do that part of the trip.

My directions will not be less accurate for this extra information, but this information will help make them better directions.

If you are not certain that you understand my directions, then you will perhaps become confused and begin to doubt that landmarks that you see correspond to landmarks I describe in my directions. You will think, "would he describe this tree like that?" or "could this red house be the pink one to which he refers; his directions are so confused that maybe he's simply being sloppy here?"

If my decisions about what is shared information are bad enough, then you—the reader—will find that my writing is difficult to read; you will try to find the correct reading of the text that makes it all clear. And, if my text is simply confusing, then you will wonder whether we agree on the facts; you will think that, if you could only know what I—the writer—knew, then the text would become crystal clear.

5. Pragmatics of Good Non-Fiction Writing

There are many ways that shared information comes into play in good non-fiction writing. Obviously facts that I assume that the reader knows ought to be facts actually known to the reader. If the facts I assume the reader knows are not clear to the reader—if they are difficult concepts, or

if the implications of the facts as they bear on my discussion are difficult
to grasp—then it is my obligation as a writer to make the facts clear, even
if that requires repetition and tutoring.

My text may introduce information that is crucial to understanding
the rest of the piece. Not only must I carefully present that material, but
in my subsequent references to it I must be sensitive to the fact that the
information was recently learned—perhaps it was forgotten or even skipped
over. I should never treat information that I have introduced the same way
that I treat assumed facts. For one thing, if I treat the information I have
introduced exactly as the information I assume the reader has known for
a while, then the reader may believe that I am talking over his head by
falsely assuming his knowledge is greater than it actually is; and maybe the
reader skimmed the presentation of the new material and doesn't realize
that the later, confusing reference to it is a reference to new and not old
information.

It is often helpful for the reader if the writer, when he refers to possibly
puzzling information, refers to the information in a clarifying way. If every
reference adds to the comfort the reader has about the material, the new
material will be better understood.

The writer has an obligation to the reader: The reader chooses to read
the piece. It is rarely the case that a reader is truly forced into reading a
piece of writing from beginning to end. The writer's obligation is to make
the reader's task easy enough that the reader will want to read the entire
piece.

6. The Language of Good Non-Fiction Writing

Beyond what I assume my reader to know, and beyond what I tell him,
there are the actual words, phrases, sentences, and paragraphs with which I
choose to pass that information to him. In bad writing the 'mental dream'
is interrupted or chafed by some mistake or conscious ploy of the writer.
Whenever a reader is forced to think about the writing, the words, the
sentence structure, or the paragraph structure, or whenever the reader has
to re-read a section of writing to understand how the words relate to each
other, it is at this point that the transfer of information from the writer to
the reader is stopped, and the dream that accompanies this transfer dies.

The dream must be re-established, and this can take extra time that could be better spent continuing a line of thought.

A second effect of such bad writing is that if a sentence has incorrect syntax, or if it is clumsy and difficult to understand, then the reader is justified in losing respect for the writer, in questioning the intelligence of the writer and his judgment, and in lowering his estimate of the importance, significance, and correctness of the entire piece of writing.

Finally, all non-fiction, and especially technical writing, requires examples and concrete details to be understandable. When we write about a computer program, we probably have thought about that program for a long time, and we have internalized its characteristics to help our own mental processes. When the reader reads our description of it, he wants to build a mental image of the program and its operation, and we hope that his mental image is similar to ours. Without specific details the reader cannot imagine the program accurately, and it is even possible that his image is inconsistent with ours. In this case, the reader will have to adjust to the newer image once he discovers the discrepancy, if he ever discovers it.

6.1 *Common Errors*

There are many common writing errors that occur; these errors render writing difficult to read with respect to the aspects mentioned earlier. The most common errors that a writer makes are errors of the basic skills of writing. I will briefly catalogue some of these errors.

Many writers excessively use the passive voice. In using the passive voice, the agent of the action is either placed at the end of the sentence ("His finger was bitten by the parrot") or else it is left out altogether ("His finger was bitten"). Perhaps the writer intends to focus the reader's attention on the injury, but the natural tendency of the reader is to imagine this action, agent and all. But if the agent is missing or introduced at the end of the sentence, the image is hazy or it is wrong; a second attempt at the image must be made by the reader, and that is when the distraction away from the dream occurs.

Beginning a sentence with an infinite-verb phrase is often a mistake; either the reader can have trouble understanding the time relationships between the elements of the sentence or else he may have difficulty understanding the logic of the statement. For example, in "taking an interrupt, the program executes the terminal handler," there may be some question about whether taking an interrupt happens concurrently with the program's executing the terminal handler or whether one event causes the other to occur. In "rapidly switching contexts, the scheduler carefully considers the next job request," there is a hint of illogicalness because 'rapidly' and 'carefully' are dissonant. The reader will pause over this statement, even if it is ultimately understandable.

Problems with diction are common. Diction refers to the choice of words and the appropriateness of that choice. Diction is the hallmark of many styles of writing. 'High diction' refers to high-brow, intellectual, or even snobbish writing. I have heard some people say that scholastic writing should not be fun to read. This reflects their attitude about the proper diction for scholastic writing. The main problems people have with diction are deciding on the proper tone for their writing task and in then sticking consistently to that tone. The sentence "the essential ingredient of an efficient topological sorting procedure is a fine set of cute hacks and clever bums" shows an inconsistent level of diction—scientific and refined at the start and casual or computer-gutter at the end. Either level of diction may be fine within a specific context, but to mix them in this way is unforgivable.

Sentence variety is important because when the sentences of the same type are strung together, the result is boredom and a lessening of the dream that keeps readers reading and understanding. Anticlimactic sentences—sentences with relative clauses at the end—can be distracting because they seem to taper off rather than getting to some point.

Unintentional rhymes and rhythms can also be distracting by causing the reader to stop absorbing the content of the writing and to focus on the writing itself. No reader of a serious paper on garbage collection would pass over this sentence without a chuckle: "Collecting spare records and gaining some space happens quite regularly and at quite a high pace."

Similarly, unintentional puns can be a problem. "The input/output bottleneck was broken by adding a separate DMA channel" contains such a pun. When the reader sees a pun or thinks of an interpretation of a sentence that is humorous, the writer is in trouble: The reader has lost the mental dream and is thinking about the pun.

Explaining events out of their natural order is a serious error: The reader must stop reading and piece together the actual sequence. This error is at the border of the language errors and the pragmatic errors, but it shares the theme of all of these errors: The reader must abandon his dream and concentrate on the writing.

6.2 *Writing and Manners*

Good writing is an act of communication between a writer and an unseen reader. Good writing is a courtesy that is expected by the reader, and if a reader puts my paper away because he cannot handle the writing, I have failed my duty to that reader. Similarly, I have no respect for a writer, regardless of his professional stature, if he will not take the time to think carefully about how he presents his work and results to me.

7. Writing Well

How can you write well? The key is to use yourself as a model of your audience. The reader does not know as much about the topic you are presenting as you do. To understand what people know you must be able to forget things you know. This forgetfulness is reasoned: You carefully reason about what you know that is not common knowledge. Then you use this reduced knowledge to see what in your text is unclear because it requires the knowledge you have that your reader may not have.

And you must be able to forget the structure of your text, so that as you read it you can successfully be a model of a reader coming upon your text afresh. One way to do this is to put time between you, the writer, and you, the later reader.

As we read, each new word causes us to move forward in parsing the text—we must understand the relationships between words in order to piece together the picture that the writer is presenting. It is possible to carefully choose words so that the reader can progress along an obstacle-free path through the words. Word choice is done when the first draft is being written and also during revisions.

You could accomplish this by reasoning about where parsing choices (and confusions) can arise and by picking words that tend to guide the reader one way over others. Sometimes it isn't possible to eliminate problems for the reader with such local choices, and global re-planning is necessary: You may have to rewrite an entire paragraph to avoid confusion in one part of a sentence.

8. Computer Writing

But I want to talk about computers doing deliberate writing. The above cautions are only a small fraction of the advice that could be given to human writers: What of computer writers? A program that writes deliberately must be able to plan and re-plan, to debug errors and inconveniences, to reason about knowledge, and to understand itself well enough to reason about why it makes certain decisions.

Writing well is difficult for a person to do, and it is also very difficult for a computer to do. As we have seen, there is an intimate relationship between the writer and his reader, although these two individuals may be separated by many miles and years.

A computer that has such a relationship with a reader is difficult to achieve. Because the writer has to share a common background with a reader (at some level) to be a successful writer, the computer must have this common background built in by the author of its writing programs. Artificial intelligence has a range of techniques for reasoning about shared knowledge and, to some degree, about plausible inferences from that knowledge.

However, the careful writer also is able to reason about the problems that the reader will have in parsing his writing. The writer is able to use himself as a model reader, after he has put his writing aside for a time. The computer cannot do this as easily, because there is no conception of 'forgetting' in current artificial intelligence paradigms, nor is there an easy way to use a natural language parser to find out where the parser has trouble with a sentence and how to correct the difficulty.

Nevertheless, there are programs that can write. I have written such a program, called *Yh*. Yh is a program that writes text, and it is one of the first attempts at a deliberate writing program. The texts it produces are explanations of the operation of simple programs. These programs have been synthesized from a description of an algorithm provided by a person during a conversation with an automatic programming system—in this case the PSI system [Green 1980].

To accomplish the writing behavior I described earlier, this program generates text from left-to-right, making locally good decisions at each step. As the generation proceeds, other parts of the program observe the generation process, and, because these parts of the program are able to make connections between distant parts of the text, they are able to criticize the result.

In other words, after the initial version of the text has been produced, further reasoning about the global nature of the choices is performed, the text is transformed, and complex sentence structure is introduced or eliminated.

There are several mechanisms in Yh designed to produce clear writing, but these mechanisms require detailed and extensive knowledge both about writing and about the subject matter of the writing to be effective. Yh has only a small amount of knowledge, but, even with this limited depth of knowledge, Yh has generated a great deal of text of good quality. However, Yh does not write uniformly well; as more knowledge is added or existing knowledge is refined, the quality of its writing will improve.

9. Background

In this section I will explain some of the philosophy behind the design of Yh. Yh is a fairly large program and has a complex control structure. Because the behavior of Yh is dependent on this structure and complexity, and because the structure and complexity are a result of this philosophy, I think it is important to spend a little time understanding it.

9.1 *How to Make Computers Write*

Researchers in artificial intelligence have been theorizing for many years about the mechanisms necessary for intelligent behavior in restricted domains, especially domains that are the realm of specialists and not laymen. One hope is that a uniform structure among these mechanisms will emerge and that this uniform structure will generalize into something which can perform a wide range of tasks.

The effect of this generalization, it is hoped, would be the creation— theoretical or actual—of a *computer individual,* a program or machine that has some of the qualities of a human mind and which encompasses nearly the full range of abilities of a normal, average person. Such a computer individual would comprise an immense body of machinery.

Rather than looking for this uniform structure within the individual mechanisms, perhaps the proper place to look for it is within the organization of an entire system. That is, perhaps individual solutions to specific problems of intelligence need be constrained to work only within their intended domain; the responsibility for selecting and relating various solutions would be left up to this uniform, overlying organization.

The driving force behind the ideas presented herein is the *fluid domain*, which will be introduced shortly.

9.2 *Complexity versus Simplicity*

One of the prevailing notions in all scientific endeavors is that simplicity is to be favored over complexity where there is a choice. When there is no other choice but a complex alternative, of course the complex alternative must be chosen.

Years ago, Herbert Simon [Simon 1969] gave us the parable of the ant on the beach, in which the complex behavior of the ant as it traverses the sand is viewed simply as the complexity of the environment reflecting in the actions of the ant. He says:

> *An ant, viewed as a behaving system, is quite simple. The apparent complexity of behavior over time is largely a reflection of the complexity of the environment in which it finds itself.*

He goes on to substitute *man* for *ant* in the above quote and attempts to justify that statement. The goal of creating an *intelligent* machine has evolved, historically, from the initial sense of simple programs demonstrating interesting behavior even though those programs are simple. This sense comes, I think, from the speed of the machine in executing the steps in a program: Even though a computer may not deliberate deeply in its processing, it can explore very many alternatives, perhaps shallowly. For many problems this extensive, but shallow, analysis may substitute effectively for deep deliberation.

9.3 *Complexity*

I want to counter Simon's parable above with a quote from Lewis Thomas's "The Lives of a Cell" [Thomas 1974]; he says, when discussing the variety of things that go on in each cell:

> *My cells are no longer the pure line entities I was raised with; they are ecosystems more complex than Jamaica Bay.*

He later goes on to compare the cell as an entity to the earth.

Each cell is incredibly complex, and our brains are composed of very large numbers of them, connected in complex ways. A conclusion consistent with this is that programs that behave like people, even in small domains, must be rather large and complex—certainly more complex than any program written by anyone so far. And to write such a large program requires an organizing principle that makes the creation of such a program possible.

9.4 *Two Aspects of Programming*

There is a useful dichotomy to help us understand how artificial intelligence programs differ from many other programs: *algorithmic programming* versus *behavioral programming*.

In algorithmic programming the point is to write a program that solves a problem that has a single solution; steps are taken to solve the problem in an efficient manner. One example of an algorithmic program is one that finds the largest prime pair smaller than 1,000,000. To be sure, writing algorithms is not simple, but it is quite different from what I call behavioral programming.

In behavioral programs the point is to produce a program that behaves in certain ways in response to various stimuli. A further requirement on such a program might be that the response is not simply a function of the current stimuli but also of all previous stimuli and responses. Examples of behavioral programs are operating systems and some artificial intelligence programs.

In writing, one could possibly write an algorithmic program to generate single sentences, but to generate a paragraph or some longer piece requires a program that can react to its previous prose output, much as people do when they write. I say 'requires,' but that obviously isn't correct, because it is certainly *possible* to write an algorithmic program to write paragraphs within selected domains—I simply mean that writing prose-generating programs is easier if there is a structure that supports the activities necessary for prose writing, and I believe that structure is a loosely-connected network of experts.

9.5 *Fluid versus Essential Domains*

I want to make a distinction between two of the kinds of domains that one can work with in artificial intelligence research: *fluid domains* and *essential domains*. The qualifiers, *fluid* and *essential*, are meant to refer to the richness of these domains.

In an *essential* domain, there are very few objects and operations. A problem is given within this domain, and it must be solved by manipulating objects using the operations available. Generally speaking, an essential domain contains exactly the number of objects and operations needed to solve the problem, and usually a clever solution is required to get the right result.

As an example of an essential domain, consider the missionaries and cannibals problem. In this problem there are three missionaries, three cannibals, a boat, and a river; and the problem is to get the six people across the river. The boat can hold three people, and if the cannibals ever outnumber the missionaries in a situation, the result is dinner for those cannibals.

If this problem actually were to occur in real life, it probably would be solved by the missionaries looking for a bridge, calling for reinforcements, or making the cannibals swim next to the boat.

An important feature of a problem posed within an essential domain is that it takes great cleverness to solve it; an essential domain is called *essential* because everything that is not essential is pruned away, and we are left with a distilled situation.

In a *fluid* domain, there are a large number of objects and a large number of applicable operations. A problem that is posed within the context of a fluid domain is typically the result of a long and complex chain of events. Generally, there are a lot of plausible-looking alternatives available, and many different courses of action can result in a satisfactory solution. Problems posed in this type of domain are usually open-ended and sometimes there is no clearly recognizable goal.

A typical fluid domain is writing. In this domain there are a large number of ways of expressing things, beginning with inventing phraseology out of whole cloth and progressing towards idioms. As I noted earlier, writing is a process of constant revision, and often that revision is centered on word choice and how those choices affect the overall structure of a piece of writing. Therefore, it does not seem likely that a computer program could avoid doing the same sorts of revisions and be as effective as a program which also did post-word-choice revision.

A key feature of writing, and of fluid domains in general, is that judgment is often more important than cleverness, and frequently the crux to solving a difficult problem is recognizing that a situation is familiar. As we write more and more, situations in which wording or fact-introduction is a problem become easier for us to spot and to repair. We use our judgment to improve the clarity of our writing.

A successful approach to take in order to solve problems in fluid domains is to plan out a sequence of steps that lead from where we start towards what appears to be the goal. These steps are *islands*, where each island is a description of a situation that we believe can be achieved adequately. We will refer to a description of the situation as the *situation description*. At each island we then apply the best techniques available for achieving that situation, given the previously achieved situations.

There are two problems we need to solve to make this method work: 1) We must be able to plan these islands without doing very much backtracking, and during the planning stage we must not be required to perform any actions that might need to be performed during the later execution stage; and 2) once the plan is completed and we are executing it, we must be able to effectively bring to bear the appropriate techniques at each island so that the island is actually achieved.

I will consider each problem a little more carefully; as I do so, I will illustrate points concerning the general problems with their realization in the writing domain.

The first problem is to build a path, perhaps a graph, of nodes where each node is a situation that we wish to establish. We hope that if we traverse the graph, establishing the corresponding situation by taking some actions, then the final situation matches the goal towards which we were aiming. Building this graph is called *coarse planning*.

In writing, each node—the islands above—could be a sentence's worth of facts that must be conveyed, or it could be several sentence's worth of facts. The point is that each island represents a set of facts which ought to be expressed as a unit—locally in some section of the text, if possible. We hope that if we could adequately express in sentences each fact in the plan, then the entire text would adequately express all the facts.

Because we may need to consider many possible graphs of nodes before a plan emerges and because we may not wish to take all of the actions to establish the situations at each node while planning, we will need to operate on abstract descriptions of the possible actions that can be taken to decide whether a node can possibly be established by future actions.

In writing, this planning stage involves making a list of the propositional contents of sentences that might be written—the graph that is produced is simply a linear list. During this planning stage a sequence of sets of predicate calculus formulas is created, where each set of formulas represents the propositional content that should be conveyed at that stage in the text. The propositional content in each set might be expressed in a single English sentence or in several. We will want to consider whether saying these sentence-contents in a given order will convey the meaning we intend before we commit ourselves to the plan.

The second problem is to find those actions that will actually establish the situations called for in our plan. Fine-grained planning may be required to establish smaller islands—or islets—within the larger given islands. The actions that are determined to be appropriate at each island are executed in order to flesh out the plan, establishing the particulars of the plan. However, once these particulars have been established, we may find that the fleshed-out plan does not work well, and then we are faced with the problem of modifying what we have so as to accomplish our goal as nearly as possible.

In writing, we will actually propose words and sentences to accomplish the propositional contents in our plan. After this stage there exists a first draft text. We might find that the words chosen do not fit well with the planned structure of the text, and that a different structure might be better. Or it might be that the structure of an earlier part of the text prevents the structure for the later part to be realized.

In order to determine that the executed plan accomplishes our goal, we must be able to observe and criticize the actions of the system as it performs the steps of the plan. This is a good way to discover the inadequacies of the techniques brought to bear at each island.

In writing, we will observe our word and sentence-structure choices to determine whether we are effectively conveying intended meaning or whether we have unintentionally expressed an unwanted meaning or connotation. One might say that the program 'reads' what it has written, although in Yh there is no parser—the program reviews a representation of the text, which is simply an elaborate parse tree for that text.

Thus there are three essentials to our method: 1) draw up a coarse plan; 2) implement the details of the plan as best as can be done; and 3) observe the processes carrying out the details of the plan in order to criticize its effectiveness and to propose changes to correct any deficiencies.

9.6 *Intelligence and Communication—Object-oriented Programming*

Suppose we had a program that exhibited a degree of intelligence; from whence would this exhibited intelligence emerge? Certainly the program code by itself is not 'intelligent,' although the intelligence of the system must emerge from that code somehow. The intelligence emerges from the program code as it is running. But, to go one step further, what in the running of that code is the source of the intelligence?

Consider a team of specialists. If a problem the team is working on is not entirely within any one person's specialty, then one might expect that they could solve it after a dialogue. This dialogue would be an exchange of information about strategies, techniques, and knowledge as well as an exchange of information about what each specialist knows, why it might be important, and why some non-obvious course of action might be appropriate.

One could say that the collective intelligence of this team emerges from their interactions as much as from each individual's expertise; some particular expertise may not be able to address very much of the problem directly, but the combination of expertise plus an overall organizing principle might better address the problem as a whole.

Also, from a practical programming point of view, if a system can be expanded mainly through the addition of another individual piece of knowledge or expertise, with responsibility for organizing that new piece of knowledge left up to the system somehow, then a large system composed of many pieces of knowledge could be created and managed.

The question, then, becomes one of supporting communication well. In Lisp, for example, in order to use a function written for a specific purpose, one has to know the name of the function and its calling sequence. This will not do for the scenario I have outlined above: Being able to address the correct or most appropriate function or expert must be accomplished flexibly.

9.7 *Object-Oriented Programming*

Object-oriented programming addresses some of the needs of the system I have outlined. In object-oriented programming one builds systems by defining objects, and the interactions between these objects is in terms of *messages* these objects send to each other.

A standard example of this style of programming is the definition of 'addition.' In a traditional programming language we can define addition as an operation performed on two numbers. The function that adds two numbers might be able to look at the types of numbers (integers, floating-point, or complex, for instance) and then decide how to add the numbers, perhaps by coercing one number into the type of the other (we add a floating-point number to a complex number by coercing the floating-point number to a complex number where the real part is the given floating-point number and the imaginary part is 0).

An orthogonal—the object-oriented—way of doing this is to consider numbers as objects which know how to add other numbers to themselves. Therefore a complex number might be sent a message saying to add to itself a floating-point number and to return the value to the sender. The complex number would then look at the type of the number sent to it and take the correct steps.

When we want to modify these systems to be able to add new types of numbers, we do different things in each system. In the traditional system we need to improve the addition program so it knows about the new types of numbers that can be added. In the object-oriented system we need to create a new type of object—the new type of number—and to provide information about how to add other sorts of numbers to it.

To make this work easily, though, it is necessary to have provided a fallback or error handler to each object. For example, if a number, x, is sent a message requesting that another number, y, be added to that number, then if x does not know what to make of y, x could send y a message to add x to it, but cautioning y that x has already tried. If y is also puzzled, then y can try another error procedure rather than simply throwing the question back to x.

With such a fallback position, we can add new data types to an object-oriented system more easily than to a traditional system.

Yh is an object-oriented system, and I will call the objects in it *experts*.

9.8 *Overview of the System*

9.8.1 *Experts*

Yh, the writing program, is organized as expert pieces of code that can perform certain tasks in writing: Some can construct sentences, some can construct phrases, some can supply words or idioms, and some can observe and criticize the operation of the rest of the system. These expert pieces of code are objects in an object-oriented system.

These experts are capable of taking some action, and each one has an associated *description* of what it does. This description is in a description language which can express features and attributes, as well as their relative importances.

Let me be a little more specific. Yh comprises a number of experts held in a database, each of which is a small program. When Yh has a task to do, it finds an expert to invoke. Each expert has an associated description of what sorts of tasks it can do, and this description is used as an index for that expert. To find an expert to do a certain task, Yh formulates a description of the task and matches that description against the description of each expert in its database of experts. The description that best matches the task description corresponds to the expert that Yh will invoke.

Yh uses these descriptions when it is planning: Yh can use the descriptions of each expert to simulate the actions of that expert and can thereby propose a sequence of experts to invoke that will accomplish some goal. The descriptions are not represented procedurally, but they are structured in such a way that an 'interpreter' can be applied to a situation description and an expert description, and produce the situation description that would result if the expert were applied in a context where the first situation description held. This interpreter assumes that the expert would do exactly what its description claims it would.

In summary, these descriptions are used during coarse planning to help determine islands and during the execution of the plan to find appropriate experts to invoke. During both of these activities a pattern matcher is used to identify the appropriate experts.

9.8.2 *Control Structure*

Yh is agenda-driven using a priority agenda. That is, the agenda contains items that have priorities attached to them. Periodically Yh scans this agenda to determine what to do next, invoking the highest-priority agenda item.

9.9 *Descriptions*

Descriptions are matched against other descriptions. The matching process is *soft* or *hybrid*, which I define to mean that matches result in pairings of attributes, bindings of variables, and a numeric measure of the strength or closeness of the match.

More specifically, each description is a set of ordered pairs called *descriptors*; the first element of each descriptor is a sentence in a simple first-order logic, and the second element is the 'measure of importance' of that sentence. This simple first-order logic contains constants, variables, functions, predicates, and some quantifiers. I will refer to the first element of a descriptor as the *propositional content* of the descriptor. The propositional content of the description is the concatenation of the sentences within the description.

Here is a partial list of the sorts of entries in the description of an expert and how they affect a match:

GOALS These are the main actions performed by the expert, expressed as sentences with associated measures of strength. The primary matching operations consider only these sentences.

PRECONDITIONS These are the pre-conditions the expert expects to be true when it is invoked. These are also expressed as sentences with associated measures of strength.

CONSTRAINTS These are predicates that must be true in order for the expert to be invoked.

PREFERENCES These are predicates with associated measures of strength. For each predicate that is true in the context of a potential match, the associated measure of strength is added to the strength of the match. If the measure of strength is a number, it can be periodically decayed.

ADDED-GOALS These are the new goals that the actions of an expert may post when that expert is invoked. The goals are stated as sentences and have associated measures of strength. For each goal, the associated measure of strength indicates how important it is to achieve that goal.

SOFT-CONSTRAINTS These predicates are exactly like CONSTRAINTS above, but each has an associated measure of strength that affects only the strength of the match.

INFLUENCES These are GOALS-like entries that only affect the strength of a match. These entries are unified against all descriptors (entries in a description) in the description being matched. If an entry unifies with another, then the measure of strength is added to the strength of the match.

COUNTERGOALS These are like GOALS above, but they represent things that are undone by the action of an expert when invoked.

The expert description as well as the situation description are expressed in this language.

9.10 *Influences*

There are two major intentions behind this style of description: inexact matching and influencing a match.

This first intention was formulated after observing that it may not always be possible to find experts with descriptions that match perfectly, and that experts whose descriptions are relevant to the goals may be able to help accomplish those goals. For example, an expert that can write a passive sentence is able to accomplish the following two goals: The expert can put the direct object at the front of the sentence, making that object more prominent; and it can keep the agent of the sentence anonymous, which is useful if the writer doesn't know the agent, for instance. One can argue that neither of these goals is more important than the other, and it can be the case that if one wanted to accomplish one or the other of these goals, the passive sentence expert might represent the best means.

The second intention was formulated after observing that there may be very many experts whose descriptions match a given situation description and which could be used to take some useful actions. For instance, there will be quite a few words that could be used to express a concept or an object, perhaps equally well. We want to be able to influence which expert is invoked. In the word-choice example, perhaps we want to avoid recently used words (using PREFERENCES), or we want to encourage the use of words with certain connotations (using INFLUENCES). If the writing program wishes to avoid sentence constructs that have been used recently in a passage, SOFT-CONSTRAINTS can be used to influence the choice of sentence constructs.

9.11 *Pattern-matching*

This section describes the pattern-matching process in a medium degree of detail; and, in particular, the mechanisms in the pattern matcher which give rise to the behavior described above will be outlined. The casual reader can skip this section.

To match two descriptions, a pairing of the descriptors of one with the descriptors of the other is produced. A pair of descriptors, d_1 and d_2, is placed in the pairing if the propositional content of d_1 unifies with the propositional content of d_2. During this pairing process, the entries labelled GOALS are the only ones considered. It may or may not be the case that each descriptor of each description is paired with one from the other, but no descriptor can be paired with more than one other descriptor. A match exists if there is a non-empty pairing.

More formally, suppose we have two descriptions, P and D, and suppose that the GOALS part of the description of P is:

$$\{(p_1, s_1) \ldots (p_n, s_n)\}$$

where each p_i is a sentence in the first-order logic and each s_i is an integer. Suppose that the GOALS part of the description of D is:

$$\{(d_1, t_1) \ldots (d_m, t_m)\}$$

where each d_i is a sentence and each t_i is an integer. Let U be a predicate on sentences where $U(f_1, f_2)$ is true iff f_1 and f_2 unify. Then, P and D match iff:

$$\exists i, j \quad 1 \leq i \leq n, \, 1 \leq j \leq m \quad \text{such that} \quad U(p_i, d_j)$$

Let *Pairing* be a set of pairs that result from a match. If $[(p_i, s_i), (d_j, t_j)] \epsilon Pairing$ and $[(p_i, s_i), (d_k, t_k)] \epsilon Pairing$, then $j = k$.

For every two descriptions there may be several pairings of GOALS entries.

Once the pairing is produced, the strength of the match is computed using the measures of importance. The basic strength of the match is computed from the pairings obtained as described above.

If

$$Pairing = \{[(p_{i_1}, s_{i_1}), (d_{j_1}, t_{j_1})], \ldots, [(p_{i_k}, s_{i_k}), (d_{j_k}, t_{j_k})]\}$$

then the basic strength of this match is a function of $s_{i_1}, t_{j_1}, \ldots, s_{i_k}, t_{j_k}$.

Define the strength of match between P and D, $Strength(P, D)$, to be the maximum of the strengths of match of all the possible pairings of descriptors in P and D.

The remainder of the entries (such as INFLUENCES) are also paired with entries from the other description, and the measures of importance are used to modify the strength of the match.

To be more specific in the case of INFLUENCES, let $(I, s) \epsilon P$ be an influence, where I is a sentence and s is a measure of strength. If

$$\exists (d, t) \epsilon D \quad \text{such that} \quad U(S, d)$$

then the strength of the match is altered by a function of s and t.

The effect of all but the GOALS portion of the description is to affect the strength of the match and not the validity of the match.

9.12 *Performance of the Matcher*

The pattern matcher performs operations on cross products. Because of this, the performance of the pattern matcher is potentially quite bad. Many of the operations, however, can be formulated in such a way that a parallel processor could greatly increase the performance of the matcher.

On the other hand, during the generation of the paragraph of text that will be shown in the example that follows, the pattern matcher was invoked approximately 5,000 times and the underlying unifier approximately 300,000 times. The total time for the generation of the paragraph was only 15 CPU minutes on a DEC KL-10A.

9.13 *Planning*

Planning is done quite simply. We start with an initial situation and a goal situation. The initial situation and the goal situation are each represented by a description, and the pattern matcher is able to use these descriptions to determine the degree of progress towards the goal.

The planner tries to find a sequence of experts that will transform the initial situation into the goal situation. To do this, the planner finds an expert whose description indicates that the expert will transform the initial situation into a situation that is 'closer' to the goal situation; P_1 is closer to D than P_2 if $Strength(P_2, D) < Strength(P_1, D)$. Yh uses the description of the chosen expert to transform the initial situation into a new situation, and the process is repeated with this new situation in place of the initial situation.

This transformation may add further goals, and it may also add entries that indicate preferences or influences over the remainder of the planning process. In this way, the current part of the plan can influence the later parts.

If the search does not appear to be proceeding towards the goal, backtracking occurs.

The initial and goal situations may also be pairs of islands within a larger plan, and often this is the case. That is, when Yh is planning some paragraphs of text on some topic, it uses other, simple, planning heuristics to lay out the sequence of topics or facts to be expressed within each paragraph. Finer-grained planning then fleshes out this plan as best it can.

9.14 *Action*

Once the plan is in place, the first expert in the list of experts found in the planning process is applied, and that expert actually updates the situation description accurately. The updating done by the planning process using the description of the expert may have been only an approximation to a detailed analysis that the expert needed to perform to decide the expert's exact effect.

At this point, if the situation that was expected to be established by the actions of this expert is, in fact, not established, Yh may apply other applicable experts to the situation until the desired state is reached.

Applicable experts are found by the pattern-matcher by searching and matching in the database of experts. An applicable expert is one whose strength of match is above a certain threshold. If no expert is above the threshold, the planner is called again to do finer-grained planning to solve the problem.

As an example from writing, suppose the initial situation is a certain state of the text and the goal state is to explain a simple additional fact. There may be some means of expressing this fact, but the means selected may have created a noun phrase that is ambiguous in its context, perhaps by using similar words to those used earlier to refer to a different object. When the situation description is updated, this ambiguity may become apparent, and some other actions might be taken to modify the text or to add further text to help disambiguate the wording.

A general-purpose function-calling mechanism is based on pattern matching descriptions—*call by description*. It is possible for an expert to ask another expert to perform some actions: The first expert puts together a situation description—which describes the current state of affairs along with the desired state of affairs—and asks the pattern-matcher and planner to find an expert or a sequence of experts to accomplish the desired state of affairs.

9.15 *The Writing Process*

With the above simple overview description of the operation of Yh, I will now explain in more detail how writing is done by Yh.

Given a set of facts to explain, Yh applies some simple heuristics to the facts to determine the order of presentation of those facts. For writing about programs the heuristics simply examine the program to determine the data structures and the flow of control.

These ordered facts are the initial islands in the planning process. A finer-grained plan is produced which partitions the facts into sentences.

That is, the finer-grained plan is a sequence of sentence schemata (declarative, declarative with certain relative clauses, etc.) along with the facts that each expresses.

At this point the writing begins with text being produced from left-to-right, all the way down to words. As the actual writing proceeds, a simple observation mechanism is used to flag possible improvements in the text. For instance, if sentences with the same subject or verb phrase appear, this is noted. The mechanism for observation is to use the pattern-matcher to locate experts that are designed to react to specific situations, such as the same subject appearing in two different sentences.

The text is represented as a parse tree. Each node of the tree contains two annotations: One annotation states the syntactic category of the subtree rooted at that node; and the other annotation contains the situation description which caused that part of the tree to be created. In general, Yh is able to randomly access any part of the tree, using as indices the syntactic annotations, the situation description (semantic) annotations, or the contents of the nodes.

When the text is complete, the experts that were triggered by interesting events—such as the same verb phrase appearing in several places—are allowed to modify the text. While this is happening, further observations are made. The process continues until a threshold of improvement is reached—that is, until there is little discernible improvement to the text.

The effect of the observation experts can be to move facts between planning islands. The initial planning stage can be regarded as only a first approximation in a series of better approximations to a satisfactory plan for expressing a set of facts in English.

When Yh starts writing there are three agenda entries, which cause the above actions to happen: 1) A coarse planning entry; 2) a plan execution entry; and 3) an observation-expert activation entry. This first entry causes the coarse planning to happen, and the second entry causes the plan to be executed (the first draft to be written). The third entry is more complicated. While the first draft is being written, observers watch the process and make suggestions. These suggestions are simply entries in a database of such entries. The third agenda item causes these entries to be processed, and any actions that need to be taken based on the suggestions contained there will be initiated by this agenda entry.

10. Example of Writing

The next few pages will present an example of Yh writing about a simple Lisp program.

10.1 *Dutch National Flag*

The Dutch National flag problem as is follows: Assume there is a sequence of colored objects in a row, where each of the objects can be either red, white, or blue; place all red objects to the left, all white objects in the middle, and all blue objects to the right.

Given the initial sequence:

B	R	W	B	R	W	B

the result is:

R	R	W	W	B	B	B

The problem is a sorting problem, and it can be done in linear time using an array and three markers into that array. The following is a simple MacLisp program that solves the problem where an array is used to the store the elements in the sequence:

```
;;; Dutch National Flag

(declare
 (array* (notype flag 1)) ;represents the Flag
                          ;can be r,b, or w.
                          ;r = red, w = white, b = blue
          (special n))     ;represents the length of the Array
```

```
;;;exchanges (flag x) and (flag y)
(defmacro exchange (x y)
 '(let ((q (flag ,y)))
      (store (flag ,y) (flag ,x))
      (store (flag ,x) q)))
```

```
;;;;tests if (flag x) is red
(defmacro redp (x) '(eq (flag ,x) 'r))
```

```
;;;tests if (flag x) is blue
(defmacro bluep (x) '(eq (flag ,x) 'b))
```

```
;;;tests if (flag x) is white
(defmacro whitep (x) '(eq (flag ,x) 'w))
```

```
;;;increments x by 1
(defmacro incr (x) '(setq ,x (1+ ,x)))
```

```
;;;decrements x by 1
(defmacro decr (x) '(setq ,x (1- ,x)))
```

```
(defun dnf ()
 (let ((l 0)(m 0)(r (1− n))) ;initialize l,m, & r
    (while (not (> m r))
            (cond ((redp m)
                   (exchange l m)
                   (incr l)(incr m))
                  ((bluep m)
                   (exchange m r)
                   (decr r))
                  (t (incr m))))
 t))
```

The flag is represented by a 1-dimensional, 0-based array of n elements, FLAG. There are three array markers, L, M, and R, standing for Left, Middle, and Right, respectively. L and M are initialized to 0; R is initialized to $n − 1$.

While M is not bigger than R the program does the following: If (flag m) is red, it exchanges (flag l) and (flag m), incrementing L and M by 1. If (flag m) is blue, it exchanges (flag r) and (flag m), decrementing R by 1. Otherwise, it increments M by 1.

In order to exchange (flag x) and (flag y), the program saves the value of (flag y), stores the value of (flag x) in (flag y) and then stores the value of the temporary in (flag x). An element of FLAG is red if it contains R, blue if it contains B, and white if it contains W.

The above three paragraphs are written by Yh from an internal representation that captures exactly what is in the above code plus the comments. The representation is similar to that which a compiler would use to represent the above computation. Rest assured, Yh is not capable of reasoning about programs—every deduction made about the program while writing the above text was trivial.

The rest of this section will explain the generation of the first paragraph.

10.2 *Overview*

Yh is started with the task of explaining the Dutch National Flag program. Yh will first produce a plan to accomplish that, which is as follows: 1) Discuss the data structures; 2) discuss the main program; and 3) discuss the macros.

The remainder of the paper will present a detailed discussion of how the paragraph which accomplishes step 1 of the plan is written. The only data structure is an array with some array markers; the plan for this portion of the text, after it has been fleshed out during the writing process, is: 1a) Discuss what the array represents; 1b) discuss the dimensionality of the array; 1c) discuss the base of the array; 1d) discuss the size of the array; 1e) discuss the array markers; and 1f) discuss the initialization of the array markers.

At the end of this part of the writing process, the paragraph is:

The one-dimensional, zero-based array of n elements, FLAG, represents the flag. There are three array markers, L, M, and R, standing for left, middle and right, respectively. L is initialized to 0. M is initialized to 0. R is initialized to $n - 1$.

While writing this first draft, experts notice that some changes should be made. After making those changes, the paragraph will be:

The flag is represented by a 1-dimensional, 0-based array of n elements, FLAG. There are three array markers, L, M, and R, standing for Left, Middle, and Right, respectively. L and M are initialized to 0; R is initialized to $n - 1$.

10.3 Starting the Process

Yh is started on the task of writing about the program described above. It is given three pieces of advice in the form of influences. Recall that an influence is a descriptor which is used to bias the pattern matcher towards choosing an expert that has a description with that descriptor in it; if a negative influence is used, then the pattern matcher will be biased towards choosing an expert that has a description with the negation of that descriptor in it.

These three pieces of advice are: 1) do not use too many adjectives; 2) collapse all sentences that share either a common subject or a common predicate as soon as they are identified; and 3) do not allow very complex sentences. This last piece of advice uses a simple complexity measure which considers sentence length, adjectival phrase length, and relative clause depth.

10.4 *Conducting an Inspection.*

I will refer to all of the functions and data structures in the above program as the *program.*

First the program is examined. Initial planning islands are established for all of the major parts of the program: the data structures and the functions. This is done by an expert that has a checklist of general features of a program that are important to discuss when explaining or describing programs. The items in the checklist have associated priorities, and the plan is to discuss the items in the checklist in priority order unless some other order is specified. That is, this checklist represents heuristics about how to write about programs.

In the case at hand, the data structures come first because they are given a higher priority by these heuristics. The functions come next with the main function, DNF, first and the macros after that. A paragraph break will be inserted between the discussion of the data structures and the discussion of the program code.

The initial plan is: 1) explain the data structures, in this case the array; 2) explain the main program, DNF; and 3) explain the macros—EXCHANGE, INCREMENT, DECREMENT, REDP, BLUEP, and WHITEP—in this order.

Yh now begins to execute that plan, and the first data structure is then examined. It is the array that represents the flag. A simple examination causes the array-describing expert to be directly invoked using call by description. This array expert knows about interesting things concerning arrays.

All relevant features of the array are retrieved. In addition, the functions that use this data structure are retrieved. All other arrays in the program are found.

The facts discovered about this array by the array expert are: 1) it represents an object to the user; 2) each of its elements is one of R, B, and W, which represent the colors of the flag; 3) three array markers are used to point to places in the array, and these markers are moved; and 4) there are no other arrays defined in the program.

Because there are no other arrays in this program, an influence is added to the initial situation description stating that the array is unique. This may result in a noun-phrase generator choosing to say 'the array' rather than some other descriptive phrase.

Now that the relevant facts about the array are known, the discussion of the array will be written.

The things that are important to talk about for an array are: what it represents, its name, its length, its base, its first element, its last element, its dimension, and the types of its elements. The array expert's overall strategy is to introduce the array as a topic of discussion and to follow up that introduction with facts about its features. The options for introducing the array are:

> The <array> represents <something>.
> There is <array description>.
> The <array> has n elements.
> The <array> is m dimensional.
> The first element of <array> is <first element>.

The notation, <form>, means that *form* is to be expressed as a phrase or a clause, and the text is substituted for <form> in the appropriate schema. In order to write any of these sentences, the array expert will invoke the simple declarative sentence expert using call by description.

10.4.1 *Simple Declaratives*

The simple declarative sentence expert knows that exophoric references—references to objects in the external world with which the reader is familiar—should be placed early in a passage. The array expert knows that the array represents the flag in the program, and this representation forms the basis of an exophoric reference. The array expert chooses to introduce the array using the first of the list of schemata above: *The <array> represents ....*

The array is an object in the Dutch National Flag program, and the flag is an object in the world. Because the flag is more concrete to the reader, the reference to the flag ought to be placed first in the sentence. To accomplish this, the simple declarative sentence expert posts a request to transform this sentence to the passive voice. This would move the noun phrase referring to the flag to the beginning of the sentence, making it the topic and formal subject.

Requests to perform passive transformations are sent on a special expert that keeps track of the various proposed passives and has the responsibility of deciding whether there would be too many passive sentences too close together.

The first sentence generated will be: *The array represents the flag.*

The simple declarative sentence expert generates the sentence left-to-right by generating the noun phrase for the subject, then the verb phrase, and finally the noun phrase for the direct object. These phrases are written by experts invoked by the simple declarative sentence expert using call by description.

Every sentence generated is annotated with the situation descriptions that were used to generate the sentence as well as the experts that were used in the process. In fact, each phrase and each word is also so annotated.

The situation descriptions used in finding the experts that generate each sentence and phrase are among the primary factors that determine wording and sentence structure. Thus, there is a correspondence between the situation descriptions and the words and sentences. While writing the first draft, these situation descriptions, along with the influences, are the sole determiners of the wording and sentence structure, and, while revisions are being made to the text, the situation descriptions are updated so that the correspondences between the situation descriptions and the words and sentences are maintained as well as possible.

If the annotations are examined in left-to-right order, a good idea of the structure and wording of the passage can be gained. This is an approximation to re-reading, which was mentioned earlier as an important aspect of how good writing is done by people.

Although this does not have the same effect as an actual re-reading under forgetfulness, the performance of Yh demonstrates that it is adequate for many writing tasks.

10.4.2 *Noun Phrases*

The noun phrase expert is fairly robust and generates interesting and appropriate noun phrases. It also generates all of the modifiers called for by the situation description. These modifiers include the determiner, adjectives, relative clauses, and post-noun modifiers such as prepositional phrases.

If the number of modifiers of a noun would make the noun phrase too long or too complex, the noun phrase generator can post further requests in the current situation description that possibly would cause other sentences to be generated in order to present the modifiers.

In the first sentence about the array, noun phrases for the array and the flag must be generated.

If the representation of an object to be generated has a unique name associated with it, the noun phrase generator will use that, unless it is necessary to add other descriptive material. As an example from fiction writing, in introducing a character to a story it is often not sufficient to use the character's name—usually the reader wants to know some simple facts about him.

In this first sentence, the name is not used because we are in the situation of introducing a new 'character,' the array. However, this name, which is FLAG, will be introduced later.

Because Yh is being used recursively to generate the subject noun phrase, there is no a priori reason to expect that the noun phrase will be a single word, or even a simple noun phrase. Had a phrase been generated, that entire phrase would be treated as a noun; if it were a verb phrase—as would be the case for an action—the result would be a gerund.

10.4.3 *Uniqueness of the Noun Phrase*

There are two considerations to be made when a noun phrase is being generated: 1) whether the noun phrase is being generated to refer to an object already referred to in the text written so far; 2) whether the noun phrase is being generated in such a way that the noun phrase itself is similar to one already used in the text to refer to an object not equal to the object being referred to now.

In order to locate the first type of reference, the annotations for all previous noun phrases are searched to find references to the same object. The second type of reference is more difficult to find. Simply stated, Yh searches all previous noun phrases and tries to match the description for the current phrase against those for all previous noun phrases. It is hoped that the internal descriptions are such that if two noun phrases have closely matching descriptions, then the noun phrases generated are similar, and hence ambiguous. This activity is the analogue of re-reading a passage.

In general, when Yh discovers that two parts of a text clash—due to ambiguities or coincidentally similar wording—Yh is capable of repairing the problem at either site, or it could choose to reformulate parts of the text to remove one or both of the offending parts.

If Yh decides that two references are the same (Case 1 above) Yh makes a request to consider combining the sentences in which they occur. In the case of ambiguous references (Case 2 above) Yh posts a request to find distinguishing descriptors. The descriptions will be scanned for the most important distinguishing descriptors, which will then be placed in prominence in the noun phrases. Other tactics such as increasing the distance between the two references might be tried also.

The next decision in writing a noun phrase is which determiner to use, *the* or *a*, or whether to use no determiner at all. If it is specified that there should be no determiner, then none is used. If there are no other noun phrases referring to the same thing, then *the* is used. If the noun phrase is plural then *a* cannot be used.

10.4.4 *Modifiers*

Let us recall where we are in the writing process: The array expert has invoked the simple declarative sentence expert, which has invoked the noun phrase expert. The noun phrase expert may invoke the adjective expert.

Any of the experts in this chain of control can specify that no adjectives should be used. This would be the case if one these experts wanted to add adjectives in some order other than that which the adjective expert would choose; if one of these experts wished to add some adjectives, it would invoke the adjective expert directly.

In the sentence, *the array represents the flag*, there are no adjectives to insert.

Under the heading of 'modifiers' are also prepositional phrases that appear after the noun phrase, as in *the dog in the yard*. The placement of all adjectives and prepositional modifiers in a noun phrase is controlled by the distance to the nearest noun phrase to the left that refers to the same object. That is, the further to the left there is a noun phrase referring to the same object, the less the negative influence there is against using these modifiers: The further away a reference to the same object, the more important it is to use a detailed noun phrase.

10.4.5 *Verb Phrases*

Verb phrases are handled very much the same way as noun phrases.

10.5 *The Array Lives*

The sentence produced thus far is:

The array represents the flag.

When the initial plan was made, no attention was paid to the details of the array, and now that the array expert has examined the array, it is about to add a number of new goals to be achieved at this planning island. In particular, the array expert wants to write about (in order of importance): the length, the name, the base, the dimension, the array markers, the element-type, the first element, and the last element. Moreover, the operations that are performed on the array and any array markers into the array are important to discuss. In the Dutch National Flag program, exchanges are performed only at the array-marker points. Fortunately, Yh knows specifically about these operations and can talk about them intelligently.

Remember that there is a negative influence against being too verbose with adjectives, which will cause some of these modifiers to be left out.

In the world there are objects, and there are qualities of those objects, which may be necessary qualities or accidental ones. In writing, mentioning an object is typically done with a noun phrase, and the qualities are expressed as modifiers. In Yh, there are two ways to influence the writing about objects and their qualities: 1) One can add influences which will increase or decrease the importance of discussing the objects or their qualities, and 2) one can add influences which increase or decrease the importance of using the means of expressing the objects or their qualities.

For example, if the influence which controls the means of expressing a quality is negative and strong enough, the quality probably cannot be mentioned—Yh is prevented from using the means to do it. If the influence which controls the importance of discussing a quality is strong enough, the quality probably will be mentioned.

If the importance of mentioning a quality is high, and the importance of not using adjectives is high, then Yh may express the quality in a separate sentence in which the quality is not expressed as an adjective. If the importance of mentioning the quality is not very high, and the importance of not using adjectives remains high, then the quality will not be mentioned. This behavior is a product of the mechanisms in the pattern matcher.

In the case at hand, the importances of mentioning some of the qualities of the array are low.

The array expert goes through this ordered list and decides facts to mention, knowing that the sentence it just generated contains the noun phrase *the array*. The first thing considered is the length; because there are a number of ways to talk about the length of an array, the decisions about how to mention the length may interact with some of the other information to discuss.

For instance, if the first and last elements are mentioned, or the base and the last element, then the length can be skipped. Which of these alternatives is used can depend on whatever aspects of the array have been discussed or whether there is some advice about what to discuss.

Given that the length is to be said directly, there are several ways to accomplish this. One is to say, *the..., length n,... array;* another is *...array... of n elements*. The first alternative is simply to add another adjective to the list of adjectives in the noun phrase so far. If this would result in an overly complex noun phrase, this alternative would be rejected.

Because I have specified to Yh that it ought not use a lot of adjectives, *...array... of n elements* is chosen, but a negative preference is added to this method, which decays with time: The other methods of introducing modifiers to a noun phrase will tend to be used if the same request is made later. Human writers do the same thing: Recently used words and sentence constructions are avoided because they distract from the mental dream by their repetition.

Yh chooses this method using call by description. The influence that I added simply is weighed along with all the other considerations by the pattern matcher. The effect of this influence is to reduce the strengths of all adjective-adding methods.

Recall that the current sentence is:

The array of n elements represents the flag.

The name of the array is next, and there are several methods that can be used: Yh could say ...,*named <name>*,... in the adjective list, Yh could add a second sentence, or Yh could use an appositive to the noun group itself. This last method is selected, again because Yh was told to avoid adjectives, yielding:

The array of n elements, FLAG, represents the flag.

Next comes the base; in this case FLAG is a zero-based array, which means that the first element has index 0. The possibilities are the same as for the name of the array. The appositive route is abandoned both because double appositives are not pleasing and because an appositive was just used, which resulted in a negative preference being attached to that technique.

Zero-based is considered a single word and is inserted by a specialist on adding adjectives to existing noun phrases. The list of adjectives is located, and the new one is added at the front of this list. Recall that the text is represented as a parse tree along with an annotation of what is at each node. To locate the adjectives, the tree is searched to find the noun phrase node for the array, and then the adjectives are located by looking at that part of the subtree.

Similarly, the modifier *one-dimensional* is appended to the front of the sequence of current adjectives. Thus far the sentence is:

The one-dimensional, zero-based array of n elements, FLAG, represents the flag.

Recall that there is a transformation pending for moving the direct object of this sentence to a more prominent position in the sentence.

10.6 *Those Pesky Array Markers*

At this point the array expert is still controlling the writing process. It is turning its attention to the array markers by invoking an array marker expert.

When an expert is controlling the writing process, it can do one of several things: It can examine the situation description and the current text and decide on specific actions, like adding a word directly to the text; it can decide to invoke Yh recursively on a situation description and place the resulting text somewhere; or it can decide to invoke a sequence of experts using call by description.

An array marker is simply an index into an array which is used to keep one's place during a computation. In the Dutch National Flag program there are three array markers: one to mark the place to put red objects, which moves to the right; one to mark the place to put blue objects, which moves to the left; and one to scan through the array examining the color of things it finds, placing them in the right place.

Once it is decided to talk about one array marker, it is often wise to discuss all three in one place. Because these array markers are similar, it might be a good idea to talk about them similarly; perhaps the sentences can collapse to form one smooth, parallel sentence.

The array marker expert checks to see whether the array marker in question has already been discussed, which would have been posted as an influence. Then the array marker expert locates the array into which the array marker is an index; knowing this array, the expert locates all of its other array markers.

The expert sets up a dispreference for using the name of the array markers as the only referencing expression, and it calls Yh recursively to try to find a way to express the stereotyped phrase, *there are n <objects>.*

The situation description that the expert uses is one which suggests a simple declarative sentence with subject (*there*), predicate noun (*objects*), and the modifier (*n*). Of course, representations of these components of the declarative sentence are used and not the words themselves. Writing this sentence is fairly straightforward: Yh adds the next sentence:

There are three array markers.

The array marker expert then decides to add the names to the right of this sentence as an ordered appositive, which will have a list of names and a parallel list of descriptions attached to the end. This is a standard way to introduce a list of objects with descriptions and names, attaching the names in a parallel construction, and, though it is very idiomatic, there is no good reason not to use this technique.

The array marker expert makes up an extended description of what it wants done: the stereotyped phrase description, the list of names and associated descriptions, and some other hints to the next writing expert to be called. Yh is then called recursively.

The stereotyped phrase expert adds the phrase,

,L, M, and R, standing for left, standing for middle, and standing for right, respectively.

Notice that the gerund form of the phrase, *stands for x*, must have been derived from the program text for the Dutch National Flag program. This derivation is performed by the parsing system in PSI, and the result is placed in Yh's dictionary.

Respectively is added to the end of the sentence. While inserting these infinite verb phrases, a verb phrase collapsing expert notices that they are the same and notes a possible collapse. Because there is an influence that states that it is better to collapse immediately than to wait, the collapsing is attempted right away.

Up to this point Yh has been lucky in that all of the things that it needed to do regarding special phrases or circumstances have been handled by an expert in that area. But luck can run out, and in the situation of collapsing these parallel phrases, there is none left. In this case the verb phrase collapsing expert can only notice that collapsings are possible, but it does not know how to actually collapse sentences with the same verb phrase! When this expert looks for another expert to actually do the collapsing, it finds only a general phrase collapsing expert. This general collapsing expert simply tries to eliminate all the common words from each phrase except the first. Thus, given the phrases, *standing for left, standing for middle,* and *standing for right* this expert will try to get rid of the phrase, *standing for,* from the second two.

The transformation, however, does not eliminate the extra words *per se,* but simply hides the words from the sentence printer, leaving the original wording available in case it is needed later: Perhaps a transformation will wish to recover that wording.

10.7 *Observing*

In the previous section I stated that one of Yh's experts 'notices' an event taking place, and earlier I stated that observing was an important part of the plan-execution part of Yh.

When any event takes place, the expert causing the event to occur formulates a description of the event and does a call by description on that description. The description states that an event is occurring, and the experts who observe events of that type are allowed to run.

For example, when noun phrases are added to the text, an announcement is made reporting that a noun phrase satisfying a certain situation description was inserted in the text by a certain expert and located at a particular place in the text. An expert that keeps track of all noun phrases is invoked and adds that information to its own database. A similar activity takes place for the verb and other sorts of phrases and words.

Recall that Yh is agenda-driven. One of the items on that agenda causes observation experts to perform activities based on what they have observed. If, for example, a noun phrase observer has noticed the same noun phrases being generated in different places, then an expert to consider merging the phrases will be eventually invoked. Additionally, observation experts are able to perform their actions right away, and this is what I asked Yh to do when I advised it to perform all collapsings immediately.

10.8 *Pondering the Issues*

Sometimes a simple examination of the explicit properties of an object does not bring forth all of the interesting things that might prove useful in writing about it. For instance, one interesting thing about an array marker is the value to which it is initialized. In the representation above this fact is not mentioned outright, but is hidden in the program code.

The array marker specialist invokes an expert that reads the code and finds out to what the various markers are initialized. Because the annotated code states the purpose of the lambda binding, it is possible to specify which *lambda*'s cause initialization rather than saving/restoring.

The line:

$$(\text{let } ((l\ 0)(m\ 0)(r\ (1-\ n))))\ \text{;initialize l,m, \& r}$$

is annotated to state that the initialization values are 0, 0, and $n-1$.

Thus, three new sentences are proposed, one for each initialization:

L is initialized to 0. M is initialized to 0. R is initialized to $n-1$.

The names, L, M, and R, are used because there is no requirement to describe fully the markers, because they have already been introduced.

To express $(1-\ n)$, a special routine is called that will convert the standard Lisp prefix notation to mathematical infix notation for external printing purposes.

As these last three sentences are generated, Yh notices that the first two have the same direct object, and all three have the same verb phrase. Additionally, the previous sentence about the array markers is noted to have used the names, L, M, and R.

10.9 *The Fun Begins*

Given that the initial paragraph looks like:

The one-dimensional, zero-based array of n elements, FLAG, represents the flag. There are three array markers, L, M, and R,

standing for left, middle and right, respectively. L is initialized to
0. M is initialized to 0. R is initialized to n − 1.

there are still some loose ends to tie up and some transformations to apply. At this stage, this paragraph is the best that Yh can do by making local decisions about paragraph structure, sentence structure, and word choice.

Let me number the sentences:

(1) *The one-dimensional, zero-based array of n elements, FLAG, represents the flag.* **(2)** *There are three array markers, L, M, and R, standing for left, middle and right, respectively.* **(3)** *L is initialized to 0.* **(4)** *M is initialized to 0.* **(5)** *R is initialized to n − 1.*

First, it might be possible to collapse sentence **(2)** with some or all of sentences **(3)**, **(4)**, and **(5)**—L, M, and R are common noun phrases. But because in sentence **(2)** L, M, and R are used as direct objects and in sentences **(3)**, **(4)**, and **(5)** they are used as subjects, the only way to accomplish such a collapsing would be by making further relative clauses to the direct objects, which would result in a sentence like:

There are three array markers, L, which is initialized to 0, M, which is initialized to 0, and R, which is initialized to n − 1, standing for left, middle, and right, respectively.

This would be a very complex sentence; this option is rejected on the grounds of complexity.

Sentences **(3)**, **(4)**, and **(5)** pose something of a problem because they are so closely related to each other. All three have the same verb phrase structure, and the first two have the same direct objects. The latter fact causes sentences **(3)** and **(4)** to be collapsed by merging the predicate parts. Therefore the subjects are conjoined with *and*, and the verb phrase is transformed into the plural. The direct object is left as it is. The situation description in the text annotations is patched to reflect the fact of the multiple noun phrase.

The new third sentence is then:

(3') *L and M are initialized to 0.*

Sentence (5) has the same verb phrase as sentence (3'), but sentence (3') is fairly complex already, so Yh choses to simply bring them closer together with a punctuation change. The last sentence of the paragraph, hence, becomes:

L and M are initialized to 0; R is initialized to n − 1.

Another option for these last three sentences is to use the parallel construction:

L, M, and R are initialized to 0, 0, and n − 1, respectively.

This is not done because it produces a sentence with the same structure as the one before it. This is determined by producing the description of the sentence that would result from the collapse of sentences (3), (4), and (5) and comparing that description with the description of sentence (2).

Finally, Yh has to transform the first sentence to the passive voice in order to change the focus from the array to the flag. The first sentence becomes:

The flag is represented by the one-dimensional, zero-based array of n elements, FLAG.

11. Alternative First Paragraphs

By increasing the dispreference of adjectives and adjusting the influences on how things such as modifiers can be introduced, the following paragraphs were generated in place of the first one:

The flag is represented by an array of n elements, FLAG. It is a 1-dimensional array. There are three array markers, L, M, and R, standing for Left, Middle, and Right, respectively. L and M are initialized to 0, the first element; R is initialized to n − 1, the last element.

The flag is represented by an array of n elements, FLAG. It is a 1-dimensional array with N elements. There are three array markers, L, M, and R, standing for Left, Middle, and Right, respectively. L and M are initialized to 0, the first element; R is initialized to n − 1.

11.1 *A Weird Alternative*

Suppose that all of the structure-producing experts were removed from Yh, leaving only the programming knowledge experts and the lexicon, what would Yh say? It would say:

> *Array N elements Flag Represent One-dimensional Zero-based Array markers Three L M R Standing for Left Middle Right L Initialize to 0 M Initialize to 0 R Initialize to n − 1*

12. Conclusion

Yh does a fair job of writing about a small class of programs, but it is not a production quality program. It does not even perform very many of the things that we saw go into good writing.

Yh does not do explicit reasoning about shared information, nor does it reason about the implications of facts introduced in the text it writes. However, in writing about simple programs very little reasoning is required, and, therefore, this is not much of a problem. There are commonsense reasoning programs that could easily be adapted for use in Yh. [Creary 1984][Gabriel 1983]

Yh does not explicitly consider whether its writing produces vivid and continuous images in the reader. Certainly there is no mechanism for Yh to experience those images itself. And Yh never actually re-reads any of its writing, although it reviews its writing using the description mechanism. The level of success of this review process is encouraging, and, combined with a commonsense reasoning expert which could reason about knowledge and belief, this technique could be sufficient for many writing tasks.

Yh takes some actions aimed at producing good writing: Yh plans its text carefully, it deliberates over word choice, and it is sensitive to potential ambiguities in its wording.

As I stated at the beginning, a writer has an intimate relationship with his human reader. Judgment, sensitivity, humor, the human facts and experiences—especially the literary experiences that help give a writer his voice—are things that I believe are difficult to give to a computer, but maybe not impossible.

References

[**Creary 1984**] Creary, Lewis G., *The Epistemic Structure of Common-sense Factual Reasoning*, Stanford Computer Science Department Memo, to appear.

[**Gabriel 1981**] Gabriel, R. P., **An Organization for Programs in Fluid Domains**, Stanford Artificial Intelligence Memo 342 (STAN-CS-81-856), 1981.

[**Gabriel 1983**] Gabriel, R. P., Creary, Lewis G., *a reasoning program written by Gabriel and Creary at Stanford University from 1982–1983*, no documentation.

[**Gardner 1984**] Gardner, John, **The Art of Fiction**, Alfred A. Knopf, New York, 1984.

[**Green 1977**] Green, Cordell, *A Summary of the PSI Program Synthesis System* in 5th **International Joint Conference on Artificial Intelligence—1977**, Cambridge, Mass, 1977.

[**Simon 1969**] Simon, Herbert A., **The Sciences of the Artificial**, MIT Press, Cambridge, 1969.

[**Thomas 1974**] Thomas, Lewis, *The Lives of a Cell* in **The Lives of a Cell**, Bantam Books, Inc., 1974.

Text Generation:
The Problem of Text Structure

William C. Mann

1 Overview

What is text generation?[1] The long term view is that it is the process of creating a technology for building computer programs that can function as authors or speakers. I call this the long term view because in the text generation programs in existence today there is very little that deserves the title of "author" or "speaker." Writing and speaking are rightly regarded as complex arts capable of high refinement and great intellectual achievement. In contrast, our programs reflect only fragments of the most basic skills.

Text generation has been studied seriously in computational linguistics only in the last five or ten years, and so it is still sorting out its goals and identifying its problems.

Part of the diversity of approaches in text generation will surely come from a problem that we face now: It is by no means clear how authors do what they do. Even though we are all exposed to text nearly every day, and manipulate it successfully, there is very little explicit knowledge of how text works.

One of the central issues involves text organization. It is evident that natural text is organized, and that its organization is essential to its function. Text has parts, arranged systematically. But what is the nature of text organization or structure? What are the parts, and what are the principles of arrangement?

We must have answers to such questions if we are to create text generators. However, there are no widely accepted answers to these questions. The answers that are available from outside of computational linguistics are partial and complex. There are logicians' answers, grammarians' answers and so forth, often representing mostly the favorite methods and assumptions of their developers -- a priori selectivity rather than comparative results.

[1]This paper was created as an invited presentation for the 1986 COLING conference. It is still largely organized as an oral presentation, and so some readers may feel, with me, that does not have all of the attributes one would desire for inclusion in a book. Nevertheless, it seems better to let it appear than not. For additional support for the positions taken here I refer readers to the more formal presentations cited. This research was sponsored in part by National Science Foundation grant IST-8408726, in part by AFOSR contract FQ8671-84-01007, and in part by DARPA contract MDA903 81 C 0335; the opinions in this paper are solely those of the author.

Also, crucially for text generation, there are no accounts of text organization at a level of detail sufficient to support computer programming. Far more detail is needed.

As a result, text generation has been inventing its own answers to these questions. It has had to.[2]

To explore the nature of text structure, we focus in this paper on two of the energetic attempts within Text Generation to describe text structure in a way that is sufficiently detailed and general to serve as a basis for programming. They are:

1. The TEXT system, and

2. Rhetorical Structure Theory

The TEXT system was developed by Kathy McKeown at the University of Pennsylvania, as the centerpiece of her PhD dissertation, and is being followed up at Columbia University and elsewhere [Paris 86]. Rhetorical Structure Theory (RST) was initially defined by Sandra Thompson, Christian Matthiessen and the author; it is under active development at USC Information Sciences Institute.[3]

This paper describes each of these lines of research in its own terms; then they are compared as text structure descriptions. The comparison is extended to the related construction processes, and finally conclusions are drawn about text structures in future text generation work.

2 TEXT Structure Description

The general task of the TEXT system was to explain the structure and terminology, but not the content, of a particular data base.[4]

---

[2]Partly because of these difficulties, some workers in text generation have concentrated on generation tasks that omit the need for extensive text organization [McDonald 80], [Bienkowski 86].

[3]Barbara Fox, Cecilia Ford, and others have made important contributions. It has been influenced significantly by [Grimes 75] and [McKeown 85]; [Mann & Thompson 87] describes its relations to other theories in detail. The support of the National Science Foundation and the Air Force Office of Scientific Research are gratefully acknowledged; the opinions in this paper are solely the author's.

[4]Terminology may be somewhat confusing in this paper, simply because some key technical terms have been used in different ways by different authors. TEXT is McKeown's system, whereas "text" refers to the communication phenomenon. Other words which will have multiple meanings include schema and identification. The problem seems unavoidable.

2.1 The Operating Environment of TEXT

The operating environment of the system included several kinds of resources:

1. Data base of naval information

2. Knowledge base of conceptual categories relevant to naval information

3. Grammar of English.

It also has specific task information, including

1. Task Categories:

   a. Define an entity

   b. Describe an entity

   c. Compare two entities

2. Particular Task Operands, classes or class members.

The knowledge base should be seen as simply a hierarchic categorial extension of the data base, necessary since the data base did not define its own categories. In describing TEXT we will describe only the parts that are expressive of text structure, not the whole system.

2.2 Defined Objects

TEXT had two kinds of defined objects:

1. Predicate Semantics

2. Schemas

The predicate semantics definitions are essentially patterns which can be matched in the data base or knowledge base. They guide the system's search for particular knowledge. For example, Figure 1 shows the pattern for the Identification predicate. In the pattern, "entity" is given, "superord" is the superordinate class category of entity, and "attr" stands for attribute. The "restrictive" and "non-restrictive" lines require finding knowledge which is respectively specific or not specific to the members of the category of <entity>. The example shows the result of matching the pattern given SHIP as the entity.

The schemas of TEXT are specifications of how expressions of predicates can be combined to form whole texts. For example, Figure 2 shows the TEXT Identification

==

given-argument: entity

        (identification <entity> <superord>
        (restrictive <attr-name> <attr-value>)
        (non-restrictive <attr-name> <attr-value>))

example:

        (identification SHIP WATER-VEHICLE
        (restrictive TRAVEL-MODE SURFACE)
        (non-restrictive TRAVEL-MEDIUM WATER))

Figure 1: Predicate Semantics
for the
Identification Predicate

==

schema in a linear notation.[5]

==

        Identification (class & attribute/function)
        {Analogy/Constituency/Attributive}*
        Particular-illustration/DB-attribute+
        {Amplification/Analogy/Attributive}
        {Particular-illustration/DB-attribute}

Figure 2: The TEXT Identification Schema
in Linear Form

==

In Figure 2, Identification refers to the Identification predicate. (It is reuse of the name, not recursion. Recursion was not implemented in TEXT.) It would be expressed in the generated text by asserting some proposition which matched that predicate. Analogy, Constituency, Attributive, Particular-illustration, DB-attribute,[6] and Amplification are names of other predicates.

---

[5]In the figure, elements in parentheses are comments, {} represent optionality, * represents zero or more repetitions, + represents one or more repetitions, and / represents alternation of the choose-one variety.

[6]my name for the Evidence predicate

For convenience schemas were also expressed in a directed graph transition network notation reminiscent of ATN grammars, as shown in Figure 3. Generation of a text is represented by passing through the graph from the entry node, named ID/, to one of the nodes which bears an arc labeled "POP" such as ID/END. The other graphs are used as subroutines.

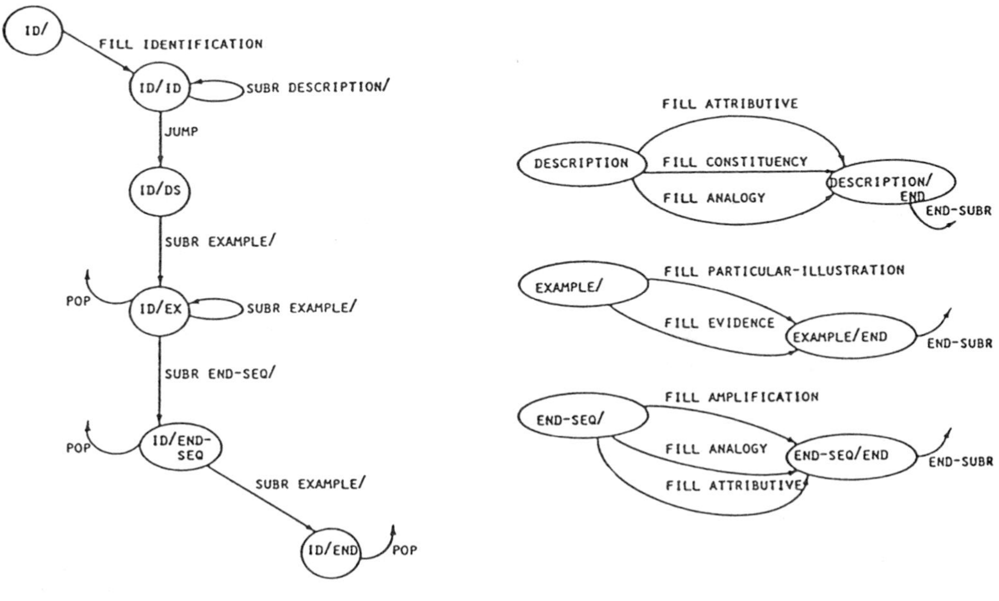

===

Figure 3: Transition Network Form of the TEXT Identification Schema

===

From the point of view of text structures, three features of the TEXT schemas are particularly significant:

1. The scale of schemas is the whole text. Texts are specified as whole units, whose structural possibilities are prespecified rather than created for the individual instance.

2. Optionality of elements is built in at the whole-text level.

3. Order of elements is prespecified.

Where do the schemas come from? They are abstracted from previous texts which are judged to be doing the same task. By studying texts from other knowledge domains, the high frequency patterns are identified and represented in the schemas.

Figure 4 shows a simple identification text generated by TEXT. It is minimal in the sense that all of the optional parts are absent.

==

The ship is a water-going vehicle that travels on the surface. Its surface-going capabilities are provided by the DB attributes DRAFT and DISPLACEMENT.

Figure 4: Sample Identification Text from TEXT

==

3 RST Structure Description

Now we turn to Rhetorical Structure Theory.[7] Most of this presentation, and most of the work on RST, is on text description rather than text construction. The early focus was entirely on description so that the constructive work would rest on a strong descriptive foundation.

3.1 Defined Objects in RST

There are four classes of defined objects in RST, shown in Figure 5. They are shown in a dependency order. All of the classes are presented below, but not in order.

==

1. Relations

2. Schemas

3. Schema Applications

4. RST Structures

Figure 5: The Classes of Defined Objects in RST

==

3.2 Schemas

Figure 6 shows the diagram conventions for the simplest RST schema. It represents graphically a configuration in which there is a span of text (represented by the whole figure) which is composed of two spans, one called the *nucleus* and the other the *satellite*. In such diagrams the nucleus is always below the vertical line. The two spans are related by a named relation.

Figure 7 shows some of the currently defined schemas of RST.[8] The first schema, the Elaboration schema, is typical in that it is defined in terms of only a single relation, in this case the elaboration relation. The second one, the Motivation/Enablement schema, is defined in terms of two relations, motivation and enablement. All of the remaining schemas shown are defined in terms of only a single relation.

Since the Elaboration and Solutionhood schemas are drawn differently, it appears

---

[7]RST was initially defined by Sandra A. Thompson, Christian M. I. M. Matthiessen and the author. Later contributions have been made by Barbara Fox and Cecilia Ford.

[8]A full presentation of schema definitions is in [Mann & Thompson 87].

==

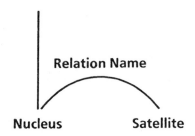

Figure 6: Simplest Generic RST Schema

==

that the schemas specify the order of the spans of which they are composed, but this is not the case. The spans are unordered in the definition, but the drawings indicate the most frequent ordering. So for example, elaboration satellites tend to follow the nucleus, but satellites in the solutionhood relation (representing presentation of a problem or question) tend to precede the nucleus.

As indicated in Figure 7, there are about 20 relations defined in the current version of RST.

Schema Applications are instances of schemas which correspond to the schema definitions according to a set of application conventions. These conventions allow multiple satellites, but require that a schema application contain only one span as nucleus.

3.3 Text Structures

RST text structures are compositions of schema applications. As an example, Figure 8 shows the RST structure diagram of a 14-unit text that appeared in a political magazine.[9] The units correspond to independent clauses.

At the top of the figure, there is an application of the Motivation/Enablement schema in which Unit 14 is the nucleus and the span of Units 1-13 is a satellite standing in a motivation relation to the nucleus. The nucleus, being a single unit, is not decomposed further.

The satellite is decomposed by an application of the Evidence schema. The

---

[9]A detailed analysis of this text appears in [Mann 84].

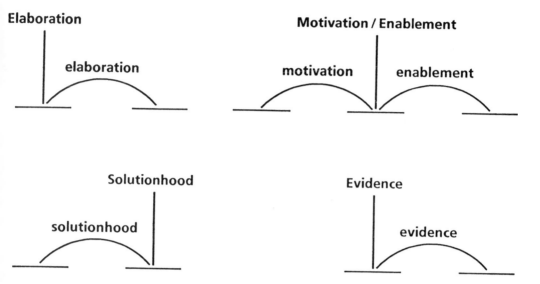

Other Defined Single-Relation Schemas

*Circumstance
*Background
*Justify
*Volitional Cause
*Non-Volitional Cause
*Volitional Result
*Non-Volitional Result
*Antithesis
*Concession

*Condition
*Otherwise
*Interpretation
*Evaluation
*Restatement
*Summary
*Sequence
*Contrast

Figure 7: Some RST Schemas

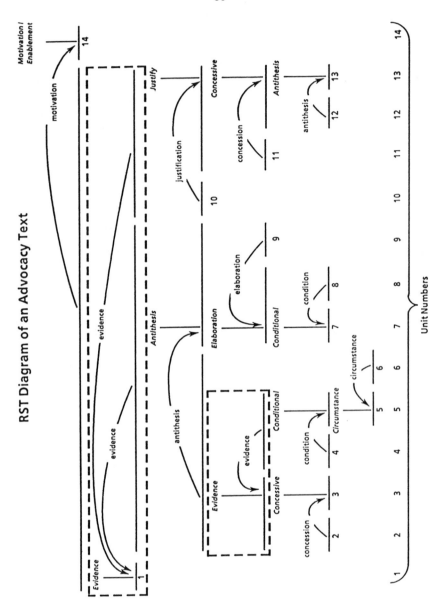

Figure 8: RST Diagram of an Advocacy Text

nucleus, which we will call the *claim*, is Unit 1, and there are two satellites, Units 2-9 and 10-13, standing in an evidence relation to the nucleus. The multiple evidence relations follow a general schema application convention that allows multiple occurrences of any relation in any schema. Within the span of Units 2-9 an Antithesis schema contains a satellite which is decomposed by another use of the Evidence schema. This use of Evidence within Evidence represents the general recursiveness of RST analysis -- that any schema can be used to decompose any span.

Notice that the top-down decomposition using schemas produces a tree structure. This particular structure contains 12 schema applications and 8 different relations.

3.4 Relation Definitions

All of the above rests on the definitions of relations. How are relations defined?

A relation definition has four fields, named in Figure 9.

===

1. **Constraints on the Nucleus**

2. **Constraints on the Satellite**

3. **Constraints on the combination of Nucleus and Satellite**

4. **The Effect**

Figure 9:   Fields of a Relation Definition

===

In describing a text, constructing an RST structure, it is necessary to decide whether a relation holds between two spans or not. It holds if its definition holds; there are no side conditions.

The decisions on whether a definition holds are plausibility judgments made by the analyst; they are based solely on the text and its context (and not, for example, on the analyst personally knowing the writer or intended reader.) Given two spans, the analyst decides whether it is plausible that each field applies.

The first 3 fields are stated as constraints which must hold for the identified nucleus and satellite spans. These constraint fields are sometimes empty.

The Effect field is a statement by the analyst that it is plausible that <u>the writer desired a particular effect</u> from the spans which the relation relates. It is not necessarily the only effect, or even the most important effect, that the writer might have intended, but if it is not plausible that the writer had the particular intent for the spans in question, then the relation definition does not hold. The Effect field of a relation definition is never empty.

The significance of the fields becomes clearer with an example. Figure 10 shows the definition of the Evidence relation.

==

1. **Constraints on the Nucleus (the *claim*):**

The reader possibly does not already believe the claim.

2. **Constraints on the Satellite (the *evidence*):**

The reader believes the satellite or will find it credible.

3. **Constraints on the combination of Nucleus and Satellite:**

Comprehending the evidence will increase the reader's belief in the claim.

4. **The Effect:** The reader's belief in the claim is increased.

Figure 10: RST Definition of the Evidence Relation

==

The constraint on the nucleus, that the reader possibly does not already believe the claim, simply insures that evidence is needed. The constraint on the satellite, that the reader believes it or will find it credible, insures that the satellite can actually serve as evidence. A non-credible span cannot function as evidence. The constraint on the combination assures that there is actually a support relation of some sort between the two in the writer's view of the reader's view.

The Effect field is a statement by the analyst that it is plausible that one reason the writer may have had for presenting the combination of nucleus and satellite spans was to increase the reader's belief in the claim. If this general statement is not plausible, then the Evidence relation does not hold.

Since the Effect field is never empty, an RST analysis is inherently a statement, for every part of a text, of a plausible reason for including each part in the text. RST is thus an explicitly functional theory, since its analyses are necessarily also accounts of the functions of the parts of a text.

The Effect field is also potentially useful in text generation, since it can help in choosing particular structures.

The kinds of conventions presented above are all that is needed to analyze a text. The analyst finds spans for which the relations hold. When they combine into schema applications, such that those applications form a tree, then the tree is an RST structure.

3.5 Related RST Studies

The methods described above have been used as the basis for a number of linguistic studies. Several of the studies below are PhD dissertations.

*Relational Propositions -- Assertions from Discourse Structure. RST relations have assertional properties, in which they convey information from the discourse structure, distinct from the clausal assertions of the text. In [Mann & Thompson 86] this phenomenon is identified, and in [Mann & Thompson 85] the link between RST and the phenomenon is made.

*Clause Combining -- Hypotaxis, Embedding and "Subordination". In [Matthiessen & Thompson 86], RST is used to establish that so-called subordination is a composite category consisting of two different phenomena.

*Clause Combining -- Antithesis Relations at Large Scale and Clause Scale. In [Thompson & Mann 87], clausal-level and large-scale antithesis relations are found to rest on the same discourse configurations.

*A Linguistic Characterization of the BBC World News Service. In [Noel 86] RST is used to characterize BBC presentational methods.

*Predicting Anaphora. In [Fox 84] RST is used in predicting when anaphora will be used.

These are ongoing studies:

*Clause Combining -- Switch Reference in Quechua

*Contrastive Rhetoric -- Comparing Structures of Essays in Chinese and English

*Rhetorical Questions in English Argumentative Prose

Overall RST is proving to be a flexible descriptive tool for discourse studies.

4 Comparing the Approaches to Structure Description

With the two sketches above we are ready to compare approaches to text structure description. To make the comparison easier, a text produced by TEXT has been analyzed in RST terms. The text is presented in Figure 11 and its RST structure in Figure 12.

Notice first of all that the only RST relation in the analysis is the Elaboration relation. The text contains 11 uses of it. This result actually holds for the TEXT system as a whole. Of the 20 or so RST relations, TEXT is using only one.

On the other hand, within Elaboration TEXT recognizes more detail and diversity in its predicates than RST does. RST has four subtypes of Elaboration: whole to part, object to attribute, set to member and set to subset. Figure 13 shows the correspondence of the two.[10]

Notice that the 16 predicates of TEXT map onto just 3 of the 4 subtypes of Elaboration. TEXT is specifying structure with a much finer grain than RST. But why? What are the benefits to TEXT of this finer grain? There are several:

1. Selectivity that is useful for particular tasks -- e.g. superordinate class information for the Identification schema.

2. Selectivity on what to say when -- predicate diversity interacts with the ordering which is inherent in schema definitions to sequence relevant information.

3. Accommodation of details of search -- e.g. attributes with and without values.

4. Basis for selecting grammatical forms for expressing the information.

Notice that none of these benefits relate to structure-building functions in RST's approach. We will see in Section 5, on text construction, that all of these functions are located somewhere outside of RST structure-building. This could be interpreted in either of two ways: that RST's present level of detail is sufficient for structure building, but needs to be supplemented to support other processes, or that RST's present level of detail is insufficient. Decisive evidence is unavailable.

The most significant differences between the text structure accounts of TEXT and RST are:

*Size of the largest structural unit -- whole text vs. RST schema

*Dual use of TEXT schemas for

    1. what constitutes an adequate answer, and

    2. text structure

(RST separates these.)

---

[10]The difference between the data base and the knowledge base in TEXT is an implementation detail which has been neutralized away in the table.

1. The cruiser and the ocean escort are surface ships.

2. The ship's surface-going capabilities are provided by the DB attributes DISPLACEMENT and DRAFT.

3. The ship has DB attributes MAXIMUM_SPEED, PROPULSION, FUEL(FUEL_CAPACITY and FUEL_TYPE), DIMENSIONS, SPEED_DEPENDENT_RANGE and OFFICIAL_NAME.

4. Ocean escorts have a DISPLACEMENT between 3400 and 4100.

5. All ocean escorts in the ONR database have REMARKS of 0, FUEL_TYPE of BNKR, FLAG of BLBL and MAST_HEIGHT of 85.

6. Ocean escorts carry between 2 and 22 torpedoes, 16 missles and between 1 and 2 guns.

7. A ship is classified as an ocean escort if the characters 1 through 2 of its HULL_NO are DE.

8. Cruisers have a PROPULSION of STMTURGRD and a LENGTH between 510 and 673.

9. All cruisers in the ONR database have REMARKS of 0.

10. Cruisers carry between 8 and 42 torpedoes, between 4 and 98 missles and between 1 and 4 guns.

11. A ship is classified as a cruiser if the characters 1 through 2 of its HULL_NO are CG.

12. The ocean escort, therefore, has a smaller LENGTH and a smaller DISPLACEMENT than the cruiser.

Figure 11: RST Analysis of a TEXT Text --
Part 1: The Text

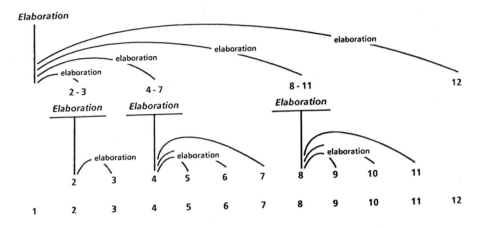

Figure 12:   RST Analysis of a TEXT Text --
Part 2: The Structure

TEXT Predicates	.......Elaboration Subtypes.......			
	Whole: Part	Object: Attribute	Set: Member	Set: Subset
Attributive				
attr + value		xxx		
disting.		xxx		
"Evidence"		xxx		
Constituency				xxx
Identification				xxx
Amplification		xxx		
Analogy				
relation		xxx		
range comp.		xxx		
Particular-Illus.				
attr + range			xxx	
attr			xxx	
Explanation		xxx		
Classification				
1			xxx	
> 1			xxx	
Inference				
(comparability)				
like		xxx		
class		xxx		
different		xxx		

Figure 13: Comparison of TEXT Predicates and Elaboration Subtypes

*Absence of relations in TEXT

*Explicit nuclearity in RST

*Fixed ordering in TEXT; free in RST.

5 TEXT and RST in Construction

Up to this point little has been said about the text generation methods associated with the text structures of TEXT and RST. Here we compare the two approaches, not explaining either in full but identifying their principal differences.

TEXT has a simple schema-follower that is well documented. It follows the transition network diagrams such as the one in Figure 3, producing one or more sentences that express the propositions of the matched predicate for each arc transition. We need not describe it in detail here.

Constructive RST has a structure-building process as one of several processes involved in developing the pre-grammatical plan for a text. Figure 14 identifies the principal kinds of processes.

In its present state of development, the processor of the procedure is human. Like a very complicated and conditional recipe, it is a procedure that a person can execute but a machine cannot. In tests, it produces identical or acceptable structures for a wide variety of natural texts.

It is now evident that the two processes of generation are very different. Since TEXT relies on predetermined text structures based on study of prior texts, it does not need to reason extensively about the need for particular text elements, nor about how to structure them. Its schemas encode both the task and the method for accomplishing the task. This produces a workable but rigid text structuring method with the major advantages of being implementable and effective in its designed domain.

RST separates text structure building from other processes, (about 8 of which are identified in Figure 14). This has the obvious advantages of flexibility and greater generality, but produces a corresponding need to implement and coordinate a diversity of processes.

Because the RST approach creates structure based on the immediate needs of the text under construction, rather than past texts, it must reason much more about the reader's state and the ways that text affects that state.

Implementation of the RST approach depends on finding suitable reductions of it which meet the needs of particular domains. This need for reduction applies both to

==

1. <u>Before</u> building RST structure:

    a. General decisions about what to accomplish, what knowledge to use. This yields a body of material to convey.

    b. Identification of the audience.

2. RST structure building, including

    a. Organizing the given body of material.

    b. Supplementing it as needed, with evidence, concessives, circumstantials, antithesis, contrast and other supporting material.

    c. Ordering nuclei and satellites.

3. <u>After</u> building RST structure:

    a. Theme control,

    b. Sentence scope,

    c. Conjunction uses,

    d. Lexical choice,

    e. Formulaic text, e.g. "Sincerely yours,",

    f. Grammatical realization.

Figure 14: RST Structure Construction and Related Processes

==

the oracles of the structure building process and to the processes related to structure building. For better or worse, in a particular text generation application much of the reduction will be forced by the limitations of the current state of the art of knowledge representation.

6 Summary

Considering both text structure and construction processes, the most important comparisons between TEXT and RST are listed in Table 1. Of these differences, the crucial one is the one highlighted -- the difference between structure derived from previous texts and structure derived from goal pursuit. These represent two competing and pervasive influences on language: prior patterns or conventions, and immediate needs.

==

1. The input to the procedure is a goal.

2. The control structure is topdown and recursive, proceeding by progressive refinement to the single clause level.

3. The procedure contains test conditions determining the need for each RST schema.

4. Use of some schemas, e.g. Conditionals, involves simple goal decompositions, whereas use of others, e.g. Evidence, involves addition of goals.

5. The procedure is based on <u>diverse and detailed appeals to the model of the reader.</u>

Figure 15:   Characteristics of the RST Structure Construction Process

==

Table 1:   Major Differences between TEXT and RST

<u>TEXT</u>   <u>RST</u>

Structure Derived   **Structure Derived**
from Previous Texts   **from Goal Pursuit**

Diversity of Operations   Diversity of
Encoded in Schemas   Processes

Narrow Task   Text Diversity

Limited\High
Linguistic Utility   Linguistic Utility

Implemented   Developmental

The first type includes fixed text and fill-in-the-blanks text as the simplest cases. The second includes many kinds of responsiveness to present needs beyond the sort represented by RST. Neither of these influences is sufficient by itself in a mature account of text structure or construction. The interactions between them are responsible for a major part of the complexity of language and communication.

It is clear that both classes of methods have important places in the text generation technology of the future. However, it is not clear what those places are. In these very early and formative days of text generation research, as it is sorting out its problems, these will form separate but interacting themes in the development of the art.

References

[Bienkowski 86] Bienkowski, Marie A., *A Computational Model for Extemporaneous Elaborations*, Cognitive Science Laboratory, Princeton University, Technical Report CSL 1, September 1986.

[Fox 84] Fox, Barbara A., *Discourse Structure and Anaphora in Written and Conversational English*, Ph.D. thesis, UCLA, 1984. To appear through Cambridge University Press.

[Grimes 75] Grimes, J. E., *The Thread of Discourse,* Mouton, The Hague, 1975.

[Mann 84] Mann, W. C., *Discourse Structures for Text Generation*, USC/Information Sciences Institute, Technical Report RR-84-127, February 1984. Also appeared in the proceedings of the 1984 Coling/ACL conference, July 1984.

[Mann & Thompson 85] Mann, William C. and Sandra A. Thompson, "Assertions from Discourse Structure," in *Proceedings of the Eleventh Annual Meeting of the Berkeley Linguistics Society*, Berkeley Linguistic Society, Berkeley, 1985. Also available as ISI/RS-85-155.

[Mann & Thompson 86] Mann, William C. and Sandra A. Thompson, "Relational Propositions in Discourse," *Discourse Processes* 9, (1), January-March 1986, 57-90. Also available as ISI/RR-83-115.

[Mann & Thompson 87] Mann, William C. and Thompson, Sandra A., "Rhetorical Structure Theory: A Theory of Text Organization," in Livia Polanyi (ed.), *Discourse Structure*, Ablex, Norwood, N.J., 1987. To Appear.

[Matthiessen & Thompson 86] Matthiessen, Christian and Thompson, Sandra A., "The Structure of Discourse and "Subordination"," in Haiman and Thompson (eds.), *Clause Combining in Grammar and Discourse*, Benjamins, Amsterdam, 1986. To Appear

[McDonald 80] McDonald, D. D., *Natural Language Production as a Process of Decision-Making Under Constraints*, Ph.D. thesis, Massachusetts Institute of Technology, Dept. of Electricial Engineering and Computer Science, 1980. To appear as a technical report from the MIT Artificial Intelligence Laboratory.

[McKeown 85] Kathleen R. McKeown, *Studies in Natural Language Processing.* Volume 2: *Text generation: Using discourse strategies and focus constraints to generate natural language text,* Cambridge University Press, Cambridge, 1985.

[Noel 86] Noel, Dirk, *Towards a Functional Characterization of the News of the BBC World News Service.* Antwerp, Belgium, 1986. Antwerp Papers in Linguistics, Number 49.

[Paris 86] Paris, Cecile L. and Kathleen R. McKeown, "Discourse Strategies for Descriptions of Complex Physical Objects," in Gerard Kempen (ed.), *Proceedings of the Third International Workshop on Text Generation*, Nijmegen, The Netherlands, August 1986.

[Thompson & Mann 87] Thompson, Sandra A. and William C. Mann, "Antithesis: A Study in Clause Combining and Discourse Structure ," in *Nominal Book Title*, Nominal Press, 1987. Submitted for inclusion in a festschrift book. Publication to be announced.

Planning Natural-Language Referring Expressions[1]

Douglas E. Appelt

1 Introduction

One major goal of artificial intelligence research in natural language generation is to develop a means of producing utterances that are natural and as close as possible to what humans would produce, given a similar domain and a similar need to communicate.

To use language with the competence of a human, it is not sufficient to have only a description of the syntactic, semantic, and discourse rules of a language: Human language behavior is part of a coherent plan of action directed toward satisfying a speaker's goals. Furthermore, sentences are not straightforward actions that satisfy only a single goal. When people produce utterances, their utterances are crafted with great sophistication to satisfy multiple goals at different communicative levels.

Figure 1 illustrates a typical situation arising when two people cooperate on a common task, in which a speaker plans an utterance that has multiple effects on the intended hearer. The speaker moves the wheelpuller in the direction of the hearer and says "Use the wheelpuller to remove the flywheel." The hearer, who is observing the speaker while he makes the request and knows the speaker is referring to the particular tool, thinks to himself, "Ah, so *that's* a wheelpuller." The speaker's gesture with the wheelpuller is an instance of *communicative pointing*, i.e., using a physical action to communicate an intention to refer to something.

In this situation, most obviously, the speaker is requesting that the hearer carry out a particular action, because the use of the imperative strongly suggests that a request is intended. Notice, however, that the speaker includes using the wheelpuller as part of his request. If he knew that the hearer did not know that he was supposed to use the wheelpuller to remove the flywheel, then his utterance was also intended to communicate the knowledge of what tool to use for the task. Also, the fact that he is *pointing* to a particular object and doing so in an obvious way communicates the speaker's intention to refer to it with the noun phrase "the wheelpuller." Because the intention to refer has been communicated, the noun phrase also communicates the fact that the intended referent is called a wheelpuller. The speaker could have said "Remove the flywheel," if he thought the hearer knew how to do it, and he could have said "Use *that thing* to remove the flywheel," if he had no goal of informing the hearer that the tool is a wheelpuller. In this case, the speaker has probably reasoned that future communication involving the wheelpuller will be necessary, and if the speaker and hearer mutually believe some description of the object other than its physical properties, it will be easier to refer to it in the future. The speaker and hearer mutually know that the phrase "the weelpuller," rather than

[1]This paper appeared in <u>Artificial Intelligence</u> Volume 25, 1985 on pages 1-33.
It is reprinted with the permission of North-Holland Publishing Company, Holland.

Figure 1: Satisfying Multiple Goals in an Utterance

"the flywheel," is intended to refer to the object of the gesture because they share sufficient knowledge of the domain to determine that the intended referent of "the flywheel" is some other object.

The satisfaction of multiple goals in utterances is more the rule than the exception in communication. There are may different combinations of goals that can be simultaneously satisfied, and utterances with such combinations are common in everyday conversation. Here are a few examples:

- *Referring and communicating additional information.* A rock climber says to a friend, "Joe and I are going to climb the Snake Dike route on Half Dome next weekend." The speaker does not use the prepositional phrase "on Half Dome" to pick out a particular Snake Dike route from several that he and the hearer mutually know about, but rather assumes the hearer has never heard of the route, and provides additional information to inform him where it is located.

- *Referring and communicating an emotional attitude.* A speaker points to an accused spy and says "That scoundrel is the one who betrayed us!" The speaker is not trying to distinguish a particular scoundrel from some set of scoundrels. Although the speaker may be attempting to inform his audience that the intended referent is a scoundrel, quite possibly he is using a pejorative expression to convey his emmotional attitude toward the intended referent.

- *Requesting and being polite.* Multiple goal satisfaction even plays a role in such coventional utterances as "Could you tell me what time it is?" In this case the speaker chooses the indirect speech act to satisfy a goal of demonstrating politeness toward the hearer, while the more direct but less polite "What time is it?" would convey the request equally well.

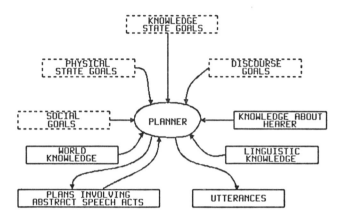

Figure 2: Overview of an Utterance Planner

These examples illustrate how a great deal of sophisticated reasoning about the effects of an utterance can be required to produce a seemingly simple sentence. A speaker capable of producing such utterances can be modeled by the process illustrated in Figure 2. The speaker, modeled by the planner in the center of the diagram, plans to satisfy physical, knowledge-state, discourse and social goals, using knowledge about the world, his own mental states and those of the hearer, and knowledge about the language. The speaker's plans can ultimately entail both physical and linguistic actions.

A planning system such as the one in Figure 2 has been implemented as part of this research and is called KAMP, which stands for **K**nowledge **A**nd **M**odalities **P**lanner. KAMP is a hierarchical planning system that uses a nonlinear representation of plans called a *procedural network* (Sacerdoti, 1977). It is capable of taking a set of axioms about the state of the world, the preconditions and effects of actions, the beliefs of different agents and a description of an agent's high-level goal, and producing a plan from the perspective of the agent that involves the performance of both physical and linguistic actions. The linguistic actions are refined until an English sentence is completely specified.

A primary consideration in the design of KAMP was to avoid dividing the language planning task into two independent processes of deciding *what* to say and deciding *how* to say it. In this view, the process of deciding how to say something is essentially a process of translation from a specification of the propositional content to the actual utterance. The propositional content remains unchanged by this process. Previous language generation systems have always made this distinction (e.g. Mann 1983; McKeown, 1985), because it allows one to separate the linguistic part of the system from everything else. Intuitively, this modularity is both theoretically and practically attractive.

In spite of its appeal, the "what-how" distinction has less merit when examined in the light of a theory of language generation based on planning. Such a theory views communication as actions directed toward satisfying goals. There are many decisions at every level of the language planning process that can be described in terms of action and goal satisfaction. At the highest level, there is planning illocutionary acts, at lower levels there is deciding how to communicate an intention to refer, and deciding how to communicate intentions about the discourse. The actions that satisfy these goals depend to different degrees on what linguistic choices are available in the current context. Thus, the planning at each level involves consideration of both linguistic rules and goal satisfaction. The distinction between "what" and "how" then becomes merely two points on a continuum between goal-satisfaction and rule-satisfaction processes, and no modularization based on this distinction is obvious. This does not, of course, imply that modularization per se is undesirable, but that the dimension along which the modules are separated is not one of "deciding what to say" and "deciding how to say it." For example the TELEGRAM grammar (Appelt, 1983) separates knowledge about the grammar and its semantics from the rest of the knowledge the system needs, but integrates the processes that uses these knowledge sources so planning plays a role in all aspects of utterance design.

Criticism of other research efforts may be somewhat unfair because the resulting limitations on what they can do, for example, the lack of ability to coordinate physical and linguistic actions, were not problems that these researchers have sought to overcome. However, designers of natural-language generation systems will ultimately have to confront these issues.

A hierarchical planner was selected as the design of KAMP because it provides for a separation between the planning of domain-level goals and actions and low-level linguistic actions as well as intermediate levels of abstraction that facilitate the integration of multiple goals into utterances. The abstraction hierarchy coincides with the spectrum of goal-satisfaction versus rule-satisfaction, which makes this design well suited to planning without a sharp distinction between "what" and "how."

This work is closely related to other recent work in artificial intelligence and linguistics. The idea of using speech acts as operators in a planning system originates with Bruce (1975), and Cohen and Perrault (1979). Evans (1981) independently developed a theory of speech acts based on situation semantics (Barwise and Perry, 1983) that shares many of the fundamental assumptions of the research reported in this article. An initial description of KAMP and utterance planning was given in two previous papers by Appelt (1980, 1982). This paper describes the system and its underlying theory as it has been fully developed and implemented.

This paper is organized in three main sections. Section 2 describes the problem that is being addressed. Section 3 describes a formal approach to axiomatizing referring actions, and Section 4 illustrates the KAMP planner with an example.

2 English Referring Expressions

Speakers use noun phrases for many different purposes, and this research has not attempted to deal with all of them. This paper will be concerned only with planning singular, specific, definite noun phrases that do not contain explicit quantifiers. Even within this narrow domain of phenomena, there exist a number of different referring intentions that a speaker may have when he utters a noun phrase, and part of a hearer's task in understanding an utterance is figuring out which one the speaker has in mind. This intention recognition process is necessary because identical noun phrases may be used in different contexts with different intentions. When a speaker utters a definite noun phrase, the hearer must decide whether the speaker intends that the hearer actually *identify* some person or object in the world to which the speaker intends to refer. The following intentions underly uses of the noun phrases under consideration:

- *Speaker intends to refer to a mutually known object.* In this case there is assumed to be a mutually known object to which the speaker intends to refer. A mutually known object is an object of which the speaker and hearer mutually know some properties. This mutual knowledge arises either out of the immediate context either by being (to use Prince's terminology (Prince, 1981)) *situationally evoked* (part of the shared context) or *textually evoked* (previously introduced to the discourse). Pronominal and anaphoric noun phrases are used to communicate intentions of this type.

- *Speaker intends that the hearer identify a referent.* The speaker may intend to refer to an object (of which he and the hearer may or may not share mutual knowledge), and intends that the hearer, based on his understanding of the speaker's intentions, perform whatever actions are necessary to identify the individual to which the speaker intends to refer. On occasion, speakers may convey this intention explicitly by means of a request to find the referent. However, this intention often underlies referring actions for which no explicit identification request is made. For example, the italicized noun phrase in "Turn left at *the third light past the large pink house on the left.*" is an example of a noun phrase that could be uttered with this intention. What distinguishes this case from the previous case is that there is not necessarily any mutual knowledge of the intended referent at the time of the utterance; in the above example, the hearer may have no prior knowledge at all of the large pink house. The speaker's implicit intention that the hearer identify the referent may require the hearer to form and execute a complex plan to make the identification. Instead of planning a description with respect to the speaker and hearer's mutual knowledge, he tries to plan a description that is *useful* for the hearer to plan an identification action. For example, a speaker does not give the hearer a useful description when he tells the hearer (whom he has just met on the bus) which bus stop to get off at by saying "Get off one stop before I do," because there is no way the hearer can use the description to form an effective plan to identify the referent, even though the noun phrase "one stop before I do" semantically denotes the right thing.

- *Speaker intends that the hearer not identify a referent.* When a definite noun phrase is used with this intention it is commonly called *attributive*. The speaker may have a discription of an individual that relates the individual to the mutual knowledge of the speaker and hearer, and the speaker may or may not know which individual satisfies that description. The hearer must realize that the speaker does not intend to say anything about a particular individual, but rather of whatever individual it is that satisfies a description. The noun phrase *John's children* (where John does not have any children yet) in the sentence "*John's children* will be very rich," is used in this manner.

According to KAMP's model of language production and understanding, a speaker uttering something implies he intends for the hearer to recognize the intended propositional content. This entails recognizing predicates and the arguments to which they are applied. These arguments are drawn from a set of so called "active" concepts. The speaker introduces concepts to this set through the performance of *concept activation actions*. These actions are frequently performed by means of *referring expressions,* which are expressions that bear a semantic denotation relationship to objects in the world. All of a speaker's physical and linguistic actions may be instrumental to conveying the intentions behind a concept activation, so while referring expressions are an important form of realization, they are not the only means that must be considered. Also, a concept can be active by means of inferential connection to active concepts even though it is not explicitly the object of a concept activation.

This paper will consider only the planning of concept activation actions in which the speaker and the hearer mutually know some facts about the object of the concept activation at the time of the speaker's utterance. An adequate formal theory of concept activation actions should account for the following phenomena: (1) How speakers reason about mutual knowledge to arrive at a description of the object, (2) How speakers use nonlinguistic means (e.g. pointing) to contribute toward the satisfaction of a goal to activate a concept, and (3) How speakers plan noun phrases that satisfy goals in addition to reference. The next section examines these questions.

3 A Formal Theory of Reference Planning

The logic that is used for the formal description of referring actions is based on Moore's logic of knowledge and action (1980). This logic consists of an *object-language* whose terms denote actions and objects in the world, and a *meta-language* whose terms also denote individuals, but which (in addition) can denote object-language terms and *possible worlds.* The object-language includes intensional operators such as **Know** and **Intend**, the semantics of which are axiomatized in the first-order meta-language in terms of possible worlds. The semantics of action-terms in the object-language are axiomatized as relations on possible worlds, were actions map one world into another, with possible worlds playing a role similar to the familiar states of a conventional logic of action (McCarthy and Hayes, 1969). The reader familiar with model-theoretic semantics will notice that the notion of possible world used here is quite different from the familiar notion of a world as a complete course of events, and should bear this distinction in mind throughout the article.

In this article, the following notational conventions will be adopted: Intensional operators (e.g. **Know**) are written in boldface type. Predicates, functions, and constants appear in lower-case type with an Initial Capital Letter. Variables appear in *lower-case italic type.* Schema variables are *UPPER-CASE ITALIC TYPE.* Most of the predicate naming conventions are taken directly from Moore (1980) to facilitate cross reference by the reader desiring more information.

A detailed description of Moore's scheme for reasoning about knowledge and action would be much too long for this article. This paper will only describe extentions to that theory that were necessary for utterance planning. The reader should bear in mind that the following predicates are used in most of the examples, and have the following meanings:

$T(w, P)$ means object language formula P is true in world w.

$D(w, x)$ is the denotation of object language term x in world w.

$K(A, w_1, w_2)$ means world w_2 is consistent with A's knowledge in world w_1.

$R(e, w_1, w_2)$ means that world w_2 is the result of event e happening in w_1.

$@(x)$ is the *standard name* of x, i.e., a term whose denotation is x in every possible world.

For the sake of simplicity, this article uses a loose notation to represent object language logical connectives and quantifiers. The same symbols will be employed to represent similar operations in both the object and the metalanguage. Moore (1980) the correspondence between object language and metalanguage, including some problems associated with quantifying into opaque contexts.

One may argue that an adequate theory of language planning must be based on a theory of *belief* rather than a theory of knowledge. Although this is a valid point, an adequate theory of belief is difficult to formalize, because once one admits the possibility of holding beliefs that are not true of the world, a theory of belief revision and truth maintainance is required. It is true that Moore's logic of knowledge can be transformed into a logic of belief by appropriately weakening the axioms (viz. the axiom that asserts reflexivity of the acessibility relation on possible worlds) so that it is no longer possible to infer P from **Know**(A, P). However, without addressing all the problems associated with belief and justification, one has really accomplished little else besides changing the word **Know** to **Believe**. Because a detailed study of reasoning about belief is beyond the scope of this research, the axioms are presented using **Know** as a first approximation to the best theory.

3.1   Reference and Concept Activation

KAMP is based on a theory of speech acts that is similar to that described by Searle (1969). According to Searle, the speaker performs some utterance acts from which the hearer recognizes the proposition that the hearer intends to convey. The speaker conveys these components of the propositional content to the hearer by means of what Searle calls *propositional acts* of referring and predicating. Then the hearer infers what the speaker wants him to do with the proposition — for example, whether it is to affect his beliefs or his future actions. This constitutes the recognition of the *illocutionary force* of the utterance.

The problem with Searle's theory is that it is too strongly sentence oriented. With the exception of conjunctions and conditionals, uttering a referring expression constitutes the performance of exactly one propositional act, and uttering a sentence constitutes the performance of exactly one illocutionary act. The KAMP theory is an attempt to move beyond the sentence oriented perspective and account for sentences that realize multiple illocutionary acts and illocutionary acts that appear to be realized over the course of several sentences. To achieve this goal it is necessary to formally decouple illocutionary acts and propositional acts from sentences and noun phrases. Toward that end, a hierarchy of linguistic actions is defined and axiomatized, and is employed by KAMP. At the top of the abstraction hierarchy are illocutionary acts. These actions are performed by means of surface speech acts. A surface speech act is realized by means of uttering a sentence.

KAMP plans concept activations, which are analogous to Searle's propositional acts, and these actions are performed by means of describing actions (realized directly as noun phrases) and communicative pointing actions. As with illocutionary acts and surface speech acts, it is possible to separate the intention communication action from its linguistic realization.

Concept activation actions and their realization will be the primary focus of this article. The verb "refer" is often used in a sense that is very close to what is meant by activating a concept.

If the subject of the verb "refer" is a linguistic expression, then what is being described is a semantic relationship similar to what one means by "denote." When subject of "refer" is an agent, then the intended interpretation is "to perform a concept activation action by means of uttering a referring expression."

KAMP represents concepts as intensional object-language expressions that denote different objects in different possible worlds. In general, it is possible for object language terms to denote different individuals with respect to each possible world. If an object language term denotes the same individual in every possible world, it is called a *rigid designator*. A rigid designator is like a proper name, and it is often convenient to use such names in the theory because they simplify the axiomatization of the domain. Under such assumptions, it is easy to show that any agent can decide whether two rigid designators denote the same individual, and they are therefore useful for describing the process of an agent reasoning about who or what something is. Because of the simplification that results, the example in this article assumes that objects have standard names despite the implausibility of people having names for every individual, (including, for example, each of the 200 identical screws in some parts bin).

3.2 Reasoning about Mutual Knowledge

The planning of concept activation actions requires not only the ability to reason about what different agents know, but also what they *mutually know*. Agents A and B mutually know that P if and only if A knows that P, B knows that P, A knows that B knows that P, B knows that A knows P, A knows that B knows that A knows that P, and so on, ad infinitum. It is insufficient in planning a concept activation for A to consider only his own knowledge and the knowledge of B, because failure to do so can result in an infelicitous reference. Clark and Marshall (1981) demonstrate that it is possible to construct examples where the definite description fails to identify the right concept for the hearer if only a finite number of assertions about the speaker's knowledge of the hearer's knowledge are considered.

Since mutual knowledge and mutual belief follow from an infinite number of facts, it is impossible to deduce mutual knowledge directly from its definition. Perrault and Cohen (1981) demonstrate that the mutual knowledge condition on referring expressions is in fact too strong. They demonstrate that A can use a definite description to refer to an object in speaking to agent B if it can be concluded that the nested assertions about A's knowledge about B's knowledge hold in all but a finite number of cases. Unfortunately, this analysis still leaves the problem of verifying an infinite number of conditions.

Nadathur and Joshi (1983) circumvent this problem by adopting a weaker condition for the use of a definite description: that the speaker believes that the hearer believes that the description denotes the object, and the speaker has no reason to believe that the chosen description is not mutual knowledge.

The KAMP theory maintains that a description used in a referring expression must be mutually believed, but admits heuristics by which mutual belief can be plausibly inferred without recourse to verifying an infinite number of conditions. Clark and Marshall call such assumptions *copresence heuristics*. According to their copresence heuristics, mutual knowledge results from three sources: (1) Common membership in a community of speakers, (2) Sharing physical proximity that enables the agents to observe, and observe each other observing, (3) Linguistic exchange of information.

In KAMP, copresence heuristics (1) and (2) above are stated directly in the axioms describing a particular communicative situation. Heuristic (3) is captured by a suitable axiomatization of illocutionary acts, described fully by Appelt (1985) that the successful performance of an illocutionary act produces mutual knowledge of its performance.

In addition to copresence heuristics, KAMP requires a logical representation of mutual knowledge from which it is possible to derive any one of the infinite consequences of an assertion of mutual knowledge. The mutual knowledge of two agents A and B is everything that is true in the *union* of the possible worlds compatible with A's knowledge and B's knowledge. Notice that the *intersection* of the propositions believed by two agents is represented by the *union* of possible worlds compatible with their knowledge. For the purpose of stating this fact formally, a pseudo-individual called the *kernel* of A and B is defined such that the set of possible worlds consistent with the kernel's knowledge is the set of all worlds consistent with either A's knowledge or B's knowledge. This leads to the following definition of mutual knowledge:

$$\forall w_1\, T(w_1, \mathbf{Mutually\text{-}Know}(A, B, P)) \equiv \forall w_2\, K(\text{Kernel}(A, B), w_1, w_2) \supset T(w_2, P).$$

The second axiom that is needed is:

$$\forall x, w_1, w_2\, K(x, w_1, w_2) \supset \forall y\, K(\text{Kernel}(x, y), w_1, w_2).$$

Axiom 3.2 states that the possible worlds consistent with any agent's knowledge is a subset of the possible worlds consistent with the kernel of that agent and any other agent. Note that because the knowledge axioms that allow one to conclude that if an agent knows P, he knows that he knows P apply to the kernel individual as well as ordinary individuals, it follows that if A and B mutually know P, then they mutually know that they mutually know P. This allows statements of the form

$$\mathbf{Know}(A, \mathbf{Know}(B, \mathbf{Know}(A, \ldots)))$$

to be derived to any arbitrary depth. Axioms 3.2 and 3.2 can be used efficiently by a first-order logic theorem prover that handles equational theories, such as that of Stickel (1983).

3.3   Reasoning about Intention

KAMP uses a possible-worlds semantics for intention that is similar to the possible-worlds semantics for knowledge and action. Reasoning about intention is crucial to utterance planning at several stages, because all actions with communicative intent (viz. illocutionary acts and concept activation actions) depend on the hearer's recognition of the speaker's intention for successful performance.

There are two levels at which KAMP describes an agent's intentions. First, an agent can intend to make a proposition true, or he can intend to perform an action. Thus,

$$\mathbf{Intend}(A, P)$$

means that agent A intends to bring it about that P, and

$$\mathbf{IntendToDo}(A, act)$$

means that A intends to perform act in the immediate future.

The semantics of **Intend** are that there is some set of possible worlds, called a *preference set* of an agent, such that for every world w in that preference set, P is true in w. This is expressed by Axiom 3.3.

$$T(w_1, \textbf{Intend}(A, P)) \equiv \exists s\, PS(A, w_1, s) \wedge \forall w_2\, (w_2 \in s) \supset T(w_2, P).$$

in which $PS(A, w, s)$ is true if and only if s is a preference set in world w of agent A.

The semantics of **IntendToDo** are similar. In that case, there is some preference set s such that for every world $w \in s$, w is the result of A performing action *act*. This is expressed by Axiom 3.3.

$$T(w_1, \textbf{IntendToDo}(A, act)) \equiv \exists s\, PS(A, w_1, s) \wedge \forall w_2\, (w_2 \in s) \supset R(\mathrm{Do}(A, act), w_1, w_2)$$

It follows directly from Axioms 3.3 and 3.3 that if an agent intends to perform an action, then he intends to bring about the effects of the action.

These two axioms give KAMP a rudimentary ability to reason about what an agent intends to bring about and what he intends to do next which is adequate for KAMP to make simple multiple-agent plans. These axioms are not claimed to come close to an adequate theory of desire or intention.

3.4 An Overview of KAMP

KAMP differs in a number of important ways from planning systems that are restricted to physical domains. The most fundamental difference is that the utterance planning system is necessarily always planning in an environment with at least one other agent, and this introduces problems of cooperating with the other agent, or thwarting its goals (Bruce 1975). The necessity of reasoning about different agents requires some means of reasoning about their knowledge, beliefs, and intentions, and how their mental states are affected by the actions that they and others perform.

The necessity of reasoning about propositional attitudes led to the adoption of the possible-worlds semantics representation described by Moore (1980). This formalism is best suited to proving that certain facts hold in a state of the world, and is not well suited to planning. Because knowledge states are represented as sets of possible worlds, straightforward application of a backward chaining algorithm to these sets in search of a plan is cumbersome at best. The design of the KAMP planner differs from other planning systems because of the need to overcome this disadvantage.

Figure 3 illustrates the operation of KAMP. KAMP solves problems by using a heuristic problem-solving method, which is successful at finding a good plan with minimal effort most of the time while preserving the option to rely on brute-force search if heuristic methods fail. KAMP has two descriptions of the actions available to the planner. One description is in the form of axioms relating possible worlds, as described above. The other description is an *action summary*, which summarizes the preconditions and effects of actions in a STRIPS-like formalism (see Fikes and Nilsson, 1971) involving preconditions and add and delete lists. The planner uses the action summaries as a heuristic guide to the selection of actions that are likely to result in a good plan. They are not intended to be complete descriptions of all the consequences of performing the action. The possible-worlds-semantics axiomatization is used to reason about whether the proposed plan is actually going to work. If the action summaries are well designed,

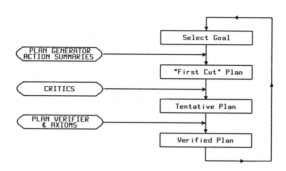

Figure 3: The Operation of KAMP

stating the effects that the action is expected to have in the most common situations in which it is performed, the planner will propose correct plans most of the time, and the search required for finding a correct plan will be significantly reduced.

The search for a plan is facilitated by the simplifications introduced by the action summaries. For example, an implicit assumption in the action summaries is that all agents know what the effects of the actions are. In some instances this assumption may not hold, and any plan that depends on this assumption will fail the verification step. The process that uses the action summaries can be viewed as a "plausible move generator" that proposes actions that are likely to succeed in achieving the goal.

KAMP uses a *procedural network* to represent the plan as it is being constructed and refined. A procedural network can be thought of as a two-dimensional data structure. The horizontal dimension is a temporal one, reflecting the partial ordering among the actions; the vertical dimension is one of abstraction, where goals and abstract actions are refined into sequences of low-level actions that can be performed directly by the agent. The connection between the planning data structure and the possible-worlds-semantics formalism is made by associating with each node in the procedural network a world that represents the state of affairs at that point. Whenever a fact must be proved to hold in the situation resulting from the execution of a series of actions, it is proved using the world associated with the appropriate node in the procedural network as the current real world.

KAMP's database contains assertions about what each agent knows, and what each agent knows that the other agents know. KAMP is not actually one of the agents doing the planning, but rather simulates how the agents would plan, given certain information about them. When KAMP plans, it "identifies" with one of the agents·and makes plans from the perspective of the agent it identifies with. This perspective makes an important difference when the planner considers the intentions of other agents. Assuming that an agent A_1 doing the planning has a particular goal to achieve, it is possible for the planner to assume that A_1 will intend to do any action that A_1 knows will contribute to achieving the goal. However, if it is necessary to incorporate the actions of another agent, A_2, into the plan, A_1 must be able to assume that A_2 will actually do the actions required of him. This amounts to showing that A_2 intends to do the action. Guaranteeing that this condition holds can lead to planning requests and commands. Once it has been established that A_2 will intend to do a high-level action, then the planner assumes that A_2 will intend to do any action that he knows will contribute toward the realization of the high-level action. Although A_2 may not have the knowledge necessary to carry out the action, it can be assumed that A_2 will execute a plan he can figure out. A_2 can ask questions of A_1, however, if A_1 can anticipate this need for information and furnish it at the time of the request, the overall plan may be simplified, and the resulting dialogue will be more natural.

When the planner is given an initial goal, it first creates a procedural network consisting of a single plan step containing the goal. The following process is then executed repeatedly until either the planner concludes that the goal is unachievable, or some sequence of executable (i.e. low-level) actions is found that achieves the goal: First, a world (serving in its role as a situation) is assigned to each node in the procedureal net reflecting the state of the world at that time (i.e. at the time *before* the action or goal named in the node is performed or achieved). The initial node is assigned W_0, the initial actual world. Then, iteratively, when the planner proposes that a subsequent action is performed in a world to reach a new world, a name is generated for the new world and the relation of the new world to its predecessor is explicitly asserted. All goal nodes that have worlds assigned are then evaluated, i.e. the planner calls on the deduction system to attempt to prove that the goal is satisfied in the assigned world. Any goal for which the proof succeeds is marked as a phantom goal, (i.e. a goal that is already satisfied) but is kept in the plan so that if actions planned at a later stage should make it no longer hold, corrective action can be taken to preserve or reachieve it.

Next, all the unexpanded nodes in the network that have been assigned worlds and that are not phantoms are examined. Some may be high-level actions for which a procedure exists to determine the appropriate expansion. These procedures are invoked if they exist, otherwise the action generator is invoked that uses the action summaries to propose a set of actions that might be performed to achieve the goal. If an action is found, it is inserted into the procedural network along with its preconditions.

Like Sacerdoti's system, KAMP uses procedures called *critics* to examine the plan globally and to determine interactions between proposed actions. A critic is a modular procedure that examines the plan for specific kinds of interactions between the effects of the actions. At the end of each cycle of expansion, each critic looks for a particular type of interaction. If the interactions occur, the critic reorganizes the structure of the plan in some way.

There is an important distinction between modifications to the plan made by critics and modifications made during the process of expanding an action to a lower level of abstraction. The process of expansion is local to an action and concerned with determining what actions can be used to achieve a given goal. The process considers only the state of the world as it is assumed to be at the time of performing an action, and what actions are available. Critics examine interactions between actions in the plan and propose changes, but do not propose new plans.

The result of separating expansion and criticism is an overall simplification of the planning process. The process of expanding actions is simpler because the many possible interactions do not have to be considered at the time of expansion. Obtaining a rough plan and refining it reduces the amount of blind search the planner has to do. The process of discovering interactions is also simpler because it does not have to be concerned with what actions to perform, only with

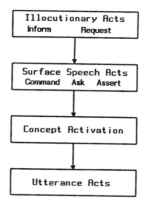

Figure 4: KAMP's Hierarchy of Linguistic Actions

the interactions between actions that have already been selected.

If the expansion of the plan to the next level of abstraction is complete, then the planner invokes the deduction system to prove that the proposed sequence of actions actually achieves the goal. If the proof is successful and the plan is not yet fully expanded to the level of executable actions, the process of world assignment is carried out again and the entire procedure is repeated.

If the proof fails, the reason is probably that the simplifying assumptions made by the action summaries were incorrect; in this case, the planner must resort to a more detailed search of the space to find a plan. Finding the best strategy for plan modification when the correctness proof fails is a good area for future research.

3.5   Planning Concept Activation Actions

As described so far, KAMP has a general ability to plan actions that affect the knowledge and intentions of agents; however for KAMP to produce language, it needs axioms and critics that capture information about linguistic actions.

Figure 4 depicts the hierarchy of linguistic actions used by KAMP. At the top of the hierarchy are such illocutionary acts as informing and requesting. These are the highest-level communicative actions. A correctly performed illocutionary act has the effect of making the speaker and hearer mutually aware that the speaker intended to perform the illocutionary act. For example, if the speaker performs the illocutionary action of informing the hearer that the box-end wrench is in the toolbox, then (as a result of the action) they mutually know that the speaker intended to do so. From this knowledge and from other knowledge that the hearer has about the speaker (e.g. whether or not he is willing to believe something the speaker says) and knowledge about the conventions of communication (e.g. the Gricean maxims 1975), he may come to believe that a particular wrench is in a particular location, thus realizing the *perlocutionary effects* of the action. A detailed description of the axioms for illocutionary acts and their relationship to perlocutionary effects is given elsewhere (Appelt, 1985) and is beyond the scope of this paper.

The next level of abstraction is that of surface speech-acts. Performing a surface speech-act entails uttering a particular sentence. The distinction between these two levels of actions can be described as follows: Saying *that* the box-end wrench is on the table is an illocutionary act. A surface speech-act realizes the illoctionary act by a *particular* utterance, in this case "The box-end wrench is on the table." (or perhaps, "The green tool is next to the platform," if the concept activation actions are realized differently. There is a one-to-one correspondence between surface speech-acts and utterances, because the former are merely abstract representations of the latter.

It is impossible to state simple axioms that describe the effects of surface speech-acts in the same manner as has been done for illocutionary acts for two reasons: The same surface speech-act can realize different illocutionary acts, depending on the context in which it is performed, and it is possible for a single surface speech-act to realize several illocutionary acts simultaneously. Because the effects of a surface speech-act depend on what illocutionary act it is being used to realize, it is impossible to describe its effects directly. The axioms need to state (1) that the hearer realizes what surface speech act has been performed, and (2) how the hearer deduces the illocutionary act from the surface speech act.

The relationship between surface speech-acts and illocutionary acts can be quite complex, although frequently the connection is quite straightforward. For example, a speaker can perform the surface speech-act of uttering a declarative sentence with propositional content P and intend that the hearer recognize the intention to inform him that P. Such speech-acts are called *direct speech-acts.* In some cases, the inferential connection between the surface speech-act and the intended illocutionary act is more complex, for example, when a speaker makes an utterance like "The door, please." and intends that the hearer recognize a request to open the door. Such actions are referred to as *indirect speech-acts,* and Allen and Perrault (1980) present a detailed analysis of how such intention recognition takes place.

KAMP does not currently plan surface speech-acts that require the hearer to make indirect interpretations, not because it is inherently incapable of doing so, but rather because indirect speech-acts are frequently planned to satisfy multiple goals, often along social dimensions and others that are very difficult to formalize. However, the ability to plan indirect speech-acts is important for the generation of plausible utterances, and the incorporation of Allen and Perrault's intention-recognition conditions into the axioms for surface speech-acts is an important area for further investigation.

Figure 5 illustrates the two components of a surface speech-act: the *intention communication* component and the *linguistic realization* component. The intention communication component is concerned with how the intentions of the speaker get communicated to the hearer. This includes communicating the intention to refer to objects or to get the hearer to identify objects. The linguistic realization component is concerned with taking the actions specified by the intention communication component and realizing them in a valid syntactic structure. A two-way channel of communication between these two components exists, because the means of communication of intention determines what linguistic structures must be chosen; in addition, the grammatical choices available constrain the possible means of intention communication.

Associated with each surface speech-act node is the syntactic structure of the sentence that constitutes its linguistic realization. Initially, these structures are only partially specified; as

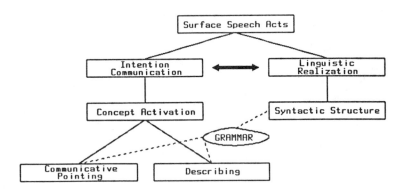

Figure 5: Components of a Surface Speech-Act

the plan is expanded to lower levels, the actions in the expansion contribute to the syntactic structure of the sentence associated with the surface speech act of which they are a part. When the plan is complete, each surface speech act node specifies a sentence, the utterance of which demonstrably satisfies the speaker's goals.

KAMP's grammar originally consisted of a relatively small number of context free rules distributed throughout the system. A grammar of basic clause structure was available to the planner when surface speech acts were planned, in expanding surface speech-acts with concept activation actions, a grammar of noun phrase constituent structure was used. Obviously, the linguistic coverage was severely limited. This was not viewed as a serious limitation, however, because the purpose of KAMP was originally to explore and develop some of the most basic relationships between utterances and their relationship to communicative intentions, and the interesting problems concerned how utterances were used in multiple goal satisfaction and integrated into a general plan of action rather than in the internal complexity of the utterances themselves.

The inadaquacy of the initial approach led to the development of the TELEGRAM grammar formalism. Currently work is in progress on constructing a larger, more robust grammar based on functional unification grammar (Kay, 1984) that provides a cleaner integration of the grammar with the planning mechanism. This work is described elsewhere (Appelt, 1985) and discussion of the details of the grammar is beyond the scope of this article.

3.6 A Formal Theory of Concept Activation

The level of abstraction below surface-speech acts in Figure 4 is that of concept-activation actions. Currently KAMP only plans concept activation-actions for which the concept is part of the speaker's and hearer's mutual knowledge. Concept activations are part of the expansion of a surface speech-act. We will consider only concept activation actions that have have realizations as noun phrases. As discussed earlier, the types of actions planned by KAMP are only a subset of the types of actions that can be realized by noun phrases, but nevertheless represents a significant subset.

As explained in Section 2, the process of understanding a speech act involves first construct-ing a proposition from a set of available concepts. This set of available concepts are called "active," and the predicate $\text{Active}(C)$ means that C is an object language term that belongs to the available set of terms for constructing the proposition the speaker is conveying by way of the surface speech act. Terms can enter the active set explicitly through the performance of a concept activation with the term as its object, or implicitly by way of inference. For example, in requesting a hearer to remove the pump from the platform in a domain involving the repair and assembly of an air compressor, if the hearer knows that the pump is attached to the platform and nothing else, the platform need not be mentioned because it is implicitly active. Therefore, it is only necessary to say "Remove the pump" for the hearer to recognize

$$\textbf{Intend}(S, \text{Do}(H, \text{Remove}(\text{pump1}, \text{platform1}))).$$

The performance of a communicative pointing action directed toward an object causes the standard name of that object to enter the set of active concepts.

The actual process of recognizing the proposition from the active concepts is not axiomatized. As a simplification, the axioms for surface speech acts state as a precondition that the terms that are part of the propositional content of the act must be active.

Axioms 1 through 3 describe what happens when an agent performs a concept-activation action (Cact). The axioms are expressed in the notation of Moore (1980). Axiom 1 describes the preconditions that the speaker and the hearer are at the same location and that the speaker intends that the hearer know that that concept is active. Axiom 2 describes the change in the set of active concepts and Axiom 3 states that the speaker and hearer mutually know that the concept activation action has taken place by specifying that the only worlds that are consistent with what the two agents mutually know are those that are the result of performing the action in some world consistent with their mutual knowledge before the action. The mutual knowledge of the action's occurance results in the mutual knowledge of the preconditions and effects holding in the appropriate states, and thereby provides a means of stating the knowledge effects of actions without the necessity of listing every consequence explicitly.

$$\forall A, B, C, w_1, w_2 \ R(\text{Do}(A, \text{Cact}(B, C)), w_1, w_2) \supset \qquad (1)$$
$$D(w_1, \text{Location}(A)) = D(w_1, \text{Location}(B)) \wedge$$
$$T(w_1, \textbf{Intend}(@(A), \textbf{Mutually-Know}(@(A), @(B), \text{Active}(@(C)))))$$
$$\forall A, B, C, w_1, w_2 \ R(\text{Do}(A, \text{Cact}(B, C)), w_1, w_2) \supset T(w_2, \text{Active}(C)) \qquad (2)$$
$$\forall A, B, C, w_1, w_2 \ R(\text{Do}(A, \text{Cact}(B, C)), w_1, w_2) \supset \qquad (3)$$
$$\forall w_3 \ K(\text{Kernel}(A, B), w_2, w_3) \supset$$
$$\exists w_4 \ K(\text{Kernel}(A, B), w_1, w_4) \wedge R(\text{Do}(A, \text{Cact}(B, C)), w_4, w_3)$$

When KAMP is expanding a concept-activation action to lower level actions, it takes into acount both the intention communication and linguistic realization components of the action.

The intention-communication component may be realized by a plan involving either physical or linguistic actions. KAMP relies on *description* as a linguistic means of communicating an intention to refer, and on *pointing* as a nonlinguistic means.

The following schema defines the preconditions of the *describe* action in a manner similar to Axiom 1:

$$\forall A, B, w_1, w_2 \, R(\text{Do}(A, \text{Describe}(B, D)), w_1, w_2) \supset \tag{4}$$
$$\exists x \, T(w_1, \textbf{Know}(A, D(@(x)))) \wedge$$
$$T(w_1, \neg\textbf{Mutually-Know}(A, B, \neg D^*(@(x)))) \wedge$$
$$T(w_1, \forall y \neg\textbf{Mutually-Know}(A, B, D^*(y)) \supset y \neq @(x))$$

Axiom 4 states the preconditions for an agent A planning to use a description D to refer to an object to an agent B. The description D is an object language predicate composed of a number of individual descriptors. It is defined as

$$D \equiv_{def} \lambda x \, (D_1(x) \wedge \ldots \wedge D_n(x)),$$

where the $D_i(x)$ are the individual descriptors that comprise the description. The symbol D^* denotes a similar expression that includes all the descriptors of D composed with the predicates that define the center of the discourse (Grosz et al., 1983). These predicates restrict the possible individuals to which the decription can apply to be only those that are relevant in the current discourse context. The general idea is that a single concept is identified as the *center* (C_b) of the discourse. As a simple approximation to a correct theory,

$$D^* \equiv_{def} \lambda y \, ((D(C_b) \wedge y = C_b) \vee (\neg D(C_b) \wedge D(y))).$$

This axiom says that if a description D is true of the center, then D^* applies only to the center, otherwise, D^* applies to the other objects, if any, of which D is true. With the addition of axioms to describe how C_b moves as the discourse progresses, KAMP can plan referring expressions that take centering into account. A full discussion of centering is beyond the scope of this article. A more detailed account of the role of centering in KAMP's description planning strategy is discussed by Appelt (1985).

The first clause in the conclusion of Axiom 4 states that the speaker must believe the description that he attributes to the intended referent actually holds. The second and third clauses state that the intended referent is the only one that is not ruled out according to the mutual knowledge of the two agents. The reason for this indirect approach is that one must allow for the case in which a speaker plans a description that serves to both identify a referent and inform the hearer of properties of that referent. In that case, descriptors $D_1(x)$ through $D_i(x)$ (called the basic descriptors) will be mutually known to identify a single object, while descriptors $D_{i+1}(x)$ through $D_n(x)$ will be believed only by the speaker. Therefore, when the hearer interprets the speaker's utterance, the description D is not known to apply to anything at all. However, if the speaker planned the description so that the basic descriptors are mutually known to pick out a single referent in context, then there will be only one object that is not *ruled out* by the description. Because the hearer knows that the speaker believes the *entire description* he then can then decide to believe the information conveyed by the additional descriptors.

KAMP chooses a set of basic descriptors when planning a describe action to minimize both the number of descriptors chosen, and the amount of effort required to plan the description. Choosing a provably minimal description requires an inordinate amount of effort and contributes nothing to the success of the action. KAMP chooses a set of descriptors by first choosing a *basic category* (see Rosch, 1976) descriptor for the intended concept, and then adding descriptors from those facts about the object that are mutually known by the speaker and the hearer, subject to the constraint that they are all linguistically realizable in the current noun phrase, until the concept has been uniquely identified.

Some psychological evidence suggests the validity of the minimal description strategy; however, one does not have to examine very many dialogues to find counterexamples to the hypothesis that people always produce minimal descriptions. According to the language generation theory embodied in KAMP, people do choose minimal descriptions for concept activations; however these descriptions can be augmented for a variety of reasons, (e.g.. to realize additional informing actions, as in the example in the next section, or to make it easier for a speaker to identify an object when an identification is requested, see Cohen 1981).

The other action that can be used to expand a concept activation action is *communicative pointing*. The following axiom describes pointing as one way of performing a concept activation action, which directly activates the concept of the object of the pointing action.

$$\forall A, B, w_1, w_2 \; R(\text{Do}(A, \text{Point}(B, X), w_1, w_2)) \supset \qquad (5)$$
$$T(w_2, \textbf{Mutually-Know}(A, B, \text{Active}(@(X))))$$

Axiom 5 says that if an agent performs a pointing action, the standard name of the object he is pointing at becomes active.

A problem with pointing actions, not dealt with here, is how it is possible to decide whether such an action has communicative intent. It is a convention of language use that utterances almost universally have communicative intent, (the exceptions being actions like muttering to oneself). However, a particular physical action may or may not have communicative intent, and KAMP does not attempt to describe how a particular perceived gesture is interpreted as communicative pointing.

Axioms 1 through 3 work together with 4 and 5 to produce the desired communicative effects. When a speaker utters a description, or points, he comunicates his intention to activate a concept, provided that the action has a suitable corresponding linguistic realization in the surface speech act.

3.7 Satisfying Multiple Goals in a Referring Expression

KAMP attempts to take advantage of opportunities to achieve multiple goals in a single utterance by recognizing situations in which *action subsumption* is possible. An important application of this principle is in the planning of referring expressions.

An action A_1 *subsumes* an action A_2 if A_1 and A_2 are part of the same plan, and action A_1, (in addition to producing the effects for which it was planned), also produces the effects for which A_2 was intended. Therefore, the resulting plan need only include action A_1 (and its expansion) to achieve all the goals.

The concept of action subsumption is particularly useful for planning linguistic actions because many options are typically available for expanding an illocutionary act into a surface utterance. Frequently, the planner can detect situations in which minor alterations to the expansion of an action will allow an action in another part of the plan to be subsumed. Although the term "minor alterations" is somewhat vague, the general idea is clear. When planning surface speech-acts, it means making a change localized to only one of the constituents of the sentence. Changes can be made to a surface speech-act during the planning that do not alter the overall structure of the sentence, but are sufficient to subsume other actions in the plan. An example of such a change that is relevant to this article is adding a descriptor to a referring expression.

Axiom 4 provides the justification subsuming informing actions by concept activation actions. For efficient planning, a good strategy is needed to recognize when action subsumption is possible. Action subsumption is an example of a global interaction between actions in a plan. Such interactions are detected by the *critics* discussed in Section 3.4. The action-subsumption critic works by first applying a set of rules to see if action subsumption may be possible. If so, it then tries several action-subsumption strategies that specify the exact modification to the plan that must be made. If the strategy is successful, then the plan is altered, and the subsumed action marked so that no further work is done by the planner to expand it.

An example of the action subsumption test rules would be "look for a situation in which a concept-activation of a concept C is being performed, and where in the same plan there is a goal that the hearer know some property holds of C." The planner attempts to (1) expand the concept activation with a describe action, and (2) incorporate the property as one of the descriptors in the describe action. Axiom 4 enables KAMP to verify the correctness of the plan modifications proposed by the critics.

This type of reasoning is what enables the speaker in the example of Figure 1 to conclude that he is informing the hearer that the object he is pointing to is a wheelpuller. The example presented in the next section illustrates how KAMP plans multipurpose referring expressions.

4   An Example of Planning Referring Expressions

KAMP's initial domain is the information required by an expert system that knows about the assembly and repair of a particular piece of equipment, and in which the user is a novice seeking assistance. There are two reasons for choosing this particular domain: First, dialogue protocols have been collected (Grosz, 1975) that provide a body of linguistic data raising interesting issues and examples of phenomena that can be explained by the theory on which KAMP is based. Second, the domain provides an ideal situation for multiple-agent planning in which communicative actions arise naturally.

Figure 6 illustrates a typical situation in which KAMP operates. This domain has two agents called Rob and John. Rob is a robot that incorporates KAMP for planning and deduction. Rob's only connection with the world is the computer terminal; thus, he is capable of performing speech acts, but no actions that directly affect the physical state of the world. John is assumed to be a person who is capable of performing both speech acts and physical actions. The particular situation for this example includes a piece of equipment to be repaired (in this case, an air compressor) and tools that are necessary for the task. The tools can be out in plain view on the table (in which case Rob and John mutually know properties such as their color, shape, size and location) or they can be stored away out of sight in the toolbox (in which case Rob may know where they are, but not necessarily John). In general, Rob is the expert and he

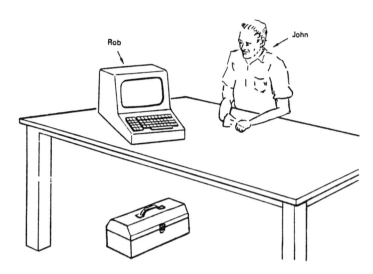

Figure 6: KAMP's Domain

knows almost everything about the situation. For example, Rob knows how to assemble the compressor; specifically, he knows how the parts fit together, what tools are needed for the various assembly operations, and where the tools are located.

This domain provides an ideal setting for studying multiple-agent planning as it relates to the production of utterances. Communication arises naturally in this domain because of the difference in knowledge and capabilities of the agents. Because Rob is incapable of performing physical actions, he must make requests of John whenever he intends to change the physical state of the world. Because Rob knows all there is to know about the task (and John knows this) John must ask questions to get the information he needs to do a task, and Rob must provide John with the information he knows he needs when he requests John to do something. Therefore, the need for communication arises in order for either agent to satisfy his goals.

The example presented in this section does not touch on every issue that arises in utterance planning, however, it touches on enough of them to give the reader a sense of how the different components of the KAMP planner fit together. The following notation is used for the illustrations in this section: Each node in the plan has some sort of boldface label (**P1**, **P2**, ..., **Pn**) to make it easier to refer to. Dotted boxes are used to represent phantom goals. The successor relation between actions is represented by solid connecting lines and hierarchical relationships by dotted lines. Each node has an associated world. For goal nodes, the world is written inside parentheses (e.g. (W_i)), to represent that the planner is to start in world W_i and find some actions to reach a world in which the goal is satisfied. For phantom nodes, the world name is not in parentheses to indicate the goal is actually satisfied within the indicated world. Action nodes have a label like "$W_i \rightarrow W_j$" to indicate that the action is a transformation relating worlds W_i and W_j. Actions will often be planned without knowing precisely what worlds they will be performed in, or precisely what world will be the result of the action. This is particularly true of actions that are represented at a high level of abstraction. Worlds are represented in the diagram as "?" if

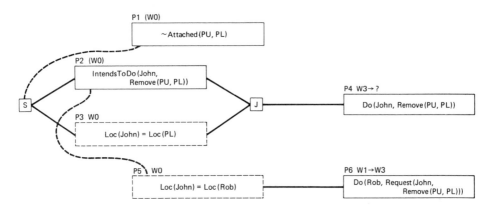

Figure 7: Rob Requests that John Remove the Pump

the planner has not yet assigned a definite world. (Note that KAMP can often reason about what is true at a given point in the plan, even though it has not assigned a world to the node, because frame axioms can be stated for high-level actions that describe some changes and leave others unspecified.) A notation like "$W_1 \to$?" is assigned to a high-level action that may be expanded to several actions at a lower level. The planner knows the action sequence will begin in W_1, but it will not know the resulting world until the action is expanded. A notation such as "? $\to$?" is used when the planner knows where in a sequence a high-level action must fall in relation to other actions in the plan, but cannot assign either an initial or final world.

KAMP requires a fairly rich description of its domain to plan communication acts. KAMP needs knowledge in five areas: Basic common-sense knowledge (e.g. Wrenches are tools, a compressor pump can only be attached to one thing at a time), basic knowledge about the objects in the domain (e.g. there is a wrench, it has an end-type of box-end, it is located in the toolbox), knowledge and mutual knowledge of agents in the domain (e.g. Rob knows the box-end wrench is located in the tool box, John does not know where the wrench is, Rob and John mutually know the pump is located on top of the table, it is universally known that all agents know their own location at all times), and descriptions of actions and their physical and knowledge-state effects, (e.g. if an agent performs an unfastening action, then he knows that he has just performed it, and the two objects that were fastened together are now no longer connected, and the agent knows this), and the basic axioms about knowledge and communication actions discussed earlier.

In the example discussed here the agents are Rob and John, the domain objects are a pump, PU, and platform, PL, mutually known to be on a table, T1, an object WR1 mutually known to be a box-end wrench, TB1 mutually known to be a toolbox and mutually known to be located under the table. The pump is mutually known to be fastened to the platform by a bolt, B1. Rob and John are initially in the same location. Because they are always in close proximity, they will always mutually know each other's location as well as their own. It is explicitly stated that John does not know what tool to use for unfastening B1, and that John does not know the location of WR1. Rob begins with the initial goal that the pump be removed from the platform:

$$\textbf{True}(\neg\text{Attached}(\text{PU}, \text{PL})).$$

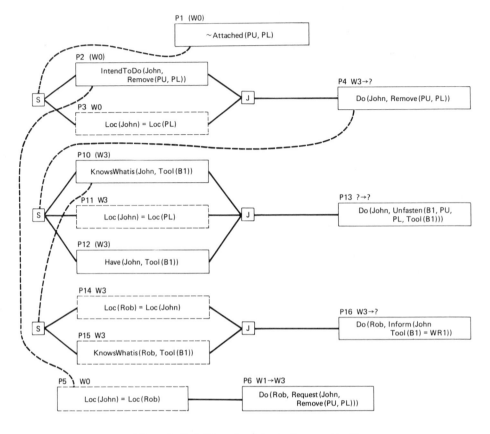

Figure 8: Rob Plans for John to Remove the Pump

Given the above goal, KAMP begins planning as described in Section 3.4 by creating a procedural network and refining the plan to successively lower levels of abstraction. Refinement to the first level of abstraction results in the plan shown in Figure 7, nodes **P1** to **P6**. KAMP has decided that Rob should request that John perform the action of removing the pump because according to the action summaries, a request is the only possible action one agent can perform to affect another's intentions. Whenever complete expansion to one level of abstraction is completed, KAMP uses the axioms to prove that the plan proposed according to the action summaries is successful.

Because the request is the only illocutionary act that has been planned so far, there is no more linguistic planning to be done at this stage. KAMP now turns its attention to expanding the REMOVE action. KAMP's axioms for remove (included as part of the general description of the domain) specify that removing is performed by unfastening any fasteners that are connecting one object to the other. This leads KAMP to include unfastening bolt B1 using the appropriate tool as part of the plan he must execute to remove the pump. This leads to the plan illustrated in Figure 8. The preconditions for John performing this action are represented by nodes **P10**, **P11**, and **P12** — that John knows what the right tool is, that John is in the same place

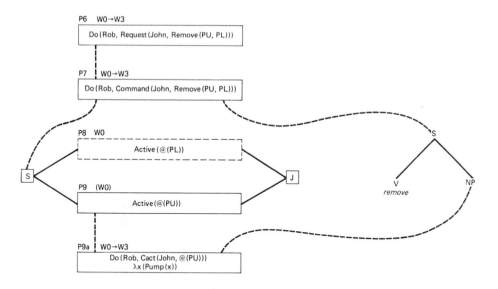

Figure 9: Expanding a Surface Speech Act

as the platform, and that John has the tool. Because John is already assumed to be in the same location as PL, the location goal, **P11** is a phantom (i.e. it is already true, but must be considered by the planner, in the event that some other action causes it to no longer hold). Rob does not know whether John has the tool, or even that John knows where the tool is located; therefore, KAMP plans for Rob to inform John that the tool for removing bolt B1 is wrench WR1 (Node **P16**).

In summary, what KAMP has done so far is formulate a plan in which John adopts Rob's goal of removing the compressor pump from its platform, and through additional planning, has discovered some information that John needs to know to carry out the plan, and has planned to provide him with this information by means of an additional informing action.

Next, the planner must expand illocutionary acts in the plan to surface speech acts. This step may require some complex reasoning about when a surface speech act will be recognized as a particular kind of illocutionary act, for example, when a question will be understood as a request to perform a physical action as opposed to a request for information. For reasons explained in 3.5, surface speech acts are assumed to be interpreted directly, so the utterance of an imperative sentence is planned to realize the request in **P6**.

KAMP reasons that enough information must be included in the utterance so the hearer will recognize the intended proposition Remove(PU, PL). This entails conveying the predicate "Remove" and activating concepts @(PU) and @(PL). As described in Section 3.6, concepts can be activated by being inferentially related to active ones as well as being activated directly. In this problem, axioms are included that state that Rob and John both know that the platform is the only object to which the pump is attached. Therefore, any action that removes the pump must remove it from the platform, and it is only necessary to say "Remove the pump" to have the hearer recognize the entire proposition.

Figure 9 illustrates the interaction between the two components of surface speech-act planning — intention communication and linguistic realization. The intention-communication component of this surface speech act consists of concept-activation goals (nodes **P8** and **P9**) for each of the concepts mentioned in the intended proposition. Because KAMP has reasoned that it does not need to mention the platform, node **P8** is marked as a phantom. The phantom action will most likely not be reflected in the final utterance, but can be noticed by critics and later reactivated if the critic decides that it could satisfy another goal by referring to the platform with an appropriate description.

The linguistic-realization component consists of choosing a basic syntactic structure for the sentence and relating it to the actions of the intention communication component. According to its grammar, the planner knows that an imperative sentence has the structure "V NP (PP)*" and associates such a structure with the surface speech act node **P7**.

KAMP now turns attention to expanding the goal node **P9**, activating the concept @(PU). Intention communication in this case is very simple, because (according to the initial axiomatization of the domain) there is only one object that is mutually believed by the speaker and hearer to be a pump. Therefore, the concept activation action **P9a** is planned, and its subordinate describe action, choosing

$$\lambda x(\mathrm{Pump}(x))$$

as a description, as described in Section 3.6.

KAMP has now reached the point at which the criticism portion of the expansion-criticism cycle begins. As explained in Section 3.4, each critic has a simple test that it applies to the plan to see if it is applicable. The action-subsumption critic's test works by examining pairs of illocutionary acts, such as the informing action **P16** and the request **P6** (see Figure 8) to see if they are connected in a way that permits action subsumption. Actions **P16** and **P6** are connected by the fact that the wrench referred to in **P16** is an instrument of the action requested by **P6**. Because the verb chosen for **P6**, remove, can take an instrument case, the critic realizes that the informing action **P16** can be subsumed by the request **P6**, provided that reference to the instrument is made explicitly in the utterance. Since the simple grammar doesn't constrain the number of adverbial PPs that appear in the sentence, the addition of a prepositional phrase is adopted as a subsumption strategy.

The action-subsumption critic must also determine whether all the preconditions for the subsumption candidate are also satisfied in the world when the subsuming action is going to be "performed". All the conditions, namely that Rob is in the same location as John, and Rob knows that Tool(B1) = WR1, are satisfied in this situation. The critic adds concept activation **P16a** of Figure 10 to the plan for intention communication, and adds the prepositional phrase with preposition *with* to the syntax tree. Once the addition is performed, then the planner reasons that the description $\lambda x(\mathrm{Wrench}(x))$ is adequate to activate @(WR1).

The subsumption of the informing action means that the hearer's knowledge will have changed by the time he executes the action of removing the pump. Because the exact effect of this additional knowledge on the plan is difficult to determine, the entire expansion of node **P4** is discarded and replanned. Figure 10 shows the procedural net after criticism by the action-subsumption critic.

KAMP now turns its attention to goal **P12**, that John has wrench WR1 in his possession. For John to have the wrench, he must know where it is, and he must go there and get it. According to our model, John does not have this knowledge, but Rob does; accordingly KAMP

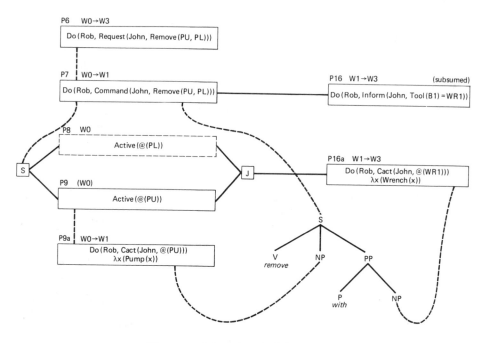

Figure 10: Subsuming the Informing Action

plans for Rob to perform an additional informing action (**P24** in Figure 11) to tell John the wrench's location.

In the next criticism cycle, the action-subsumption critic finds a situation analogous to the one with informing action **P16**. Action **P17** is a candidate for subsumption by the request because it informs the hearer of a property of one of the case arguments of the main verb being planned for the request. As in the previous case, the informing action is relocated so that it follows the request, and the part of the plan that may be affected by the hearer's new knowledge is discarded and replanned, as before. The description used in the concept-activation action **P16a** is then augmented with the new descriptor to yield

$$\lambda x \left[(\text{Wrench}(x) \wedge (\text{Loc}(x) = \text{Loc}(\text{TB1}))) \right]$$

and modifying the linguistic realization, shown in Figure 12 to attach a prepositional phrase to the noun phrase referring to the wrench.

The plan is completed when the planner plans a concept-activation of TB1, using the description $\lambda x(\text{Tool-box}(x))$. In the completed plan, Rob says to John "Remove the pump with the wrench in the toolbox." Before the plan is actually adopted and executed, KAMP verifies that it will actually work, since the action summaries employ simplifications that may in some cases lead to the formulation of an incorrect plan. In this case the verification is possible because according to Axiom (8), the hearer acquires the knowledge through the describe actions associated with concept activation **P16a** that would have been provided by inform actions **P16** and **P24** had they not been subsumed.

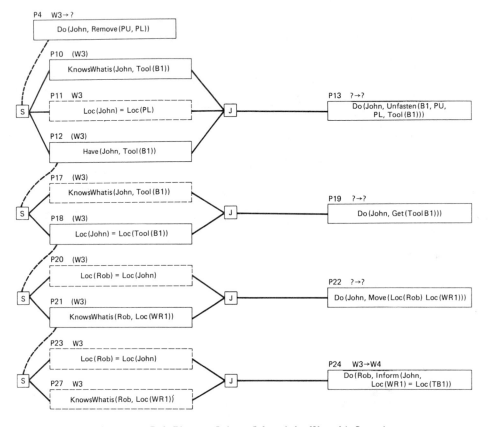

Figure 11: Rob Plans to Inform John of the Wrench's Location

5 Conclusion

This research has focused on how speakers plan referring expressions that can be coordinated with physical actions and that may satisfy multiple goals. Producing such utterances given only a description of a speaker's goals is not a simple process; it requires a powerful system that is capable of general reasoning about agents' beliefs and intentions. It is difficult to envision any alternative to utterance planning that will account for the wide range of behavior observed in human communication.

The KAMP system is an important vehicle for the investigation of a theory of language generation based on planning. Adapting KAMP from a general-purpose hierarchical planner to a language planner involved axiomatizing the various linguistic actions (illocutionary acts, surface speech-acts, describing, pointing and concept activation) in terms of the possible-worlds formalism, incorporating these axioms and action summaries into KAMP and designing plan critics that focus on interactions typical of linguistic actions. The result of incorporating these capabilities into KAMP is a system capable of producing English sentences with complex referring expressions as part of an agent's plan.

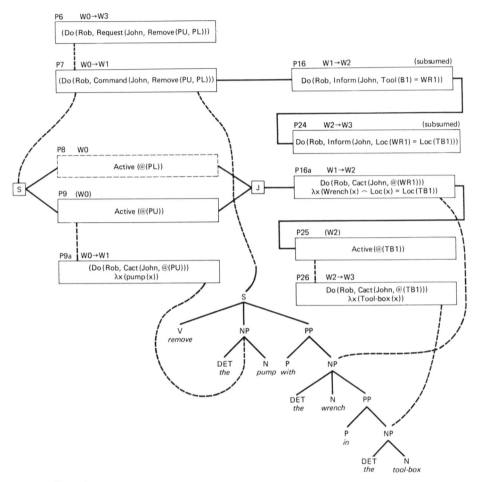

Figure 12: Incorporating the Wrench's Location into the Referring Expression

Several important research issues in planning referring expressions have been raised by the work done on KAMP, but have received only cursory examination to date. The linguistic coverage of the grammar needs to be extended considerably, and the work on TELEGRAM has been an important step in that direction. As has been cited earlier, there are a number of different purposes for which speakers use noun phrases. Not only are the concept activation actions examined in depth in this article realized by noun phrases, but also identification requests, attributive uses of definite descriptions, and a variety of other phenomena. It will be an important test of the theory to see if these other actions can be axiomatized and easily accomodated within this general framework.

KAMP has proven to be a useful tool for the investigation of planning referring expressions and utterances in general, and promises to be useful in developing a speech-act theory to account for many aspects of natural language use.

6 Bibliography

Allen, James and Perrault, C.R., Analyzing intention in utterances, *Artificial Intelligence* **15** (1980) 143–178.

Appelt, Douglas E., A planner for reasoning about knowledge and action, *Proc. of the Nat. Conf. on Artificial Intelligence*, (1980) 131–133.

Appelt, Douglas E., Planning natural-language referring expressions, *Proc. of the 20th Annual Meeting of the Assoc. for Comp. Ling.*, (1982) 108–112

Appelt, Douglas E., TELEGRAM: A grammar formalism for language planning, *Proc. of the Eighth Int. Joint Conf. on Artificial Intelligence* (1983) 595–599.

Appelt, Douglas, *Planning English Sentences*, Cambridge University Press, Cambridge, UK (1985).

Barwise, Jon and John Perry, *Situations and Attitudes* MIT Press, Cambridge, MA, (1983).

Bruce, Bertram C., Belief systems and language understanding, *BBN Technical Report No. 2973* (1975).

Bruce, Bertram C. and Newman D., Interacting plans, *Cognitive Science* **2** (1978) 195–233.

Clark, Herbert, and Marshall C., Definite reference and mutual knowledge, in Joshi, Sag, and Webber (Eds.), **Elements of Discourse Understanding**, Cambridge University Press, Cambridge (1981) 10–63.

Cohen, Philip and Perrault, C. R., Elements of a plan based theory of speech acts, *Cognitive Science* **3** (1979) 177–212.

Cohen, Philip, The need for identification as a planned action, *Proc. of the Seventh Int. Joint Conf. on Artificial Intelligence* (1981) 31–36.

Deutsch (Grosz), Barbara, Typescripts of task-oriented dialogs, *SRI International AI Center Tech. Note No. 146.* (1975)

Evans, David, *Situations and Speech Acts: Toward a Formal Semantics of Discourse*, Ph.D. dissertation, Department of Linguistics, Stanford University (1981).

Fikes, Richard E., and Nilsson, N., STRIPS: a new approach to the application of theorem proving to problem solving, *Artificial Intelligence* **2** (1971).

Grice, H. P., Logic and conversation, in Davidson (Ed.), *The Logic of Grammar*, Dickenson Publishing co., Encino, CA (1975).

Grosz, Barbara J., Focusing and description in natural language dialogs, in Joshi, Sag, and Webber (Eds.), *Elements of Discourse Understanding: Proceedings of a Workshop on Computational Aspects of Linguistic Structure and Discourse Setting*, Cambridge University Press, Cambridge (1980) 84–105.

Grosz, Barbara J., Joshi, A., and Weinstein S., Providing a unified account of definite noun phrases in discourse, *Proc. of the 21st Annual Meeting of the Assoc. for Comp. Ling.* (1983) 44-50.

Kay, Martin, Functional unification grammar: A formalism for machine translation, *Proc. of the Tenth Int. Conf. on Comp. Linguistics* (1984) 75-78.

McCarthy, John and Hayes P., Some philosophical problems from the standpoint of artificial intelligence, in Meltzer and Michie (Eds.), *Machine Intelligence* **4**, Edinburgh University Press, Edinburgh, (1969).

McKeown, Kathy, *Text Generation: Using Discourse Strategies and Focus Constraints to Generate Natural-Language Text,* Cambridge University Press, Cambridge, UK (1985).

Mann, William C. and Matthiessen, Christian, NIGEL: A systemic grammar for text generation, *University of Southern California Information Sciences Institute Technical Report ISI/RR-83-105* (1983).

Moore, Robert C., Reasoning about knowledge and action, *SRI International AI Center Tech. Note No. 191* (1980).

Nadathur, Gopalan, and Joshi, A. K., Mutual beliefs in conversational systems: their role in referring expressions, *Proc. of the Eighth Int. Joint. Conf. on Artificial Intelligence* (1983) 603-605.

Perrault, C. R. and Cohen, P., It's for your own good: a note on inaccurate reference," in Joshi, Sag, and Webber (Eds.), **Elements of Discourse Understanding,** Cambridge University Press, Cambridge (1981).

Prince, Ellen F., Toward a taxonomy of given-new information, in Cole (Ed.), *Radical Pragmatics*, Academic Press, New York, NY (1981).

Rosch, Eleanor, Mervis, C., Gray, W., Johnson, D., and P. Boyes-Braem, Basic objects in natural categories, *Cognitive Psychology* **8** (1976) 382-439.

Sacerdoti, Earl, *A Structure for Plans and Behavior*, Elsevier North-Holland, Inc., Amsterdam (1977).

Searle, John, *Speech Acts: An Essay in the Philosophy of Language,* Cambridge University Press, Cambridge, UK (1969).

Stickel, Mark E., Theory resolution: building in nonequational theories, *Proc. of the Nat. Conf. on Artificial Intelligence* (1983) 391-397.

SURFACE TRANSFORMATIONS DURING THE GENERATION OF
WRITTEN GERMAN SENTENCES

Stephan Busemann

FOREWORD

This contribution describes a system for surface transformations (SUTRA), which handles
many of the complex syntactic and morphological phenomena of German - distinguishing
between processes which code meaning and those which ignore meaning.

With the implementation of SUTRA, the natural language dialog system HAM-ANS has at its
disposal a component which is independent of domain of discourse and can transform HAM-
ANS' numerous communicative capabilities into grammatically well-formed German sentences.

SUTRA was not conceived of as a part of the HAM-ANS system, but rather as an easily
adaptable, system-independent module which can be interfaced to any natural language
system which generates the structures that SUTRA processes. The language fragment to
be generated by a partial grammar in any given instance is represented separately and
can therefore be easily extended.

Thus SUTRA does not represent an attempt to implement any particular theory of grammar,
but aims instead at a general description of the grammatical phenomena involved in any
particular fragment of German. Appropriate descriptions are to be found primarily in
the less recent linguistic literature (e.g., GLINZ 1952, DUDEN 1973, ENGEL 1977). The
theoretical framework of this literature is not at the center of present-day linguistic
research, but its coverage of a broad range of linguistic phenomena meets the needs of
SUTRA far better than many more recent works in linguistics which treat a limited range
of phenomena. These theories have yet to be generalized to cover an entire language.

Research on HAM-ANS is currently being supported by the German Ministry of Research
and Technology (BMFT) under contract 08IT15038.

1. INTRODUCTION AND OVERVIEW

In the last two decades, natural language (NL) interaction with computer systems in the field of Artificial Intelligence (AI) research has undergone a particularly rapid development. The first priorities in this research were the development of techniques for analyzing NL inputs, for storing them in the form of internal representations and evaluating them. In the initial stages, less attention was paid to the problem of how NL could be generated from evaluated internal representation structures particularly since human hearers can correctly interpret communicatively inadequate and ungrammatical utterances on the basis of their world knowledge and contextual information.

In many NL systems, the techniques employed were poorly grounded in semantics and pragmatics. For example, predetermined text schemas were instantiated according to the results of their evaluation. In the process, the structure of all responses was predetermined and knowledge about the particular dialog situation was rarely utilized. In the direct verbalization of portions of the knowledge base, it was necessary to accept the shortcoming that the quality of the utterance was to a great extent dependent on the structuring of the knowledge (MANN et al. 1982, p. 2).

With increasing complexity of NL systems and knowledge bases, the disadvantages of these methods for generating language became evident. Since these disadvantages were often extremely prejudicial to the acceptance of NL systems (cf. WAHLSTER 1982, p. 265), the development of general procedures for generating communicatively adequate responses came to the fore.

At the present time, greater attention is being paid to the development of independent NL generation systems. The research activities in this field can be broken down into two areas:

- How are the content and 'gestalt' of an utterance produced?
- How is the NL form of an utterance produced?

While the production of the 'gestalt' involves, among other things, problems of word choice and sentence structure, the NL form of an utterance involves producing its syntactically and morphologically correct surface structure.

In a number of important contributions, the generation of communicatively adequate utterances as a result of planning processes on different levels is discussed (COHEN 1978, DAVEY 1978, APPELT 1981, McKEOWN 1982). Important aspects considered are overanswering (cf. WAHLSTER et al. 1982), ellipsis (cf. JAMESON, WAHLSTER 1982), and verbalization of portions of the knowledge base for the purpose of explaining earlier utterances (cf. WAHLSTER 1981). These generation problems are for the most part directed at the first question.

The communicative achievements of a NL generation system can only be realized as grammatically well-formed surface structures by employing *syntactic tools*. These tools realize grammatical phenomena and are completely independent of the content and the "origin" of the structures processed. It is the need for such tools that is meant when the grammar is referred to as a bottle-neck or filter at the output of a (text) generation system (MANN et al. 1982, p. 5).

In this report, which takes up the second question, tools are provided for a fragment of German which inflect specified word stems and specify the necessary morpho-syntactic information (abbr.: MSI) for this process.

These tools were implemented in the SUTRA (SUrface TRAnsformations) system and are utilized in the NL dialog system HAM-ANS (HOEPPNER et al. 1983, 1984).

The following is an overview of the contents of this contribution:

Chapter 2 treats the fundamental preconditions for the utilization of SUTRA and contains an abstract description of the system.

In Chapter 3, the form and content of the interface to a hypothetical NL generation system is described. The partial grammar of German is illustrated with examples.

Chapter 4 describes the knowledge sources used in SUTRA - the rules for sentence constituent positioning, the inflection rules and the word lexicon entries necessary for SUTRA.

This knowledge is used in the transformation of the structures described in Chapter 3 into sentences of the German language. The detailed description of the step-by-step transformation in Chapter 5 serves at the same time as an exhaustive description of the system.

In Chapter 6, limitations of the system are discussed and some prospects for further development are outlined.

The utilization of SUTRA in HAM-ANS and technical data on programming environment and implementation are covered in Chapter 7 which is followed by numerous examples of performance in Chapter 8 summarizing most of the system's capabilities.

2. SURFACE TRANSFORMATIONS IN A NATURAL LANGUAGE GENERATION SYSTEM

First we will consider some aspects of language structure which speak for an independent component for surface transformations. After sketching some related work, the properties of the generation process critical for the design of SUTRA are discussed. The third part of the chapter contains an overview of the system focusing on the relationship between desired capabilities and the characteristics of the processes necessary for their realization.

2.1 SEPARATE COMPONENTS FOR SURFACE TRANSFORMATIONS

The necessity for a separate component for surface transformations motivated in the introduction is not characteristic of all languages. For languages with relatively few inflections (e.g., English), the problems outlined are simpler than for languages with a rich inflectional system (e.g., German). For this reason, most English and American systems do not include an interface between syntactic and morphological processes like the one proposed here for German.

But, up till now, even systems that generate German have not included a separate component for surface transformations.[1] A research group at the Department of Medical Cybernetics at the University of Vienna is, however, pursuing an apparently related approach (cf. BUCHBERGER 1982, HORACEK 1983).

A separate generation component on the basis of a complete form lexicon with semantic and syntactic information has been developed within the scope of the speech recognition system at the University of Erlangen-Nuremberg (REITHINGER 1984).

Kempen and Hoenkamp in their incremental procedural grammar (IPG) for a fragment of the Dutch language separate "lexico-syntactic" from "morpho-phonological" processes (KEMPEN, HOENKAMP 1982). A similar distinction is made in SUTRA (cf. 5.10). Thus it was possible to perform an interesting experiment. In order to interface the morphological transformations in SUTRA to the syntactic procedures of the IPG, it was necessary to transfer the morphological procedures written in UCI-LISP from the PDP-10 computer of the Department of Computer Science at the University of Hamburg to Franz LISP (FODERARO 1980) which is available on the department's VAX-11 computer. After minor adjustments in the IPG (Dutch and German have related grammars) and the construction of a partial lexicon for German, the IPG generated German sentences.[2]

In the field of automatic translation research, syntaxes of fragments of German, French, Russian and English had already been developed some time earlier by BROCKHAUS et al. (1976). Evidently the results of this work have not yet been applied to AI systems. It contains important fundamentals for the morphological processes in SUTRA (cf. 5.11.3).

2.2 THE CONCEPTION OF SUTRA AS A COMPONENT OF NATURAL LANGUAGE GENERATION SYSTEMS

How is a system for surface transformations to be integrated into the generation process? In (BUSEMANN 1982), it was suggested that the generation procedure should be sub-

---

[1] MORIK (1982) compares the generation components of NL systems in the Federal Republic of Germany.

[2] This work was done by H. Schotel (University of Nijmegen) and the author in approx. five man-weeks.

divided into two components (cf. Fig. (2-1)). This division corresponds to the two questions posed in the introduction.

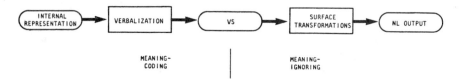

Fig. (2-1): Subdivision of the Generation Process

First the internal representation of an utterance is *verbalized*. In this process, its meaning is mapped onto structures of the German language. This requires, among other things, processes for word choice (cf. GOLDMAN 1975), for the expansion of system-internal object identifiers into noun phrases (cf. WAHLSTER et al. 1978), and the generation of explicit syntactic constituents which delimit the scope of the MSI items (cf. 2.3).

Although the meaning of an utterance is not changed in the process of verbalization, this can be seen as a *meaning coding* process since NL structures result. The output is a grammatically specified form of the utterance - the *Verbalized Structure* (VS).

In the VS, all transformations which were *initiated* but not yet completed during verbalization are specified in MSI form. Among these are ellipsis, pronominalization, and certain aspects of word order such as those that are involved in the realization of coherence relations and emphasis or focus marking.

In the second part of the language generation process, i.e., during the application of *surface transformations*, the VS is processed by the syntactic and morphological tools until a grammatically well-formed sentence results. Since all transformations in this component function without knowledge of meaning they are termed *meaning ignoring* transformations.

The division into meaning-coding and meaning-ignoring processes in language generation makes it possible to design a flexible module independent of both the particular NL system and the domain of discourse. The only connecting link between this module and the NL generation system (besides the interface) is the module's access to the word lexicon.

2.3 THE FUNCTION AND DESIGN OF SUTRA

The last component of a NL generation system to be activated has the task of generating grammatically well-formed sentences.

For German, this involves carrying out numerous inflectional processes. These are implemented on the basis of different MSI which must, in part, be determined previously by grammatical processes.

SUTRA processes a VS representing a sentence. The system works in two steps. Its over-all structure is shown in Figure (2-2). The first step realizes syntactic transforma-tions on the basis of MSI specified in the VS, orders sentence constituents with the aid of separate, context-sensitive knowledge and makes explicit some additional MSI necessary for word inflection. The final result of the syntactic processes forms a fur-ther intermediate representation of the generated utterance, the *Preterminal String* (PS).[1] The PS contains bundles of MSI which are assigned to word stems by utilizing grammatical agreement features. It forms the input structure for the second step in which context-free morphological processes use the specified MSI to generate the inflec-tional morphemes from a further separate knowledge source and attach them to the stems.

While the PS is linearly ordered, a hierarchical syntactic constituent structure is necessary in the VS in order to assure the proper assignment of the syntactic transfor-mations to those constituents which they operate on. This is suggested in Figure (2-3) where an example of processing a VS with an embedded sentence is given. The syntactic

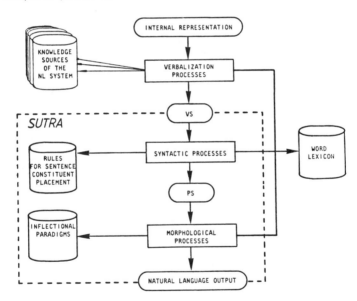

Fig. (2-2): Surface Transformations in the Generation Process

---

[1] The PS differs from the presentation by v. HAHN et al. (1980) and WAHLSTER (1982), where an intermediate representation without MSI is described which, however, can-not by itself serve as a basis for word inflection.

processes (in Fig. (2-3), only subject-verb agreement, generation of discontinuous verb constituents, and positioning of sentence constituents are mentioned) can proceed in a fixed, predeterminate order, each generating as its result the modified VS required for the next process. In Figure (2-3), the unmodified parts are represented by dots. First, the syntactic transformations apply to the main clause, then to the embedded object clause. The resulting PS contains various MSI items.

What then is the source of the MSI represented in a PS? There are three sources: The MSI is either contained explicitly in the VS, or implicitly in the VS, or it is contained in the word lexicon. Let us consider the three possibilities more closely.

Only that information which was required by the NL system for evaluation and earlier phases of generation appears *explicitly* in the VS. Some of this information is carried over to the PS, e.g., mood (labeled m:, cf. Fig. (2-3)), while other parts are processed by the syntactic transformations and no longer appear in the PS, as for example voice (v:), which, in the case of passive, brings about the generation of non-finite verb constructions, or pronominalization instructions (pro:), which prepare the generation of the corresponding pronouns (cf. 5.6).

Verb tense (t:) is also processed by a syntactic transformation which generates among other things[1], a new, "morphological" tense indication (present or imperfect). This indication appears explicitly in the PS.

If we view such a process as a step in the transformation of a piece of semantic information (here perhaps: the time of occurrence of an event) into its surface realization as an inflectional suffix, it can be seen how it is transformed into syntactic and later morphological information in the course of the generation process. Looking at the process in this way also brings to light relationships between semantics, syntax and morphology.

Implicit in the VS is that information that was not utilized in earlier processing phases, e.g., for the construction of the internal representation or for the verbalization of an utterance. Examples are person (labeled p:, cf. 5.2.2), surface case (labeled k:, cf. 5.9.1) and type of determination (labeled d:, cf. 5.9.2). This information appears explicitly in the PS because it too is involved in guiding word inflection processes. The implicit information can also be viewed as the coding of semantic information, which firsts assumes an explicit form as MSI when this is necessary for syntactic reasons.

Since both types of MSI - explicit and implicit - are determined by the meaning of an utterance or part of an utterance, they can be classified as *variables*. In contrast, the lexical MSI is termed *constant* since it represents invariable characteristics of

---

[1] In addition, the generation of non-finite verb constituents may be necessary (see 5.5).

VERBALIZED STRUCTURE:

```
(sent-s (verb (v: ACTIVE) (m: IND) (t: PRES) BEHAUPT)
        (object-s
         (sent-s (verb (v: ACTIVE) (m: KON) (t: PERF) ANHALT)
                 (case-slot S-TIME (ap-s RECHTZEITIG))
                 (case-slot S-LOCATIVE (pp-s VOR (np-s (n: SG) D ROT AMPEL)))
                 (case-slot S-AGENT (np-s (n: SG) (pro: PRN) FAHRER))))
        (subject-p (np-s (n: SG) D FAHRER (attr-gen (np-s (n: SG) D GELB WAGEN))))))
```

SYNTACTIC PROCESSES:

Subject-verb agreement changes the constituent *verb*.

(... (verb (p: 3) (n: SG) (v: ACTIVE) (m: IND) (t: PRES) BEHAUPT) ...)

During the *generation of discontinuous verb constituents*, the constituent *verb* is replaced yielding

(... (finite (p: 3) (n: SG) (m: IND) (t: PRES) BEHAUPT) ...)

Positioning of sentence constituents changes the order on top level
from: *finite, object-s, subject-p*
to: *subject-p, finite, object-s*

> SYNTACTIC PROCESSES for the object clause:
>
> The constituent S-AGENT is *selected as subject* and renamed.
> *Subject-verb agreement* changes the constituent *verb*.
> (... (verb (p: 3) (n: SG) (v: ACTIVE) (m: KON) (t: PERF) ANHALT)
> ... (subject-p (np-s (n: SG) (pro: PRN) FAHRER)))
>
> *verb* is replaced through the *discontinuous verb constituents*
> (... (finite (p: 3) (n: SG) (m: KON) (t: PRES) HAB)
>   (infinite ((vinfin: PPRF) ANHALT)) ...)
>
> *Positioning of sentence constituents* changes the order
> from: *finite, infinite, s-time, s-locative, subject-p*
> to: *subject-p, s-time, s-locative, infinite, finite*

PRETERMINAL STRING of the whole clause:

```
((k: NOM) (g: MAS) (n: SG) (d: DEF) (DETDEF D) (NOM FAHRER)
 (k: GEN) (g: MAS) (n: SG) (d: DEF) (DETDEF D) (ADJ GELB) (NOM WAGEN)
 (p: 3) (n: SG) (t: PRES) (m: IND) (VRB BEHAUPT) (MARK ,)
 (XXX DASS) (k: NOM) (g: MAS) (n: SG) (p: 3) (PERSPRN)
 (XXX RECHTZEITIG)
 (PRP VOR) (k: DAT) (g: FEM) (n: SG) (d: DEF) (DETDEF D) (ADJ ROT) (NOM AMPEL)
 (vinfin: PPRF) (VRB ANHALT)
 (p: 3) (n: SG) (t: PRES) (m: KON) (VRB HAB) (MARK ,))
```

MORPHOLOGICAL PROCESSES transform the PS into the NL UTTERANCE:

DER FAHRER DES GELBEN WAGENS BEHAUPTET, DASS ER RECHTZEITIG VOR DER
ROTEN AMPEL ANGEHALTEN HABE.
[The driver of the yellow car claims that he in time in front of the
red traffic lights stopped had.]

Fig. (2-3): Example of Processing in SUTRA with some Intermediate Results
(dots stand for the unmodified parts of the VS)

lexemes. Insofar as it is relevant for the inflection of word groups (i.e., where agreement is involved) lexical MSI (e.g., gender of a noun) is made explicit in the PS (label g:). Other constant information is only relevant for individual word stems and is thus first determined by the corresponding inflectional processes (e.g., the declension class of a noun (cf. 5.11.1.1)).

The three kinds of MSI represented in the PS are thus derived either from explicit indications in the VS or extracted from parts of the VS with the aid of grammatically motivated procedures, or taken from the word lexicon.

The conception of SUTRA sketched above requires access to two components of a NL generation system - the verbalization component and the word lexicon (see Fig. (2-2)). While the interface to the verbalization component requires a complete definition of its syntax and semantics, the syntax of the lexicon access in SUTRA is not predetermined, but rather taken over from the NL generation system, which has the necessary basic processes at its disposal. The semantics of the lexicon access is specified by the categories of the constant MSI (cf. 4.1).

Because of the exclusively linguistic demands SUTRA places on the NL generation system, SUTRA can be interfaced to any NL generation system that generates verbalized structures and supplies the necessary constant MSI.

3. THE INTERFACE TO A NATURAL LANGUAGE GENERATION SYSTEM

The interface to a NL generation system is not designed to be limited to a particular fragment of German, on the contrary, it should be possible to extend it to embrace additional grammatical constructs. For this reason partial grammars such as the one which generates the language fragment discussed in this chapter should be declaratively defined as in Appendix A.

The input to SUTRA must contain, in addition to the canonical word stems, the variable MSI. The nature and extent of these depends on the grammatical construct to be generated and must therefore also be easily extendable. The scope of the MSI is defined through syntactic constituents and hence limited to that portion of the utterance that is relevant to them.

In the following section, the hierarchical structure of the constituents utilized will be presented. The description of the MSI in the input follows. Finally, the fragment of German to be generated will be discussed.

3.1 THE HIERARCHICAL STRUCTURE OF THE INTERFACE

The basic sentence concept has been borrowed from valency and dependency grammar and is supplemented by the hierarchical constituent structure (see Appendix A). The constituents carry identifiers corresponding to their syntactic role.[1]

In SUTRA, the identifiers refer to grammatical characteristics of the constituent in question. In this manner *sent-s* triggers the processing of a simple sentence by SUTRA. Each sentence consists of an a priori indeterminate number of sentence constituents. Sentence constituents are those parts of the input which can be permuted with the aid of the *permutation test* (GLINZ 1952) and are thus subject to the rules for positioning sentence constituents (cf. 4.2).

Sentence constituents carry partly semantic, partly syntactic identifiers. The semantic identifiers correspond to the names of deep cases (see the definition of DEEP-CASE-LABEL in Appendix A), which, in HAM-ANS, are filled and verbalized as sentence constituents. In SUTRA, they are only used for sentence constituent positioning and for extraction of MSI about surface case, just like syntactic identifiers (see the definition of SENTENCE-CONSTITUENT).

In SUTRA, sentences which consist of subject, copula and predicate complement (cf. BUSEMANN 1982, 6.3.1) can be processed as well as those which are represented with a fully instantiated case frame (FILLMORE 1968) in the NL generation system. In HAM-ANS, both forms of representation are used, while in SUTRA a uniform representation is employed allowing, among other things, considerable simplification of the sentence constituent positioning process (cf. 4.2). The VS in (3-1)[2] was verbalized from a case-frame representation, while the verb in (3-2) has its origins in a copula (compare also the VS in Fig. (2-3)).

```
(3-1) (sent-s
        (verb (v: ACTIVE) (m: IND) (t: PERF) ABBIEG)
        (case-slot S-AGENT (np-s (n: SG) D GELB PERSONENWAGEN))
        (case-slot S-SOURCE (pp-s VON (np-s (n: SG) D OSTSTRASSE)))
        (case-slot S-GOAL (pp-s IN (np-s (n: SG) D SUEDRING)))
        (case-slot S-TIME (ap-s GERADE)))
```

   Der gelbe Personenwagen ist gerade von der Oststraße in den Südring abgebogen.
   [The yellow car has just from Oststraße onto Südring turned off.]

```
(3-2) (sent-s (subject-p (np-s (n: PL) SCHMETTERLING))
        (verb (v: ACTIVE) (m: IND) (t: PRES) SEIN)
        (predicative (np-s (n: PL) BUNT INSEKT))
        (modifier (ap-s IMMER)))
```

   Schmetterlinge sind immer bunte Insekten.
   [Butterflies are always brightly colored insects.]

---

[1] The explicit naming of constituents is also utilized by McDONALD (1981, p. 25).

[2] Translations of the sample sentences are put into brackets. They follow closely the German syntax in order to provide an impression of the discussed phenomena to the reader who is not familiar with the German language.

In contrast to the first sentence type (3-1), a VS for copula-sentences like (3-2) contains a constituent which is already marked as subject (*subject-p*). This is necessary since in (3-2) SUTRA could not decide unambiguously which constituent should become subject and which predicate noun. This choice is not arbitrary as (3-3) and (3-4) demonstrate.

(3-3) Butterflies are always brightly colored insects.

(3-4) Brightly colored insects are always butterflies.

object-p and *indobj* make it possible to explicitly specify a direct or an indirect object without making use of the semantic identifiers, e.g., S-RECIPIENT.

The direct object can be an embedded clause (*object-s*, cf. Fig. (2-3)), in which case the recursive definition initiates the syntactic processing of that clause. The sentence constituent labeled *subclause* makes it possible to process a variety of subordinate clauses that are introduced with a conjunction.

The identifiers beginning with *pp, np* and *ap* indicate coordinate and simple prepositional, noun or adjective phrases which are not only immediate constituents of sentence constituents. Noun phrases, for example, are also constituents of prepositional phrases. Furthermore, noun phrases may contain (in final position) an attribute whose *attr* label indicates that the embedded constituent (marked with *sent, pp* or *np* labels) is to be interpreted as a relative clause, prepositional attribute or genitive attribute (cf. the example in Fig. (2-3)). The labels *comparison* and *elision* control the comparison of the embedded adjective and the elision of the embedded sentence constituent or noun.

Further examples are to be found in sec. 3.3.

3.2 CANONICAL WORDS AND MORPHO-SYNTACTIC INFORMATION IN THE VERBALIZED STRUCTURE

The word stems in the VS are defined as canonical forms of which inflectional endings can be added. They usually consist of the largest common base for all possible forms (verbs may have additional bases; cf. 5.11.3). Verb stems can, for example, be defined as *infinitive forms without the infinitive morpheme EN or N* (e.g., *LAUF* [run], *RECHN* [calculate], *MOGEL* [cheat]). The verb *SEIN* [be] with the stem *SEIN* is the only exception.

In its present stage of development SUTRA only orders the constituents of a clause. The order of word stems within sentence constituents is implicitly assumed to be the terminal word order. A linguistically motivated linearization procedure for word groups would require, in particular, a further subcategorization of noun phrases as, e.g., in (KEMPEN, HOENKAMP 1982), but even this would not suffice. Engel's procedure for distinguishing among adverbial specifications, e.g., *SCHON LANGE NICHT MEHR* in (3-5) (from ENGEL 1977, p. 201) requires knowledge about the semantic and pragmatic context which is not available in SUTRA. For this reason, the word order in the example could not be reconstructed, if, for example, the word order in the underlying VS were specified alphabetically.

(3-5) *Deshalb haben die Kinder   schon   lange   nicht mehr damit   gerechnet.*
      Thus   have the children already long time no more   on that counted.
      [So, the children haven't counted on that for a long time.]

Furthermore, there are no syntactic rules that can be used to determine an unambiguous order in (3-6). Thus the succession of coordinate constituents in a VS is likewise considered terminal.

(3-6) Fritz traveled by way of Hamburg, Hannover, Kassel, Fulda and Frankfurt.

The VS explicitly contains only the MSI that SUTRA cannot arrive at with the aid of morphosyntactic or lexical knowledge. Since this MSI is based on knowledge that was required at an earlier stage in the generation process, the VS can be characterized as free of redundancies. The list (3-7) contains the MSI which must be explicitly specified in the VS (cf. the definitions of MSI and WORD in Appendix A):

(3-7) • Mood, tense and voice of the verb
      • Number in noun phrases
      • Pronominalization in noun phrases
      • Formulation of sentence constituents as relative pronouns
      • Comparison of adjectives (usually positive)
      • Elision of sentence constituents
      • Elision of the noun in a noun phrase

Voice, mood and tense determine a number of morphosyntactic transformations applied to the verb stem. The category number is not assigned to a specific word stem (e.g., a noun) but rather to an entire noun phrase taking into account the requirement for grammatical agreement between the noun and nominal adjuncts in German. In order to compare adjectives, it is necessary to have information about the degree of comparison (comparative or superlative).

The decision as to whether a noun phrase should be formulated as a pronoun or not is made during verbalization and carried out in SUTRA. SUTRA does not treat reflexives at present. Similarly, decisions regarding the permissibility of sentence constituent and noun deletion are made during verbalization and carried out in SUTRA. The elision of nouns prior to the surface transformations would not be an adequate solution since this would not allow for gender agreement between nouns and their modifiers within the noun phrase. SUTRA could no longer establish grammatical gender as a lexical feature of nouns.

3.3 THE FRAGMENT OF GERMAN TO BE GENERATED

In order to limit necessary extensions of the interface if SUTRA is adapted by an NL system, the fragment to be generated by SUTRA is based on a compilation of linguistic capabilities which a broad natural language AI system should be able to evaluate (MORIK 1982). Most of the grammatical phenomena which are necessary for these capabilities can be represented in the interface and processed by SUTRA. They are listed in (3-8):

(3-8) • Placement of the finite verb in first position (yes-no questions)
- Placement of finite verb in second position (main clauses)
- Placement of finite verb in end position (subordinate clauses)
- Coordination of sentences, phrases and of individual words
- Prepositional phrases
- Noun phrases with:
  - attributive adjectives
  - postposed genitive attribute
  - postposed prepositional attribute
  - attributive relative clauses; the relative pronoun replaces a noun phrase which is
    - a sentence constituent
    - embedded in a prepositional phrase
- Adjective and adverbial phrases (negation, proforms, adverbial modifiers)
- Verb constructions with six tenses; active, passive; indicative, subjunctive
- Personal pronouns
- Indefinite pronouns
- Possessive pronouns
- Ellipsis
- Comparison of adjectives and adverbs

List (3-9) contains a number of important phenomena (cf. Morik's (1982) list) that SUTRA cannot yet process. These phenomena more closely define some of the points listed in (3-8). Processing them would require expansion of the constituent structure and, in some cases, of the stock of MSI.

(3-9) • WH-Questions
- Imperatives
- Appositives to noun phrases
- Infinitival subordinate clauses   (cont. on next page)

- Relative clauses
  - as subject or object complements
  - whose pronoun replaces a genitive attribute
  - introduced by other elements than inflected forms of the stem
- Reflexive verbs and reflexive pronouns
- Preposed genitive and prepositional attributes
- Modal auxiliaries
- Adjective and noun valency

The following examples show some additional restrictions on the partial grammar de-
limited in Appendix A and illustrate how the hierarchical constituent structure, the
MSI and the canonical words are represented in a VS.

(3-10) Who has caused the accident?

(3-11) (sent-s
          (subject-p
            (np-s (n: SG) D FAHRER
                  (attr-gen (np-s (n: SG) D GELB WAGEN))))))

        Der Fahrer des gelben Wagens.
        [The driver (of) the yellow car.]

Verbalized structures can be grammatically complete or *elliptical* if sentence constituents are deleted, as in (3-11), or nouns are marked, as in (3-13). If SUTRA is
adapted to a NL dialog system, generating elliptical utterances is required to answer
questions like (3-10) or (3-12) in a communicatively adequate manner.

(3-12) Which car was parked behind the small tree?

(3-13) (sent-s (subject-p (np-s (n: SG) D GELB (elision AUTO)))))

        Das gelbe. [The yellow.]

If an elliptical VS contains a verb a sentence constituent capable at becoming subject
must also be present. A VS like (3-14) is ill-formed and should not be generated by
the verbalization component. The attempt to generate (3-15) from (3-14) would fail
in any case because SUTRA would try to generate a finite verb form which, in this
instance, would not be possible since subject-verb agreement (in number and person) is
not possible. Even if the subject were present and marked as deletable, the desired
result (3-15) would not be generated, rather an additional finite verb form would be
produced.[1]

---

[1] On the marking of sentence constituents for the generation of ellipses see 5.3.

(3-14) (sent-s (v: ACTIVE) (m: IND) (t: PERF) GEH))

(3-15) *Gegangen.* [Gone.]

A further restriction affects the generation of relative clauses. In (3-16) the noun
phrase to be relativized is marked by (pro: REL). In German, relative pronouns that
replace a genitive attribute (cf. (3-11)) are placed before the head of the genitive
attribute. Generating these would require certain noun phrase word order modifications
which, at present, are not performed in SUTRA. Thus preposed genitive attributes cannot
be generated from a VS constructed according to the syntax defined in Appendix A.
We'll come back to this problem in section 6.1.

```
(3-16) (sent-s
        (subject-p
         (np-s (n: PL) D ZWEI BAUM
             (attr-rel
               (sent-s
                 (verb (v: ACTIVE) (m: IND) (t: PRES) PARK)
                 (case-slot S-AGENT (np-s (n: SG) EIN GRUEN AUTO))
                 (case-slot S-LOCATIVE
                             (pp-s ZWISCHEN (np-s (n: PL) (pro: REL)
                                                D ZWEI BAUM)))))))))
```

Die zwei Bäume, zwischen denen ein grünes Auto parkt.
[The two trees between which a green car is parked.]

Another phenomenon concerning the head noun in a noun phrase occurs in (3-17). Here,
KEIN is not only a quantifier, it also replaces the noun phrase *KEIN STUHL* [no chair].
In order to find the necessary gender information for the inflection of *KEIN*, the
head noun of the embedded attribute is chosen (here: *STUHL*).

```
(3-17) (sent-s
        (subject-p
         (np-s (n: SG) KEIN
             (attr-prp (pp-s VON (np-s (n: PL) D DREI STUHL)))))))
```

Keiner von den drei Stühlen.
[None of the three chairs.]

```
(3-18) (sent-c (sent-s (subject-p (np-c (np-s (n: SG) D BETT)
                                    UND
                                    (np-s (n: PL) D SESSEL)))
                       (verb (v: ACTIVE) (m: IND) (t: PRES) SEIN)
                       (predicative (ap-s HART)))
               ABER
               (sent-s (subject-p (np-s (n: SG) EIN SOFA))
                       (verb (v: ACTIVE) (m: IND) (t: PRES) SEIN)
                       (predicative (ap-s SEHR WEICH))))
```

Das Bett und die Sessel sind hart, aber ein Sofa ist sehr weich.
[The bed and the easy-chairs are hard, but one sofa is very soft.]

Sentences and phrases can be coordinated (cf. their definitions in Appendix A). An example for the coordination of sentences and noun phrases is given in (3-18).

The deletion of the subject and the finite verb form has not yet been provided for. Hence a VS for a coordinate sentence like (3-19) cannot be processed.

(3-19) The knave of hearts has stolen the tarts and taken them all away.

The coordination of adjectives and quantifiers is possible overall in SUTRA since they inherit the same MSI, as in (3-20).

```
(3-20) (sent-s (case-slot S-LOCATIVE
                      (pp-s IN (np-s (n: SG) DIES ODER JEN
                                SCHOEN ALT BERUEHMT STADT)))))
```

> *In dieser oder jener schönen, alten, berühmten Stadt.*
> [In this or that beautiful, old, famous city.]

In SUTRA, attributive adjectives can be compared (3-21). In the case of predicate adjectives, only comparisons like (3-23), not those like (3-22), are possible because the than-phrase depends on the adjective, not on the verb. The adjective is represented in an adverbial phrase, as in (3-23), which cannot govern phrasal constituents (cf. Appendix A). This problem touches upon the representation of adjective valencies which are not dealt with in SUTRA (cf. (3-9)).

```
(3-21) (sent-s
         (subject-p (np-s (n: SG) D
                                   (comparison (cmp: SUP) ALT)
                                   (elision WEINROEMER)))
         (verb (v: ACTIVE) (m: IND) (t: PRES) SEIN)
         (predicative (np-s (n: SG) D
                                   (comparison (cmp: SUP) SCHOEN)
                                   (elision WEINROEMER)))))
```

> *Der älteste ist der schönste.*
> [The oldest is the most beautiful (wine goblet).]

(3-22) *Der grüne ist schöner als der blaue.*
       [The green is more beautiful than the blue.]

```
(3-23)
       (sent-s
         (subject-p (np-s (n: SG) D ROT (elision WEINROEMER)))
         (verb (v: ACTIVE) (m: IND) (t: PRES) SEIN)
         (predicative (ap-s (comparison (cmp: SUP) TEUER))))
```

> *Der rote ist am teuersten.*
> [The red is the most expensive.]

4. THE KNOWLEDGE SOURCES REQUIRED FOR SUTRA

In SUTRA, there are two separate knowledge sources. The first consists of rules for *positioning sentence constituents*. The other provides *inflectional morphemes* with the aid of morphological features. In addition, SUTRA has access to the *word lexicon* of the NL system.

In principle, the lexical MSI could also be stored in a separate knowledge source belonging to SUTRA in order to make the module independent of the NL system. However, two considerations recommend using the NL system's word lexicon. For one thing, the constant MSI are accessed by means of lexical word stems, for another, SUTRA, in contrast to a NL system, is not bound to particular domains of discourse so that the scope of a separate SUTRA word lexicon would only be arbitrarily delimitable.

In the following sections, the demands placed on the word lexicon will be described and the two knowledge sources internal to the module will be explained. In Chapter 5 we will go into the grammatical knowledge contained in the individual transformations and the methods for explicating MSI.

4.1 DEMANDS PLACED ON THE WORD LEXICON

In (4-1), the constant MSI necessary for the processing of the verbalized structures described in Chapter 3 are listed.

(4-1) • Word class
   • Gender of nouns
   • Case governed by prepositions
   • Declension information for nouns
   • Conjugation information for verbs
   • Comparison information for adjectives

It should be clear from this list that SUTRA does not require a complete-form lexicon. The individual types of lexical information will be considered in more detail below.

4.1.1 The Word Class System

Word classes are necessary in SUTRA for two reasons. First of all, lexical MSI is in part dependent on word class (e.g., gender is characteristic of nouns and case i.a. is governed by prepositions). Secondly, word classes determine the selection of different inflectional paradigms. Neither aspect requires a great deal of differentiation so that SUTRA requires only a relatively small word-class system (4-2).

(4-2)
- Verbs, auxiliaries, modal verbs   VRB
- Nouns   NOM
- Attributive adjectives   ADJ
- Definite article (*D*)   DETDEF
- Indefinite article (*EIN*), *KEIN*   DETIND
- Quantifiers and Determiners in article position DETQ
- Relative pronouns   RELPRN
- Personal pronouns   PERSPRN
- Possessive pronouns   POSSPRN
- Prepositions   PRP
- Remaining noninflecting stems   XXX

This subclassification must be differentiated from the word-class systems used in NL systems, in which word classes play an important role in the analysis. For parsing, it is necessary to introduce finer distinctions, for instance, in the class of remaining non-inflecting stems XXX. Grouping these words as a class in SUTRA makes it possible to convert the preterminal word stems assigned to this class unchanged into terminal word forms.

SUTRA operates under the assumption that an unambiguous accessing of the lexicon is always possible. This is not, however, always the case: for example, *SEIN* belongs both to the word class VRB (in the reading *to be*) and to the word class POSSPRN (in the reading *his, its*). In addition, many verb stems are also canonical noun forms.

Both problems, the difference in word class systems and unambiguous lexicon accessing, make an adapter necessary. This adapter converts the word-class system of the NL system into the system presented in the list (4-2) and replaces some pointer to a lexicon entry with the associated canonical form that is processed by SUTRA (cf. 3.2). In HAM-ANS (as well as in the examples in this paper) the canonical forms serve by themselves as keys to lexicon entries. Thus the HAM-ANS lexicon need not contain more than one entry for a particular canonical form.

4.1.2 General and Special Lexical Features

General features are those lexical characteristics of word stems that must be represented in the PS. Among the categories mentioned in (4-1), in addition to word class, the gender of nouns and the cases governed by prepositions are general features which are required in the respective entries.

The prepositional cases form a list of all those surface cases in which a word governed by a preposition can be inflected. The appropriate case for a given occasion is selected as described in 5.9.1.

The *special* features refer to inflectional information for nouns, verbs and adjectives. This information in its form and degree of detail, is required in order to satisfy special demands made by SUTRA.

For nouns an indication of *declension type* is necessary because the MSI about case, number and gender is not sufficient for determining inflectional morpheme precisely. The lexicon must also contain information on *verb types* which determines the degree of irregularity of a verb and hence the necessity of further lexical *conjugation information* on ablauted stem forms, perfect participle, separable prefix and choice of auxiliary. Adjectives are associated with a *comparison class* which makes it possible to unambiguously determine comparative morphemes. For adjectives with irregular comparison, comparative and/or superlative base forms are utilized. The utilization of the special features will be described in sec. 5.11.

4.1.3 Accessing HAM-ANS' Word Lexicon

HAM-ANS' word lexicon is composed of a mixture of complete forms and stem forms (HOEPPNER et al. 1984). The MSI in (4-1) is associated with word stems so that SUTRA does not access other lexemes. For each stem, there is exactly one lexicon entry so that the problem of unambiguous accessing is not posed by HAM-ANS.

Table (4-3) shows how the word classes necessary for generation in HAM-ANS (HOEPPNER 1981) are projected onto the SUTRA word classes. Relative pronouns (cf. (4-2)), are generated by SUTRA.

All lexical MSI with the exception of word class can be directly processed by SUTRA. Appendix B contains an excerpt from HAM-ANS lexicon.

4.2   KNOWLEDGE ABOUT THE POSITION OF SENTENCE CONSTITUENTS

Since the order of sentence constituents and not the order of words is computed in SUTRA, the ordering rules refer to sentence constituent identifiers. Some of these correspond to more than one type of sentence constituent (e.g., INDOBJ represents those constituents which contain *indobj* and S-RECIPIENT; SUBJECT represents those constituents labelled *subject-p* and *subject-s*). The rules are controled through a set of parameters. Hence the 'normal' word order of a sentence is generated in the same way as any deviation from the norm specified by the parameters. Deviations for emphasis, focus, coherence relations or stylistic reasons are not considered in this paper. Such rules would require additional pragmatic or semantic features to be represented in the interface. They could also be applied by another component of the NL system (perhaps a 'style expert') which would take control of sentence constituent placement by setting additional parameters.

(4-3)

	HAM-ANS	SUTRA
Verb	VRB	
SEIN, HAB, WERD	AUX	VRB
Noun	NOM	NOM
Attributive adjective	ADJ	
Attributive quantifying adjective	DET	ADJ
Attributive perfect participle	PAR	
Article and quantifier	DET	DETDEF / DETIND / DETQ
Personal pronoun	PRN	PRN
Possessive pronoun	POSSPRN	POSSPRN
Preposition	PRP	PRP
Predicate adjective	ADJ	
Predicate perfect participle	PAR	
Adverb	ADV	
Verb prefix	VRBZ	
Conjunction	KON	XXX
Subordinating conjunction	NSKON	
Interjection	ITJ	
Cardinal number	ZWT	
Negation particle	NEG	

In the basic pattern of the main clause, the subject is always in the forefield (cf. DU-
DEN 1973, § 1501 ff.). All other constituents with the exception of verb constituents
are placed in the middle field or the end field (cf. Fig. (4-1)). The rules are defined with the aid of the principle that the *structurally necessary* sentence constituents in the middle field are positioned as far as possible from the finite verb which
is always in the second position (HELBIG, SCHENKEL 1969).[1] In SUTRA, the basic patterns
for each sentence constituent are defined by determining for each cooccuring sentence
constituent whether that constituent stands before or after the constituent in question.
It is assumed that each identifier occurs no more than once in a sentence. This requirement is motivated by FILLMORE (1968) for language processing directed by case
frames. At present, the rules are controled by the following parameters:

- Sentence type (FRONT, CENTRAL, LAST)
- Formulation as relative pronoun (T, F)
- Formulation as personal pronoun (T, F)

---

[1] Structural necessity can be determined with the *deletion test* (GLINZ 1952) which
checks each sentence constituent to determine whether the remainder of a sentence
would be grammatical if that particular constituent were deleted.

FORE-FIELD	finite verb const.	MIDDLE FIELD			infinite verb const.	END FIELD
Peter	hat	seinen Eltern	gestern	nichts	gesagt	außer der Wahrheit
[Peter	has	his parents	yesterday	nothing	said	but the truth]

Fig. (4-1): Structure of the German Declarative Sentence (according to DUDEN 1973)

Sentence type refers to the position of the finite verb and is calculated from an input parameter for SUTRA (the default value is CENTRAL). In the (recursive) processing of dependent clauses, LAST is entered automatically. The position of other sentence constituents is not influenced by sentence type.

If a noun phrase is to be formulated as a relative pronoun (in accordance with (3-8)), the corresponding sentence constituent is positioned at the front of the (relative) clause. Note that in this case sentence type is LAST. This interdependence of parameters can be utilized in the positioning rules (cf. Appendix C).

In certain cases, pronominal formulation of a noun phrase changes the position of some sentence constituents. For instance, a pronominal direct object must be positioned before the indirect object, as in (4-5). In the positioning rules utilized in SUTRA - Appendix C contains an excerpt - the ordering with respect to this pronominal formulation of a noun phrase is considered only in connection with the cooccurrence of direct and indirect objects.

(4-5) *Karl gibt seiner Schwester ein Buch.*
   [Karl gives his sister a book.]

   Karl gibt es seiner Schwester.
   [Karl gives it (to) his sister.]

4.3   MORPHOLOGICAL KNOWLEDGE

The inflection of word stems is carried out on the basis of MSI found in the PS or the lexicon. In this process, knowledge from MSI about the generation of an inflectional morpheme (or the complete form in case of personal pronoun generation) is utilized within an inflectional paradigm. This knowledge is coded into decision trees whose nonterminal nodes represent MSI and whose terminal nodes represent inflectional morphemes or pronominal forms.

In SUTRA, the following paradigms are used:

- Comparison
- Adjective inflection
- Inflection of quantifiers and possessive pronouns
- Noun inflection
- Personal pronoun generation
- Inflection of the definite article and relative pronoun
- Verb inflection

For verb inflection (5.11.3), the dynamic calculation of a *segment type* specifying the basic form of the verb to be used is necessary. The knowledge necessary for this is coded in a similar manner.

A list of MSI items whose number and order correspond to the structure of the tree in question directs the breadth-first search through the tree which has been coded as LISP list progressing from left to right. This search procedure functions most efficiently when frequently used paths through a tree are placed at the beginning of the corresponding LISP list. The terminal nodes of the accessible subtrees are not always distinguished from one another beyond a certain depth. In such cases, only one subtree is specified. Its root is marked by the special nonterminal ELSE:.
Appendix D contains all of SUTRA's inflectional paradigms.

5. THE TRANSFORMATION OF THE VERBALIZED STRUCTURE

The term transformation (cf. CHOMSKY 1957, 1965) is used in SUTRA for deletion, replacement, extension and permutation of constituents of an initial structure. Meaning is not changed in these processes. The application of transformations in SUTRA is deterministic.

The structures to which the transformations apply are not deep structures in the Chomskyian sense, but rather grammatically prestructured intermediate representations of utterances. The resulting structures often form the basis for further transformations as was indicated in Figure (2-3).

While Chomsky transforms tree structures into tree structures, in SUTRA, tree structures can be transformed into other trees (cf. 5.4) or into nonhierarchically organized (linear) strings (cf. 5.10).

SUTRA transformations do not confirm exclusively to a particular model of grammar but are chosen solely according to the requirements of modular structuring thereby simplifying the language generation process. This simplification argument is emphasized by Rohrer who in turn bases his position on Chomsky (ROHRER 1971, p. 57).

In SUTRA syntactic oriented transformations generate a linear string, the PS, from the hierarchically structured VS. This string is then put into its final form by morphological transformations.

In Chapter 2, it was noted that the MSI in the VS is not sufficient for many transformations. The necessary supplementary information is either taken from the word lexicon (see 4.1), derived with the aid of knowledge-based rules (see 4.2, 4.3) or extracted from the VS by utilizing linguistic knowledge. The task of the transformations is to inspect or to consume the MSI relevant to them and to specify explicitely the MSI required for later transformation (see 2.3).

Figure (5-1) contains an overview. The individual transformations frequently initiate other operations which are not shown here. The arrows indicate the temporal order of processing, while the dashes mean that no a priori order of transformations can be stated.

The following sections describe the functioning of the transformations and explain how they are triggered, what additional MSI they require and how this is determined. The order of operations in Figure (5-1) will be maintained in the presentation insofar as possible.

5.1 DETERMINATION OF THE SUBJECT

Even in the valency grammar oriented approach utilized in SUTRA, the subject receives special treatment based on agreement in number and person with the finite verb.

In a number of cases, a marked subject is already present in the VS (cf. (3-2)). If this is not the case, the voice of the verb determines which sentence constituent will become the subject: In the active voice S-AGENT is replaced by the syntactic identifier *subject-p*, in the passive voice, *object-p* is replaced by *subject-p*. If the VS does not contain an appropriate identifier, an elliptical structure is assumed and no subject is generated.

The voice of the verb is indicated in the sentence constituent *verb* in accordance with the definition of the interface. This definition requires the presence of a *verb* in the VS during the process of subject determination. In the case of elliptical statements in which the verb is to be deleted, this deletion is not permitted until the subject has been determined. Sec. 5.3 will take this point up in more detail.

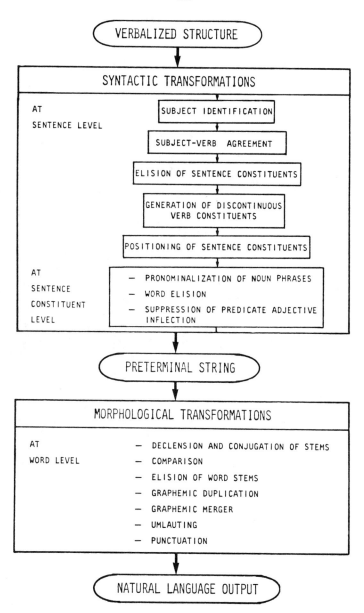

Fig. (5-1): The Transformation Steps in SUTRA

5.2 SUBJECT-VERB AGREEMENT

The subject and the finite verb agree in number and person. The verb takes its number information from the subject. In addition, the grammatical person of the subject is bequethed to the verb.

Hence the existence of a subject is a prerequisite for subject-verb agreement in SUTRA. Ellipses without a subject but with a (non-finite) verb form cannot be generated (cf. 3.3.1).[1]

If the subject is a subordinate clause, rather than a noun phrase as in (5-1), third person singular is assigned to the verb.

```
(5-1) (sent-s
        (case-slot S-RECIPIENT (np-s (n: SG) D GAST))
        (verb (v: PASSIVE) (t: PAST) (m: IND) SAG)
        (object-s (sent-s (subject-p (np-s (n: SG) D BETT))
                          (verb (v: ACTIVE) (m: KON) (t: PRES) SEIN)
                          (predicative (ap-s ZIEMLICH HART))))))
```

Dass das Bett ziemlich hart sei, wurde dem Gast gesagt.
[That the bed rather hard was, was to the guest told.]

Subject-verb agreement is always realized if a non-deletable verb is present. In the following sections, the methods for extracting number and person from noun phrases will be described.

5.2.1 Determination of Number

Number is explicitly indicated in the VS for every simple noun phrase (cf. def. of NOUN-PHRASE type SIMPLE in Appendix A). It need not, however, always correspond to the number of the embedding sentence constituent. Divergences can occur in coordinated noun phrases where number is dependent on the conjunction: with *UND* number is plural, with *ODER*, the number of the last noun phrase is the determining factor.

The coordination of subject complement clauses is an exception since in this case *UND* does not cause pluralization:

(5-2) That the bed was hard and that the shower didn't work was told to the guest.

5.2.2 Determination of Person

The grammatical person of a noun phrase is determined by its word stem. If the noun

---

[1] An extension to the system for generating such structures would have to take into account that the subject may not be deleted until subject-verb agreement has taken place.

phrase contains one of the two special stems (*SYSTEM*, *USER*), the first and second person are generated, respectively. In all other cases, third person is involved.

The special stems have the sole function of making grammatical person explicit. Although only the third person singular personal pronouns are inflected for gender, the fact that other personal pronouns also have a gender is illustrated by the gender agreement of the relative pronoun in (5-3):

(5-3) *Du,* $\left\{ \begin{matrix} der \\ die \end{matrix} \right\}$ *niemals zu spaet kam, hast verschlafen?*

    [You who have never arrived late have overslept?]

This phenomenon cannot be handled in SUTRA if the gender carrying noun to be replaced is not in the lexicon.

5.3   ELISION OF SENTENCE CONSTITUENTS

Elliptical utterances can be implicitly generated in SUTRA because incomplete VS's are processed, as for example in (3-13).

Explicit sentence constituent elision is necessary with the *verb*. For this process the deletable sentence constituents must be marked by *elision*. After subject deter- mination and realization of subject-verb agreement, all sentence constituents marked in this way are deleted.

A more efficient approach involves introducing default assumptions about verb voice at this point, as, for example, when the NL generation system only produces active sen- tences. This enables SUTRA to generate the ellipsis (5-6) from the structure (5-5) without *verb*. Without this assumption, the underlying structure would have to have the form (5-4).

```
(5-4) (sent-s
        (elision (verb (v: ACTIVE) (m: IND) (t: PERF) ABBIEG))
        (case-slot S-AGENT (np-s (n: PL) ZWEI GELB POSTWAGEN))
        (case-slot S-GOAL (pp-s IN (np-s (n: SG) D OSTSTRASSE)))))
```

```
(5-5) (sent-s
        (case-slot S-AGENT (np-s (n: PL) ZWEI GELB POSTWAGEN))
        (case-slot S-GOAL (pp-s IN (np-s (n: SG) D OSTSTRASSE)))))
```

(5-6)   *Zwei gelbe Postwagen in die Oststrasse.*
    [Two yellow mail trucks onto Oststrasse.]

5.4 GENERATION OF DISCONTINUOUS VERB CONSTITUENTS

In processing the sentence constituent *verb*, a number of operations are initiated which

- evaluate the indication of verb voice and then delete it,
- evaluate syntactic tense information and replace it with morphological tense information,
- separate a possible prefix from the verb stem depending on sentence type, voice and tense of the verb.

During the evaluation of voice and syntactic tense, it is determined whether the verb stem must be replaced by an auxiliary. In this case, the generation of a non-finite form is prepared. Figure (5-2) summarizes the various combinations that can occur in German.

The finite components are represented on two lines. In the upper line, the place holder for the verb stem (<verb>) is found unless it was necessary to replace it by an auxiliary *(SEIN, WERD)*. If this auxiliary is determined with the aid of constant MS1 (Name: KONJUG - PAUX in Appendix B) then this is noted by <paux>. The lower line contains the morphological tense that will later direct the inflection of the finite verb stem as either present (PRES) or imperfect (PAST).

The non-finite parts of the verb are represented in a single line, if a prefix separable from the stem of the finite verb assumes the position of the non-finite constituent. This can only occur in the present or imperfect active when the finite verb does not stand in final position in the sentence (subordinate clause). The braces indicate, that not all verbs have separable prefixes. In the two-line representations, the lower line contains conjugation information for the verb stem above it, determining whether a perfect participle (PPRF) or an infinitive (INF) is to be generated.

In SUTRA, the generation of discontinuous verb constituents is modeled by replacing the sentence constituent *verb* with two new sentence constituents with the identifiers *finite* and *infinite*.

finite labels the finite verb constituent which contains the verb stem, the morphological tense and the indications of person, number and mood from *verb*.

infinite labels the non-finite verb constituent which is formed from the stems in their terminal order and the conjugation information assigned to them, or which consists of a separated prefix. These options are mutually exclusive (see Figure (5-2)). Separable prefixes are contained in the lexicon entries of verbs (in Appendix B: KONJUG - VRBZ) and thus permit the reduction of the finite verb stem. If the finite verb is in final position, the non-finite constituent can be empty.

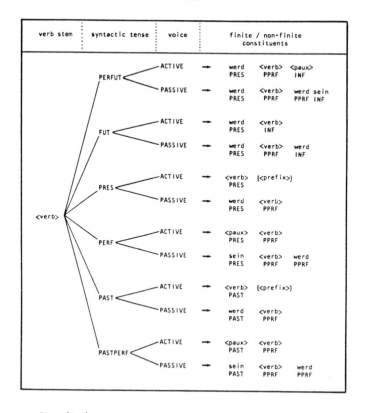

Fig. (5-2): Generation of Discontinuous Verb Constituents

Two examples should suffice to illustrate the functioning of the transformation. They contain a *verb* from the VS, from which representations for its finite and non-finite constituents are generated. In (5-7) the future perfect passive of *AUFSTELL* is generated and in (5-8) the present active of the same verb.

(5-7) (verb (n: SG) (p: 3) (v: PASSIVE) (m: IND) (t: PERFUT) AUFSTELL)

➡ ((finite (n: SG) (p: 3) (t: PRES) (m: IND) WERD)
    (infinite ((vinfin: PPRF) AUFSTELL) ((vinfin: INF) WERD)
        ((vinfin: INF) SEIN)))

wird aufgestellt worden sein   [will have been set up]

(5-8) (verb (n: SG) (p: 3) (v: ACTIVE) (m: IND) (t: PRES) AUFSTELL)

➡ ((finite (n: SG) (p: 3) (t: PRES) (m: IND) STELL) (infinite AUF))

stellt auf   [sets up]

5.5 POSITIONING OF SENTENCE CONSTITUENTS

Sentence constituents which have not been deleted are now recorded on the basis of the knowledge described in sec. 4.2. For this process, the three parameters for sentence type and pronominalization must be made availabe.

SUTRA can be parameterized as to which type of sentence is to be generated: for interrogatives, FRONT is defined, for declaritives CENTRAL and for subordinate clauses LAST.

The other two parameters are fixed by examining each sentence constituent for MSI about pronominal formulation. If a noun phrase is to be replaced by a relative pronoun, this is indicated in the VS by (pro: REL). The formulation of a noun phrase as a personal pronoun is indicated by (pro: PRN).

5.6 PRONOMINALIZATION IN NOUN PHRASES

The generation of personal pronouns is initiated by the MSI (pro: PRN). Gender and person are added in order to make possible the later generation of terminal forms. Grammatical person is calculated as described in sec. 5.2.2. In the first and second persons, personal pronouns receive no overt gender marker. Otherwise noun stems are involved and their gender is fixed.

After this, all word stems and the marking (pro: PRN) are deleted and (PERSPRN) is introduced as inflectional information. For example:

(5-9) (np-s (n: SG) (pro: PRN) DIES SCHOEN GARTEN)

➤ (n: SG) (g: MAS) (p: 3) (PERSPRN)

With relative pronouns, whose generation is triggered by (pro: REL), the process is similar. At least the head noun and the number of the noun phrase must be available so that number and gender agreement between the relative pronoun and its antecedent can be realized. Grammatical person is not relevant. The word stem and the marker (pro: REL) are deleted and the stem D along with the word class RELPRN is introduced. In (3-16), the entire antecedent noun phrase is repeated. In (5-10), the same noun phrase is used.

(5-10) (np-s (n: PL) (pro: REL) D ZWEI BAUM)

➤ (n: PL) (g: MAS) (RELPRN D)

5.7   WORD ELISION

Parallel to ellipsis generation on the sentence level, ellipses can also be generated
on the sentence constituent level: both implicitly through omission of the word in the
VS and explicitly through marking the word with *elision*. The explicit method is obligatory for nouns since the gender of the deletable noun is necessary for the inflection of the remaining stems in the noun phrase. After gender agreement has been realized within the noun phrase, the marked noun is deleted.

5.8   SUPPRESSION OF PREDICATE ADJECTIVE INFLECTIONS

Whether adjectives are inflected or not is dependent on their grammatical role. As
attributive adjectives they are inflected, as predicate adjectives they are, however,
uninflected. Syntactically, the difference can be seen in the kind of phrases in
which the adjectives occur. While attributive adjectives occur only in noun phrases,
predicate adjectives are limited to adjective phrases. At the point of word inflection, these features are, however, no longer available; word class directs the choice
of inflectional paradigm.

The remainder class XXX was introduced for words which are not inflected (4.1.1.).
All predicate adjectives are relegated to this class so that their stems appear as
terminal word forms in the NL output.

5.9   EXTRACTION OF FURTHER MORPHOSYNTACTIC INFORMATION

The following sections explain what additional MSI is still necessary for the application of the word-inflection transformations and how this information is determined.

Each word stem is assigned a word class from the NL system's word lexicon which is
projected onto a SUTRA word class by a filter relation as in (4-3). Lexical gender is
determined for each noun.[1] Both of these items of constant MSI appear in the PS. For
each preposition, the list of cases it governs is taken from the lexicon. This serves
as a restriction in determining the surface case of a sentence constituent.

The following sections describe how surface case and type of determination are extracted and punctuation marks inserted.

5.9.1 Surface Case

A syntactic case is determined for each sentence constituent. The sentence constit-

---

[1] In examples (5-9) and (5-10), gender has already been determined.

uent identifiers associated with an inherent syntactic case feature and the list of
lexically permissible cases governed by a preposition serve as the sole basis for
making this determination. In this manner, an unambiguous surface case can be determined (BUSEMANN 1982, p. 43ff). The procedure is based on determining the intersection S between the a priori surface case c (see Table (5-15)) and the list Cp of
cases governed by the preposition in question. This list is considered empty if a
sentence constituent contains a noun phrase instead of a prepositional phrase.

If S is non-empty, it contains exactly one element, c, which is selected. If S is
empty, and Cp non-empty, the first element of Cp is selected. If both S and Cp are
empty, c is selected.

A single example should suffice to illustrate this process. The deep cases S-LOCATIVE
and S-GOAL are linked a priori to the surface cases Dative (DAT) and Accusative (AKK)
respectively. The list of cases governed by the preposition *AUF* is (DAT AKK). Thus we
arrive at the following surface realizations.

(5-11) (case-slot S-LOCATIVE (pp-s AUF (np-s (n: SG) D STRASSE)))

    auf der Strasse
    [on the street]

(5-12) (case-slot S-GOAL (pp-s AUF (np-s (n: SG) D STRASSE)))

    auf die Strasse
    [onto the street]

There is, however, an important restriction involved in this process which is not
explicitly represented in SUTRA: The process is not context free, but rather requires
supplementary information about the verb for whose valency a surface case is to be
determined.

Hence verbs must be lexically classified in such a way that an unambiguous a priori
surface case can be assigned to each deep case within a class. The verbs *FRAG* and
ANTWORT in (5-13) and (5-14) belong to different classes because the *indobj*-slots in
each instance receive different case features in the surface structure (the surface
representations of *indobj* are printed in capitals).

(5-13) *Karl fragte SEINEN FREUND, was er sich zum Geburtstag wünsche.*
    [Karl asked HIS FRIEND what he wanted for his birthday.]

(5-14) *Fritz antwortete SEINEM FREUND, daß ihm sechs Richtige im Lotto gerade*
    willkommen seien.
    [Fritz answered HIS FRIEND that six correct numbers in the lottery would
    be just the thing.]

This sort of classification appears to be practicable, e.g., on the basis of the valency dictionary of HELBIG and SCHENKEL (1969).

Up till now, this kind of structuring has not proved to be necessary for HAM-ANS since case frames are at present used exclusively for motion verbs which constitute a separate class. For this reason, SUTRA does not employ explicit verb classification and relies instead on assignment of deep cases to surface cases as illustrated in Table (5-15).

The upper half of the table contains the semantically oriented names (cf. def. of DEEP-CASE-LABEL in Appendix A) while the identifiers in the lower portion are syntactic labels.

(5-15)

Constituent Identifier	Surface Case
S-AGENT S-INSTRUMENT S-LOCATIVE S-RECIPIENT S-SOURCE S-TIME	Dative
S-GOAL S-PATH	Accusative
subject-p predicative	Nominative
attr-gen	Genitive
attr-prp indobj	Dative
object-p	Accusative

5.9.2 Type of Determination

Type of determination takes account of the fact that adjectives may receive different inflectional features when they follow determiners. The value of the type of determination is dependent on word class. With DETDEF or DETQ, the value is DEF, with DETIND or POSSPRN, it is INDEF. If an adjective is not preceded by any of the stems of these four classes, the value is WITHOUT (cf. (5-16) through (5-18)).[1]

(5-16)   WITHOUT: *mit vielem kaltem Wasser*
                     [with a lot of cold water]
                DEF: *mit dem vielen kalten Wasser*
                     [with all that cold water]

(5-17)   INDEF: *kein kalter Rotwein*
                     [no cold red wine]
                DEF: *jener kalte Rotwein*
                     [that cold red wine]

---

[1] The type of determination in SUTRA has the same function as Esau's functional marking for noun phrases (ESAU 1973), which is only taken over by the first element, if this element is 'capable of it'.

(5-18)   WITHOUT: *mit starkem Kaffee*
                   [with strong coffee]
              INDEF: *mit deinem starken Kaffee*
                   [with your strong coffee]

Concerning its morphological behavior, the determiner *VIEL* (along with a few others)
belongs to the word class ADJ.

The type of determination is established for each simple noun phrase and fixed in the
PS.

5.9.3   Punctuation Marks

SUTRA has a number of simple rules for punctuation at its disposal. Punctuation within
a sentence is restricted to commas. These are inserted in coordinated constituents. In
contrast to other constituents, coordinated sentences receive a comma before the conjunction as well. Commas are also generated at the beginning and the end of each subordinate clause. There possible conflicts with sentence final punctuation must be
taken into consideration. Depending on sentence type, final punctuation my be a period
or a question mark.

If a punctuation mark is to be inserted, an element with the form (MARK <mark>)
appears in the PS since the concatenation with the preceding word, which is neces-
cary for orthographical reasons, is not possible until the word has been inflected.

An unsolved problem in SUTRA is the insertion of commas between attributive adjectives
because in some cases, contextual knowledge is needed.[1] This is illustrated in (5-19)
and (5-20) (cf. DUDEN 1980, p. 37).

(5-19) another strong move
       (a previously mentioned move was also strong)

(5-20) another, strong move
       (the previously mentioned move was weak)

In SUTRA, commas are placed after the first adjective in every sequence of two adjectives inasfar as they do not appear in different degrees of comparison.

5.10   THE INTERFACE BETWEEN SYNTACTIC AND MORPHOLOGICAL TRANSFORMATIONS

The transformation in the upper box in Figure (5-1) transform the hierarchical VS into

---

[1] This and similar problems can be handled by available knowledge at another point
in the language generation process (cf. 6.3).

a linear PS with the same meaning. The PS forms an additional interface which principally serves the function of modularizing processes, thus increasing the transparency
of the system. The generation of a PS requires the syntactic processes to make explicit all the MSI which must be made available to the morphological transformations. From
this point on, the constituent structure is no longer necessary and is thus not reflected in the PS. However, the interface 'PS' ((5-23) is a complex example; see also
Figure (2-3)) is not the only possibility for separating the syntactic from the morphological transformations. Word inflection can also be carried out on the basis of
MSI annotated at different levels of the constituent tree, as in MUMBLE (McDONALD 1981)
or in IPG developed by KEMPEN and HOENKAMP (1982). With the latter method, a linear
string appears after word inflection thus allowing for incremental generation of text.
With an interface like 'PS', on the other hand, a further level of representation is
provided that seems to be better suited for replacement transformations applying to
word stems of different syntactic constituents in those cases where only a linear and
not a hierarchical structure is necessary for the transformation. For example, in the
case of dative, singular and feminine, *ZU DER* [to the] is contracted to *ZUR*. In
HAM-ANS, the inverse process is handled on a similar level during analysis (cf. HOEPP-
NER et al. 1984). At present, however, SUTRA does not utilize the PS for this kind of
transformation.

5.10.1 The Preterminal String

The PS contains all the MSI that was either already present in the input structure
(e.g., mood) or which had to be generated. This is - with the exception of the lexical
inflection features - exactly the MSI which is necessary for the subsequent morphological transformations. It is summarized in Table (5-21).

The scope of the items is implicitly indicated by the direction in which they are
read and limited by a change in the value of the same category, which must be
explicitly specified. The categories in Table (5-21) marked with an asterisk are an
exception in that they only apply to the next stem.

(5-21)

	Category	Meaning	Possible Values
*	cmp:	degree of comparison	KOMP SUP
	d:	type of determination	DEF INDEF WITHOUT
	g:	gender of nouns	FEM MAS NTR
	k:	surface case	AKK DAT GEN NOM
	m:	mood	IMP IND KON
	n:	number	PL SG
	p:	person	1 2 3
	t:	morphological tense	PAST PRES
*	vinfin:	type of non-finite verb form	INF PPRF PPRS

Because the scope of the MSI was limited by the hierarchical arrangement of the syntactic constituents in the VS, no limitations were placed on their being positioned on a particular level. In the PS, however, all the items of MSI which are to apply to a word stem must be positioned to the left of that word stem.

The PS (5-23) illustrates the result of the syntactic transformation of the VS (5-22) for the sentence (5-24).

```
(5-22) (sent-s
        (verb (v: PASSIVE) (m: IND) (t: PAST) ABREISS)
        (case-slot S-TIME (ap-s GESTERN)))
        (object-p
          (np-s (n: SG) D (comparison (cmp: KOM) ALT) BRAUN HAUS
                (attr-rel
                  (sent-s
                    (case-slot S-AGENT
                                (np-s (n: SG) (pro: PRN) *USER*))
                    (verb (v: ACTIVE) (m: IND) (t: PASTPERF) WOHN)
                    (case-slot S-TIME
                                (pp-s VOR (np-s (n: PL) VIEL JAHR)))
                    (case-slot S-LOCATIVE
                                (pp-s IN (np-s (n: SG) (pro: REL) HAUS)))))))))
```

```
(5-23) ((k: NOM) (g: NTR) (n: SG) (d: DEF) (DETDEF D)
         (cmp: KOM) (ADJ ALT) (ADJ BRAUN) (NOM HAUS) (MARK /,)
         (PRP IN) (k: DAT) (g: NTR) (n: SG) (RELPRN D)
         (k: NOM) (g: MAS) (n: SG) (p: 2) (PERSPRN)
         (PRP VOR) (k: DAT) (g: NTR) (n: PL) (d: WITHOUT)
         (ADJ VIEL) (NOM JAHR)
         (vinfin: PPRF) (VRB WOHN)
         (p: 2) (n: SG) (t: PAST) (m: IND) (VRB HAB) (MARK /,)
         (p: 3) (n: SG) (t: PAST) (m: IND) (VRB WERD)
         (XXX  GESTERN) (vinfin: PPRF) (VRB ABREISS))
```

(5-24) *Das aeltere braune Haus, in dem du vor vielen Jahren gewohnt hattest, wurde gestern abgerissen.*

[The older brown house, in which you many years ago lived had, was yesterday torn down.]

5.10.2 On the Representation of Agreement Relations

The bequethal of MSI can only be represented in a linear structure in a natural way if there is a continuous scope for the inherited property which embraces both the bequething and the inheriting word stem. For the agreement of noun, adjective and article in gender, number and case, this requirement is met. Subject-verb agreement cannot, however be represented in this way, which is why the bequethed MSI was copied (see 5.2). The same holds for the agreement in number and gender between the relative pronoun and its antecedent phrase (see (5-23)) as well as for case agreement between subject and predicate noun (see (3-2)). A more detailed discussion of the representation of agreement in German is to be found in BUSEMANN (1982, sec. 6.4).

5.11 THE INFLECTION OF WORD STEMS

Since German has a rich inflectional system where even many irregularities forms can be caputred by rules, it is worthwhile to perform word inflection in a procedural way rather than by lexicon lookup as it might be suitable for English which has relatively few inflections.

The basic principle involved in the inflection of word stems[1] is quite straightforward: With the aid of the inflectional paradigms (Appendix D), inflectional morphemes specific to word classes are determined and suffixed to the word stem. Numereous irregular forms, however, make this last transformation complicated. In a number of cases, the stem must be umlauted or merged with the ending. In some instances, the last grapheme of the stem must be doubled, an *E* elided or inserted.

The rest of the chapter describes the inflection of nouns, adjectives, verbs and other stems in SUTRA.

5.11.1 The Declension of the Noun

For noun inflection, it is necessary to establish a classification embracing the various inflectional morphemes that a German noun can take for any given item of MSI. In addition, stems may be umlauted and the final consonant reduplicated.

The most obvious classification method is oriented around plural forms. ENGEL (1977) set up a schema of twenty classes which in addition to exceptions like *HERZ* [heart] and *FRIEDE* [peace] also encompasses numerous irregular words of foreign origin. The schema used in SUTRA includes a few exceptions but needs only thirteen word classes, also defined primarily by plural form. In contrast to Engel's schema, stems requiring umlaut can be precisely listed.

The schema should, moreover, prove itself in practical use by being easy to handle, e.g., when updating the lexicon. Thus the class names correspond to the nominative plural marking of their elements for mnemonic reasons. In German there are six different morphemes of this type, namely: *E, EN, ER, N, S* and the zero-allomorph (*).

Nouns in *EN* and *N* which take a genitive singular in *S* are assigned to the classes EN_G and N_G, respectively. If they have *EN* or * as genitive singular marker they belong to the classes EN_S and N_S, respectively. The suffixes _G and _S are reminiscent of the terms *gemischt* [mixed] and *schwach* [weak] with which the inflectional

---

[1] Another work in the field of automatic translation presents a formalism for generating all of the inflectional forms of German (KUNZE, RUEDIGER 1968). I learned of this work after the implementation of the morphological transformations in SUTRA was finished.

paradigms are referred to in many traditional grammars of German (e.g., DUDEN 1973, §400ff).

With nouns in *, those without dative plural marking are categorized separately with **. The necessary umlauting of many stems in the categories *, **, E and ER is facilitated by the introduction of four further classes *_U, **_U, E_U, and ER_U. Figure (5-3) contains examples illustrating this classification schema. The inflectional paradigm for nouns is based on these declension types, which are contained in the word lexicon (Name: DEKLIN).

declension type	stem (NOM SG)	NOM PL	DAT PL
*	Zimmer room	Zimmer	Zimmern
*_U	Vater father	Väter	Vätern
**	Wagen auto	Wagen	Wagen
**_U	Garten garden	Gärten	Gärten

declension type	stem (NOM SG)	NOM PL
E	Tisch table	Tische
E_U	Hand hand	Hände
ER	Kind child	Kinder
ER_U	Haus house	Häuser
S	Radio radio	Radios

declension type	stem (NOM SG)	NOM PL	GEN SG
N_S	Seife soap	Seifen	Seife
N_G	Auge eye	Augen	Auges
EN_S	Frau woman	Frauen	Frau
EN_G	Fleck spot	Flecken	Flecks

Fig. (5-3): Declension Types for Nouns

There are apparently only a few exceptions which cannot be correctly inflected with this schema: Buchstabe-Buchstabens [letter] (similarly Friede [peace], Name [name] Same [sperm]) also Herr-Herrn [Mr.] Herz-Herzen [heart].[1]

Nouns whose plural forms require a different stem are not generated. The following are a few examples of plurals not embraced by the system:

Album-Alben [album], Atlas-Atlanten [atlas], Baby-Babies [baby], Bronchitis-Bronchitiden [bronchitis], Bus-Busse [bus], Firma-Firmen [firm], Index-Indices [index], Lexikon-Lexika [lexicon], Schema-Schemata [schema], Tempus-Tempi [tempos], Tempora [tenses].

The umlauting of noun stems is triggered by the declension types. In forming the plural, an E is inserted after the last umlautable vowel (A,O,U) except in the diphthong AU, where E is inserted between the vowels (cf. Fig. (5-3)).

---

[1] These are mostly historical relicts of masculine and neuter n-stems with an N in the oblique cases. In general these have an irregular form in the genitive and dative singular.

If a stem ends in <consonant>IN (and its gender is feminine) or in NIS, the last grapheme is doubled in the plural (in the case of NIS in the genitive singular as well) under the assumption that the I is unaccented (5-25). In (5-26), however, duplication is suppressed since the gender is neuter.

(5-25) Spielerin - Spielerinnen [player (fem.)]
       Bildnis - Bildnisse [picture]

(5-26) Benzin - Benzine [gasoline]

5.11.2 The Inflection of the Adjective

Adjectives are formed by declension and/or comparison. With both operations, the elision of the final E of the stem is necessary in many cases.

In stems ending in AUER, EUER and <consonant>EL, the last E is deleted. Although the speaker has freedom of choice with TEUER-TEUERE or TEURE [expensive], elision is obligatory in many cases, e.g., in NOBLE [elegant], EDLE [noble] or variable [variable].

Elision is also employed in the inflection of verbs and possessive pronouns as well as in the declension and comparison of adjectives.

In the comparison of adjectives, the comparative markers are suffixed to the stem before the adjective (if used attributively) is declined. The superlative of predicate adjectives is formed in SUTRA in a standard fashion as illustrated in (5-27).

(5-27) AM <stem><superlative marker>EN

Since the superlative marker varies very irregularly between ST and EST and since the stem must be umlauted in some cases, adjectives are divided into four comparison classes analogous to the nominal types: ST (e.g., SCHNELL-AM SCHNELLSTEN [fast]),

ST_U (e.g., JUNG-AM JÜNGSTEN [young]), EST (e.g., RASCH-AM RASCHESTEN [quick]) and EST_U (e.g., GESUND-AM GESÜNDESTEN [healthy]).

These classes are contained in the word lexicon (Name: KOMP) except in a few special cases where explicit comparative base forms are listed under KOMP (see Appendix B).

In the dynamic formation of comparatives, a check is made to see if an E should be elided (5-28).

(5-28) sauer - saurer - am sauersten [sour]

5.11.3 The Conjugation of the Verb

In German, there are about two hundred irregularly conjugated prefixless verbs (cf.
DUDEN 1973, §290; BROCKHAUS 1975b). Verbs with separable prefixes do not differ in
their morphological behavior from verbs without prefixes. Prefixed verbs can thus
be traced back to non-prefixed verbs for the purpose of determining their conjugation.

A relatively complex conjugation schema is necessary in order to enable generation of
the ablaut and umlaut patterns which occur. As a first step, the *base forms* are
determined. These serve as bases to which the inflectional morphemes can be suffixed.

After presenting a typology for German irregular verbs, we will look at further irregularities requiring graphemic insertion, merger and elision. Based on a two-leveled
graphemically oriented approach for the conjugation of prefixless verbs developed by
BROCKHAUS (1975a), a considerably simpler schema involving eleven *verb types* is developed here. The simplification does, of course, demand a certain price, which must
be paid through the introduction of a number of additional operations which will be
described in the following sections.

The verb type (cf. Appendix B: KONJUG - VTYP) consists of a number from 1 to 11. The
verbs in class 1 are the regular or weak verbs. The classes 2 to 11 reflect, in numerical order, the increasing irregularity in the inflection of the verb stems listed
in Appendix E.

In order to encompass all umlauting and ablauting verb stems, five *segment types* are
defined. In addition to Brockhaus's four types VGFA, VGFB, VGFC, and VGFD, the category
SOND is introduced for special handling of the completely irregular verb *SEIN* [be].

The segment types refer to the possible base forms of a verb in the word lexicon. The
verb type indicates which segment types a verb includes.

The VGFA-segment is identical to the lexical stem. The VGFB-segment is the largest
common initial segment of those forms which take it as a base (cf. Fig. (5-4)). The
VGFC-segment is identical to the first person singular imperfect.[1] The VGFD-segment
is identical to the first person singular of the past subjunctive. The SOND-segment is
empty. This indicates that complete forms are generated for *SEIN* and not endings.

With the aid of Fig. (5-4) (coded under %VERB_SEGMENT_TYPES in Appendix D), verb type,
tense, number and person can be used to determine the segment type which in turn is
used to access the corresponding base form of the verb.

---

[1] BROCKHAUS 1975a defines the VGFA and the VGFC segments in a somewhat different way.

137

Verb type	Present PL Imper. PL Subj. I Infinitive Pres.part.	1. Present Singular	2./3. Present Singular	Imperative Singular	Past	Subj. II
1	VGFA	VGFA	VGFA	VGFA	VGFA	VGFA
2	VGFA	VGFA	VGFA	VGFA	VGFC	VGFA
3	VGFA	VGFA	VGFA	VGFA	VGFC	VGFC
4	VGFA	VGFA	VGFA	VGFA	VGFC	VGFD
5	VGFA	VGFA	VGFB	VGFA	VGFC	VGFC
6	VGFA	VGFA	VGFB	VGFA	VGFC	VGFD
7	VGFA	VGFA	VGFB	VGFB	VGFC	VGFD
8	VGFA	VGFB	VGFB	VGFA	VGFA	VGFA
9	VGFA	VGFB	VGFB	VGFA	VGFC	VGFA
10	VGFA	VGFB	VGFB	VGFA	VGFC	VGFD
11	SOND	SOND	SOND	SOND	VGFC	VGFD

Fig. (5-4): The Distribution of Verb Segment Types

Figure (5-4) contains all of the 29 inflectional forms with the exception of the perfect participle. Many perfect participles can hardly be derived with the aid of rules (cf. BROCKHAUS 1975a). Hence all perfect participle forms are contained in the lexicon entries (see Appendix B under KONJUG - PPRF).

At this point of the conjugation process, the appropriate stem and morpheme are already determined. Before the morpheme can be suffixed to the stem, the following checks have to be made.

a) Graphemic insertion:

If the morpheme begins with *S* or *T* and the base form possesses certain characteristics, an *E* is inserted between the base form and the inflectional morpheme. These characteristics are:

- base form ends in *D* or *T*
  (e.g., *bindet, bietest, standet, tatest*
  [he binds, you offer, you (pl.) stood, you did])

- base form ends in *BN, DN, FN, GN, TM* etc.

  (e.g., *ebnest, ordnest, öffnest, segnest, atmest*
  [you smooth, put in order, open, bless, breathe])

- base form is a VGFC-segment and ends in *S* or *Z*

  (e.g., *rissest, schmolzet* [you tore, you (pl.) melted])

b) Graphemic Merger:

Table (5-30) contains a list of cases in which the inflectional morpheme is merged with the stem. The asterisk stands for the portion of the base form or the morpheme which is not affected.

(5-30)

Base Form	Morpheme	Merged Form
*ST	ST →	*ST
bläst	*st*	*bläst* [you (sg.) blow]
*S	S* →	*S*
vergiss	*st*	*vergisst* [you (sg.) forget]
*Z	S* →	*Z*
reiz	*st*	*reizt* [you (sg.) irritate]
*T	T* →	*T*
birst	*t*	*birst* [it bursts]
*E	E* →	*E*
konnte	*en*	*konnten* [we could]

c) Graphemic elision:

The elision of *E* in base forms in *EL* and *ER* has two aspects. If the inflectional morpheme is *E*, the last *E* of the base form must be elided. Two examples are given in (5-31).

(5-31) *versauer* + *e* → *versaure*   [I'm rotting away]
      mogel   + *e* → *mogle*   [I cheat]

If the ending begins with *E*, but is not identical to *E*, the *E* of the ending and not of the stem is elided.

(5-32) *versauer* + *en* → *versauern*   [we are rotting away]
      mogel   + *en* → *mogeln*   [we cheat]

There are a few forms that cannot be captured by the verb typology described above and must be generated separately. They are listed below.

soll [I, he shall] (otherwise regular!);
wird, will, darf, kann, muß, mag, weiß
[he becomes, wants, may, can, must, likes, knows].

5.11.4 The Inflection of Other Stems

Determiners are inflected according to two paradigms (see Appendix D). The schema
%DETDEF_RELPRN_MORPHEMES includes the morphemes for the definite article as well as
for the relative pronoun. On the other hand, the stems of the word classes DETIND and
DETQ are inflected with the aid of the schema %QUANTIFIER_MORPHEMES, the type of determination being used as a decisive feature for the choice of the inflectional ending.

The same schema is used to decline the possessive pronoun taking INDEF as the type of
determination since the inflectional morphemes are the same as those for DETIND. For
the stems of possessive pronouns the additional possibility of *E*-elision must be taken
into account.

6. LIMITATIONS AND PROSPECTS FOR FURTHER DEVELOPMENT

In this chapter, we will first discuss a number of critical processes for determining
limitations and alternatives for the further development of SUTRA. Taking the addition
of further transformations as an example, we will then discuss possibilities for extending capabilities within the framework of the considerations sketched in Chapter 2.

6.1 PERSPECTIVES ON THE RULES FOR SENTENCE CONSTITUENT PLACEMENT

As a result of the contextual dependency of the rules, the positioning of sentence
constituents takes place on the sentence level of the transformational process (cf.
Fig. (5-1)), the necessary information for the ordering process being secured through
a pointed examination of the sentence constituent in question, in order to determine
whether, for example, it contains MSI for ponominalization. Later on, this MSI has
to be examined again, e.g., during generation of a pronoun. An alternative to this
top-down approach would be to assign a position to a constituent at a later point on
the basis of the results of a complete analysis of that constituent (cf. KEMPEN,
HOENKAMP 1982, p. 25f). This *bottom-up process* would aviod the double examination of
individual items of MSI, but would require the retention of information on the sentence constituent level.

This trade-off alone should hardly speak in favor of the second method even under consideration of an increased number of parameters (e.g., for placement of deictic expres-

sions so as to produce text coherence or consideration of emphasis) because this requires a number of additional global data structures for storing the parameters arising
from the analysis. It is only in the case where word order within sentence constituents
is to be altered that the bottom-up method might enjoy a clear advantage over the top-
down process, namely, if word order within sentence constituents depends on the same
parameters as sentence constituent positioning (e.g., (pro: REL) could trigger rules
for word as well as sentence constituent placement; as in (6-1)).[1]

(6-1)   Storks are nesting on the *roof of the house.*
        The house on *whose roof* storks are nesting, ...

Word order within sentence constituents was assumed as a given. Nevertheless, it is
influenced by some transformations, e.g., formulation of a genitive attribute as a
relative pronoun. This is one of the rare cases in colloquial German where a preposed
genitive has to be generated (6-1). Word order changes of this kind would require, in
advance, an expensive analysis of the constituents embedded in a noun phrase and could
probably be performed more efficiently utilizing a bottom-up approach similar to the
one mentioned above. At present, SUTRA does not generate proposed genitive attributes
at all.

Another problem which arises in connection with sentence constituent placement concerns
the occupancy of the end field. A more natural placement of sentence constituents in
(5-1) would position the subordinate clause after the non-finite verb form, as in (6-2).

(6-2)   The guest was told that the bed was rather hard.

The observation that sentence constituents tend to be placed in the end field because
of their complexity is not taken into account in SUTRA since this is more a matter of
stylistic, rather than grammatical positioning. With increasing grammatical complexity
of the language fragment to be generated, a stylistic check becomes more and more
necessary.

6.2   ON THE LEXICAL CODING OF MORPHOSYNTACTIC INFORMATION

The word lexicon is supposed to contain all those items of MSI that are inherent features of a lexeme. It is then unnecessary for these to be included in the input structure
nor do they have to be extracted from the input structure.

The helping verb used for forming the periphrastic perfect tenses (see Appendix B:
KONJUG - PAUX) is not, however, an invariable feature of the verb stem, as (6-3) and
(6-4) illustrate.

---

[1] In addition, the article whose position is assumed by the relative pronoun is deleted
in (6-1).

(6-3)   *Er IST nach Hause gefahren.*
[He has driven home.]

(6-4)   *Er HAT den Wagen in die Garage gefahren.*
[He has driven the car into the garage.]

Why then was lexical assignment chosen for SUTRA? One reason is the obvious lack of unambiguous rules for the periphrastic perfect of intransitive verbs (cf. DUDEN 1973, §178f). In addition to difference in usage between the northern and southern parts of the German-speaking area idiosyncrasies often make a principled choice of helping verb impossible. With verbs of motion, point of view plays the decisive role. If the duration of the motion is placed in the foreground, *HAB* is used (6-5), if the emphasis is on change of location, *SEIN* is used (6-6).

(6-5)   *Wir haben die ganze Nacht über getanzt.*
[We danced the whole night long.]

(6-6)   *Wir sind quer durch den Saal getanzt.*
[We danced across the room.]

Another reason for lexical assignment is the conjecture that a verb classification as suggested in sec. 5.9.1 provides a better basis for the choice of auxiliary. Intransitive verbs are immediately separated from transitive verbs and their valencies can provide information about the 'point of view' in each instance.

Since SUTRA is suited for processing sentences in any domain of discourse, an interactive component which updates HAM-ANS' word lexicon was found to be necessary. This component requests missing constant MSI from the user and processes the information secured in such a way that it remains accessible during the dialog and can be integrated into the lexicon if desired. Most items of lexical MSI can be entered correctly even by inexperienced users with the help of the mnemonic classification schemas for noun declension and adjective comparison types. Conjugation information is acquired simply by asking the user for the verb stem which is used to automatically determine the verb type on the basis of the lists of irregular verbs contained in Appendix E.[1] Further Information needed for verb inflection (cf. the categories under the indicator KONJUG in Appendix B) is then queried by the component.

For each entry a plausibility test is performed by checking the inputted values for their syntactic permissibility. When an erroneous input is detected the user is asked for correction.

---

[1] In this process, the prefixless verbs not listed in Appendix E are classified as regular (type 1). The user is only requested to enter a prefix, if any.

6.3   PUNCTUATION BETWEEN ADJECTIVES

In sec. 5.9.3, it was demonstrated that SUTRA's handling of the punctuation between preposed attributes of a noun is inadequate. Let us consider examples (5-19) and (5-20) again.

(5-19)   another strong move

(5-20)   another, strong move

According to DUDEN (1973, p. 37), a comma is inserted before the last of a series of adjectives if this adjective forms a *unit of meaning* with the noun.

In a NL generation system, it is possible to decide whether such units of meaning are present. Let us suppose that four concepts in the knowledge base of the NL system (let us call them A, B, C, and D) are verbalized to *another, strong, move,* and *strong move.*

The verbalization of the concepts A, B and C produces two attributes (A and B) of a noun (C). (5-20) is generated. If on the other hand, the concepts A and D are to be verbalized, the unit of meaning D leads to the generation of (5-19).

Knowledge about this sort of distinction is not taken into account in the definition of the interface as in Appendix A, and is thus lost. Representation of the concept *unit of meaning* in the VS is not difficult[1] and solves the problem of punctuation between attributive adjectives.

6.4   ON THE INTEGRATION OF FURTHER TRANSFORMATIONS

As soon as lexical indications about kind of valency are available, it becomes possible to integrate a number of further transformations into SUTRA which are also described by CHOMSKY (1965). The examples of Subject-to-Object Raising[2], Equivalent NP-Deletion (EQUI) and Coordinated Coreferential Subject Deletion (CCSD) show that this would mean assigning fundamental tasks of the verbalization component of the NL generation system to SUTRA. This would involve shifting the interface to SUTRA to a deeper level of the generation process.

In the following two sections we will briefly sketch some of the problems. A possible solution is presented in sec. 6.4.3.

---

[1] The most obvious approach simply involves using parentheses.

[2] In more recent work, Chomsky rejects Subject-to-Object Raising (cf. CHOMSKY 1977, p. 107 fn., CHOMSKY 1981, p. 38, p. 146 fn., p. 148 fn.).

6.4.1   Subject-to-Object Raising and Equi-NP Deletion

A verb classification as suggested in sec. 5.9.1 makes it possible to decide, for example, whether for the structures (6-7) and (6-9) (which are identical with the exception of the verb: *GLAUB* [to believe] vs. *SEH* [to see]) a subordinate clause (6-8) or an infinitive construction with Subject-to-Object Raising (6-10) should   be generated.

```
(6-7) (sent-s (case-slot S-AGENT (np-s (n: SG) D MUTTER))
              (verb (v: ACTIVE) (m: IND) (t: PRES) GLAUB)
              (object-s
                (sent-s (case-slot S-AGENT (np-s (n: SG) D SOHN))
                        (verb (v: ACTIVE) (m: IND) (t: PRES) WASCH)
                        (object-p (np-s (n: SG) D AUTO))))))
```

(6-8) *Die Mutter glaubt, daß der Sohn das Auto wäscht.*

   [The mother believes, that the son the car washes.]

   'The mother believes that the son is washing the car.'

```
(6-9) (sent-s (case-slot S-AGENT (np-s (n: SG) D MUTTER))
              (verb (v: ACTIVE) (m: IND) (t: PRES) SEH)
              (object-s
                (sent-s (case-slot S-AGENT (np-s (n: SG) D SOHN))
                        (verb (v: ACTIVE) (m: IND) (t: PRES) WASCH)
                        (object-p (np-s (n: SG) D AUTO))))))
```

(6-10) *Die Mutter sieht den Sohn das Auto waschen.*

   [The mother sees the son the car wash.]

   'The mother sees the son washing the car.'

In (6-9), a surface realization with a subordinate clause is also possible. Stylistic questions are involved in that the rather abrupt form (6-11) could be generated for both examples. Here the dependence of the subordinate clause, which has main clause word order, is expressed solely by its position in the sentence.

(6-11) *Die Mutter sieht (glaubt, ...) der Sohn wäscht das Auto.*

   [The mother sees (believes, ...) the son is-washing the car.]

Analogous to (6-9), the processing of (6-12) allows for a choice between a subordinate clause (6-13) or an *extended infinitive construction with 'zu'* (EQUI) (6-14).

```
(6-12) (sent-s (case-slot S-AGENT (np-s (n: SG) D SOHN))
               (verb (v: ACTIVE) (m: IND) (t: PRES) VERSPRECH)
               (case-slot S-RECIPIENT (np-s (n: SG) D MUTTER))
               (object-s
                 (sent-s
                   (case-slot S-AGENT (np-s (n: SG) D SOHN))
                   (verb (v: ACTIVE) (m: IND) (t: PRES) WASCH)
                   (object-p (np-s (n: SG) D AUTO))))))
```

(6-13) *Der Sohn verspricht der Mutter, dass er das Auto wäscht.*
[The son promises the mother that he the car will-wash.]

(6-14) *Der Sohn verspricht der Mutter, das Auto zu waschen.*
[The son promises the mother, the car to wash.]

It is quite apparent that SUTRA would have to make the stylistic decisions and perform the pronominalization in (6-13) and the deletion in (6-14) *by itself*. No MSI is available in the input structure to initiate such operations.

For the latter two, a necessary prerequisite is lacking, namely, the explicit representation of *reference identity* which the pronominalization and the deletion process must be based on. Thus with (6-15), not only (6-16), but also (6-17) may be intended.

```
(6-15)(sent-s (case-slot S-AGENT (np-s (n: SG) D SOHN))
              (verb (v: ACTIVE) (m: IND) (t: PRES) BEHAUPT)
              (object-s (sent-s
                        (case-slot S-AGENT (np-s (n: SG) D SOHN))
                        (verb (v: ACTIVE) (m: IND) (t: PRES) WASCH)
                        (object-p (np-s (n: SG) D SOHN)))))
```

(6-16) *Der Sohn behauptet, sich gewaschen zu haben.*
[The son claims, himself washed to have.]

(6-17) *Der Sohn behauptet, ihn gewaschen zu haben.*
[The son claims, him washed to have.]

Before suggesting how SUTRA could be extended in a consitent way in order to cope with reference identity let us look at a related phenomenon, CCSD.

6.4.2   Coordinated Coreferential Subject Deletion

As HERINGER (1970, p. 27ff.) has pointed out, errors can arise in coordination which are also due to problems of reference identity. As a prerequisite for the application of the coordination rule (CHOMSKY 1965, p. 212, A3), the string of symbols for the subjects of the two sentences to be coordinated must be identical (cf. CHOMSKY 1965, p. 137). Heringer cites an example from BIERWISCH (1963, p. 121), in which the transformation works properly (6-18). He then gives a structurally identical example for which the transformation is clearly not permissible (6-19).

(6-18) *the car is fast* and *the car is comfortable*
       becomes *the car is fast and comfortable*

(6-19) *many cars are big* and *many cars are small*
       becomes *many cars are big and small*

The permissibility of CCSD is dependent on reference identity of the subjects, which is apparently present in (6-18). Analogously reference identity with indefinite quantifiers like *many* in (6-19) means that the same subset of the objects in question must be involved in order for the transformation to function properly. In (6-19), this requirement cannot be met because of the oppositional pair *big-small*.

The next section suggests how information about the different kinds of reference can be made available to SUTRA by extending the system in a compatible way.

6.4.3   An Extension of the Verbalized Structure

In a NL generation system which generates noun phrases on the basis of *extensions*, the reference of a given noun phrase is known. As a result, all that is necessary in order to transmit this knowledge to SUTRA is a suitable extension of the definition of the VS.

In the case of definite descriptions (e.g., (6-15) to (6-18)), this can be accomplished with associated *individual constants*. A generalization of this approach to indefinite descriptions (e.g., (6-19)) is conceivable through the association of *equivalence classes* instead of individual constants. These equivalence classes group together noun phrases that refer to the same subset of a closed set of extensional objects. Identical verbalizations in different equivalence classes are thus not coreferential.

The intensional (generic) reading of noun phrases is also distinguished in this approach, since such noun phrases do not appear in any equivalence class. This can be easily represented in the extension of the VS outlined.

In SUTRA, it can then be decided whether EQUI or CCSD is permissible: The transformations can be applied if the noun phrases in question have the same form and if the individual constants (or the equivalence classes) associated with them are identical.

This extension is exemplary since it fits in precisely with the philosophy of SUTRA (see Chap. 2): The meaning independent application of both transformations is only possible after reference identity has been made explicit in the VS.

7.   THE IMPLEMENTATION AND INTEGRATION OF SUTRA IN THE HAM-ANS SYSTEM

The generation component of the HAM-ANS dialog system generates German sentences for structures of the internal representation language DEEP (JAMESON et al. 1980). Initially the inflection and punctuation component of the predecessor system HAM-RPM (v. HAHN et al. 1980) was utilized. This component proved, however, to be too inflexible for the greater demands placed on it by HAM-ANS, in which three different domains of discourse (traffic scene, fishery data base, and hotel reservation situation) generate extremely varied sentence patterns (HOEPPNER et al. 1983).

The demand for a new domain-independent component in a NL system with a very broad spectrum of communicative capabilities provided optimal preconditions for the design, implementation and testing of SUTRA.

In the following sections, we will discuss aspects of the adaptation of SUTRA to HAM-ANS.

7.1   INTERFACES TO COMPONENTS OF HAM-ANS

In the HAM-ANS system itself, the verbalization component had to be adapted for the production of VS. In addition, the constant MSI had to be integrated into the word lexicon.

The system-specific sentence constituent identifiers verbalized in HAM-ANS are integrated as DEEP-CASE-LABEL in the definition of VS which is otherwise independent from HAM-ANS. In this way, it is possible to provide for free exchange of the identifiers which facilitates the integration of SUTRA into NL systems other than HAM-ANS.

Accessing the word lexicon utilizes procedures which are used in HAM-ANS for lexical analysis. In this process, the complete lexicon entry is not loaded into the main storage before a particular part of an entry is searched for. After it is loaded, it is available in the form of the LISP property LEX-DTA of the lexeme.[1] For SUTRA, the accessing of constant MSI in HAM-ANS takes the form of a search in property lists - a standard method in LISP (cf. MEEHAN 1979, Chap. 13).

Three different components in HAM-ANS make use of SUTRA. In addition to the verbalization of the internal representations of utterances, it is necessary to provide for NL presentation of portions of domain-specific knowledge sources (e.g., with metaquestions) and of accesses to an inference memory (e.g., with demands for an explanation). For examples see HOEPPNER and MARBURGER (1984, p. 70 and p. 37).

In answers to yes-no questions or in case a presupposition violation occurs HAM-ANS requires, in addition to the elaborated utterance, the generation of a particle (JA, NEIN, or DOCH). SUTRA receives a third parameter besides the VS and the sentence type which governs the selection of the appropriate particle. It is placed at the head of the terminal string generated by SUTRA and a comma is inserted.

7.2   ON THE INTERPRETATION OF VERBALIZED STRUCTURES

In the 1983 version of SUTRA, input structures which did not correspond exactly to the syntax defined in Appendix A did not necessarily trigger an error indication or cause processing to be broken off, nor did they always lead to an ill-formed NL output.

---

[1] This efficient automatic disc access in HAM-ANS is carried out with the aid of the ATTACH package (JAMESON 1980).

Although this behavior is not logically incorrect, it obscured the behavior of the NL system as a whole and was thus a hindrance to transpareny.

After a partial reimplementation of the program (January 1984), only those structures are now processed which fit the patterns defined in Appendix A. This has been achieved by employing procedures from the HAM-ANS' EBNF-interpreter based on the pattern matcher of the programming language FUZZY.

In HAM-ANS, the transparency of the generation process as a whole is considerably enhanced because both parts, verbalization and surface transformations (cf. Fig. (2-1)), are controlled by this same interpreter. Thus the different constructions which represent an utterance in the course of its generation are processed by the same operators. For example the VS generated during verbalization by the interpreter's synthesis operator BUILD is broken down by the analysis operator TAKE and fed to the syntactic processes of SUTRA.

It is, however, now necessary to include the EBNF interpreter if SUTRA is to be transported.

7.3 TECHNICAL DATA

SUTRA is implemented in UCI-LISP (MEEHAN 1979) in the 1983 version and FUZZY (LEFAIVRE 1978) in the 1984 version. The system runs under the TOPS10 operating system on the DECsystem 1070(KI-10) computer of the University of Hamburg Computer Science Department and encompasses ca. 6 Kwords (à 36 bit) of interpreted code in approx. 70 procedures and 1.5 Kwords of data readable in LISP.

An early version of SUTRA's morphological processes has been implemented in Franz LISP (FODERARO 1980) (cf. sec. 2.1). The complete 1984 version of SUTRA has been transported onto a Symbolics 3600 Lisp Machine, embedding FUZZY in Zetalisp. This was achieved using the translation system ULM (cf. NEBEL 1984).

SUTRA can only be started in the environment of the NL system because access to a word lexicon is required. In HAM-ANS, the access to the disc areas which contain some necessary procedures for lexical analysis, the lexicon and SUTRA itself is provided by way of the ATTACH package. SUTRA's knowledge sources have to be read into the main storage.

Run time required varies with the complexity of the VS to be processed. In the 1983 version, a simple VS, e.g., (3-2), required ca. 1.6 seconds CPU time while a complexer VS, e.g., (5-22), demanded approx. 4.5 seconds CPU time.[1]

---

[1] The measurements were made on an almost 'empty' machine.

8.   SAMPLES OF PERFORMANCE

The following examples illustrate most of SUTRA's capabilities. The structures are derived from a terminal session which was recorded on disc with the aid of DSKLOG (MEEHAN
1979, p. 128).

Examples (8-1) to (8-5) are responses to user questions taken from dialog sequences
with the HAM-ANS system (HOEPPNER, MARBURGER 1984). HAM-ANS generates a considerably
more limited language fragment than the one defined in Appendix A. For example, passive
and adjective comparison are not employed and the lexemes used display only a few of
the morphological irregularities handled in SUTRA.

HAM-ANS does, nevertheless, contain the most highly developed generation component for
German implemented in an NL system at present. The syntactic differences between VS's
and the corresponding structures in the dialog sequences described by HOEPPNER and MAR-
BURGER (1984) are due to the effects of the partial reimplementation of SUTRA. In the
January 1984 version:

- nonterminal symbols are written in lowercase letters and in part indicated
  in a different way.
- sentences with a copula are represented in VS's with a sentence constituent
  verb,
- only those VS's are processed which satisfy the definition in Appendix A.

Examples (8-6) to (8-10) demonstrate capabilities of SUTRA that were not yet required
by HAM-ANS as of January 1984.

For each sample sentence, the underlying VS and PS is given. VS (8-1a) represents a coordinate sentence whose second clause corresponds to an elliptical sentence (cf. JAMESON,
WAHLSTER 1982). The PS for the first clause is (8-1b), for the second clause (8-1c).

```
(8-1a) (sent-c
          (sent-s (subject-p (np-s (n: SG) EIN GROSS STUHL))
                  (predicative (ap-s NICHT))
                  (verb (v: ACTIVE) (m: IND) (t: PRES) ZUR/ VERFUEGUNG/ STEH))
          ABER
          (sent-s (subject-p (np-s (n: SG) EIN SESSEL)))))


(8-1b) ((k: NOM) (g: MAS) (n: SG) (d: INDEF)
         (DETIND EIN) (ADJ GROSS) (NOM STUHL)
         (p: 3) (n: SG) (t: PRES) (m: IND) (VRB STEH)
         (XXX NICHT) (XXX ZUR/ VERFUEGUNG))


(8-1c) ((k: NOM) (g: MAS) (n: SG) (d: INDEF) (DETIND EIN) (NOM SESSEL))


(8-1d) EIN GROSSER STUHL STEHT NICHT ZUR VERFUEGUNG. ABER EIN SESSEL.

       [A large chair is not available, but an easy-chair.]
```

Grammatically the prepositional phrase *ZUR VERFÜGUNG* behaves like a separable prefix of *STEH*. From the point of view of SUTRA *ZUR VERFÜGUNG STEH* can thus be classified as a verb.

Example (8-2) contains a prepositional attribute. The gender of the embedding noun phrase is taken from the attribute noun phrase. The noun carrying gender is elided.

```
(8-2a) (sent-s
          (subject-p
            (np-s (n: SG) EIN
                  (attr-prp (pp-s VON (np-s (n: PL) D VIER
                                            (elision SITZGELEGENHEIT))))))))
          (verb (v: ACTIVE) (m: IND) (t: PRES) SEIN)
          (predicative (ap-s RELATIV BEQUEM)))


(8-2b) ((k: NOM) (g: FEM) (n: SG) (d: DEF) (DETQ EIN)
         (PRP VON) (k: DAT) (g: FEM) (n: PL) (d: DEF) (DETDEF D) (XXX VIER)
         (p: 3) (n: SG) (t: PRES) (m: IND) (VRB SEIN)
         (XXX RELATIV) (XXX BEQUEM))

(8-2c)  EINE VON DEN VIER IST RELATIV BEQUEM.

         [One of the four is relatively comfortable.]
```

EIN is the indefinite pronoun here and thus assigned to the word class DETQ. The type of determination is DEF.

In (8-3), we have an attributive relative clause whose subject is relativized.

```
(8-3a) (sent-s
          (subject-p (np-s (n: SG) KEIN DING))
          (verb (v: ACTIVE) (m: IND) (t: PRES) SEIN)
          (predicative
           (pp-s AUF (np-s (n: SG) D COUCHTISCH
                           (attr-rel
                            (sent-s
                              (subject-p (np-s (n: SG) (pro: REL)
                                               D COUCHTISCH))
                              (verb (v: ACTIVE) (m: IND) (t: PRES) SEIN)
                              (predicative
                               (pp-s NEBEN (np-s (n: SG) D SESSEL))))))))))


(8-3b) ((k: NOM) (g: NTR) (n: SG) (d: INDEF) (DETIND KEIN) (NOM DING)
         (p: 3) (n: SG) (t: PRES) (m: IND) (VRB SEIN)
         (PRP AUF) (k: DAT) (g: MAS) (n: SG) (d: DEF)
         (DETDEF D) (NOM COUCHTISCH) (MARK /,)
         (k: NOM) (g: MAS) (n: SG) (RELPRN D)
         (PRP NEBEN) (k: DAT) (g: MAS) (n: SG) (d: DEF)
         (DETDEF D) (NOM SESSEL)
         (p: 3) (n: SG) (t: PRES) (m: IND) (VRB SEIN))

(8-3c)  KEIN DING IST AUF DEM COUCHTISCH, DER NEBEN DEM SESSEL IST.

         [Nothing is on the coffee table which next-to the easy-chair is.]
```

150

VS (8-4a) contains an elliptical sentence (the PS for this is shown in (8-4b)) without a verb. Since HAM-ANS does not generate passive contructions, the AGENT-slot is choosen as subject (cf. 5.3). The PS for the second clause is given in (8-4c).

```
(8-4a) (sent-c
        (sent-s (case-slot S-AGENT
                    (np-s (n: SG) EIN GELB (elision PERSONENWAGEN)))
                (case-slot S-SOURCE
                    (pp-s VON (np-s (n: SG) D HARTUNGSTRASSE)))
                (case-slot S-GOAL
                    (pp-s IN  (np-s (n: SG) D SCHLUETERSTRASSE))))
        ABER
        (sent-s (verb (t: PERF) (v: ACTIVE) (m: IND) ABBIEG)
                (case-slot S-AGENT (np-s (n: SG) D GRUEN KOMBI))
                (modifier (ap-s VORHER NICHT)))))
```

```
(8-4b) ((k: NOM) (g: MAS) (n: SG) (d: INDEF)
        (DETIND EIN) (ADJ GELB)
        (PRP VON) (k: DAT) (g: FEM) (n: SG) (d: DEF)
        (DETDEF D) (NOM HARTUNGSTRASSE)
        (PRP IN) (k: AKK) (g: FEM) (n: SG) (d: DEF)
        (DETDEF D) (NOM SCHLUETERSTRASSE))
```

```
(8-4c) ((k: NOM) (g: MAS) (n: SG) (d: DEF)
        (DETDEF D) (ADJ GRUEN) (NOM KOMBI)
        (p: 3) (n: SG) (t: PRES) (m: IND) (VRB SEIN)
        (XXX VORHER) (XXX NICHT) (vinfin: PPRF) (VRB ABBIEG))
```

```
(8-4d) EIN GELBER VON DER HARTUNGSTRASSE IN DIE SCHLUETERSTRASSE,
        ABER DER GRUENE KOMBI IST VORHER NICHT ABGEBOGEN.
```

> [A yellow one from Hartungstrasse into Schlueterstrasse,
> but the green station wagon has before not turned-off.]

The ellipsis (8-5c) contains coordinated noun phrases. Again the AGENT constituent becomes the subject.

```
(8-5a) (sent-s
        (case-slot S-AGENT (np-c (np-s (n: SG) EIN ALT FRAU)
                                 UND
                                 (np-s (n: SG) EIN JUNG MANN))))
```

```
(8-5b) ((k: NOM) (g: FEM) (n: SG) (d: INDEF)
        (DETIND EIN) (ADJ ALT) (NOM FRAU)
        (XXX UND)
        (k: NOM) (g: MAS) (n: SG) (d: INDEF)
        (DETIND EIN) (ADJ JUNG) (NOM MANN))
```

```
(8-5c) EINE ALTE FRAU UND EIN JUNGER MANN.
```

> [An old woman and a young man.]

The remaining examples presume capabilities not covered by HAM-ANS. In (8-6a), a passive construction is required causing the object phrase to be selected as the subject. The AGENT-slot is verbalized as a prepositional phrase.

```
(8-6a) (sent-s
         (case-slot S-AGENT
             (pp-s VON (np-s (n: SG) D GEGNERISCH DAME)))
         (object-p
             (np-s (n: SG) D GEFESSELT SPRINGER
                   (attr-prp
                      (pp-s AUF (np-s (n: SG) D LANG DIAGONALE)))))
         (verb (v: PASSIVE) (m: IND) (t: FUT) ERBEUT))
```

```
(8-6b) ((k: NOM) (g: MAS) (n: SG) (d: DEF)
         (DETDEF D) (ADJ GEFESSELT) (NOM SPRINGER)
          (PRP AUF) (k: DAT) (g: FEM) (n: SG) (d: DEF)
          (DETDEF D) (ADJ LANG) (NOM DIAGONALE)
         (p: 3) (n: SG) (t: PRES) (m: IND) (VRB WERD)
         (PRP VON) (k: DAT) (g: FEM) (n: SG) (d: DEF)
          (DETDEF D) (ADJ GEGNERISCH) (NOM DAME)
         (vinfin: PPRF) (VRB ERBEUT) (vinfin: INF) (VRB WERD))
```

(8-6c) DER GEFESSELTE SPRINGER AUF DER LANGEN DIAGONALE WIRD VON DER GEGNERISCHEN DAME ERBEUTET WERDEN.

> [The pinned knight on the long diagonal will by the opponent queen be captured.]

In the following examples the main clause contains a direct and indirect object.

```
(8-7a) (sent-s
         (object-p (np-s (n: SG) EIN GROSS ZEITVORTEIL))
         (modifier (ap-s UNGEWOLLT))
         (subclause WEIL
           (sent-s
             (verb (v: ACTIVE) (m: IND) (t: PASTPERF) VERSCHLAF)
             (case-slot S-AGENT
                        (np-s (n: SG) (pro: PRN) GROSSMEISTER))
             (object-p (np-s (n: SG) D PARTIEBEGINN))))
         (case-slot S-RECIPIENT (np-s (n: SG) D GEGNER))
         (case-slot S-AGENT (np-s (n: SG) D GROSSMEISTER))
         (verb (v: ACTIVE) (m: IND) (t: PAST) GEB))
```

```
(8-7b) ((k: NOM) (g: MAS) (n: SG) (d: DEF)
         (DETDEF D) (NOM GROSSMEISTER)
         (p: 3) (n: SG) (t: PAST) (m: IND) (VRB GEB)
         (k: DAT) (g: MAS) (n: SG) (d: DEF)
         (DETDEF D) (NOM GEGNER)
         (XXX UNGEWOLLT)
         (k: AKK) (g: MAS) (n: SG) (d: INDEF)
         (DETIND EIN) (ADJ GROSS) ZEITVORTEIL) (MARK /,)
         (XXX WEIL)
          (k: NOM) (g: MAS) (n: SG) (p: 3) (PERSPRN)
          (k: AKK) (g: MAS) (n: SG) (d: DEF)
          (DETDEF D) (NOM PARTIEBEGINN)
          (vinfin: PPRF) (VRB VERSCHLAF)
         (p: 3) (n: SG) (t: PAST) (m: IND) (VRB HAB))
```

(8-7c) DER GROSSMEISTER GAB DEM GEGNER UNGEWOLLT EINEN GROSSEN
ZEITVORTEIL, WEIL ER DEN PARTIEBEGINN VERSCHLAFEN HATTE.

[The grandmaster gave the opponent unintentionally a large
time-advantage because he the beginning-of-the-round overslept had.]

The VS (8-8a) requires pronominalization of all noun phrases. Thus the order of sentence
constituents in (8-8b) differs from (8-7b). The VS is generated as a question because
the sentence type is FRONT (this is not shown here; cf. 4.2).

(8-8a) (sent-s
           (case-slot S-AGENT (np-s (n: SG) (pro: PRN) GROSSMEISTER))
           (indobj (np-s (n: SG) (pro: PRN) GEGNER))
           (object-p (np-s (n: SG) (pro: PRN) ZEITVORTEIL))
           (modifier (ap-s WIRKLICH UNFREIWILLIG))
           (verb (v: ACTIVE) (m: IND) (t: PERF) GEB))

(8-8b) ((p: 3) (n: SG) (t: PRES) (m: IND) (VRB HAB)
           (k: NOM) (g: MAS) (n: SG) (p: 3) (PERSPRN)
           (k: AKK) (g: MAS) (n: SG) (p: 3) (PERSPRN)
           (k: DAT) (g: MAS) (n: SG) (p: 3) (PERSPRN)
           (XXX WIRKLICH) (XXX UNFREIWILLIG)
           (vinfin: PPRF) (VRB GEB))

(8-8c) HAT ER IHN IHM WIRKLICH UNFREIWILLIG GEGEBEN?

[Has he it him really unvoluntarily given?]

'Did he really give it to him unvoluntarily?'

Example (8-9) contains an object complement clause which consists of subject, copula
and a noun phrase representing a *predicate nominative* which is followed by a genitive
attribute.

(8-9a) (sent-s
           (object-s
             (sent-s (subject-p (np-s (n: SG) D ZEITNOT))
                     (verb (v: ACTIVE) (m: KON) (t: PERF) SEIN)
                     (predicative
                       (np-s (n: SG) D URSACHE
                             (attr-gen (np-s (n: SG) D DEBAKEL))))))
           (case-slot S-TIME
                       (pp-s NACH (np-s (n: SG) D NIEDERLAGE)))
           (case-slot S-AGENT
                       (np-s (n: SG) (pro: PRN) GROSSMEISTER))
           (verb (v: ACTIVE) (m: IND) (t: PAST) BEHAUPT))

(8-9b) ((k: NOM) (g: MAS) (n: SG) (p: 3) (PERSPRN)
           (p: 3) (n: SG) (t: PAST) (m: IND) (VRB BEHAUPT)
           (PRP NACH) (k: DAT) (g: FEM) (n: SG) (d: DEF)
           (DETDEF D) (NOM NIEDERLAGE) (MARK /,)
           (XXX DASS)
           (k: NOM) (g: FEM) (n: SG) (d: DEF) (DETDEF D) (NOM ZEITNOT)
           (k: NOM) (g: FEM) (n: SG) (d: DEF) (DETDEF D) (NOM URSACHE)
           (k: GEN) (g: NTR) (n: SG) (d: DEF) (DETDEF D) (NOM DEBAKEL)
           (vinfin: PPRF) (VRB SEIN)
           (p: 3) (n: SG) (t: PRES) (m: KON) (VRB SEIN))

(8-9c) ER BEHAUPTETE NACH DER NIEDERLAGE, DASS DIE ZEITNOT DIE
       URSACHE DES DEBAKELS GEWESEN SEI.

       [He claimed after the defeat that lack of time the
       cause of the debacle was.]

The last example shows comparison with attributive and predicate adjectives.

(8-10a) (sent-s
          (subject-p (np-s (n: SG) D GESPIELT ZUG))
          (modifier (ap-s (comparison (cmp: SUP) EINFACH)))
          (verb (v: ACTIVE) (m: IND) (t: PAST) GEWINN)
          (subclause OBWOHL
            (sent-s
              (verb (v: ACTIVE) (m: IND) (t: PAST) STECK)
              (subject-p (np-s (n: PL) (comparison (cmp: KOM) ELEGANT)
                               MOEGLICHKEIT))
              (case-slot S-LOCATIVE
                         (pp-s IN (np-s (n: SG) D STELLUNG))))))))

(8-10b) ((k: NOM) (g: MAS) (n: SG) (d: DEF)
         (DETDEF D) (ADJ GESPIELT) (NOM ZUG)
         (p: 3) (n: SG) (t: PAST) (m: IND) (VRB GEWINN)
         (cmp: SUP) (XXX EINFACH) (MARK /,)
         (XXX OBWOHL)
         (k: NOM) (g: FEM) (n: PL) (d: WITHOUT)
          (cmp: KOM) (ADJ ELEGANT) (NOM MOEGLICHKEIT)
         (PRP IN) (k: DAT) (g: FEM) (n: SG) (d: DEF)
          (DETDEF D) (NOM STELLUNG)
         (p: 3) (n: PL) (t: PAST) (m: IND) (VRB STECK))

(8-10c) DER GESPIELTE ZUG GEWANN AM EINFACHSTEN, OBWOHL ELEGANTERE
        MOEGLICHKEITEN IN DER STELLUNG STECKTEN.

        [The played move won the easiest though more elegant
        possibilities in the position were.]

        'The move played was the easiest to win though there were
        more elegant possibilities in the position.'

APPENDIX

A. THE SYNTACTIC DEFINITION OF THE VERBALIZED STRUCTURES

The following declarative definition of the partial grammar was accomplished with the
aid of a software package from the system HAM-ANS, which employs a syntax based pattern
matcher, thus permitting the interactive definition, the alteration and interpretation
of expressions in extended Backus-Naur form (EBNF). The EBNF formalism is used in
HAM-ANS for processing expressions in the representation languages DEEP and SURF
(JAMESON et al. 1980).

The syntactic definition makes it possible to generate and recognize all the structures
that SURTA can process, but also includes meaningless and ungrammatical structures (e.g.,

those with three subjects). Where alternative definitions of a nonterminal are given, the *type* preceded by a semicolon is specified after each definition thus permitting an unambiguous selection. The type indications within a definition allow different instantiations of one nonterminal (see definitions of the type COORDINATE). The identifiers in lowercase letters at the beginning of definitions increase the efficiency of the matching process at cost of redundancy (e.g., *np-c* precedes a compound noun phrase, *np-s* a simple one; *object-p* precedes an object phrase, *object-s* an object sentence).

The *plus sign* means that the preceding nonterminal may appear more than once. Nonterminals enclosed in *pointed brackets* are optional. An *asterisk* means that the preceding nonterminal is optional, but can also appear more than once. A *period* causes the preceding nonterminal to be checked immediately if it matches the corresponding definition.

The definition for WORD of the type LEXICON generates a local binding environment in FUZZY in which a check is carried out to see whether the current part of the input is an entry in HAM-ANS' word lexicon.

```
<adjective-phrase>
    ::=  (ap-c <adjective-phrase>.+ ;FIRST-ONES
          <word> ;CO-CONJ
          <adjective-phrase> ;LAST-ONE)              ;COORDINATE
    ::=  (ap-s <word>+ ;WORDS)                          ;SIMPLE

<attribute>
    ::=  (attr-rel <sentence>)                  ;RELATIVE-CLAUSE
    ::=  (attr-gen <noun-phrase>)                      ;GENITIVE
    ::=  (attr-prp <prepositional-phrase>)       ;PREP-SUPPLEMENT

<deep-case-label>
    ::=  S-AGENT | S-GOAL | S-INSTRUMENT | S-LOCATIVE | S-PATH |
          S-RECIPIENT | S-SOURCE | S-TIME

<inf-verb-const>
    ::=  (<msi> ;VINFIN <word> ;VERB)

<msi>
    ::=  (v: <msi-voice>)                               ;VOICE
    ::=  (m: <msi-mood>)                                 ;MOOD
    ::=  (t: <msi-tense>)                               ;TENSE
    ::=  (n: <msi-number>)                             ;NUMBER
    ::=  (pro: <msi-proform>)                         ;PROFORM
    ::=  (cmp: <msi-comparison>)                   ;COMPARISON
    ::=  (p: <msi-person>)                             ;PERSON
    ::=  (vinfin: <msi-vinfin>)                      ;INFINITE
    ::=  (d: <msi-det>)                               ;DET-TYPE
    ::=  (g: <msi-gender>)                             ;GENDER
    ::=  (k: <possible-cases>)                          ;CASES

<msi-case>
    ::=  AKK | DAT | GEN | NOM

<msi-comparation>
    ::=  KOMP | SUP
```

```
<msi-det>
    ::= DEF | INDEF | WITHOUT

<msi-gender>
    ::= FEM | MAS | NTR

<msi-mood>
    ::= IMP | IND | KON

<msi-number>
    ::= SG | PL

<msi-person>
    ::= 1 | 2 | 3

<msi-proform>
    ::= REL | PRN

<msi-tense>
    ::= FUT | PAST | PASTPERF | PERF | PERFUT | PRES

<msi-vinfin>
    ::= INF | PPRF | PPRS

<msi-voice>
    ::= ACTIVE | PASSIVE

<noun-phrase>
    ::= (np-c <noun-phrase>.+ ;FIRST-ONES
         <word> ;CO-CONJ
         <noun-phrase> ;LAST-ONE)                    ;COORDINATE
    ::= (np-s <msi> ;NUMBER
         {<msi>. ;PRO-TYPE}
         <word>.+ ;WORDS
         {<attribute>. ;ATTRIBUTE})                  ;SIMPLE

<part-of-speech>
    ::= ADJ | VRB | PERSPRN | DETDEF | DETIND | DETQ | NOM |
        PRP | POSSPRN | RELPRN | XXX

<phrase>
    ::= <prepositional-phrase>.
    ::= <noun-phrase>.
    ::= <adjective-phrase>.

<possible-cases>
    ::= (<msi-case>.+ ;CASES)                         ;PP
    ::= <msi-case>                                    ;NP

<prepositional-phrase>
    ::= (pp-c <prepositional-phrase>.+ ;FIRST-ONES
         <word> ;CO-CONJ
         <prepositional-phrase> ;LAST-ONE)           ;COORDINATE
    ::= (pp-s <word> ;PREPOSITION <noun-phrase>)     ;SIMPLE

<sentence>
    ::= (sent-c <sentence>.+ ;FIRST-ONES
         <word> ;CO-CONJ
         <sentence> ;LAST-ONE)                       ;COORDINATE
    ::= (sent-s <sentence-constituent>.+
         ;SENTENCE-CONSTITUENTS)                     ;SIMPLE
```

```
<sentence-constituent>
    ::=  (elision <sentence-constituent>)                    ;ELISION
    ::=  (modifier <adjective-phrase>)                       ;SENT-MOD
    ::=  (case-slot <deep-case-label> ;NAME <phrase>)        ;CASE-SLOT
    ::=  (subject-p <noun-phrase>)                           ;SUBJECT
    ::=  (subject-s <sentence>)                              ;SUBJ-SENT
    ::=  (predicative <phrase>)                             ;COPULA-PRED
    ::=  (object-p <noun-phrase>)                            ;DIRECT
    ::=  (object-s <sentence>)                               ;OBJ-SENT
    ::=  (indobj <noun-phrase>)                              ;INDIRECT
    ::=  (subclause <word> ;SUB-CONJ <sentence>)           ;SUBORDINATE
    ::=  (verb <msi>.3-5 ;MODALITY <word> ;VERB)             ;VERB
    ::=  (finite <msi> ;PERSON
          <msi> ;NUMBER
          <msi> ;MORPH-TENSE
          <msi> ;MOOD
          <word> ;FINITE-ROOT)                              ;FINITE
    ::=  (infinite <word>.)                                  ;PREFIX
    ::=  (infinite <inf-verb-const>.+ ;CONSTITUENTS)         ;INFINITE

<word>
    ::=  (elision <word> ;NOUN)                              ;ELISION
    ::=  (comparison <msi> ;GRADE <word> ;ADJECTIVE)
                                                             ;COMPARISON
    ::=  (*LOCAL (*R ?WORD (AND (ATOM !WORD) (WORTART !WORD))))
                                                             ;LEXICON
    ::=  (<part-of-speech>. <word> ;LEXEME)                  ;CLASSIFIED
```

B. AN EXCERPT FROM HAM-ANS' WORD LEXICON

In the following examples, only the parts of a lexical entry which SUTRA makes use of
are given. Each *part* is identified with a *name*, which is followed by a *value*. The value
itself consists either of the information sought or of another *part* which also consists
of a name and a value.

Each entry contains a wordclass (Name: WORTART). The declension type for the noun is
indicated with DEKLIN, the gender of the noun with GENUS. The name of the list of possible cases governed by prepositions is FLEXION. Verbs include conjugation information
under the indicator KONJUG, which is subdivided into a number of separate entries.
These have the following meanings:

Name		Constant Information
VTYP	:	Verb type ("degree of irregularity")
VGFB, VGFC, VGFD:		Verb base form
PPRF	:	Perfect participle form
PAUX	:	Auxiliary for the perfect tenses
VRBZ	:	Verb prefix

The comparison class of adjectives is under the name KOMP. The comparative and superlative forms of some adjectives are irregular and cannot be dynamically calculated. In

such cases, forms with the names KOMPARATIV and SUPERLATIV are listed instead of comparison class. The following excerpt form the lexicon contains all of these exception.

```
`  ABBIEG    ((WORTART VRB)
              (KONJUG (VTYP 4) (VGFC ABBOG) (VGFD ABBOEGE)
                      (PPRF ABGEBOGEN) (PAUX SEIN) (VRBZ AB)))
`  ARBEIT    ((WORTART VRB)
              (KONJUG (VTYP 1) (PPRF GEARBEITET) (PAUX HAB)))
`  ALT       ((WORTART ADJ) (KOMP EST_U))
`  DASS      ((WORTART NSKON))
`  GROSS     ((WORTART ADJ) (KOMP (KOMPARATIV GROESSER)
                                  (SUPERLATIV GROESST)))
`  GUT       ((WORTART ADJ) (KOMP (KOMPARATIV BESSER)
                                  (SUPERLATIV BEST)))
`  HAB       ((WORTART AUX)
              (KONJUG (VTYP 6) (VGFB HA) (VGFC HATTE)
                      (VGFD HAETTE) (PPRF GEHABT) (PAUX HAB)))
`  HAUS      ((WORTART NOM) (GENUS NTR) (DEKLIN ER_U))
`  HOH       ((WORTART ADJ) (KOMP (KOMPARATIV HOEHER)
                                  (SUPERLATIV HOECHST)))
`  NAH       ((WORTART ADJ) (KOMP (KOMPARATIV NAEHER)
                                  (SUPERLATIV NAECHST)))
`  NEBEN     ((WORTART PRP) (FLEXION (DAT AKK)))
`  SEIN      ((WORTART AUX)
              (KONJUG (VTYP 11) (VGFC WAR) (VGFD WAERE)
                      (PPRF GEWESEN) (PAUX SEIN)))
`  VIEL      ((WORTART ADJ) (KOMP (KOMPARATIV MEHRER)
                                  (SUPERLATIV MEIST)))
```

C. AN EXCERPT OF THE RULES FOR SENTENCE CONSTITUENT PLACEMENT

The rules are defined as packages for each of currently fifteen identifiers which
stand for sentence constituents. Some of them correspond to more than one sentence
constituent. In each package the position of the corresponding sentence constituent is
defined relative to any possible cooccurring constituent. Each rule in a package consists of evaluatable UCI-LISP code preceeded by the representative(s) to which the rule
may be applied. PUT-LEFT! and PUT-RIGHT! are interpreted as position a constituent
before or after the sentence constituent the package is associated with. An unambiguous
ordering of constituents is guaranteed by the completeness and symmetry of the rules
as well as the explicit representation of undefined combinations. In particular, the
positioning is independent of the order in a VS.

The rules allow parameterization. The Boolean variables LAST?, CENTRAL?, and FRONT?
indicate the position of the finite verb (cf. 4.2). The Boolean functions RELATIVE?
and PRONOMINAL? indicate whether the constituent belonging to their argument is to be
formulated as a relative or personal pronoun. THE-FORMER identifies the constituent
belonging to the package while THE-LATTER indicates the one to which the relevant rule
may be applied.

Some of the packages are listed below.


```
FINITE
 ((SUBJECT (COND [FRONT? PUT-RIGHT!] [T PUT-LEFT!])))
 (SUBCLAUSE PUT-RIGHT!)
 ((S-AGENT S-GOAL INFINITE S-INSTRUMENT S-LOCATIVE MODIFIER
   OBJECT S-PATH PREDICATIVE INDOBJ S-SOURCE S-TIME)
  (COND [LAST? PUT-LEFT!] [T PUT-RIGHT!])))


INDOBJ
 ((FINITE (COND [LAST? PUT-RIGHT!] [T PUT-LEFT!])))
 (SUBJECT (COND [(RELATIVE? THE-FORMER) PUT-RIGHT!]
               [T PUT-LEFT!]))
 ((INFINITE MODIFIER SUBCLAUSE) PUT-RIGHT!)
 (OBJECT (COND [(RELATIVE? THE-LATTER) PUT-LEFT!]
               [(RELATIVE? THE-FORMER) PUT-RIGHT!]
               [(PRONOMINAL? THE-LATTER) PUT-LEFT!]
               [T PUT-RIGHT!]))
 ((S-AGENT S-GOAL S-INSTRUMENT S-LOCATIVE S-PATH S-SOURCE
   S-TIME)
  (COND [(RELATIVE? THE-LATTER) PUT-LEFT!] [T PUT-RIGHT!]))
 (PREDICATIVE UNDEFINED))


INFINITE
 ((SUBCLAUSE PUT-RIGHT!)
 (FINITE (COND [LAST? PUT-RIGHT!] [T PUT-LEFT!])))
 ((S-AGENT S-GOAL S-INSTRUMENT S-LOCATIVE MODIFIER OBJECT
   S-PATH PREDICATIVE INDOBJ S-SOURCE SUBJECT S-TIME)
  PUT-LEFT!))


MODIFIER
 ((FINITE (COND [LAST? PUT-RIGHT!] [T PUT-LEFT!])))
 ((INDOBJ SUBJECT) PUT-LEFT!)
 ((INFINITE SUBCLAUSE) PUT-RIGHT!)
 (OBJECT (COND [(RELATIVE? THE-LATTER) PUT-LEFT!]
               [(PRONOMINAL? THE-LATTER) PUT-LEFT!]
               [T PUT-RIGHT!]))
 ((S-AGENT S-GOAL S-INSTRUMENT S-LOCATIVE S-PATH PREDICATIVE
   S-SOURCE S-TIME)
  (COND [(RELATIVE? THE-LATTER) PUT-LEFT!] [T PUT-RIGHT!])))


OBJECT
 ((FINITE (COND [LAST? PUT-RIGHT!] [T PUT-LEFT!])))
 (SUBJECT (COND [(RELATIVE? THE-FORMER) PUT-RIGHT!]
               [T PUT-LEFT!]))
 ((INFINITE SUBCLAUSE) PUT-RIGHT!)
 ((MODIFIER INDOBJ S-TIME)
  (COND [(RELATIVE? THE-FORMER) PUT-RIGHT!]
        [(RELATIVE? THE-LATTER) PUT-LEFT!]
        [(PRONOMINAL? THE-FORMER) PUT-RIGHT!]
        [T PUT-LEFT!]))
 ((S-GOAL S-INSTRUMENT S-LOCATIVE S-PATH S-SOURCE)
  (COND [(RELATIVE? THE-LATTER) PUT-LEFT!] [T PUT-RIGHT!]))
 ((S-AGENT PREDICATIVE) UNDEFINED))
```

```
PREDICATIVE
 ((FINITE (COND [LAST? PUT-RIGHT!] [T PUT-LEFT!]))
  ((INFINITE SUBCLAUSE) PUT-RIGHT!)
  ((MODIFIER SUBJECT S-TIME)
   (COND [(RELATIVE? THE-FORMER) PUT-RIGHT!] [T PUT-LEFT!]))
  ((S-AGENT S-GOAL S-INSTRUMENT S-LOCATIVE OBJECT INDOBJ
    S-SOURCE S-TIME)
   UNDEFINED))


 S-SOURCE
  ((FINITE (COND [LAST? PUT-RIGHT!] [T PUT-LEFT!]))
   ((INFINITE SUBCLAUSE) PUT-RIGHT!)
   ((S-PATH S-GOAL)
    (COND [(RELATIVE? THE-LATTER) PUT-LEFT!] [T PUT-RIGHT!]))
   ((S-AGENT S-INSTRUMENT MODIFIER OBJECTE INDOBJ SUBJECT
     S-TIME)
    (COND [(RELATIVE? THE-FORMER) PUT-RIGHT!] [T PUT-LEFT!]))
   ((PREDICATIVE S-LOCATIVE) UNDEFINED))


 SUBCLAUSE
  (((S-AGENT FINITE S-GOAL INFINITE S-INSTRUMENT S-LOCATIVE
     MODIFIER OBJECT S-PATH PREDICATIVE INDOBJ S-SOURCE
     SUBCLAUSE SUBJECT S-TIME)
    PUT-LEFT!))


 SUBJECT
  ((FINITE (COND [FRONT? PUT-LEFT!] [T PUT-RIGHT!]))
   ((INFINITE MODIFIER SUBCLAUSE) PUT-RIGHT!)
   ((S-AGENT S-GOAL S-INSTRUMENT S-LOCATIVE OBJECT S-PATH
     PREDICATIVE INDOBJ S-SOURCE S-TIME)
    (COND [(RELATIVE? THE-LATTER) PUT-LEFT!] [T PUT-RIGHT!]))))
```

D. THE INFLECTIONAL PARADIGMS

The tree structure of the inflectional schemas listed below is reflected in their bracketing. Nonterminal nodes have preceding opening brackets while terminal nodes have following closing brackets. The leaves with the exception of those in %PERSONAL_ PRONOUN_FORMS and %VERB_SEGMENT_TYPES correspond to inflectional morphemes. The zero-allomorph is represented by NIL.

The recursive tree search operates in a top-down, breadth-first manner. It is guided by an ordered list of MSI items supplied by a morphological process. The succession of this MSI corresponds exactly to the MSI encoded at the different levels in the respective decision tree. The search process terminates when a list of two atoms is found, returning the second atom as its result.

For each schema listed below the sequence of MSI categories is specified, thus indicating which kind of MSI is encoded at the different levels of the tree.

Comparison: *degree of comparison, type of comparison*

```
%ADJECTIVE_COMPARISON_MORPHEMES
 ((KOM (ELSE: ER))
  (SUP (ST ST) (ST-U ST) (ELSE: EST)))
```

Adjective inflection: *number, gender, case, type of determination*

```
%ADJECTIVE_MORPHEMES
 ((SG (MAS (NOM (DEF E) (ELSE: ER))
           (DAT (WITHOUT EM) (ELSE: EN))
           (ELSE: EN))
      (FEM (GEN (WITHOUT ER) (ELSE: EN))
           (DAT (WITHOUT ER) (ELSE: EN))
           (ELSE: E))
      (NTR (GEN EN)
           (DAT (WITHOUT EM) (ELSE: EN))
           (ELSE: (DEF E) (ELSE: ES))))
  (PL (ELSE: (GEN (WITHOUT ER) (ELSE: EN))
             (DAT EN)
             (ELSE: (WITHOUT E) (ELSE: EN))))))
```

Verb inflection: *segment type, tense/mood, number, person*

```
%VERB_MORPHEMES
 ((VGFA (INF EN)
        (PAR1 END)
        (IMP (SG E) (PL T))
        (PRES (SG (1. E) (2. ST) (3. T)) (PL (2. T) (ELSE: EN)))
        (IMPF (SG (2. TEST) (ELSE: TE)) (PL (2. TET) (ELSE: TEN)))
        (KON1 (SG (2. EST) (ELSE: E))(PL (2. ET) (ELSE: EN)))
        (KON2 (SG (2. TEST) (ELSE: TE)) (PL (2. TET) (ELSE: TEN))))
  (VGFB (PRES (SG (1. NIL) (2. ST) (3. T)))
        (IMP (SG NIL)))
  (VGFC (IMPF (SG (2. ST) (ELSE: NIL)) (PL (2. T) (ELSE: EN)))
        (KON2 (SG (2. EST) (ELSE: E)) (PL (2. ET) (ELSE: EN))))
  (VGFD (KON2 (SG (2. ST) (ELSE: NIL)) (PL (2. T) (ELSE: N))))
  (SOND (INF SEIN)
        (PAR1 SEIEND)
        (IMP (SG SEI) (PL SEID))
        (PRES (SG (1. BIN) (2. BIST) (3. IST))
              (PL (2. SEID) (ELSE: SIND)))
        (KON1 (SG (2. SEIEST) (ELSE: SEI))
              (PL (2. SEIET) (ELSE: SEIEN))))))
```

Inflection of the definite article and of relative pronouns:
number, case, gender, DET/REL-switch

```
%DETDEF_RELPRN_MORPHEMES
 ((SG (NOM (MAS ER) (FEM IE) (NTR AS))
      (GEN (FEM (DET ER) (ELSE: EREN)) (ELSE: (DET ES) (ELSE: ESSEN)))
      (DAT (FEM ER) (ELSE: EM))
      (AKK (MAS EN) (FEM IE) (NTR AS)))
  (PL (GEN (ELSE: (DET ER) (ELSE: EREN)))
      (DAT (ELSE: (DET EN) (ELSE: ENEN)))
      (ELSE: IE)))
```

Generation of verb segment types: *tense/mood, number, person, verb type* (cf. Appendix E)

```
%VERB_SEGMENT_TYPES
  ((PRES (PL (ELSE: (11. SOND) (ELSE: VGFA)))
         (SG (1. (8. VGFB) (9. VGFB) (10. VGFB) (11. SOND) (ELSE: VGFA))
             (ELSE: (11. SOND) (1. VGFA) (2. VGFA) (3. VGFA)
                    (4. VGFA) (ELSE: VGFB))))
   (KON1 (ELSE: (ELSE: (11. SOND) (ELSE: VGFA))))
   (IMPF (ELSE: (ELSE: (1. VGFA) (8. VGFA) (ELSE: VGFC))))
   (KON2 (ELSE: (ELSE: (1. VGFA) (2. VGFA) (3. VGFC) (5. VGFC)
                       (8. VGFA) (9. VGFA) (ELSE: VGFD))))
   (IMP (SG (ELSE: (7. VGFB) (11. SOND) (ELSE: VGFA)))
        (PL (ELSE: (11. SOND) (ELSE: VGFA))))
   (INF (ELSE: (ELSE: (11. SOND) (ELSE: VGFA))))
   (PAR1 (ELSE: (ELSE: (11. SOND) (ELSE: VGFA))))))
```

Noun declension: *declension type, number, case, gender*

```
%NOUN_MORPHEMES
  ((* (SG (GEN (FEM NIL) (ELSE: S)) (ELSE: NIL))
      (PL (DAT N) (ELSE: NIL)))
   (*_U (SG (GEN (FEM NIL) (ELSE: S)) (ELSE: NIL))
        (PL (DAT N) (ELSE: NIL)))
   (** (SG (GEN S) (ELSE: NIL)) (PL NIL))
   (**_U (SG (GEN S) (ELSE: NIL)) (PL NIL))
   (E (SG (GEN (FEM NIL) (ELSE: ES)) (ELSE: NIL))
      (PL (DAT EN) (ELSE: E)))
   (E_U (SG (GEN (FEM NIL) (ELSE: ES)) (ELSE: NIL))
        (PL (DAT EN) (ELSE: E)))
   (EN_S (SG (NOM NIL) (ELSE: (FEM NIL) (MAS EN))) (PL EN))
   (EN_G (SG (GEN S) (ELSE: NIL)) (PL EN))
   (ER (SG (GEN ES) (ELSE: NIL)) (PL (DAT ERN) (ELSE: ER)))
   (ER_U (SG (GEN ES) (ELSE: NIL)) (PL (DAT ERN) (ELSE: ER)))
   (N_S (SG (NOM NIL) (ELSE: (FEM NIL) (MAS N))) (PL N))
   (N_G (SG (GEN S) (ELSE: NIL)) (PL N))
   (S (SG (GEN (FEM NIL) (ELSE: S)) (ELSE: NIL)) (PL S))))
```

Personal pronoun generation: *number, person, case, gender*

```
%PERSONAL_PRONOUN_FORMS
  ((SG (1. (NOM ICH) (GEN MEINER) (DAT MIR) (AKK MICH))
       (2. (NOM DU) (GEN DEINER) (DAT DIR) (AKK DICH))
       (3. (NOM (MAS ER) (FEM SIE) (NTR ES))
           (GEN (FEM IHRER) (ELSE: SEINER))
           (DAT (FEM IHR) (ELSE: IHM))
           (AKK (MAS IHN) (FEM SIE) (NTR ES))))
   (PL (1. (NOM WIR) (GEN UNSER) (ELSE: UNS))
       (2. (NOM IHR) (GEN EUER) (ELSE: EUCH))
       (3. (DAT IHNEN) (GEN IHRER) (ELSE: SIE)))))
```

Inflection of quantifiers and possessive pronouns:
number, gender, case, type of determination

```
%QUANTIFIER_MORPHEMES
  ((SG (MAS (NOM (INDEF NIL) (ELSE: ER)) (GEN ES) (DAT EM) (AKK EN))
       (FEM (NOM E) (AKK E) (ELSE: ER))
       (NTR (GEN ES) (DAT EM) (ELSE: (INDEF NIL) (ELSE: ES))))
   (PL (ELSE: (GEN ER) (DAT EN) (ELSE: E)))))
```

E. THE INFLECTIONAL TYPES OF THE IRREGULAR VERBS

The following list contains the prefixless irregular verbs of German (verb type 2 to
11). Discontinuous irregular verbs can be derived from similarly conjugated verbs in
this list. Their verb type remains unchanged. Sources used are DUDEN (1973) and BROCK-
HAUS (1975).

Type	Stems
2	brenn kenn nenn renn send wend
3	befleiß beiß bleib bleich dünk gedeih geh gleich gleit greif häng hau heiß kneif kreisch leid leih meid pfeif preis reib reiß reit ruf scheid schein scheiß schleich schleif schleiß schmeiß schneid schrei schreib schreit schweig spei spleiß steig streich streif treib weich weis zeih
4	beginn beweg bieg biet bind bitt bring denk ding dring erkies find flieg flieh fließ frier gär geling genes genieß gewinn gieß glimm heb klimm kling komm kriech kür lieg lüg mißling pfleg riech ring rinn saug schaff schall scher schieb schieß schind schließ schling schnaub schwimm schwind schwing schwör sied sing sink sinn sitz spinn sprieß spring steck steh stieb stink trief trink trüg tu verdrieß verlier wäg web wieg wind wring zieh zwing
5	blas brat fall fang halt laß lauf rat schlaf stoß
6	back fahr grab hab lad sauf schlag trag tret werd
7	befehl berg berst brech dresch empfehl eß echt felcht freß gebär geb gelt gescheh helf les lösch melk meß nehm quell schelt schmelz schreck schwell seh sprech stech stehl sterb treff verderb vergeß wachs wasch werb werf
8	woll
9	dürf könn müß
10	mög wiß
11	sein

ACKNOWLEDGEMENTS

I would like to thank Wilfried Brauer, Wolfgang Hoeppner and Wolfgang Wahlster for
numerous helpful comments on my diploma thesis which this contribution is based on,
and Russell Block for translation and many useful suggestions. Thanks goes also to
Brigitte Biester, Wenjer Hsu, Maren Mühlenberg, Astrid Scherff and Silke Vogt for
their aid in typing and editing this report.

REFERENCES

APPELT, D.E. (1982): Planning Natural Language Utterances to Satisfy Multiple Goals. Ph.D. Dissertation, Stanford University, Stanford, CA.

BIERWISCH, M. (1963): Grammatik des deutschen Verbs. Studia Grammatica 2, Berlin.

BROCKHAUS, K. (1975a): Flexion der deutschen Verben. In: Brockhaus et al. 1976, Part 2. Working Paper B7.

BROCKHAUS, K. (1975b): Liste der irregulären Verben des Deutschen. In: Brockhaus et al. 1976, Part 2. Working Paper B8.

BROCKHAUS, K., HAUENSCHILD, C., HOEFLING, J., HUCKERT, E., MAIER, R. (1976): Forschungsbericht 1.11.1973 - 31.3.1976. Sonderforschungsbereich 99 ("Linguistik"). Teilprojekt A2 ("Automatische Übersetzung"), Heidelberg.

BUCHBERGER, E. (1982): Generierung natürlichsprachlicher Sätze aus einem semantischen Netz. University of Vienna, Dept. of Medical Cybernetics, Report 82-05.

BUSEMANN, S. (1982): Probleme der automatischen Generierung deutscher Sprache. University of Hamburg, Research Unit for Information Science and Artificial Intelligence, Memo ANS-8.

CHOMSKY, N. (1957): Syntactic Structures. Den Haag.

CHOMSKY, N. (1965): Aspects of the Theory of Syntax. Cambridge.

CHOMSKY, N. (1977): Essays on Form and Interpretation. Amsterdam.

CHOMSKY, N. (1981): Lectures on Government and Binding. Dordrecht.

COHEN, P.R. (1978): On Knowing What to Say: Planning Speech Acts. University of Toronto, Technical Report 118.

DAVEY, A. (1978): Discourse Production. A Computer Model of Some Aspects of a Speaker. Edinburgh.

DUDEN (1973): Duden. Grammatik der deutschen Gegenwartssprache. 3. Auflage, Mannheim.

DUDEN (1980): Duden. Rechtschreibung der deutschen Sprache und der Fremdwörter. 18. Auflage, Mannheim.

ENGEL, U. (1977): Die Syntax der deutschen Gegenwartssprache. Berlin.

ESAU, H. (1973): Form and Function of German Adjective Endings. In: Folia Linguistica 6, 1973, 1/2. pp. 136-145.

FILLMORE, C.J. (1968): The Case for Case. In: Bach, E., Harms, R.T. (eds.): Universals in Liguistic Theory. New York.

FODERARO, J.K. (1980): The Franz Lisp Manual. University of California at Berkeley, Dept. of Computer Science.

GLINZ, H. (1952): Die innere Form des Deutschen. Bern.

GOLDMAN, N.M. (1975): Conceptual Generation. In: Schank, R.C. (ed.): Conceptual Information Processing. Amsterdam.

v. HAHN, W., HOEPPNER, W., JAMESON, A., WAHLSTER, W. (1980): The Anatomy of the Natural Language Dialogue System HAM-RPM. In: Bolc, L. (ed.): Natural Language Based Computer Systems. München.

HELBIG, G., SCHENKEL, W. (1969): Wörterbuch zur Valenz und Distribution deutscher Verben. Leipzig.

HERINGER, H.J. (1970): Theorie der deutschen Syntax. Linguistische Reihe, 1. München.

HOEPPNER, W. (1981): Zum Wortklassensystem in HAM-ANS. University of Hamburg, Research Unit for Information Science and Artificial Intelligence, Working Paper 5.

HOEPPNER, W., CHRISTALLER, T., MARBURGER, H., MORIK, K., NEBEL, B., O'LEARY, M., WAHLSTER, W. (1983): Beyond Domain-Independence: Experience with the Development of a German Language Access System to Highly Diverse Background Systems. In: Proc. of the 8th IJCAI, Karlsruhe, pp. 588-594.

HOEPPNER, W., MARBURGER, H. (1984): Dialog Sequences with HAM-ANS: Commented Examples of the System's Performance. University of Hamburg, Research Unit for Information Science and Artificial Intelligence. English Version of Memo ANS-16.

HOEPPNER, W., MORIK, K., MARBURGER, H. (1984): Talking it Over: The Natural Language Dialog System HAM-ANS. To appear in: Bolc, L. (ed.): Cooperative Interactive Systems. Berlin, Springer.

HORACEK, H. (1983): Generierung im System VIE-LANG: Linguistischer Teil. University of Vienna, Dept. of Medical Cybernetics, Report 83-04.

JAMESON, A. (1980): ATTACH: A Package for Accessing LISP Programs and Data from Disk. University of Hamburg, Research Unit for Information Science and Artificial Intelligence. Memo RPM-12.

JAMESON, A., HOEPPNER, W., WAHLSTER, W. (1980): The Natural Language System HAM-RPM as a Hotel Manager: Some Representational Prerequisites. In: Wilhelm, R. (ed.): GI-10. Jahrestagung Saarbrücken, Berlin, pp. 151-171.

JAMESON, A., WAHLSTER, W. (1982): User Modelling in Anaphora Generation: Ellipsis and Definite Description. In: Proc. of the 1st ECAI, Orsay, pp. 222-227.

KEMPEN, G., HOENKAMP, E. (1982): An Incremental Procedural Grammar for Sentence Formulation. University of Nijmegen, Internal Report 82 FU 14.

KUNZE, J., RUEDIGER, B. (1968): Algorithmische Synthese der Flexionsformen des Deutschen. In: ZPSK 21, pp. 245-303.

LeFAIVRE, R. (1978): FUZZY Reference Manual. Rutgers University, Computer Science Department.

MANN, W.C., BATES, M., GROSZ, B., McDONALD, D.D., McKEOWN, K.R., SWARTOUT, W.R. (1982): Text Generation: The State of the Art and the Literature. University of Southern California, Information Science Institute, Report ISI/RR-81-101.

McDONALD, D.D. (1981): Natural Language Generation as a Computational Problem: an Introduction. University of Massachusetts at Amherst, COINS Technical Report 81-33.

McKEOWN, K.R. (1982): Generating Natural Language Text in Response to Questions about Database Structure. Ph.D. Dissertation, University of Pennsylvania, Philadelphia.

MEEHAN, J.R. (1979): The New UCI-LISP Manual. Hillsdale.

METZING, D. (1981): Plädoyer für Kasus wiedereröffnet - für die Künstliche Intelligenz? In: Pleines, J. (ed.): Beiträge zum Stand der Kasustheorie, Tübingen, pp. 193-210.

MORIK, K. (1982): Differenzstudie zu früheren sprachverarbeitenden Systemen der Bundesrepublik Deutschland. University of Hamburg, Research Unit for Information Science and Artificial Intelligence, Report ANS-6.

NEBEL, B. (1984): ULM: Ein UCI-LISP-Lispmaschinen-LSIP Übersetzungssystem. University of Hamburg, Research Unit for Information Science and Artificial Intelligence, Memo ANS-22.

REITHINGER, N. (1984): Generierung von Antworttexten für das Erlanger Spracherkennungssystem. Master Thesis, University of Erlangen-Nürnberg.

ROHRER, C. (1971): Funktionelle Sprachwissenschaft und transformationelle Grammatik. München.

WAHLSTER, W. (1981): Natürlichsprachliche Argumentation in Dialogsystemen. KI-Verfahren zur Rekonstruktion und Erklärung approximativer Inferenzprozesse. Berlin.

WAHLSTER, W. (1982): Natürlichsprachliche Systeme. Eine Einführung in die sprachorientierte KI-Forschung. In: Bibel, W., Siekmann, J.H. (eds.): Künstliche Intelligenz.
   Berlin, pp. 203-283.

WAHLSTER, W., JAMESON, A., HOEPPNER, W. (1978): Glancing, Referring and Explaining
   in the Dialogue System HAM-RPM. In: American Journal of Computational Linguistics.
   Microfiche 77, pp. 53-67.

WAHLSTER, W., MARBURGER, H., JAMESON, A., BUSEMANN, S. (1983): Over-Answering Yes-No-
   Questions: Extended Responses in a NL Interface to a Vision System. In: Proc. of
   the 8th IJCAI, Karlsruhe, pp. 643-646.

VIE-GEN
A Generator for German Texts

E. Buchberger
H. Horacek

1. Overview

VIE-GEN is a generator that produces German text from a semantic representation. It is a component of the German language dialogue system VIE-LANG [2], implemented in INTERLISP. The input to VIE-GEN is part of the episodic layer of the semantic network SEMNET, its outputs are German sentences. The generator is not restricted to single sentences, it contains features for creating coherent structures (e.g. generation of anaphora and gapping). VIE-GEN is designed to suit the idiosyncracies of the German language: it is able to produce various alternative word orderings (in German word order is not as strict as e.g. in English), it considers syntactic differences between main clauses and dependent ones and it is able to correctly produce all inflectional forms being found in German.

In order to be able to handle all these features, VIE-GEN performs its task in two steps which shall be referred to as verbalization phase and realization phase, respectively. The input to the verbalization phase is a part of the episodic layer of the semantic net, which is to be supplied by the dialogue component. This reflects the nearly classical distinction between "what to say" (decided by the dialogue component) and "how to say it" (decided by the generator) (e.g. [11]). The verbalization process is strongly data driven, its main sources of information being discrimination nets (DNs) and the so-called syntactico-semantic lexicon (SSL). By application of the DNs and by evaluating the SSL an intermediate structure (IMS) is created, forming the input to the realization phase.

The IMS is a tree, whose nodes represent either single words (terminals) or groups of words, i.e. constituents (nonterminals) together with their features. The "lexeme"-property of a node contains the canonical form of the word (actually a pointer to a lexicon entry so that morphological data can be accessed in the last step of processing) or, in the non-terminal case, a list of pointers to the dependent nodes. Admissible features are the complement type, an identifying marker that carries information about the individuated source concept (in SEMNET) the node stands for (used as a link for phrase heads and playing an important role in the generation of anaphora and gapping), number, tense, preposition (prepositional phrases are treated like noun phrases, the only difference being in the preposition feature being bound to a non-NIL value) and some others. Details on the IMS are to be found in a separate chapter below.

The task of the realization phase is the production of surface sentences out of the IMS. This task is divided into the following subprocedures:

- The predicates (in the grammatical sense) of the IMS are split into their finite and non-finite parts (in German, the predicate often is a discontinuous constituent)
- All constituents of a sentence are sorted in a standard order. The most interesting parts of this subtask are the partitioning of the IMS into sentences, maintaining their connections, and selection of appropriate types of sentences.
- Transformations are applied to these sentences, reordering the constituents in case of questions and subordinate phrases and the generation of gapping or anaphora.
- Noun phrases are linearized.
- In a last step, morphologic synthesis is performed.

2. The Embedding System VIE-LANG

VIE-GEN is the generation component of the German language dialogue system VIE-LANG [2]. VIE-LANG receives German texts as input and maps them onto the semantic net SEMNET [18] by means of its parser VIE-PAR [14]. A dialogue component is being developed which decides how to react to the input, based on a partner model [8] and dialogue strategies. Finally, the generator VIE-GEN maps the result of this step, which is assumed to be a coherent graph of individuals of SEMNET with no islands, onto a German text.

There are two data structures in VIE-LANG that play an important non-local role: The semantic net SEMNET and the syntactico-semantic lexicon (SSL).

2.1 The Semantic Network SEMNET

VIE-LANG uses the semantic network SEMNET as meaning representation [18], structurally similar to the structured inheritance (SI) network formalism by Brachman [1]. SEMNET maintains a clear separation between structure and content. The number of different structural elements (nodes and arcs) is kept very small, such that the net is accessed only by a small number of functions. [17].

The net consists of concepts which are connected with each other by roles. A role, together with the concept to which it is linked (the so-called value-restriction), is referred to as an attribute. An attribute describes a property of a concept, where the value-restriction indicates the range of possible fillers and the role describes the function of the filler with regard to the concept [16]. Thus, a concept together with its attributes may be considered as a frame (Fig. 1).

The concepts of SEMNET represent semantic primitives in the sense of Wilks [19], complex notions are formed from these primitives by means of the above described linkage in form of roles. Furthermore, concepts form a super-subconcept hierarchy in which a subconcept inherits all those attributes of its superconcepts that are not explicitly modified.

The frame-like notation is taken advantage of by a case grammar. The uniform structure of the net permits to regard each role of a concept as a case, a fact already stressed by Charniak [3] who pointed out that cases can be seen as slots in a frame. Data concerning the mapping from surface elements to entities in the net and vice versa is contained in the syntactico-semantic lexicon.

Apart from the conceptual level the net also incorporates episodic knowledge in form of individuals which are linked to concepts. Individuals are described by values tied to the corresponding roles of the superordinated concept. Entities at the episodic level are created by the parsing process (there are a few a priori individuals like a representation of the dialogue system itself, the current date and the like); elements of the episodic level selected by the dialogue component form the input for the generator.

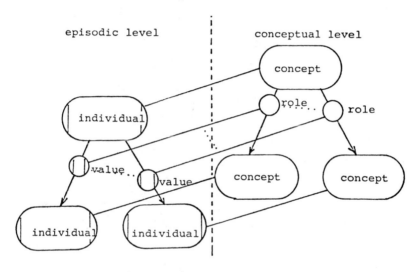

Fig.1: Structure of SEMNET

2.2 The Syntactico-Semantic Lexicon (SSL)

The SSL serves to facilitate the mapping between surface expressions in natural language and structures in the semantic net. It is used by the parser as well as the generator.

The lexicon captures the correspondence between roles in the net and cases in a case grammar, as this relation is not a fixed one. (E.g.: the verb 'erhalten' in the meaning 'to receive' relates the subject to the role RECIPIENT, the verb geben ('to give') relates it to SOURCE).

The entries of the SSL are word-senses, each consisting of a number of pairs, denoted by 'Left Side' (LS) and 'Right Side' (RS). LSs describe features of the surface sentence. Most features refer to syntactic properties, e.g. constituents of a given surface case, infinitive constructions, lexical categories, surface words, and some features indicate selectional restrictions.

RSs refer mostly to structures within the semantic net. There is no one-to-one correspondence between word-senses and conceptual primitives. To represent word (or phrase) meanings, primitives are linked forming more complex structures. By definition there is one distinguished concept in each RS 'the root concept' which is the central element of the representation. All other structures referenced in an RS are linked to it.

3. The Verbalization Phase

The task of the verbalization phase is to select appropriate words for the part of the episodic layer of SEMNET that has been selected as output structure by the dialogue component. Furthermore, it has to represent correctly dependencies between these words. The chosen words as well as their dependencies are shown in the IMS, so, technically speaking, the verbalization phase has to transform part of SEMNET to an IMS. The problem of word selection is not trivial, as neither individuals nor even concepts can be mapped to words one-to-one. This is due to the use of semantic primitives [19], so that e.g. verbs like give, lose, buy, receive, etc. are all represented in SEMNET by the same concept OBJTRANS. The difference is to be found in the different ways this concept is linked to other ones. So in order to decide for a specific word, not only one concept in SEMNET has to be considered, but its environment as well. Generally, this holds true for all types of words, in particular for verbs. Therefore, special attention has been given to the correct selection of verbs, as these play a central role in a sentence. Furthermore, the verb determines its constituents in an idiosyncratic way. These dependencies are captured by the syntactico-semantic lexicon as described above.

The mentioned facts led to a strongly data driven design of the verbalization phase, its two main sources of information being discrimination nets (DNs) and the syntactico-semantic lexicon (SSL). Whereas DNs are used only by the generator, the SSL is used as well by the parser of VIE-LANG.

In a rough sketch, the process of verbalization may be depicted as follows: The dialogue component provides the generator with a coherent graph consisting of marked nodes and values in the episodic layer of SEMNET. First, the discrimination net of its root node is selected and applied. When this root node is an individual of an actional concept (which usually is the case), the DN returns a verb-sense, that is, an entry in the SSL, which is processed immediately afterwards. The SSL may select new root nodes which form the input to a recursive call to the verbalization phase. The old root nodes are saved on a stack (current individual stack). When recursion terminates, that is, a DN returns one or more words without further recursive call, the stack is popped and DNs of marked values of the current root node that have not been considered up to now are processed. Let us take a closer look at the involved data structures and processes. (Actually, most of the processes are contained in the data structures.)

3.1 Discrimination Nets (DNs)

The idea of using DNs for generation purposes goes back to Goldman [5]. He proposed to use them for the selection of verb-senses starting from a "primitive act" in the Conceptual Dependency (CD) [12] representation. Essentially, a DN is a binary tree with a predicate at each branching point, responsable for the choice of which branch to take. Its leaf nodes are word-senses. In VIE-GEN, DNs are used in a more general way:

- In adapting DNs to our form of knowledge representation, SEMNET, we made use of an advantage of KL-ONE like nets, namely, the clear intensional-extensional distinction as pointed out by Matthiessen [10]: in SEMNET, DNs responable for the selection of word-senses for individuals are attached to concepts so that when the generator is processing an individual from the episodic layer of SEMNET, it looks up the DN attached to the corresponding concept.

- DNs in VIE-GEN do not only cover actional primitives but all sort of concepts in the net (e.g. objects) and even roles. This way, not only verbs, but also nouns, adjectives, prepositions and so on are realized by means of DNs. The attachment of DNs to roles also facilitates the processing of optional constituents.

- Not all of the concepts necessarily have DNs attached to them. This is made possible by the use of the super/subconcept hierarchy property of SEMNET. If there is no DN attached to the current concept, the generator scans the hierarchy to find a DN for a more general concept which might be suitable.

- Other than the classical DNs which return only one word-sense, some of our DNs return more than one acceptable solution, a feature which proves useful for the creation of paraphrases.

An example of a DN, which selects a verb-sense for the concept "OBJTRANS", is shown in Fig. 2.

3.2 Processing of the SSL

The SSL consists of productions in the form Left Side (LS) -> Right Side (RS). Whereas the parser handles these productions in their "natural" direction from left to right, the generator has to evaluate them in the opposite way: items like those created by the parser (individuals of SEMNET) are the input for the generator, items that the parser treats as (syntactic) tests (e.g. presence of words with certain syntactic cases) are treated as syntactic actions by the generator [13].

The RSs mainly specify net elements that have to be present and the LSs syntactic properties that have to be met by the words associated with the structure being addressed by the corresponding RS. These associated words are selected by DNs, resulting in a recursive process. Each RS selects a net structure headed by an individual CURIND (the individual acting as case filler) and the LS passes to the IMS the corresponding syntactic data together with the result of a recursive call to the verbalization phase, with CURIND as new root node. Thus, the dependencies in the IMS arise almost naturally from the

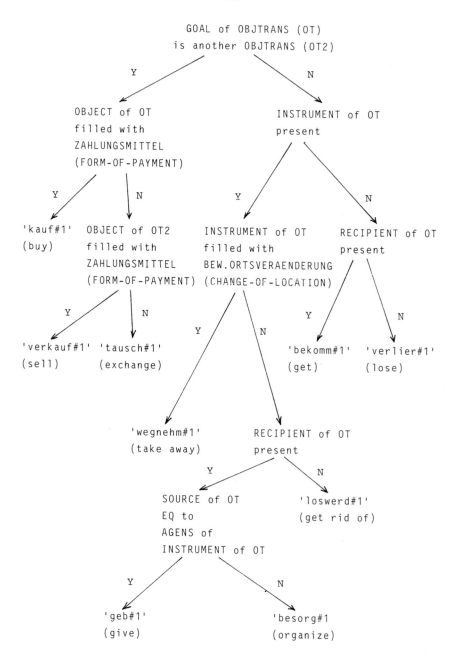

Fig. 2: Discrimination net for OBJTRANS

dependencies in SEMNET, controlled by the SSL. If a constituent itself is to be realized by a verb (plus environment), the same process takes place once more (i.e. a recursive verbalization is performed), if the DN of a constituent returns a noun, recursion most often will terminate there (sometimes nouns have dependent cases, too.) We will show the use of the SSL by the generator by means of an example. The input to the verbalization phase is shown in Fig. 3.

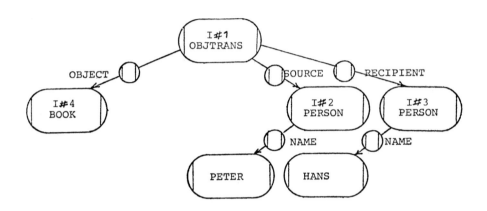

Fig. 3: Episodic layer of SEMNET for
'Hans bekommt das Buch von Peter.'
('John gets the book from Peter.')

Let us assume the DN of OBJTRANS to already have selected "bekomm#1" (to get) with the meaning of "to receive a physical object from someone" (as opposed to e.g. "to get kicked"). The SSL entry for this verb-sense is shown in Fig. 4.

```
(BEKOMMEN
 (1 ((AND (CASE E1) (RESTR OWNABLE-OBJ))
     --> ((IND OBJTRANS) (VAL + OBJECT *)))
    ((AND (CASE E0) (RESTR ANIMATE))
     --> ((VAL + RECIPIENT *)))
    ((AND (CASE E3) (RESTR ANIMATE) (PREP VON))
     --> ((VAL + SOURCE *))))
 (2 ...) ...)
```

Fig. 4: part of SSL entry for BEKOMMEN

As noted above, the generator processes each of these three pairs from right to left, starting with the action (IND OBJTRANS). (IND is read by the parser as "create individual".) The generator treats this as a null action, as OBJTRANS1 is the current root node, and it has already been put on the stack for the current individual. The next action, (VAL + OBJECT *) selects the element attached to the OBJECT link of the current root node (denoted by +) and puts it onto the stack. Now the generator proceeds with the LS of the production rule: CASE E1 (interpreted by the parser as: find a phrase in accusative case) passes to the IMS the complement type information E1 and identifying marker I#4 together with the result of a recursive call to the verbalization phase with the current individual (BOOK1, the one on top of the stack) as new root node. In handling the recursive call, the generator tries to pick the DN for the concept the current root node is an individual of (i.e., BOOK). BOOK has no DN attached to it, so the superconcept hierarchy is walked through, until a DN is found. In this case, it is attached to "BILDERZEUGENDES_OBJEKT" ("PICTURE PRODUCER"), specifying to use the name of the object, that is, "Buch". This terminates the recursive call. The successful completion of this task also removes BOOK1 from the stack for the current individual. The action (RESTR OWNABLE-OBJECT) results in a no-op for the generator, as this information has already been processed in the DN when deciding to use the verb-sense "bekomm#1" (for the parser, RESTR means to check whether the constituent meets a certain value restriction). As for the second LS-RS pair, PERSON has a DN attached to it, returning the name of the person as result. The last constituent is created in a similar way. The resulting IMS is shown in Fig. 5.

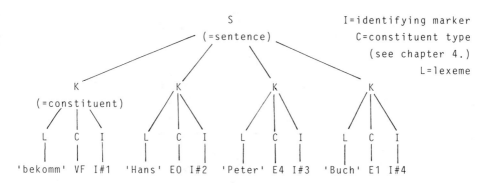

Fig. 5: IMS for 'Hans bekommt das Buch von Peter.'
('John gets the book from Peter.')

3.3 Processing of Roles

Not all of the constituents of the final sentence will be reflected by the case-frame contained in the lexicon. Let us look at what will transform into a prepositional phrase. In the sentence "Ich warte auf ihn" ("I wait for him") the preposition "auf" is specific for the verb with this meaning, therefore it appears in the case-frame. A different case is "Er gibt ihm das Buch auf der Strasse" ("He gives the book to him in the street") where "auf der Strasse" is not typical for the verb but is simply a locative specification which can be used with many verbs. Note that therefore the lexicon entry (Fig. 4) does not provide for this case. On the other hand, there are verbs that require a locative as e.g. "wohnen" ("to live"): "Er wohnt in Wien" ("He lives in Vienna"). In this case, data for the mapping will be contained in the lexicon entry "wohnen". (These observations are based on the linguistic work of Engel [4], who distinguishes between "Ergaenzungen" (verb-specific) and "Angaben" (non-verb-specific).)

This problem is solved by attaching information about mappings of non-verb-specific elements to their respective roles (in this example the role "LOCATION"). When all obligatory constituents (captured by SSL entries) have been processed, roles of the processed concepts resulting in optional constituents are worked upon. Adverbials often tend to be generated the same way. The same will hold for parts of noun phrases (adjectives and other dependants).

3.4 Creation of Paraphrases

Earlier papers on generation have stressed the fact that a generator should always try to select the most specific wording for a fact to be expressed. This is very plausible, if a fact appears for the first time, but when it occurs repeatedly, paraphrases seem appropriate. (The most usual case, use of anaphora (like personal pronouns), is incorporated into the transformation part of the realization phase.)

Creation of paraphrases in VIE-GEN is accomplished by one of the above mentioned features of its DNs: instead of returning only one result, some of our DNs return additional expressions that may be used as a paraphrase, especially, if the main result consists of more than one word or is a compound noun. The realization component of the generator selects an alternative when the main result has already been used. A less expensive implementation would be to create the structure for a paraphrase only when explicitly triggered by demand. On the other hand, control is very easy this way and the additional effort is partially compensated by a reduction of search. Moreover, the decision for usage of a paraphrase is not only caused by multiple reference of this concept in the semantic network. Portioning of text from the deep structure on may require an anaphor, which can be realized by this paraphrase.

There are different ways to create a paraphrase all of which are supported by the fact, that a semantic network is the basic data structure (the following list contains theoretically acceptable solutions, albeit not all of them have been implemented in VIE-GEN up to now):

1. Choosing some property already mentioned by the user or obviously known to him due to his general world knowledge. In general, this applies to roles of objects or persons ('the pope', 'the big building with the flags').

2. Utilizing some class the concept belongs to, by the corresponding generic (if the instantiation was verbalized by its name, 'Vienna' -> 'the town'), or by the superconcept's name, if it is not too general ('the city hall' -> 'the building').

3. Verbalizing just the root concept of the involved subtree, ignoring the roles which require additional words: ('general assembly' -> 'assembly', 'x gave y to z' -> 'the transfer').

4. Verbalizing just the name of the role and selectional restriction instead of the object attached to the role. Note, that the user is intended to interpret the name of the role as a designation for its filler ('recipient', 'buyer').

In general, case (1) is preferable to all the others. But, most of the time, the features necessary for a realization are not available. Cases (3) and (4) are very probably correct concerning comprehension. They are usually accompanied by a demonstrative pronoun. The suitability of a verbalization (realized by a fixed value to keep things simple) is a further decision criterion additionally available in the discrimination nets. The selection of case (2) is sometimes critical, but it is necessary if no other realization is possible. Some effort has then to be put into additional tests, in order to ensure unambiguity.

4. The Intermediate Structure (IMS)

The IMS is structured in form of a tree. Its basic elements (nodes) are word markers, describing single words or groups of words and many of their features in the actual instance. They can be composed to noun phrases, prepositional phrases or adjective phrases which are treated the same way throughout this paper. Either word markers or noun phrases form constituents, filling the slots of a verb's case frame. (The verb itself is considered as a part of its case frame here.) If complete sentences bear a case role, they finally have to be realized by a subordinate phrase. A node being a marker for a single word contains its canonical form and is a terminal node. Otherwise it contains pointers to its successors.

The classes of words contained in the IMS as generated by the verbalization phase are verbs, nouns, adjectives, numerals and adverbs. Pronouns appear only after application of certain transformations. Words belonging to other classes are all specifiers of a phrase and are implicitly included in their phrase head (e. g. determiners in the corresponding noun). Determiners and prepositions become proper words only when linearizing a noun phrase.

Each marker and also each constituent has at least at its disposal:

- its **canonical form** or pointers to its components respectively, called **'lexeme'** from now on

- a **complement type** for case bearers of a noun phrase and their depending components. It can be omitted for such parts of a noun phrase where the case is inheritable. This feature is also used for verbs to mark them as 'VF' and 'VN' for the finite and non-finite part respectively

The following complement types are used (closely resembling those proposed by Engel [4]):

VF ..... Verb finite part
VN ..... Verb non-finite part
EO ..... Subject
IO ..... Actor in a passive form clause

Objects without prepositions:
E1 ..... Surface case is accusative
E2 ..... Surface case is genitive (owner)
E3 ..... Surface case is dative

Objects with prepositions:
E4 ..... Unique preposition, determined by the verb
E5 ..... Indicating a location
E6 ..... Indicating a direction

Complement types indicating an identification:
E7 ..... like 'Peter ist mein Freund' (Peter is my friend).
E8 ..... like 'Das Gebaeude ist gross' (The building is big).

Complement types of non-verb-specific constituents:
IC ..... Causal, conditional or consecutive
IT ..... Temporal
IL ..... Local
IF ..... Final
IK ..... Concomitance

- an 'identifying marker', which indicates the key of the individual from the semantic net of which the current IMS node is a verbalization. It is used to distinguish identical from different persons or objects. If the node represents a state or an action, knowledge about the same or different meaning is expressed this way. Additionally, this feature is used as link for phrase heads

Some other properties, available (mostly) in terminal nodes and depending on the word class, are:

- a **negation** feature

- a **reference** feature, indicating whether the node represents an object marked as question, a definite object or an indefinite one. For verbs only 'marked as question' is useful

- **number** and **gender**, if they are not inheritable or derivable from the lexeme's entry in the lexicon

- **tense** and **mode** for verbs, defaults are present and indicative

- **preposition** and **surface case** if they are not derivable from the complement type, and if the preposition does not demand a unique case

- **degree of comparison** for adjectives

One or more independent noun phrases or sentences can be joined by means of a junctor and are treated as a single constituent or sentence.

Available junctors are:

1) AND, OR, TIMEQ, TIMESEQ:
ordinary junctors, they are treated in the procedure which partitions the IMS into clauses (see chapter 5.2). TIMEQ combines simultaneous events, TIMSEQ forms a chain of events in their temporal order. For both of them, the temporal context has to be expressed explicitly.

2) XOR:
contains alternative verbalizations for the same individual from the semantic net, one of which is selected during the first step in the realization phase (see chapter 5.1). They have a different structure, but identical content ('the big house', 'the house is big').

3) SOR:
contains alternative verbalizations for the same individual from the semantic network, where a new information is introduced or the information is reduced. The first one is to be used when introducing the individual, the others can be used for later occurences (see chapter 5.1). This way, paraphrasing is realized ('John', 'the president'; 'a meeting took place', 'that event').

Representation of a complex NP:

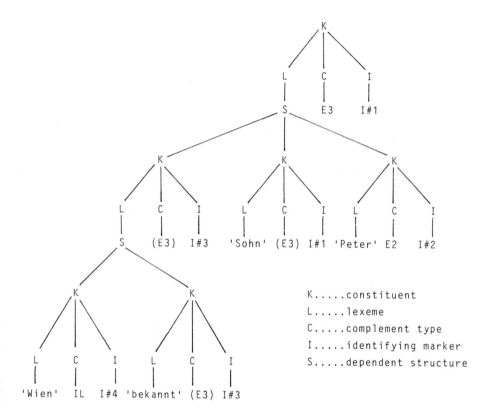

K.....constituent
L.....lexeme
C.....complement type
I.....identifying marker
S.....dependent structure

corresponds on the surface to

'dem in Wien bekannten Sohn von Peter'
('to the son of Peter, well-known in Vienna')

Note the significance of the identifying marker for recognition of 'Sohn' as the head of the noun phrase for the realization of the adjective phrase. A wrong interpretation would yield 'im bekannten Wien' ('in well-known Vienna').

Representation of a dependent clause:
(and its different syntactical realizations)

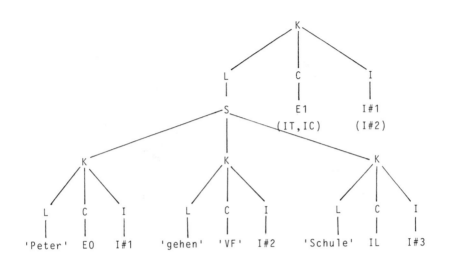

If the identifying marker on top level is I#1 (I#2) 'Peter' ('gehen')
is interpreted as the case bearer. This yields: (Case E1) :

Relative clause (for I#1) :
1. .... Peter, der in die Schule geht ...
(...... Peter, who goes to school ...)

'dass'-clause (for I#2) :
2. ...., dass Peter in die Schule geht ...
(......... , that Peter goes to school ...)

for cases different from E1 and identifying marker I#2 we get:

Temporal clause (IT):
3. .... , wenn Peter in die Schule geht
(........... , when Peter goes to school)

Causal clause (IC):
4. .... , weil Peter in die Schule geht
(........... , because Peter goes to school)

5. The Realization Phase

5.1 Choice among alternatives in the IMS

1) Choice of alternatives from an 'XOR'

A lexeme whose header is an 'XOR' is replaced by the locally best choice from its elements with regard to the following preferences of the element's structure:

1. an adjective phrase consisting of an adjective or of a corresponding word and at most one additional modifier ('big', 'very big').

2. a clause consisting of three components at least (not counting the subject).

3. any other clause (simple ones, 'John is tall', 'Jack owns that book').

4. a complex adjective phrase

2) Selection of a variation from an 'SOR'

The alternatives of an SOR are treated nearly as synonyms. They are used to realize different paraphrases (see chapter 3.4). A lexeme whose header is an 'SOR' is replaced by one of its elements depending on the position in which this lexeme occurs. If it occurs for the first time, its first element is chosen, if it occurs for the second time, the second one is chosen and so on. If the number of occurences exceeds the number of elements the selection process is continued in a cyclic way excluding the first element in case it is a clause. As the path through the IMS leads from left to right in a depth-first manner, the order of occurences of a lexeme corresponds to the order of clauses they belong to, when partitioning the IMS.

5.2 Partitioning of the IMS into Clauses

The IMS is partitioned into those parts which contain a finite verb on top level (clauses). This task is necessary, because dependent clauses can occur at any place in the case frame and would therefore appear in the interior of the superordinated clause at the surface [6]. For reasons of readability they have to occur in front of or after the clause they depend on (except for relative clauses). Additionally, the occurence of many dependent clauses can create problems of readability. To avoid this undesirable fact, all but one of the clauses depending on the same superordinated clause are changed into a main clause on the surface. This rule is applied recursively to the whole IMS.

A similar approach is chosen when a dependent clause is a structure headed by the junctors 'AND' or 'OR' (joining clauses again, of course).

Some possible cases:

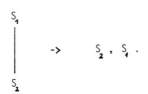

where S_2 is a (simple) dependent clause, and S_1 its superordinated clause. S_2 precedes it and remains subordinated.

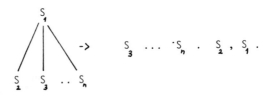

In case of several dependent clauses, one of them remains subordinated, the other ones become main clauses. The choice is taken according to their type.

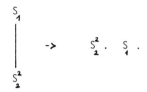

$$S_1 \quad \rightarrow \quad S_2^2 . \; S_1 .$$

If the dependent clause itself contains another dependent clause, it becomes a main clause anyway.

$$S_1 \quad \rightarrow \quad S_2 , \;\; .. \; S_n . \; S_1 .$$
$$\text{AND}(S_2 \;.. \; S_n)$$

$$\text{AND}(S_1 , \; S_2 , \; .. \; S_n) \quad \rightarrow \quad S_1 , \; S_2 . \; ... \; S_n .$$

Examples for structures containing a junctor

A dependent clause will precede its superordinated one after slight modifications. Its genuine place will be replaced by the case bearer for a relative clause and by an anaphor corresponding to the complement type otherwise. If a dependent clause remains dependent (except to relative clauses), the anaphor is not created, in case of a relative clause, this clause will be inserted immediately after the case bearer.

The decision for a super- or subordinated clause is made as follows: ·

type of clause	subsumptive	relative
criterion	identifying marker of the verb is the link to the main clause	identifying marker of a constituent (other than verb) is the link to the main clause

Actions that have to be taken depend on whether the dependent clause remains subordinated or not:

In case the dependent clause remains subordinated:

	Insertion of a conjunction,	constituent is replaced by a relative pronoun
action in subord. clause	Insertion of a conjunction,	constituent is replaced by a relative pronoun
action in superord. clause	omission of the constituent	replacement of constituent by its case bearer

In case the dependent clause becomes a main clause:

action in dependent clause	none	none
action in superord. clause	replacement of the constituent by an anaphor	replacement of constituent by its case bearer

By these means the tree has been changed into a series of sentences that transformations can work on. Furthermore, there is a list of marks to distinguish relative clauses from all others and a further list with junctors to be applied (NIL from a dependency or no relation). A third list contains information about necessary punctuation marks. They are inserted. later on in the linearization phase (chapter 5.4). taking care of the following special cases: If a relative clause follows the whole sentence it is depending on, their punctuation marks are exchanged. Additionally, a check is performed, if the subject or the verb of a sentence has been gapped. In such a case the preceding punctuation mark is omitted.

5.3 Transformations

Transformations are realized by means of a production system. In contradiction to other systems (e.g. by Katz [7]) we stress the treatment of multiple clauses. Its rules are pairs in the form conditions --> actions. Conditions as well as actions are joined by an implicit 'and'. Apart from triggering the actions, the condition part selects a constituent (constituents) to which the actions are applied. Conditions consist of a flag, specifying whether presence or absence of a constituent shall be tested, a level mark, specifying whether only the top level or all levels shall be taken into account, and comparisons that shall be drawn between properties of constituents and fixed values or properties of other constituents. Transformations in VIE-GEN are obligatory in the sense that if all of the conditions are fulfilled, the corresponding actions are performed.

The following actions are admissible:
- Omitting a constituent
- Moving a constituent to another place
- Exchanging places of two constituents
- Changing qualities of a constituent

Normally, all constituents referenced by the actions have to be identified unambiguosly, but there are actions that allow a multiple match for some constituents.

Some properties call for special treatment: As some features occur only for one specific property, the formalism would become very complex if a general solution were to be proposed. We therefore decided to treat them as exceptions. An example is the creation of a possessive pronoun. In this case, the lexeme depends on person, number and gender of the referent. As the rules do not allow the change of a quality 'X' induced by a quality 'Y', the relevant qualities of the referent are saved under other names: 'refperson' etc. The lexeme is changed into 'poss' independently. After the transformations are all executed, the corresponding lexeme is selected by the next task. A further speciality is the property 'number' of a constituent headed by a junctor, which is plural by default.

In VIE-GEN, transformations are applied to single sentences and to adjacent ones. In most cases of anaphora generation and in all cases

concerning generation of gapping two adjacent sentences are involved.
There is a well defined set of transformations applied in a fixed order
which is essential for correct handling (e.g. agreement of verb and
subject - this is treated as a transformation in our system - has to be
performed after an eventual passivation rule which changes the
subject).

At present the data base containing rules for transformations consists
of nine rules for single sentences and of the same number for adjacent
ones. Some rules are divided into subrules, which are evaluated like
XOR-operations or like the COND-statement in LISP. In the following
enumeration encircled numbers indicate successfully matched
constituents, whereas encircled asterisks stand for constituents whose
absence is required. A multiple match is only allowed for the first
and the last constituent of the conditional part, their treatment being
different. If the last constituent yields a multiple match, the
actions are applied to all of them. If the first constituent's match
was multiply sucessful, the rest of the rule is evaluated for all those
matches separately.

Rules for a single sentence:

1) Omission of an 'obvious' reflexive

① Subject (E0)
② Indirect object (E3) with same identifying marker as ①

Then: Omit ②.

If the beneficient of an action is the same person as the actor,
this fact can be seen as default and is usually not stated
explicitly, which is achieved by this rule.

Ich kaufe mir ein Buch.
(I buy a book for myself).

↓

Ich kaufe ein Buch.
(I buy a book).

2) Mode change

2.1) Subrule for using the passive voice

(1) Verb finite part, mode is different from imperative, the verb
     is in a special list (allowing usage of the passive voice)

Again, two subrules are treated, (both concerned with constituent
(1)), the first one is activated when the subject is unpersonal.

2.1.1) Passive voice usage induced by unpersonal subject

(2) Direct object (E1)
(3) Unpersonal subject ('es', 'jemand', 'etwas')
(4) Verb non-finite part

    Then: Mark the verb parts as passive forms,
           Change the case of (2) into the subject case,
           Omit (3).

Jemand verkauft das Auto.
(Someone sells the car).

           ↓
Das Auto wird verkauft.
(The car is sold).

2.1.2) Passive voice usage induced by an object to be focussed

(2) Direct object, focussed
                   (the focus marker is assumed to have been
                   set by the dialogue component)
(3) Subject
(4) Verb non-finite part

    Then: Take same actions as in case 2.1.1, but instead of
           omitting (3) exchange (1) and (3) and change the case
           of (3) to E1.

This way, usage of the passive form is the preferred focussing
method.

2.2) Subrule for imperative treatment

2.2.1) Polite form

(1)   Verb finite form, in imperative mode, form is polite
(2)   Subject

    Then: Set (1) into the plural form,
           Replace the lexeme of (2) by 'Sie'.

2.2.2) Regular form

(1)   Verb finite part, in imperative mode
(2)   Subject

    Then: Make (1) and (2) agree in number and person,
           Omit (2).

3) Question treatment and constituent movement

3.1) Question treatment

(1)   Verb finite part, is marked as question
                      (the question marker
                      originates from SEMNET)

Again three subrules are distinguished:

3.1.1) The subject is the constituent marked as question

(2)   Subject, is marked as question

    Then: Take no action, all is in right order.

3.1.2) Any other constituent (except the verb)

(2)   Subject
(3)   Any constituent marked as question, on top level

    Then: Move (2) after (1) and (3) in front of (1).

3.1.3) Yes/No-question

② Subject

  Then: Exchange ① and ②.

3.2) Constituent movement

① Verb finite part (not in question here)
② Any top level constituent, which is focussed
③ Subject (therefore ② is not the subject)

  Then: Move ③ after ① and ② in front of ①.

4) Treatment of reflexive pronoun

① Subject
② Any top level constituent, with same identifying marker as
   ①

  Then: Change the lexeme of ② to the reflexive pronoun and
      make it agree in number, gender and person with ①.

5) Treatment of possessive pronoun

① Subject
② Any non top level constituent with same identifying marker as
   ① in the owner case

  Then: Same action as above, but select the   possessive
      pronoun as new lexeme.

6) Treatment of relative clauses (link is on top level)

① Any top level constituent, marked as relative link

Two subrules exist, covering the fact that the relative link is
the subject or some other constituent:

6.1) The relative link is different from subject

(2)   Subject (therefore (1) is not the subject)

    Then: Move (2) in front of (1) and save its number and gender
              before   the lexeme is changed into the relative
              pronoun.

6.2) Subject is the relative link

(2)   Verb finite part (a dummy condition)

    Then: Same action as above without the movement.

The relative link has to be the first word in the relative clause anyway.

7) Treatment of relative clauses (link is not on top)

(1)   Any non top level constituent, marked as relative link

Now the same subrules as above are distinguished:

7.1) Relative link is not the subject

(2)   The top level constituent (1) belongs to
(3)   Subject (therefore different from (2))

    Then: Move (2) in front of (3),
              Change the lexeme of (1) to the relative pronoun after
              saving its gender (sufficient for 'dessen' or
              'deren').

7.2) The relative link is the subject

(2)   Same as above, now the subject itself

    Then: Perform the same changes as above, the movement is
              unnecessary.

8) Subordinate phrase verb movement

(1) Verb finite part of a subordinate clause
(2) Verb non finite part

Then: Move (1) behind (2).

The verb is in the last position in German subclauses anyway.

9) Agreement of verb and subject

(1) Verb finite part
(2) Subject

Then: Make number and person of (1) agree with (2).

This rule is applied to each non-imperative clause.

Rules for two adjacent sentences:

1) Infinitive constructions

(1) Subject

Now, purposive meaning is distinguished from other dependencies:

1.1) Infinitive construction with purposive meaning

(2) Conjunction , introducing a purpose clause
(3) Subject , has same identifying marker as (1)
(4) Verb finite part
(5) Verb non finite part

Then: Change the lexeme of (2) ('damit') to 'um',
       Omit (3) and (5),
       Change the form of (4) to the infinitive.

Peter faehrt nach Wien, damit Peter die Stadt besichtigt.
(Peter travels to Vienna, so that Peter visits the town).

Peter faehrt nach Wien, um die Stadt zu besichtigen.
(Peter travels to Vienna in order to visit the town).

1.2) Regular infinitive construction

② Conjunction is 'dass'
③ Subject , has same identifying marker as ①
④ Verb finite part is of a specific class (the list of verbs allowing such infinitive constructions)
⑤ Verb non finite part

Then: Same actions as above, but omit ② instead of changing it.

Peter moechte, dass Peter den Kuchen isst.
(Peter wants that Peter eats the cake).

Peter moechte den Kuchen essen.
(Peter wants to eat the cake).

2) Subject reduction

① Subject , junctor is 'and'
② Subject , has same identifying marker as 1

Then: Omit ②.

Peter kauft ein Buch und Peter schenkt Hans das Buch.
(Peter buys a book and Peter gives the book to John).

Peter kauft ein Buch und schenkt Hans das Buch.
(Peter buys a book and gives the book to John).

3) Verb gapping

① Verb finite part , junctor is 'and'
② Verb finite part , has same identifying marker as ①
③ Verb non finite part

Then: Omit ② and ③.

Peter bekommt ein Buch und Hans bekommt eine Schokolade.
(Peter gets a book and John gets a chocolate).

↓

Peter bekommt ein Buch und Hans eine Schokolade.
(Peter gets a book and John a chocolate).

For transformations 4 to 7 each constituent is required to be not yet pronominalized.

4) Personal pronoun, antecedent is a subject

① Subject
② Any constituent on top level with same identifying marker as
①

Then: Save person, number and gender from ② and change the
lexeme to the personal pronoun.

Peter trifft Hans, der Peter eingeladen hat.
(Peter meets John, who invited Peter).

↓

Peter trifft Hans, der ihn eingeladen hat.
(Peter meets John, who invited him).

5) Possessive pronoun, antecedent is a subject

① Subject
② Any constituent not on top level with same identifying marker
as ①, in the owner case

Then: Same action as above, but select the possessive pronoun.

Peter trifft Hans, der der Freund von Peter ist.
(Peter meets John, who is the friend of Peter).

$\downarrow$

Peter trifft Hans, der sein Freund ist.
(Peter meets John, who is his friend).

6) Possessive pronoun, other antecedent

(1) Any constituent , not on top level in the owner case

6.1) No ambiguity arises

(2) Any constituent on top level with same identifying marker as (1)

(*) Any constituent with same number and gender as (1)

Then: Same action as above but with constituent (1).

Maria trifft Hans, sie besuchen den Vater von Hans.
(Mary meets John, they visit the father of John).

$\downarrow$

Maria trifft Hans, sie besuchen seinen Vater.
(Mary meets John, they visit his father).

6.2) Ambiguity arises, other pronoun is selected

(2) Same as above ((*) does exist now !)

Then: Same as above, select the disambiguative possessive pronoun ('dessen', 'deren').

Peter trifft Hans, sie besuchen den Vater von Hans.
(Peter meets John, they visit the father of John).

$\downarrow$

Peter trifft Hans, sie besuchen dessen Vater.
(Peter meets John, they visit John's father).

7) Personal pronoun, other antecedent

  (1) Any constituent
  (2) Any constituent with same identifying marker as (1)
  (*) Any constituent with same number and gender as (1)

    Then: Same as above, select the personal pronoun.

Maria trifft Hans, Hans lernt fuer eine Pruefung.
(Mary meets John, John studies for an examination).

Maria trifft Hans, er lernt fuer eine Pruefung.
(Mary meets John, he studies for an examination).

If (*) exists, no pronoun is generated, appropriate rules for 'dieser', 'jener' ('this', 'that') have not yet been considered.

8) 'Auch'-insertion

  (1) Any constituent on top level in the second clause
  (*) Any constituent on top level in the second clause (this clause has been reduced to a single constituent)

    Then: Insert 'auch' ('too') after (1).

Peter spielt und Hans spielt.
(Peter plays and John plays).

            (Transformation 3 is applied first)

Peter spielt und Hans. (ungrammatical)

            (Transformation 8)

Peter spielt und Hans auch.
(Peter plays and John plays too).

9) Object inversion after pronominalization

①   Direct object, pronominalized
②   Indirect object

Then: Exchange ① and ② .

Peter kauft Hans ein Buch.
(Peter buys John a book).

Peter kauft es Hans (ihm).
(Peter buys it for John (him)).

5.4 Linearization

The linearization phase takes care of the transduction of complex constituents (NP's, PP's and AP's) into a series of word markers representing only single words after this phase. Moreover, syntactical features like number and gender are inherited to dependent parts of a constituent. The creation of proper words for expressing the complement type, question and negation features is performed resulting in the creation of determiners, prepositions and negations.

Four types of phrases are distinguished:

1) **Verb part**

Verb -> (neg) Verb

where 'neg' is introduced when the non-finite verb part is treated, in case the negation feature of the verb in the IMS is set. The realization of the parts of the verb is postponed till the morphology phase.

2) **Noun phrases or prepositional phrases**

NP   ->   (Det) (AP)* CB (NP)*

resulting in determiner, adjective phrases, the case bearer itself and depending noun phrases. If the noun phrase is a structure with a junctor, the word expressing the kind of junctor is to be inserted between the last but one and the last noun phrase that the junctor is combining. If there are more than two such phrases, the other ones are separed by commas. Additionally, inheritance of complement type, preposition and determiner information is required.

3) Adjective phrase

$$AP \quad \rightarrow \quad (NP)^* \, Adj$$

resulting in depending noun phrases and the adjective itself.

4) Determiner part

$$Det \quad \rightarrow \quad (Neg) \; (Praep) \; (Det)$$

The determiner (derived from the constituent's reference) can be definite, indefinite or in question. It is realized by 'der', ('die', 'das', 'die'), 'einer' ('eine', 'eines', '-') and 'welcher' ('welche', 'welches', 'welche') respectively. In case of a proper name a determiner is only created when there is another dependent phrase like ('der grosse Peter'), contrary to ('Peter'). If the negation feature is accompanied by an indefinite reference 'keiner' ('keine', 'keines', 'keine') is selected instead of 'einer', otherwise the negation feature is expressed by 'nicht'.

If a constituent, whose question feature is set, is an indefinite pronoun ('jemand', 'etwas'), it is changed into 'wer' or 'was' respectively or a corresponding form ('wessen' for the owner case). An appropriate word has to be selected at this stage for some classes of pronouns the canonical form of which depends on number, gender and person. Additionally, a negation feature can require a change of the word ('etwas' → 'nichts'). After this stage a slight reordering is performed for relative clauses, which are inserted immediately after the constituent they are depending on. There is an exception to this rule: if the link in the superordinated clause is the last constituent disregarding verbs, the relative clause follows the superordinated clause.

As the finite and the non-finite part of a verb normally appear at separated places in a German sentence, the complexity of the problem increases further. We generate both parts separately only at their occurence. An exception is made for verbs containing a particle, as this part is split from the rest of the form in present tense and imperfect and it takes the place of the non-finite part ('weitergehen' -> 'geht' ... 'weiter'). Therefore the particle (or the other part of the form) is stored until it is actually used. Creation of other tenses does not raise such problems. Only the usage of 'haben' or 'sein' for composed tenses has to be distinguished, the rest is straight forward.

In German, the rules for the use of capital letters are quite numerous and present problems even to native writers. We decided to use a simplified approach, writing all substantives with capital letters as well as the first word of an utterance and all words immediately following a '.', '!' or '?'.

Details on the morphological lexicon are to be found in [15], which contains also the complete tables.

6. Future Work

Up to now, VIE-GEN is able to produce text rather than single sentences and to express subtle features of the net structure by selection of appropriate words, correctly maintaining the dependencies between them. A lot of syntactic constructions can be generated, text coherence is supported by consideration of anaphora, gapping and paraphrases.

As mentioned above, many of the involved processes are strongly data-driven. The incorporation of new data therefore will play a crucial role toward better performance of the generator. As preparation and input of data by hand is a tedious task, methods for automatic data acquisition are currently being studied. One of these is the use of the SSL for the automatic support of generation of DNs [13]. Additionally, the development of strategies for learning SSL entries from examples would be quite fruitful. This seems to be a vast field for possible innovations.

5.5 Morphology

In this final step each lexeme is transformed into a single unambiguous form according to the associated syntactical information. An exception is the non-finite part of a verb, which can yield from none to three words depending on tense and voice.

As German is a language rich in inflexional forms, a morphological lexicon is used. It contains the canonical form of each word together with morphological data (e.g. word category, type of inflexion). Irregular forms are stored explicitly. The morphological lexicon, which is used also by the parser of VIE-LANG, was augmented for generation purposes using data by Kunze and Ruediger [9]. Some modifications have been performed on this data, although not impairing the completeness of forms to be generated.

Three classes of inflexion are distinguished:

Substantival inflexion class

All substantives belong to that class except to those which are derivable from a participle. Due to the explicit storage of irregular plural forms (e.g.: 'Atlas' - 'Atlanten') a significant reduction in different inflexion classes was obtained compared to [9].

Adjectival inflexion class

This class contains all inflecting words with the exception of verbs and those belonging to the substantival inflexion class. The fact, that the adjective flexion in German also depends on the preceding words belonging to the same phrase is taken into account ('das grosse Haus', but 'ein grosses Haus').

Verbal inflexion class

There exist short procedures for synthesis of each of the following forms: infinitive, imperative, present and perfect participle as well as indicative and conjunctive for present tense and imperfect. All other tenses and all voices are composed by application of these basic procedures.

Some extensions of the transformational part will prove useful.
Automatic support is required because of the ease to change the rules
or to introduce new ones. Most extensions will improve the ability to
generate anaphora and gapping. The heuristics responsible for
partitioning and for selection of alternatives have to be tested
extensively leading to the correction of eventually occuring
undesirable results.

Appendix: Abbreviations

Abbreviation	Meaning	Chapter
CURIND	Current individual	3.2
DN	Discrimination net	3.1
E1,...,E8	Complement types	4.
IC,IT,IL,etc.	Non-verb-specific complements	4.
IMS	Intermediate structure	4.
LS	"Left side" of an SSL-entry	2.2
RESTR	Value restriction for individuals of SEMNET	3.2
RS	"Right side" of an SSL-entry	2.2
SEMNET	Semantic network of the system VIE-LANG	2.1
SOR	Marker for alternative verbalizations	4.,5.1
SSL	Syntactico-semantic lexicon	2.2
VF	Finite part of verb	4.
VIE-GEN	Generator of the system VIE-LANG	1.
VIE-LANG	Vienna Language Understanding System	2.
VN	Non-finite part of verb	4.
XOR	Exclusive OR	4.,5.1

References

[1] Brachman R.J.: A Structural Paradigm for Representing Knowledge, Bolt Beranek and Newman Inc., Rep. 3605, Cambridge, MA,; 1978.

[2] Buchberger E., Steinacker I., Trappl R., Trost H., Leinfellner E.: VIE-LANG - A German Language Understanding System, in Trappl R.(ed.), Cybernetics and Systems Research, North-Holland, Amsterdam; 1982.

[3] Charniak E.: The Case-Slot Identity Theory, Cognitive Science, 5(3)285-292; 1981.

[4] Engel U.: Syntax der deutschen Gegenwartssprache, Erich Schmidt Verlag; 1977.

[5] Goldman N.M.: Computer Generation of Natural Language from a Deep Conceptual Base, Stanford AI Lab Memo AIM-247; 1974.

[6] Horacek H.: Zur Generierung zusammenhaengender Texte, in Neumann B.(ed.), GWAI-83, Springer, Berlin; 1983.

[7] Katz B.: A Three-Step Procedure for Language Generation, MIT, AI Memo No.599; 1980.

[8] Kobsa A., Buchberger E., Steinacker I.: Funktion, Inhalt und Aufbau von Partnermodellen in natuerlichsprachigen Dialogsystemen, Bericht 82-08, Inst.f.Med.Kybernetik, Univ.Wien; 1982.

[9] Kunze J., Ruediger B.: Algorithmische Synthese der Flexionsformen des Deutschen, Zeitschrift fuer Phonetik, Sprachwissenschaft und Kommunikationsforschung 21,245-303; 1968.

[10] Matthiessen C.M.I.M.: A Grammar and a Lexicon for a Text-Production System, in Proceedings of the 19th Annual Meeting of the ACL, 49-55; 1981.

[11] McKeown K.R.: The Text System for Natural Language Generation: An Overview, in Proceedings of the 20th Annual Meeting of the Association for Computational Linguists, University of Toronto, Toronto, Canada, 113-120; 1982.

[12] Schank R.C.: Conceptual Information Processing, North-Holland, Amsterdam; 1975.

[13] Steinacker I., Buchberger E.: Relating Syntax and Semantics: The Syntactico-Semantic Lexicon of the System VIE-LANG, in Proceedings of the First Conference of the European Chapter of the ACL, Pisa, Italy; 1983.

[14] Steinacker I.: VIE-PAR, ein semantisch gesteuerter Parser zur Analyse deutscher Saetze in einem sprachverstehenden System, Dissertation, Technische Universitaet Wien; 1984.

[15] Trost H., Buchberger E.: Lexikon, morphologische Analyse und Synthese im System VIE-LANG, Bericht 81-02, Inst.f.Med.Kybernetik, Univ.Wien; 1981.

[16] Trost H., Steinacker I.: The Role of Roles: Some Aspects of World Knowledge Representation, in Proceedings of the 7th International Joint Conference on Artificial Intelligence, Univ.British Columbia, Vancouver, Canada; 1981.

[17] Trost H.: Struktur und Zugriffsroutinen der Datenstruktur SEMNET, Institutsbericht 82-13, Inst.f.Med.Kybernetik, Univ.Wien; 1982.

[18] Trost H.: SEMNET - Ein semantisches Netz zur Darstellung von Umweltwissen in einem natuerlichsprachigen System, Dissertation, Technische Universitaet Wien; 1983.

[19] Wilks Y.: Good and Bad Arguments about Semantic Primitives, Communication and Cognition, 10(3/4); 1977.

GENERATION OF SENTENCES FROM A SYNTACTIC DEEP STRUCTURE WITH A SEMANTIC COMPONENT

Heinz-Dirk Luckhardt

In this paper, the generation component of the SUSY machine translation system is described. In doing this, the author attempts to explain some basic differences in natural language generation in MT and AI. This more general discussion concentrates on the aspect of syntactic and/or semantic representation, especially on the status of deep semantic cases in natural language processing. The presentation of the SUSY generation component includes detailed descriptions of the data base for generation and its manipulation as well as the generation process and some linguistic aspects of generation.

0. General framework and background

0.1 Environment

The SUSY MT system is being developed since 1974 by the A2-project of the special research unit 'Elektronische Sprachforschung' (SFB100) at the University of the Saar in Saarbrücken. Although the name is still the same as in 1974, it now stands for a host of new strategies and subsystems that include SUSY-II, that commands a new parsing strategy and data structure called S-graph (cf. Maas (1981)). SUSY-II is a new core system that competes with the one described in 0.3, but shares the system environment with it. The systems are run on a Siemens computer, some subsystems have been migrated to a Univac. The translation speed is estimated at 15.000 - 30.000 words per hour CPU-time.

Like most MT systems SUSY is subdivided into analysis, transfer, and generation (synthesis) subsystems, of which only the last one will be discussed in detail, i.e. parsing strategies or the interface between analysis and transfer will not be mentioned. Moreover, no time will be dedicated to the description of SUSY's lexicon system. Some remarks about the system philosophy concerning analysis, transfer, and generation may be useful.

0.2 Characteristics

I. Multilinguality

This has two aspects:

a. Analysis and generation are independent of each other, i.e. we can use the same analysis output for the generation of sentences in more than one target language (TL), and the generation process does not take the source language (SL) into account.

b. There is only <u>one</u> analysis module and <u>one</u> generation module for all languages, i.e. the procedures are externally controlled by sets of language-specific parameters.

II. Extendibility

This means that new (European) languages can easily be integrated. To date the following languages can be analysed: German, Russian, English, French, and Esperanto, and the following can be generated: German, English, and French. The disparity may be explained by the fact that the dictionaries for parsing cannot be used for generation, so that for each language a new generation dictionary has to be created. This has been done only for three languages.

III. Heterogeneity

Heterogeneous means that rules for different classes of linguistic phenomena can be formulated in different ways and do not have to be homogeneous, i.e. they do not have to be formed according to the same strict rule formalism. This principle follows from the insight that language cannot be moulded into only one pre-defined rule schema. However comfortable it may be to let the parser work on just one rule format, it seems to be obvious that different problems have to be tackled by different means. These means are:

- Programmed rules -

One should not complelety forgo the possibility of programming rules (i.e. of formulating them in a higher programming language), as this still is the fastest, the most flexible and most direct way of expressing linguistic knowledge. There are some prerequisites, however:

o as many data as possible should be kept externally to make
   the control structure transparent

o the programs themselves must be transparent by using a
   mnemonic data manipulating language

o the data must be organised in a way that makes their
   manipulation easy.

- Phrase structure grammars for parsing -

If the linguistic facts that are to be described by rules are clear-cut and well-defined and if it is more important to get a complete description than to get it quickly, a PS-grammar may be employed. In SUSY the way in which main clauses, subclauses, discontinuous clauses, etc. interact is described by means of a PS-grammar that is exactly the same (and has been tested) for German, Russian, English, French, and Esperanto; i.e. the inventory of clause types and the PS-rules are language-independent, the means for the identification of clauses and clause boundaries are language specific (cf. Luckhardt 1985). The PS-rules are restricted to function only in certain contexts.

- Linguistic characteristics -

If we define the set of those rules that are common to all languages as the interlingual core of SUSY and the set of those rules that differ in at least two languages as its interlingual body, there is a control structure for the interlingual body that we shall call linguistic characteristics of a language. To put it in a different way: the parser can be controlled externally by defining - for each language - the path to follow in every case of deviating rules (cf. 3.4).

- External rules -

External rules are used in many different ways in a number of modules. All of these rules are easily accessible, i.e. extendible and improvable. They determine

o   the combinability of words within NPs
o   the combinability of verbal elements
o   the weighting of sequences of words
o   the default translation of prepositions
o   the generation of articles and pronouns
etc.

- External control -

of intermediate results and of the number of translational variants per sentence of analysis according to text type

IV. Modularity

The MT process is broken down into analysis, transfer, and generation - as usual - and into linguistically motivated smaller units.

V. Data structure

The Data structure is a network with pointers. For every accepted reading of a sentence one network is built up that may be regarded as a blackboard from which a process reads the structures already accepted and onto which it writes new ones (cf. Luckhardt 1985a). The network is described in more detail in 1.1.

VI. Interface structure (IS)

The interface structure is a syntacto—semantic deep structure without reference to a specific language pair.

VII. Easy information access

This means easy access for the rule writer to any node in the interface structure and a wide range of opportunities to display intermediate stages of analysis.

VIII. Linguistic data system

There is an external description of linguistic data for analysis, transfer, and generation.

IX. Lexicon system

There is a compound lexicon system with all lexicons and their entries having the same internal structures, notwithstanding their different uses, contents, and languages. The modularity of SUSY is reflected in the lexicon system, as there are separate dictionaries for the morpho—syntactic analysis, the lexico—semantic analysis, the lexical transfer, the lexixo—semantic generation, and the morpho—syntactic generation. The largest lexicon is that for the German morpho—syntactic analysis: 140,000 entries. There are lexicons for

morphosyntactic analysis

Here the entries are word stems and forms with information about their morphological and syntactic behaviour and with their 'lemma name' (basic form) assigned. The disparity in size reflects the relative amounts of effort that have gone into the various languages to date:

German: 140,000 entries
English: 5,200 entries
French: 9,400 entries
Russian: 15,000 entries

lexico—semantic analysis

These dictionaries contain rules for source language lemmas that have to disambiguated or that trigger disambiguation procedures or procedures for the detection of idiomatic expressions:

```
German:        5,000 entries
English:       3,000 entries
Russian:       2,600 entries
French:          500 entries
```

lexical transfer between two languages

These dictionaries support the translation of the source language lemma names into the target language and hold information about the syntactic transfer between the two languages (e.g. translation of valencies which differs from the standard translation):

```
German-English:       3,600 entries
English-German:       4,300 entries
French-German:        9,000 entries
Russian-German:       9,000 entries
```

morphosyntactic generation

These dictionaries contain information about how the target language words behave syntactically (e.g. what kind of infinitive they can take as a complement) and how they inflect (e.g. entries of verbs carry information about the length of their detachable prefix: aufarbeiten; and entries of nouns tell the generation module how the plural is formed: Stadt - Städte):

```
German:       11,000 entries
French:        8,500 entries
English:       2,000 entries
```

X. High degree of determinism

The SUSY-parser follows an intermediate path between the two extremes

- follow all paths possible (non-determinism)
- follow just one path (determinism)

Generation operates deterministically.

XI. Syntax plus semantics

The question as to the relation between syntax and semantics is nearly as old as MT itself. In SUSY it has been tackled in the following manner:

1. phase:	purely syntactic analysis (1972-1977)
2. phase:	semantic analysis on the basis of the output of
	the syntactic analysis (1977-1982)
3. phase:	integration of semantic procedures into the
	process of syntactic analysis (1982-1986)

The overall philosophy was to tackle the problems first with syntactic means and to exhaust the possibilities of syntactic analysis, and then to solve the remaining problems by means of semantic procedures. This has lead to the following insights:

1. The primacy of syntax for the representation of the output of the analysis is - from our point of view - not contestable.
2. Semantics seems to be, first of all, indispensable for the dissolution of syntactic ambiguities.
3. Secondly, semantics is indispensable for the dissolution of lexical ambiguities and idioms, and this can be done after the syntactic analysis.
4. Thirdly, semantics is indispensable for the representation of relations between predicates and adverbial complements and perhaps also between the constituents of compounds, for the representation of synonymous structures, for choosing the correct target language equivalents, etc.

0.3 The SUSY-(sub)processes

Here is a short account of the (sub)processes of SUSY and the tasks they fulfill.

Morphological analysis (WOBUSU)

   (dictionary look-up, inflectional analysis, analysis of compounds
   and derivations, analysis of unidentified words)

Disambiguation of word classes (DIHOM)

   (automatic elimination of word class variants in certain
   contexts, weighting of sequences of word classes, output
   of up to 12 (i.e. the 12 best) non-ambiguous word
   sequences for 1 sentence)

Segmentation of sentences (SEGMENT, PHRASEG)

   (detection of clause boundaries, analysis of the relations
   between the clauses)

Analysis of noun phrases (NOMA)

  (analysis of simple and complex NPs, analysis of English
  string compounds)

Analysis of verbal phrases (VERA)

  (combination of verbal elements, deep syntactic representation of verbal phrases, e.g. active and passive forms
  have the same representation)

Complementation of valency frames (KOMA)

  (differentiation between valency-bound and non-valency-
  bound constituents, filling of valency frames, transformation of surface syntactic into deep syntactic
  description)

Lexical and semantic disambiguation (SEDAM)

  (dissolution of lexical and semantic ambiguities, transformation of prepositions into an interlingua)

Transfer

  (replacement of SL words by TL words, translation of
  valencies, insertion of articles, elimination of
  multiple negations, transfer of structure of untrans-
  latable words: "zielsprachlich" = "of the target language")

Semantic synthesis

  (transformation of interlingua expressions into TL prepositions)

Syntactic synthesis

  (Generation of linear sequences of pre-terminal nodes for
  the TL from the IS)

Morphological synthesis

  (Generation of word forms from the pre-terminal nodes)

0.4 Generation in AI and MT

As far as generation is concerned, AI and MT differ considerably. From the discussion of generation in AI in Wahlster (1982) we can derive the following criteria of differentiation.

(a) In AI, some systems operate with prefabricated texts or excerpts from knowledge bases, i.e. without a proper generation component. This is impossible in MT.
(b) In AI generation, a semantic representation has to be verbalised. In MT, for reasons discussed below, there always is a (semanto-) syntactic representation to generate target language sentences from.
(c) In MT, the choice of TL words is, first of all, governed by the corresponding SL word and, secondly, by its individual context, but not by means of a dialogue memory, of rules of inference, or conceptual knowledge, as in dialogue-oriented AI models.
(d) The basic problem for generation in MT is the difference of structures and concepts in SL and TL. This problem could disappear as a means of differentiation between MT and AI, if a parser in MT was able to generate representations on a level where differences between SL and TL disappear. Such a level cannot be reached by a universal MT system, and it might be claimed that MT systems have to generate texts that they cannot be said to have understood.

Differences of structure and concept entail a number of problems of which the definition of tasks of analysis, transfer, and generation is the most prominent. This definition meets with the following difficulties that have especially become obvious during the preparatory phase of the European Community's MT system EUROTRA.

(1) The need to differentiate vs. the economy of representation

Modern MT systems are not restricted to one language pair, so the parser must not take the TL into account, but produce a representation of the SL text that is irrespective of the TL. So, e.g., there must not be any parsing rules for an SL that perform tasks that aim at a certain TL. This is a task for the interlingual transfer that deals with language-pair specific differences.

(2) The need to keep transfer small.

Principle (1) clashes with the need to keep transfer small. This is necessary, because for n languages in a system there are n modules and n generation modules, but n x (n-1) transfer modules. So, for reasons of economy, the transfer modules and dictionaries ought to be kept small, as there are so many of them.
So, the division of labour has to respect that analysis ought to produce a rather shallow representation and that transfer ought to be kept small. This would leave generation with most of the differentiations still to be done. As this is impossible - I shall demonstrate that below - a compromise has to be found.

Here is a small example:

If we want to translate the German adjective 'groß' into English, there is no use in analysing it any deeper, as the possible concepts of 'groß' in German do not coincide with English as well as, e.g., French concepts. So, the job ought to be done in transfer. But then we must have access to the semantic features of the TL, which would contradict the principle of small transfer. If the problem is carried along into generation, the system ends up with rules for differentiating a SL concept in generation which clearly is undesirable.

The compromise found for SUSY has the following aspects:

The principle of small transfer has been slackened, i.e. there are rules for structural transfer. The level of representation for analysis is defined by every rule writer who decides to write a rule for semantic differentiation in analysis. This is done in a way that the representation gives access to the overall concept <u>and</u> its specified subconcept. So, the rule writer in transfer is free to translate the general or the specific concept. This approach has not yet been realised completely insofar as there still is no access to TL features in transfer so that some ambiguous concepts still have to be carried through to semantic generation.

1. A syntactic deep structure with a semantic component

1.1 The syntactic data base for generation

Generation operates on the interface structure (IS) produced by the transfer module which in turn operates on the IS produced by the analysis module, so first of all we shall take a closer look at the IS. As mentioned above, the IS is a network with pointers. It differs from the IS that serves as interface between the different analysis modules in that it contains neither structural nor word ambiguities, and that, of course, the SL lexical units have been replaced by those of the TL.

The IS is made of

P-nodes (predicates)
N-nodes (noun phrases)
T-nodes (terminals)

e.g.: <u>The young teacher laughed.</u>
(cf. <u>Fig. 1</u>)

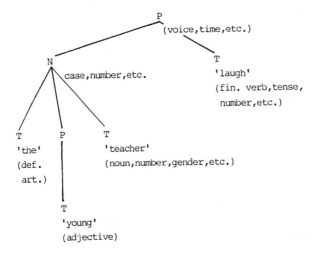

<u>Fig.1</u>

Every node is specified by a decoration (a set of variable/value-pairs) that holds the information pertaining to that node. The P- and N-nodes also have relational labels that define their position in the net. A T-node can be replaced by a set of sister T-nodes. The entry node to the net is defined as

a) The one P-node that has no father
b) if a) is not true (e.g. for titles without predicate, i.e. for sentences that are specified as belonging to a special type of text): the leftmost N-node.

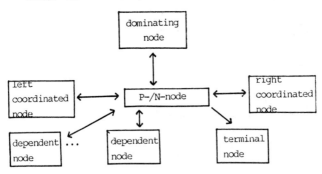

<u>Fig. 2</u>

Fig. 2 shows how a P-/N-Node is embedded into the IS. The example in Fig. 3 demonstrates how the predicate 'sang' is embedded in the IS of the sentence 'Mary danced and sang':

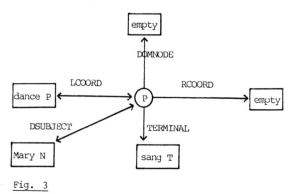

Fig. 3

The basic difference between P- and N-nodes is that an N-node can point to more than one terminal node, a P-node cannot. This net has some characteristics that have to be mentioned:

a. There are no relations between sister nodes. Sisters have access to one another only via the father node.
b. A father node points to its daughters via <u>fixed relation labels</u> (11 labels for N-nodes, 15 for P-nodes), so that the process operating on the net has to look through all of these fixed relation labels, if it wants to find, e.g., a certain NP without knowing what relation label it carries. On the other hand, it is very easy to access a <u>specified</u> dependent node as you just state the relation's name (deep subject, deep object, etc.), which is the usual use of the IS.
c. The pointers are subspecified in such a way as to indicate whether they point to a P- or an N-node. This is not true for coordinated nodes, as they must be of the same kind, which is a deficiency for certain - not very common - constructions.
d. There cannot be a left-coordinated and a dominating node at the same time. A node with a coordinated node to its left has no dominating node and vice versa.

1.2 Semantic vs. syntactic representation

1.2.1 On deep semantic cases in Machine Translation

a. Some basic positions in MT and AI

a.1 How much semantics?
MT: as much as necessary
AI: as much as possible

Semantics is vague - the vaguer something is, the less it is formalisable - the less formalisable something is - the less it can be used in MT. Questions of semantics cannot be answered in a binary fashion.

a.2 How much syntax?
MT: as much as possible
AI: as little as possible

Syntax is concrete and formalisable. Syntax is nearer to the surface. Syntax can control the parser in a considerably safe fashion without man being forced to intervene.

a.3 How much interaction?
MT: possibly none (during run time)
AI: as much as necessary

Interaction is time-consuming. MT systems are made for high through-put. It can seldom be easily defined where and when man is to intervene in the process of parsing.

a.4 What field of discourse?
MT: well-defined and large enough for a useful and economic application
AI: as large as possible and describable with a justifiable effort

For MT, it is difficult to define fields of discourse, and uneconomic to build an MT system for a special field of discourse. AI systems are almost by definition created for special fields of discourse.

a.5 What kind of input?
MT: almost any, user has no influence on its production
AI: user formulates input

An MT system must parse almost any input. The user mostly has no influence on the text production. The user of an AI system formulates the input himself.

b. Syntactic and/or semantic representation

Two types of structure are 'represented' that can be differentiated by means of their function:

- structures that are produced by the user <u>before</u> parsing: linguistic and world knowledge
- structures that are produced in the parsing process by the machine (and that in AI may become part of the knowledge base <u>after</u> parsing): analysis structures

The interplay between these factors will be dealt with in b.2 ff.

b.2 Syntactic Representation

There have been attempts to do parsing without syntax, but they have remained very restricted or have already been given up, as e.g. in the PLANES system which has received a syntactic component in its follow-up JETS. I shall assume that for an MT system a syntactic component will be indispensable. Also for semantic representation by case frames a syntactic valency frame cannot be dispensed with (I shall deal with that in b.4). Such a valency frame will look like this:

verb

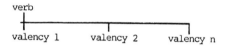

valency 1   valency 2   valency n

This is the standard form of a valency frame the application of which presupposes that, e.g., passive clauses have been transformed into active ones. In order to be able to apply the following valency frame

öffnen

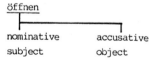

nominative   accusative
subject   object

the parser must transform the sentence "Das Fenster wurde von mir geöffnet" ('The window was opened by me') into "Ich öffnete das Fenster" ('I opened the window'). Such a syntactic representation would also be true for "Der Schlüssel öffnete die Tür" ('The key opened the door'). This raises one of the most controversial questions of MT, i.e.: how much does the MT system really have to "know", e.g. do we have to differentiate the above two syntactic representations? It is obvious that semantics <u>is</u> necessary, e.g. to differentiate "fällen (Baum)" ('cut down' a tree) and "fällen

Entscheidung)" ('make' a decision). Where semantics ought to be used and to what an extent will be discussed in b.4.

b.3 Semantic Representation

A basically semantic representation is used in Stuttgart by Laubsch and Hanakata, who are developing a generation system for German (project SEMSYN). This is a very special case, as they do not have to worry about parsing. They are furnished with semantic representations produced by the Japanese ATLAS/U system (Fujitsu), cf. Fig. 4.

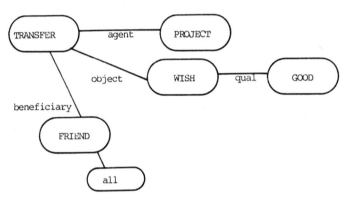

("Das Projekt sendet allen Freunden die besten Wünsche")
Fig. 4

b.4 Syntacto-semantic representation

This is where I shall deal with the interplay between syntax and semantics. First of all, I should like to touch on a number of problems of case theory and its application to MT.

Semantic deep cases are relatively rarely used in MT systems (in comparison with AI systems). Exceptions are METAL (cf. Slocum 1983) and the above-mentioned SEMSYN generation system. Why do MT researchers renounce the use of deep cases? To answer that question, we must take a look at case theory. The most important aspects of criticism of case theory are mentioned and discussed by Fillmore (1981, 23ff.):

1. Case theory is a purely notational variant to other grammar theories

Everything that can be expressed by it can also be expressed in a different way. One does not gain much by using cases like Experiencer, Agent, Instrument, etc.

2. Case Theory is irrelevant for the description of language,

because it is at best a pure taxonomy. Against this argument Fillmore advances the argument that case theory was not meant to be a complete grammar model.

Fillmore holds arguments 1. and 2. to be irrelevant, but he accepts 3. and 4. as presenting serious problems:

3. A level of deep structure as demanded by the Standard Theory
   is necessary

This argument is accepted by Fillmore.

4. There is no generally accepted set of cases

It may even be claimed that deep cases cannnot be strictly and universally defined and formulated at all, as they cannot be delimitated. This arguments disqualifies cases for MT, for: what are they good for, if there is no generally accepted set of cases for all languages concerned? (cf. discussion of Eurotra study below).

A further point of criticism is advanced by Seyfert (1981, 153):

5. Deep cases only repeat part of the meaning of the predicate

"The predicate itself attributes characteristics to its arguments (grammatically speaking: the NPs), and therefore we understand sentences also in a figurative sense:

   Alfred putzt seine Reputation"
   ('Alfred polishes his reputation')

We understand this sentence as being ironic, because we know that 'polishing' is a purely mechanical manipulation. In order to understand it we do not need abstract conceptions of agents, instruments, objects, etc.; all we need is the meaning of 'polish' and the knowledge of which NP refers to the polisher and which NP refers to the thing being polished. To clarify this we may use 'subject' and 'direct object' or 'agent' and 'patient' or 'source' and 'goal' or 'controller' and 'controlled'. We recognize that the predicate attributes characteristics to its arguments and that this represents a very specific accomplishment, if we consider - vice versa - which characteristics NPs impose on the verb:

   "Alfred verb Schuhe".

We can say nothing about it. It may stand for:

Alfred putzt Schuhe. ('Alfred polishes shoes')
Alfred liebt Schuhe. ('Alfred loves shoes')
Alfred kennt Schuhe. ('Alfred knows shoes')
...

If we do not understand the predicate, we do not understand anything."
(Seyfert 1981, 153; translation by myself)

6. The explication of deep cases must very often be done by force

This last argument has a pragmatic background: it explains certain problems encountered when incorporating deep cases into MT. It is a fact that the existence of cases has been proved by means of a very small number of case frames that are repeated in many publications on case theory, e.g. "to open". But: how does the great majority of verbs for which no intuitively simple, unambiguous, and reasonable case frame can be produced fit into the theory? Or more important: what are the practical consequences for the creation of dictionary entries? Seyfert presents an example:

"... if we think of physiological function verbs like in 'Alfred coughs', 'sweats', 'stutters': is Alfred an agent? That depends on the circumstances. Alfred may cough spontaneously ('experiencer' ?) or deliberately ('agent' ?)). It does not make much sense to maintain two different role structures her. The sentence 'Alfred coughs' gives no clue as to its actual meaning, no decision about agentivity/non-agentivity is possible. Case grammar, however, forces us to make a decision."
(Seyfert 1981, 155; translation by myself)

What we need for the (automatic) analysis of natural language is not a theory that explains singular phenomena, like the nature of action/process-verbs (to break, to open, etc.), but one that is 'of a piece'. This is no longer true for case theory, at least since Fillmore withdrew the notion of case grammar and defined case theory as a number of arguments for the assumption that there is a sentence level with case structures. But the above arguments and the development of case theory suggest that case theory never was made 'of a piece'. Above all, this is demonstrated by the fact that every researcher who concerned himself with case theory developed a different list of case labels. And such lists tend to change even from one field of discourse to another, as the ET-7-D study (cf. below) has shown. The difficulty of defining and delimiting case roles becomes especially obvious, when a set of labels has to be evaluated for a large corpus of sentences from different fields. This has been shown in 1981 and 1983/84 in the framework of the European MT system Eurotra. In 1981 the ET-7-D project of the German Eurotra group (vgl. Freigang/Gerhardt/Luckhardt/Maas-/Thiel (1981)) has tried to develop a hierarchically structured set of case roles. This study and further tests by all Eurotra groups (English, French, Danish, Belgo-Dutch, Italian, and Greek) in 1983/84 have shown that

(a) the assignment of case roles to complements is based on intuition and is very difficult to formalise

(b) this assignment is even more difficult to achieve, if it is done on the basis of a detailed predicate classification, than in loose connection with a rough classification (like: action, process, state). This was shown on the basis of a conceptual (cf. Ruus/Spang-Hanssen (1982)) and a case-oriented predicate classification (cf. Longacre (1976)).

(c) the existence of case roles and their usefulness for MT could not be proved.

The application of case roles in the parsing process is a controversial matter. The only MT system that has deep cases in its repertoire is METAL, but there are no details how they are used. They are not used as a means of disambiguation during the parsing process (cf., Slocum (1983)).

What can deep cases achieve in the parsing process? Fillmore seems to think that we have to understand a sentence, before we can determine subject and object (cf. Fillmore (1977)). Does that mean – if we assume that the meaning of a sentence is best be described by means of deep cases – that cases roles are determined, before subject and object are determined? This cannot be true, and the analysis of (1) and (2) can prove this:

(1) Die Tür öffnet Dir kein Schlüssel.
    (No key will open that door for you)
(2) Die Tür kann von Dir mit keinem Schlüssel geöffnet werden.
    (This door cannot be opened by you with any key)

Theses examples were chosen, because the case frame of 'öffnen' (to open) has most frequently been used to prove the existence of deep cases. Two frames for the assignment of cases may look like the following (their application presupposes that passive sentences have been transformed into active ones):

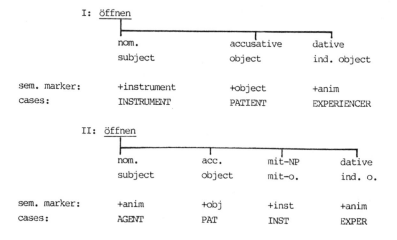

I: öffnen

	nom. subject	accusative object	dative ind. object
sem. marker:	+instrument	+object	+anim
cases:	INSTRUMENT	PATIENT	EXPERIENCER

II: öffnen

	nom. subject	acc. object	mit-NP mit-o.	dative ind. o.
sem. marker:	+anim	+obj	+inst	+anim
cases:	AGENT	PAT	INST	EXPER

How can (1) and (2) be assigned their cases by means of these frames? This can only be done by comparing the complements to the slots in the frames, but: what case is assigned to 'Dir' in (1)? The parser first of all has to determine 'Dir' as the indirect object, and he can do this only by recurring to the surface case 'dative'. And, of course, we cannot directly derive the deep case from the surface case, as, e.g. for (2), only the passive transformation creates the basis for the assignment of deep syntactic cases. So, the natural order is

surface case - synt. deep case - sem. deep case

This was an example for the 'computation' of deep cases for one of the standard examples of case theory. Computation is more difficult for:

(3) Von dir hätte ich das nicht erwartet.
    (I shouldn't have expected that of you)
(4) Von Dir hätte ich gleich nach Hause gehen sollen.
    (From you (your home) I should have gone home straight away)
(5) Dem Sänger war eine ganze Seite gewidmet.
    (A whole page was dedicated to the singer)
(6) Dem Sänger war eine ganze Seite zu wenig.
    (A whole page was not enough for the singer)
(7) Mit diesem Verhalten macht er sich nur Ärger.
    (This behaviour will cause trouble for him)
(8) Mit diesem Verhalten rechnete keiner.
    (This behaviour wasn't expected by anybody)
(The English phrases are just translations and do not reflect the linguistic problem)

What about the von-phrase of 'erwarten', the indirect object of 'widmen', or the mit-phrase of 'rechnen'? All these complements cannot be easily assigned a deep case. The rule-writer is forced to assume a definite deep case, although this may run counter to his intuition, e.g, one of the following cases may be argued for:

von-complement of 'erwarten'

PATIENT = the one concerned
EXPERIENCER = the one who makes an experience
AGENT = the one who does something that we did not expect
SOURCE = the source of the action that we did not expect
GOAL = the one the expectation aims at

indirect object of 'widmen'

EXPERIENCER = the one who makes an experience
RECIPIENT = the one who receives the dedication
GOAL = the one the dedication aims at

<u>mit-complement</u> of 'rechnen'

PATIENT = the thing or person concerned
GOAL = the thing or person the expectation is aimed at

There must be reasons for the differentiation between PATIENT, EXPERIENCER, and GOAL, or they would not have been defined (cf. Longacre (1976)). But for the three verbs above they had better have been merged into one. Thus, the necessity of introducing or eliminating cases even changes from one verb to another. This is obvious, for every verb has a meaning of its own and <u>cases are just a part of their meaning</u>. It seems that cases are especially difficult to define for those complements that constitute a certain meaning of a verb, like the mit-phrase for the meaning 'strong expectation' of the verb 'rechnen'. Such complements constitute a very important part of the meaning of the verb, so that it is quite natural that it is difficult to separate them from the verbal meaning by isolating them and giving them a case role that does not mean anything. For it does not make any sense to give the mit-phrase in (8) the roles PATIENT, EXPERIENCER, GOAL, RANGE, etc. That would be the same role as for the underlined NPs in (9) and (10):

(9) <u>An dieser Aufgabe</u> rechneten sie stundenlang.
    (They were busy with this exercise for hours)
(10) <u>Diese Aufgabe</u> kann niemand rechnen.
     (This exercise cannot be solved)

This would efface the difference in meaning, i.e. on the case level no differentiation would be possible any more. The surface NP and its preposition are indispensable as a criterion for differentiation. This is also illustrated by Anderson's well-known example:

(13) Bees are swarming in the garden.
(14) The garden is swarming with bees.
(Anderson (1971))

These sentences do <u>not</u> mean the same, but the case roles AGENT and LOCATION would efface this difference.

These are some of the problems the integration of case roles into MT is confronted with. If we dispense with case theory as a means of description for the semantic analysis, what is the alternative? This should take into account a notion that is characteristic of semantics: vagueness or fuzzyness. The possibility of defining fuzzy frames for the analysis is blocked by the dichotomy obligatory/optional that is demanded by case and valency grammarians. If we maintain it for the analysis of natural language sentences, we have to create valency and case frames for the analysis dictionaries that are so strict that the parsing algorithm will reject many sentences from randomly chosen texts. For MT, the obligatory/optional dichotomy has to be rejected insofar as it defines the (un)grammaticality of sentences. The sentence 'Blinde sehen mit den Händen' must not be rejected on the basis of a 'sehen'-case frame that demands the semantic marker 'viewing instrument' for the mit-phrase, that 'Hände', of course, does not have. As an ideal, such frames should not reflect the (always restricted) competence of the rule-writer, that will surely be falsified by the performance of millions of text writers the texts of which will be processed by the respective MT system. In order to approach this ideal, rules and frames must not be formulated too restrictively. According to Helbig/Schenkel the following sentences are ungrammatical:

Er sieht nach. Er sieht. Er baut auf.

But of course, they are not. As a consequence, the frames of 'nachsehen', 'sehen', and 'aufbauen' must not ask for an <u>obligatory</u> deep object, but allow for an <u>optional</u> one. This notion of vagueness is accounted for in the valency-theoretical approach of SUSY that dispenses with the <u>obligatory</u> filling of frames during the analysis. The constituents of a sentence are distributed among the valencies of a predicate. This has not lead to wrong assignment of constituents in many cases, as one might have expected. This may be explained by the fact that SUSY normally parses well-formed natural language sentences, and does not have to distinguish between correct and false sentences. Semantics is introduced for the choice between different lexical meanings, and here the notion 'obligatory' makes sense, as for certain verbal meanings complements are obligatory (in order to distinguish the meanings of 'sehen': 'sehen können' vs. 'sehen (erblicken)'). So, the semantic component comes into play, when a meaning has to be differentiated, as above has been demanded for 'fällen'. Then, however, it is safer to operate with syntactic deep cases and semantic categories, than with vague deep semantic cases. So, if the syntactic analysis has created a syntactic deep structure, the semantic analysis can <u>interpret</u> it. Nobody can predict how text writers will use the verb 'fällen'. If a rule-writer creates the following frame:

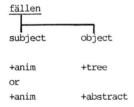

fällen

subject   object

+anim   +tree
or
+anim   +abstract

the sentence 'Diese Entscheidung hat den Minister gefällt' cannot be analysed. The frame or the syntactic deep structure ought to look like this:

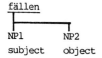

fällen
NP1   NP2
subject   object

This structure may be interpreted in the semantic analysis:

NP2 marked as +abstract:
‐‐‐‐‐‐‐⇓‐‐‐‐‐‐‐‐‐‐‐‐‐‐‐‐
fällen = fällen (abstract)

NP2 marked as +concrete:
‐‐‐‐‐‐‐⇓‐‐‐‐‐‐‐‐‐‐‐‐‐‐‐
fällen = fällen (absägen)

The interplay between syntactic and semantic component in SUSY is described in Fig. 5.

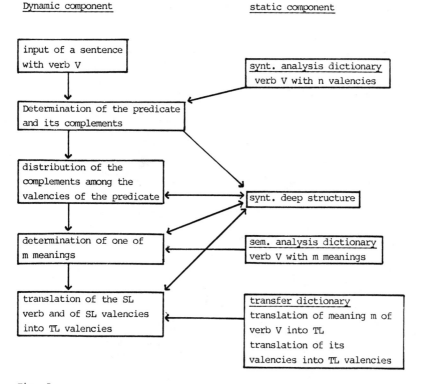

Dynamic component   static component

Fig. 5

1.2.2 Syntacto-semantic representation in SUSY

The following examples may demonstrate how in SUSY nouns, adjectives, verbs, and prepositions are disambiguated and represented by means of their syntactic environment and semantic markers. The rules presuppose a deep syntactic structure in which the algorithm can move about. Among others the following structures are implemented:

⇒ means: this node (or: its governor)
        triggers the rule

→ means: navigation in the tree
        'lemma' roughly corresponds to the notion of 'lexical unit', e.g. 'goes'
        is part of the lemma 'go'

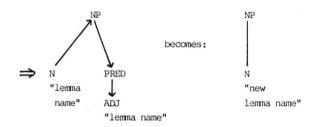

e.g.: <u>kalte Ente</u> (= a special kind of drink)

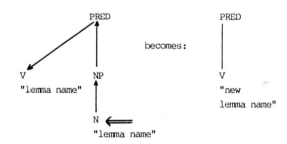

e.g.: <u>Abstand nehmen</u> (= to refrain from)

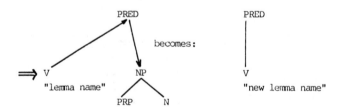

e.g.: <u>in Angriff nehmen</u> (= to tackle)

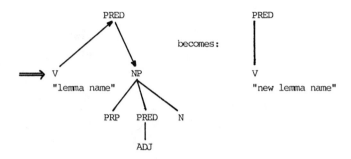

e.g.: <u>auf die leichte Schulter nehmen</u> (= to pooh-pooh)

This rule type operates on those constructs where the meaning of complements is absorbed by the verbal meaning. In these cases pure lemma names are turned into meaning units of a higher level, i.e. concepts, that may be directly translated into the target language:

Abstand nehmen (von) = to refrain (from) // in Angriff nehmen = to tackle

By the next class of rules lexemes are disambiguated by means of their syntacto-semantic context:

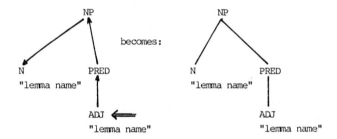

e.g.: <u>großer</u> Buchstabe (= capital letter)

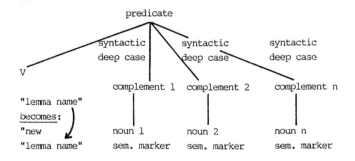

228

For "ablösen", e.g., the different frames are:

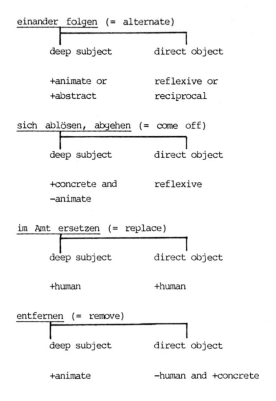

einander folgen (= alternate)

     deep subject   direct object

     +animate or   reflexive or
     +abstract   reciprocal

sich ablösen, abgehen (= come off)

     deep subject   direct object

     +concrete and   reflexive
     -animate

im Amt ersetzen (= replace)

     deep subject   direct object

     +human   +human

entfernen (= remove)

     deep subject   direct object

     +animate   -human and +concrete

Rules of description

Above all, these are used to describe the meaning of compounds and derivations. They are necessary in those cases where it may be assumed that a translational unit of the source language does not correspond to a translational unit (concept) of the target language. Such a unit can be decomposed into subconcepts that do correspond to concepts of the target language. In most cases this is done by assigning a synonymous structure to a word or structure in the following manner:

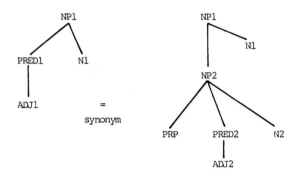

e.g.: hochwertiges Geschenk = Geschenk von hohem Wert
      (high value present = present of high value)

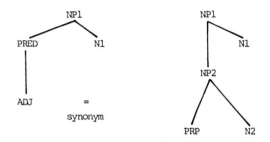

e.g.: erfolgloser Versuch = Versuch ohne Erfolg
      (unsuccessful attempt = attempt without success

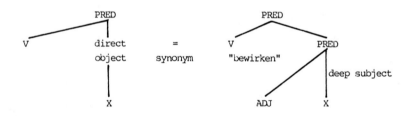

e.g.: stärken(X) = bewirken(stark sein(X))
      (enforce (X) = cause (strong be(X)))

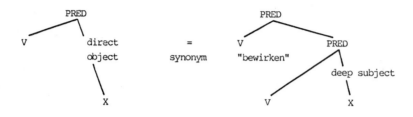

e.g.: tränken(X) = bewirken(trinken(X))
      (water(X) = cause(drink(X)))

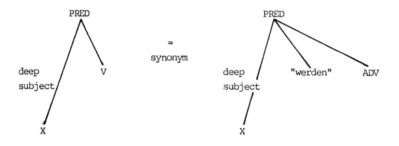

e.g.: wachsen(X) = werden(groß,X)
      (grow(X) = become(big,X))

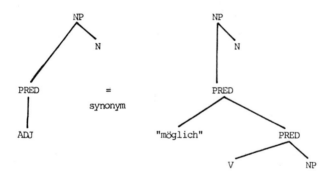

e.g.: lesbares Wort = möglich(lesen(Wort))
      (readable word = possible(read(word)))

e.g.: Gehörloser = taub(Mensch)
      (deaf person)

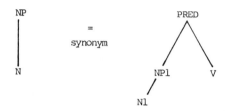

e.g.: Zuckerproduktion = produzieren (Zucker)
      (sugar production = produce(sugar))

2. SEMSYN – semantic synthesis

2.1 Area of application

SEMSYN performs semantic and lexical disambiguation and structural transfer. SEMSYN is the second instantiation of a control mechanism that also performs the semantic analysis of the SL (SEDAM). SEDAM and SEMSYN are two production systems with the same control mechanism, the same type of data base, i.e. the IS, and two different sets of rules. It is the task of SEMSYN to prepare the IS in such a way that SYNSYN can operate on it. In particular, SEMSYN produces the TL prepositions from a semantic Interlingua and generates TL structures that differ from those of the SL.
What is the control mechanism like? It is roughly made up of two separate processes, one for N-nodes and one for P-nodes. The selection of rules depends on the following factors:

- the rule and the node in question both have to be of the same kind (P / N).
- the trigger for trying out a rule is the congruence of the lexical unit (LU) of the T-node under the P-/N-node in question and the LU under which the rule is filed in the rule set. The latter is organised like a dictionary so that the access to the rules and addition/correction of rules is extremely easy, as this can be done by the usual SUSY lexicon handling system.

What are the rules like? A rule consists of a conditions and an assignments part. The conditions part always contains the LU of the core of the node at that the rule is directed, and the conditions for applying it. The assignments part contains the LUs that have to be assigned and other assignments to the node(s) in question, structural changes,etc.

Examples

Prepositions:

We do not have to regard the valency-bound prepositional phrases, as they have already been handled during transfer. SEMSYN generates TL prepositions from an interlingua into which all prepositions of non-valency-bound NPs of the SL text have been transformed during SEDAM. Prepositions are treated as predicates, in order to keep the control mechanism simple. The structure to be expected is shown in Fig. 6.

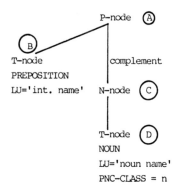

Fig. 6

The rule looks like this:

conditions: LU of B = 'interlingua name' and
                   wordclass of D = NOUN and
                   wordclass of B = PREP and
                   PNC-CLASS of D = n
assignments: LU of B := 'target language preposition'

PNC-CLASS stands for 'preposition-noun combination class', i.e. nouns are classified according to the prepositions with which they combine.

This is a simplified formal representation, it does not respect the possibility of defining more complex conditions, like those which may be necessary, if the TL preposition is not only determined by the PNC-Class of the noun, but also by some other features like 'existence of a numeral under the node in question' (Fig. 7).

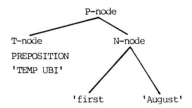

| TEMP UBI August | in August |
| TEMP UBI first August | on August first |

Fig. 7

Here are some other examples: 'until' may be used with a negation ('not until') and then has a different meaning than 'until' without negation. The German preposition 'unter' can only be used in the sense of 'among', if the phrase is in the plural (unter den Geschenken = among the presents).

One more word about the interlingua. It contains around 40 expressions like:

LOC UBI = place
LOC QUO = goal (locative)
LOC UNDE = point of departure
LOC QUA = path
TEMP UBI = instant
...

CAUSE, FINAL, CONCERN, etc. and has first been used in the European MT project EUROTRA, under development in the countries of the European Community. Some labels can be subspecified by UBI, QUO, UNDE, QUA under the following definition:

	−source	+ source
− goal	UBI	UNDE
+ goal	QUO	QUA

Nouns:

Let us regard the translation of the english noun 'absorptance' into the french one 'coefficient d'absorption'. Transfer has produced an IS as in Fig. 8. This must be transformed into the structure in Fig. 9.

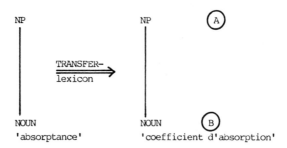

Fig. 8

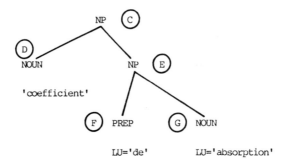

Fig. 9

We need a rule like the following:

```
conditions:      LU of B = 'noun x'
assigments:      LU of D := 'noun y' ; SYNTCLASS of E := NP;
                 LU of G := 'noun z' ; SYNTCLASS of F := PREP;
                 LU of F := 'de' ; SYNTCLASS of G := NOUN;
```

For rules of this kind we have defined macro rules that allow us to produce all structures of the same kind, and there are many. The macro rules, that carry names (here: KPDE for the above explicit rule), look like this:

```
LU = noun x
KPDE =    ⟨ noun y,noun z ⟩
```

LU = coefficient d'absorption
KPDE = 〈 coefficient,absorption 〉

LU = cone d'admission
KPDE = 〈 cone,admission 〉

LU = séquence de recette
KPDE = 〈 séquence,recette 〉

etc.

Verbs

Verbs can be disambiguated in SEDAM, TRANSFER, or SEMSYN, as demonstrated above. Disambiguation rules ought to be applied where a verb is known to be ambiguous (in TRANSFER) and where there is access to TL semantic features (in SEMSYN). The optimal solution therefore would be an integration of TRANSFER and SEMSYN which is planned for the near future (cf. 0.4). A different approach is to treat ambiguous verbs in the analysis, i.e. in SEDAM which is realized for verbs like "überschreiten". The IS may after the syntactic analysis look like the one in Fig. 10.

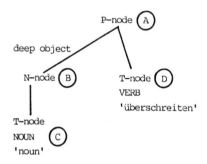

Fig. 10

Then in SEDAM the following rule will be applied:

conditions: LU of D = 'überschreiten' and
                   B is deep object of A
assignments: if SEMFEATURE of C = ABSTRACT,
                      then LU of D =: überschreiten (ABS),
                      else LU of D =: überschreiten (CON)

The transfer lexicon contains TL equivalents for both 'überschreiten (ABS)' (= surpass) and 'überschreiten (CON)' (= cross).

2.2 Depth of semantic analysis and generation

The SEDAM-/SEMSYN- rules have shown that in SUSY - apart from the PNC-classes - only very primitive semantic features are used and that a semantic interlingua is employed only for the description of the meaning of non-valency-bound prepositional NPs. Why this is so has already been discussed in the section on deep semantic cases. I should like to give some more arguments for the SUSY approach to semantics.

a. Economy of differentiation

Working with a small set of semantic features like +/- abstract, +/- animate, etc. has shown that a considerably high degree of disambiguation can be achieved with that set, if it is applied to a syntactic deep structure like that of SUSY, whereas even a very high degree of differentiation of semantic features will not lead to a substantially higher degree of disambiguation. E.g., in order to translate the English transitive verb 'to grow' into German, you can roughly differentiate the meanings "(Kartoffeln) anbauen" (grow potatoes), "(einen Geschmack) entwickeln" (grow a taste) and "sich (einen Bart) stehen lassen" (grow a beard) using the features + abstract, +plant, and + concrete. This differentiation will lead to a certain amount of correct translations, but you would not manage to generate, e.g., "Rosen züchten". If you add +/- edible, you still would not get 'Champignons züchten' right. Moreover, if you give 'chrysanthemum' the feature -edible, to get 'Chrysanthemen züchten' right, you will not be able to translate a recipy for 'chrysanthemum salad', which for some people is a delicacy. At this point you might start wondering, where this all will lead you to, e.g. to assigning a feature 'not edible for some, a delicacy for others'? Even if this will be accepted, there can never be a system of semantic features that would lead to a differentiation of the different meanings of, e.g., 'to control': beherrschen, eindämmen, bekämpfen, kontrollieren, überwachen, beaufsichtigen, prüfen, regeln, leiten, lenken, führen, verwalten, bewirtschaften, planen, steuern, regulieren, etc. We may as well refrain from developing a more specific system of semantic features, as we cannot imagine what the semantic features of the deep objects in the following examples have to look like, in order to disambiguate 'to control':

to control industry = die Industrie beherrschen
to control a fire = ein Feuer eindämmen
to control an experiment = ein Experiment kontrollieren
to control growth = das Wachstum regeln
to control consumption = den Konsum lenken
to control prices = Preise binden
to control a rocket = eine Rakete steuern.

b. Semantic description of arguments

Semantic representation systems are usually advertised using verbs like kill, hit, give, sell, break, open, etc. the arguments of which very nicely can be assigned, e.g., Fillmore's cases. But that is not the usual brand of verbs encountered when analysing and translating 'normal' texts like scientific or technical reports, bulletins, etc. Here the parser very often meets with vague or even semantically empty verbs like bestehen, (sich) ergeben, hervorgehen, betragen, aufweisen, ausstehen, gelingen, bilden, nennen, beruhen, sich einstellen, zeigen, darstellen, zulassen, sich erweisen, and erreichen. These are the verbs from a randomly chosen technical text, and there is no use of describing the arguments in terms of Agent, Patient, Recipient, etc. It does not make more sense to give the deep subject of "bestehen" (consist in) the case 'Experiencer' or whatever, than just to operate with the notion 'deep subject'. It might even lead to confusion, if NPs like 'of the proposal' (like in 'They approved of the proposal') or 'on the proposal' (like in 'They decided on the proposal') are both assigned a case like 'Patient' from which then the translation "den Vorschlag" (Sie billigten den Vorschlag) and "für den Vorschlag" (Sie entschieden sich für den Vorschlag) would have to be generated. The translation via the patient-label is much less obvious and intuitive than just translating the of-object by a direct deep object and the on-object by a für-object at the same time, when translating 'approve' by "billigen" and 'decide' by "sich entscheiden" (cf. Luckhardt/Maas (1983)). Here a constrastive approach seems to be more appropriate than a deep semantic description which would not make dictionary or generation process writing easier.

c. Semantic constraints

It has already been shown by the chrysanthemum-example that semantic restrictions may be dangerous, but we can give some more evidence. Case grammar supposedly accounts for the ungrammaticality of sentences like

* John and a hammer broke the window.
(Samlowski (1976,62)).

i.e. only noun phrases in the same case may be conjoined. That this is too strong a constraint can be shown by the following sentences:

Der Revolverheld und seine Pistole verschafften sich Achtung.
   (= Der Revolverheld verschaffte sich Achtung mit seiner P.)
   (The gunner and his pistol made themselves respected)

Kubrick und sein Film erregten Aufsehen.
   (= Kubrick erregte mit seinem Film Aufsehen)
   (Kubrick and his film caused a sensation)

It surely is necessary to introduce constraints for the disambiguation of syntactic structures like in

I saw the girl with the telescope.

but such constraints cannot be formulated easily. A semantic system of constraints, e.g., for the detection of coordinated NPs like in:

Au cours de la 49ième campagne, on à observé sur des enregistrements des fluctuations anormales dans les signaux de température et des évolutions inhabituelles du bruit acoustique.

has not been developed. The same is true for determining the function of NPs as a nominal attribute or a verbal complement like in:

...Hartsilber mit 2% Kupfer verwendet.

...Hartsilber mit Erfolg verwendet.

...Legierungsgehalt bei Abkühlung untersucht.

...Glühen bei diesen Temperaturen erfolgen muß.

...die Temperaturen bei den meisten Stählen anwenden.

A first tentative explanation of such differences is given in Luckhardt (1983), where the notion of sublanguage is used.

d. Semantic explanation

The ALPAC report of 1966 demanded a broadening of the linguistic basis for MT, especially further research into semantics was supposed to be necessary. This has been done in the last 15 years, but the results are not such that they can be used for the improvement of MT. Most semantic theories "give explanations", i.e. make language phenomena intellectually comprehensible. This is - to be true - often done in a formal manner and very often can be computerised, but not in an efficient and (linguistically) economic way. For MT it is hardly relevant

- to make inferences like
  Peter showed the book to Mary. = Mary saw the book.
- to explain why sentences sound odd:
  John and a hammer broke the window.
- to account for the complexity of sentences like
  The very beautiful young woman the man the girl loved met on a cruise ship in Maine died of cholera in 1962.

It could improve MT only then, if the conclusions drawn could effectively be used for the disambiguation of sentences, for the detection of pronoun reference, etc. Unfortunately, semantic theories have either been solitary monoliths in the linguistic landscape (with the links to the world severed) or too complex for practical use.

These are some of the reasons for the reluctance to employ a more elaborate semantic system in SUSY. They surely are controversial, but the reader should be aware of the fact that SUSY is not solely being developed to prove theories, but to create the basis for a practicable MT system. We are not saying that you can do the latter without the former, but our work is controlled by real-life texts rather than by theoretical problems. What a practicable MT system has to cope with, when doing practical work, can be shown by a number of typical MT problems that cannot be solved purely syntactically and for that a semantic solution has not been found, either:

(a.) (as mentioned above) determination of the function of NPs:

    attrib. : Er verwendet Hartsilber <u>mit 2 % Kupfer</u>.

    circ. : Er verwendet Hartsilber <u>mit Erfolg</u>.

(b.) (as mentioned above) disambiguation of word meaning, e.g. 'to control', 'control', "Leitung", etc.

(c.) detection of string compounds:

    c.1 When turning over <u>control operators</u> will switch to zero.
    c.2 Parliament submitted to the <u>Council proposals</u>.
    c.3 <u>Case ejection door</u> locks immediately.

Are the underlined constituents string compounds (like in c.3 and perhaps also in c.1 and c.2) or do they constitute different NPs (as perhaps in c.1 and c.2) or are they even part of different clauses (as perhaps in c.1) ?

(d.) (as mentioned above) coordination of NPs:

    Leitung der Versuchsdurchführung und <u>Beachtung</u> der Spezifikationen.

Which NP is the underlined NP coordinated with and how can the decision be formalised?

Most of these problems are not such that a linguist would like to turn his attention to them, as they do not seem to be 'interesting', but they are part of the everyday work of computerlinguists working in the field of MT.

3. SYNSYN – syntactic generation

3.1 Handling the syntactic data base

The 1974-version of the SUSY generation process was a phrase structure grammar, as the output of analysis was then surface-oriented. With the introduction of a transformational component in 1976 and the definition of dependency grammar as the theoretical basis of the system, it became necessary to adapt generation to the new kind of IS, in that e.g. deleted complements have been reconstructed, complex verb phrases have been transformed into simple predicates with complex decorations, and the passive constructs have been transformed into active ones.

An example for an IS that is input to SYNSYN is given in <u>Fig. 11</u>.

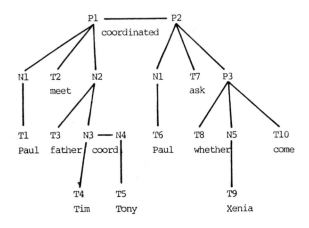

<u>Fig. 11</u>

This is, e.g., the IS for 'Paul met the father of Tim and Tony and asked, whether Xenia had come.' Here is the control structure of the processing of the above nodes:

(The article is not represented as a node in the IS, but as a feature '+definite' at the node N2. As a rule, this feature is used for the generation of the article, if this does not contradict (lexical) rules of the TL (cf. 3.4))

1. P1
2. N1,T2,N2
3. N1
4. T1
5. T2
6. N2
7. the,T3,N3
8. N4
9. the,T3
10. T4
11. T5
12. P2
13. N1,T7,P3
14. T6
15. T7
16. T8,N5,T10
17. T8
18. T9
19. T10

The list shows the sequence of all first elements of the push-down store, where nodes are kept during the process. Where there is more than one node on one level (N1,T2,N2), the nodes are sisters to one another, and it is on this level that the word order within a sentence is determined. The store or rather stack is used in the following way: P1 and P2 are put into the stack in the inverse order of their appearance, first P2, then P1:

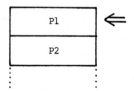

P1 is expanded:

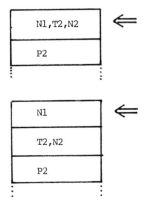

etcetera

Before P2 is expanded, all of the nodes above it in the stack have to be processed. The process ends, when the stack is empty. The process shows that the nodes are not moved around in the IS to map the SL word order onto the TL word order ('rearranged') , but the TL sentence is generated all on its own. The example may suggest that the surface form of the TL text will mimic that of the IS. This is the case only for this simple sentence and is purely accidental (cf. 3.2).

3.2 Differences of structure

When such a sequence N1,T2,N2 has been put on the stack, there still is access to the dominating node P1. This is necessary, e.g., to determine the word order in German. If P1 represents a main clause and T2 is its finite verb, the sequence may remain as it is. If P1 represents a subordinate clause, T2 is moved towards the end: N1,N2,T2. The filling of the stack elements is controlled by the external linguistic characteristic (LICA, cf. below) of the respective language. The stack elements are structured in such a way that their filling automatically produces a standardised sentence frame. LICA and the stack element structure make it possible to generate the correct word order for the different languages. Thus the following sentences are produced:

	N1	T2		N2	N3
German:	Dann	sind	die	Knoten	Brüder.

	N1	N2		T2	N3
English:	Then	the nodes		are	sisters.

	N1	T1	T2	T3	T4
English:	The stack	will	have	been	emptied

	N1	T1	T4	T3	T2
German:	Der Keller	wird	geleert	worden	sein

I should also like to demonstrate how those structures are handled that differ in SL and TL, e.g. prenominal participial modification vs. (postnominal) relative clause. If the generation algorithm comes to a structure

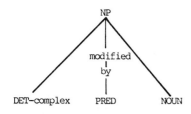

(which is the same for, e.g.:
'einige dadurch erzeugte Strukturen'
and
'einige Strukturen, die dadurch
erzeugt worden sind')

it generates for English:

DET + NOUN + PRED, e.g:
'some structures generated by the system'
or
DET + P + NOUN, e.g.:
'some generated structures'

for German:

DET + P + NOUN, e.g.:
'einige durch das System generierte Strukturen'
or
DET + NOUN + P, e.g.:
'einige Strukturen, die das System unter diesen
Bedingungen genereriert hat'

Realisation and position of P are, for each language, determined by the number of its complements, i.e. for English all augmented participial constructions are postponed, for German only the complexer ones with more than one complement.
Another example for a structural change is the change of voice. The decision active/passive may be

a. lexicon-driven: e.g., if a German verb is translated by an English verb that cannot be used in the passive
b. rule-driven: e.g., for predicates without a deep subject, but with a deep object the passive voice is chosen

c. SL-driven: there are some features of the SL surface text that are kept in the IS. One of them is voice. In order to generate TL structures that come as close to the SL structure as possible, predicates are generated in the passive, if their SL voice was passive and the TL verb may be used in the passive.

3.3 The SYNSYN process

This was a description of some abstract and concrete structures and their processing. Now I should like to give a description of the SYNSYN-process and its subprocesses.

a. Take first element from stack. Call it X.
b. Apply process SYN to X. The result is a
   sequence Y = (Y1, Y2,...,Yn).
c. Invert Y, i.e. construct Y' = (Yn, Yn-1, ..., Y2, Y1). Put the components of Y' into stack, one after the other (first = Yn, last = Y1).
d. Take first element from stack. Call it X.
e. If X is terminal, apply process TERMINALS to X and go to d.
   If X is non-terminal, goto b.
   If X is empty, SYNSYN is finished for this structure (sentence).

The process SYN is subdivided into the subprocesses shown in Fig. 12.

SYN = | COORDINATED NODES
      | O
      | COMPLEMENTS
      | O
      | SENTENCE TYPES
      | O
      | SENTENCE STRUCTURES
      | O
      | GENERATE VERBS
      | O
      | DELETE COMPLEMENTS IN COORDINATED PHRASES

Fig. 12

COORD   puts those nodes into the stack that are coordinated with the node in X

COMP   puts the dependent nodes of X into the stack and – if X is an N-node – generates its terminal and pre-terminal elements Tn

SENTYPE   decides whether the nodes in the stack are to be realised as infinitive clauses, adverbial clauses, etc.

SENSTRUC   determines the internal structure of X (e.g. order of phrases), if it is a clause

GENVERB   generates verbal phrases

DELCOORD   deletes noun phrases that have already been generated in a coordinated clause

TERMINALS   puts the terminal and pre-terminal nodes in the final order of their generation onto a file that is handed over to MORSYN.

This is a very rough representation of what is done in SYNSYN. Some linguistic and technical aspects are treated in more detail in the following paragraphs.

3.4 Linguistic aspects of generation

Syntactic constructions generated

The question as to what syntactic structures can be handled would only be relevant, if SYNSYN mapped SL-structures onto TL-structures, which it does not do. In principle, SYNSYN can handle all incoming structures, no matter how complex the IS may be. The linearisation of the IS is completely based on the TL grammar. The TL description may be considered as consisting of two elements:

- the universal grammar that contains the linguistic elements common to all TLs treated. This includes the detection of pronoun reference, the realisation of complement clauses, the default patterns for the generation of word order (subject-predicate-object, PRP-DET-ADJ-N, etc.), etc.
- the specific grammar that contains the external linguistic description specific to that TL (cf. below).

Multilinguality aspect

As has been said before, there is only one subprocess for syntactic generation for all three TLs (German, English, French) that has access to an external linguistic description of the target language. So in cases of diverging TL structures the process is informed about how to proceed, e.g.

- whether to generate future tense verb forms synthetically like in French or analytically like in German
- whether to generate verbal affixes like in German (<u>ab</u>arbeiten) or in English (grow <u>up</u>)
- whether to generate possessive relative phrases like in English (the father of whom) or in German (dessen Vater)
- how to generate the deep subject in passive clauses:

      by-phrase (English)

      par-phrase (French)

      von-phrase (German)

- how to generate the dative

      like in German: dative

      like in English: to-phrase

      like in French: à-phrase

- whether to generate the order of adverbial phrases like in German or like in English
- whether to admit just one argument or circumstantial standing in front of the predicate

(like in German):

      Er arbeitete gestern...; or

a circumstantial and an argument (like in English):

      Yesterday he worked...

etc.

Automatic derivation and composition

The subprocess SGKOMP generates compounds (for languages that have compounds). When generating German, attribute structures normally remain as they are. Some constructions, however, are transformed into compounds:

$$\text{system of translation} \neq \text{System von Übersetzung}$$
$$\Downarrow$$
$$\text{Übersetzungssystem}$$

This transformation is necessary insofar as in English-German transfer in most cases the type of article is not changed (cf. below). This leads to the formulation of the first condition for the transformation:

a) NP2 may have no article (cf. Fig. 13), where NOUN3 = NOUN2 + infix + NOUN1

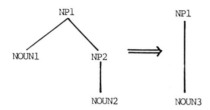

Fig. 13

Further conditions are:

b) NP2 may contain only a noun and may not have an attribute
c) for German NP2 may have the prepositions 'von' or 'für'.

If these conditions are fulfilled, the procedure goes as follows:

1. The NP1-NP2 pointer is deleted;
2. An infix is generated, following this algorithm:
2.1 The infix depends on the genitive suffix of NOUN2 and its end grapheme;
    If the genitive suffix is not zero, go to 2.2, else:
    if NOUN2 ends in -e and can have plural forms, the infix is 'n', as in:
        Hose-n-traeger
        Trasse-n-führung
    if NOUN2 ends in -s/-ß/-z, the infix is zero, as in:
        Orgasmus-schwierigkeit
    if NOUN2 does not end in -e, the infix is 's', as in:
        Hoffnung-s-schimmer
        Zivilisation-s-schaden
2.2 If the genitive suffix is not '-ses', go to 2.3;
    the infix is zero, as in:
        Geheimnis-verrat
2.3 If the genitive suffix is not -n/-en/-ns or -ens, go to 2.4;
    the infix is the genitive suffix, as in:
        Bauer-n-aufstand
        Bär-en-fänger
        Name-ns-gleichheit
2.4 The remaining genitive suffixes are -s and -es. If NOUN2 does not end in a vowel
    and the number is plural, the plural suffix is chosen as infix, as in:
        Pferd-e-stall
        Büch-er-wand
        Kleid-er-sammlung
    else: the zero suffix is chosen, as in:
        Weg-biegung
        Schrank-wand
        Auto-schlosser   (false for: Tod-es-verachtung)

The procedure is recursive so that compounds of any length may be generated. In evaluating this procedure, one should take into account three aspects:

1. The procedure is triggered by attribute constructions. Lexicalised compounds have not been taken into account.
2. The procedure is not expected to generate 100 % correct compounds. It is meant to turn 100 % wrong attribute constructions into a very high number of correct compounds. It is not meant to present a flawless linguistic model for composition, either.
3. There is no consistent formalisable description of the formation of infixes in German compounds. Differences like 'Treue-erweis' and 'Liebe-s-entzug' cannot be accounted for.

Similar tasks are fulfilled by the SNOADJ subprocess. It inspects noun phrases as to the possibility of transforming them into adjectives like 'Käse aus Bulgarien' = 'bulgarischer Käse'.

The activation of the derivational component of SNOADJ is also necessary for noun phrases the governor of which is a verb or adjective. So it is possible to derive (lexicon-driven)

> 'Hitze' from 'heiß'
> 'Dummheit' from 'dumm'
> 'Berechnung' from 'berechnen'
> 'evaluation' from 'evaluate'
> 'dumping' from 'dump'
> 'Attentat' from 'Anschlag verüben'

etc.

Automatic detection of pronoun reference

In linguistics, pronominalisation is a controversial topic that has been treated in many theoretical discussions. In MT, pragmatic solutions are required, in order to solve this problem. The subprocess SPORE represents a pragmatic solution on the basis of a preference weighting. The operational area of SPORE is the whole interface structure (cf. Fig. 14).

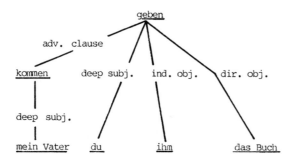

Wenn mein Vater kommt, gibst du ihm das Buch.

Fig. 14

The detection of the referent of a pronominal NP is based on the assumption that the probability of a noun phrase NP1 being the referent of a pronominal noun phrase NP2 decreases with increasing distance between NP1 and NP2. So, in the above example 'mein Vater' is the most probable referent for 'ihm'. The NPs in the sentences before that have a lower weight.

The procedure:
For every sentence, the NPs are collected and assigned a complement-specific weight. When the generation process proceeds to the next sentence, the weights of the sentences before are lowered. If the weight of an NP drops below a specific value, it is no longer regarded as a possible referent.

Collection of possible referents:
The procedure first addresses the predicate P0 dominating NP:

P0

NP

For possessive pronouns, first the dominating NP is addressed (e.g., for 'der Herr und sein Hund'). Fig. 15 shows which nodes are addressed after that.

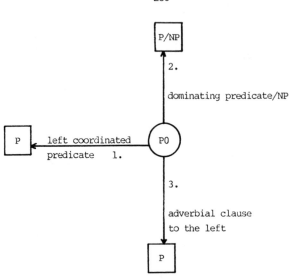

Fig. 15

All these addresses are collected and the following operations are performed on them in the given order:

For predicates:

>seek
>1. left coordinated predicate
>2. dominating predicate/NP
>3. deep subject
>4. direct objects
>5. prepositional objects
>6. adverbial adjunct

For NPs:

>seek
>1. genitive attribute
>2. prepositional attributes
>3. dominating predicate

Each of the complements stored receives a weight depending on its syntactic function. Furthermore the path to its referent is weighted. The values of the complements are logarithmicised and added for each path. The highest weight, e.g., is given to the deep subject of the left coordinated predicate, the lowest to an adverbial phrase in an adverbial clause to the left of PO. The procedure has mainly been tested, with good results, for Russian-German.

Generation of articles

The SL articles are disregarded in generation, only the values +/- definite and zero of the category 'definiteness' of each NP are taken into account. Depending on these the TL articles are generated, unless

(a) the preposition of the NP demands a certain type of article, e.g.:
   aus Furcht
   for fear
(b) the adjective of the NP demands a certain type of article, e.g.:
   der längste Tag
   eine solche Frage
(c) the noun of the NP demands a certain type of article, e.g.:
   der Rhein, die Schweiz, switzerland, Deutschland, das heutige
   Deutschland, der Umgang
(d) the NP is an apposition, e.g.:
   eine Million Blumen
   or a certain type of prepositional attribute, e.g.:
   Bedarf an Material

Standard matrix for the generation of NPs

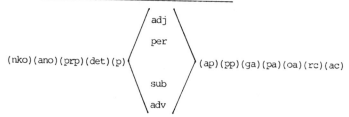

$$(nko)(ano)(prp)(det)(p) \left\langle \begin{matrix} adj \\ per \\ sub \\ adv \end{matrix} \right\rangle (ap)(pp)(ga)(pa)(oa)(rc)(ac)$$

nko = coordinate conjunction
ano = NP-modifying adverb
det = determiner (complex)
p = adjective/participle (complex)
adj = adjective (terminal)
per = pronoun
sub = noun
adv = adverb
ap = apposition
pp = postposition
ga = genitive attribute
pa = prepositional attribute
oa = other attribute
rc = relative clause
ac = attributive clause

Standard matrix for the generation of clauses

(cc)(ds1) p (dio1)(dio2)(av)(do1)(do2)(po)(go)(ds2)

cc = conjunction (complex)
ds1 = deep subject
p = predicate
dio1 = deep indirect object 1
dio2 = deep indirect object 2
av = free adjuncts
do1 = deep direct object 1
do2 = deep direct object 2
po = prepositional objects
go = genitive object
ds2 = attribute to the deep subject

Lexicon

Some general statements on dictionary making can be given (for more details, see Krebs/Luckhardt (1983)):

- the less explicit the information in the dictionary is, the more explicit the rules in the process of dictionary look-up must be, e.g. if the entry for the verb 'modify' has no information about its ending, the process must derive it automatically.
- the content of the dictionary depends on the nature of the process by that it is used. If the formation of passive is allowed, the verbs must carry information about whether they can be passivised or not. If the process includes rules for derivation, the entries must inform about what suffixes a stem can take. If the process operates on a deep syntactic structure, verb entries must contain information about the nature of the complement clauses it can take, in particular, whether it can take an infinitive clause or whether it has to be a that-clause, and what the deep subject in an infinitive clause is like.
- the creation of lexicon entries is the more time-consuming the more explicit the semantic representation is. So, for a large MT system with large dictionaries as much as possible has to be achieved by syntatic means and methods. This is one of the major aspects that distinguish MT and KI.
- the SUSY lexica are organised as a linguistic knowledge base with links between the lexica and between the entries within them.

lexical unit	information
1. (created ex nihilo)	def. article,neuter,nominative,singular

2.	
paper	noun,nominative,singular,morph.info.
3.	
(created ex nihilo)	aux.,finite,type 'to be',present tense, indicative,third person,singular
4.	
almost	fixed form
5.	
finish	verb,past participle,morph. info.

Fig. 16

4. MORSYN - morphological synthesis

The output of SYNSYN is represented as a file that contains terminal and pre-terminal nodes in the final target language order. MORSYN (which stands for morphological synthesis) has access to the generation dictionary and its morphological information. A formalised example for an input file is given in Fig. 16.

As the process is to a large extent language-independent, there is some redundant information in the output, as you do not need so much information for the generation of an english definite article. The MORSYN-process consists of a language-independent superprocess and language-dependent subprocesses for the generation of german, english, french, and Esperanto nouns, verbs, and adjectives.

5. Extensions to the system

The last remarks concern the extensibility of the system for a new language. If a new target language is to be integrated, the following steps have to be taken:

- delineation of lexicon information
- creation of a semantic lexicon, a generation lexicon, and at least one (bilingual) transfer lexicon
- setting-up of the linguistic characteristics
- adaptation of a number of language-dependent ramifications in the SYNSYN-subprocess
- writing the morphological subprocesses

This will produce a prototype version of the generation process for that language, that, of course, has to be tested and gradually stabilised.

Bibliography

Blatt, A., Luckhardt, H.-D., Truar, M. (1984). Evaluation of Linguistic Specifications LS.1 Concerning Semantic Relations. In: Eurotra-Report ETL-4-D. Commission of the European Communities. Luxembourg

Charniak, E., and Y. Wilks (eds.,1976). Computational Semantics. Amsterdam: North-Holland P.C.

Fillmore, Ch. (1981). Die Wiedereröffnung des Plädoyers für Kasus. In: J. Pleines (ed., 1981). Beiträge zum Stand der Kasustheorie. Tübingen, 13-44

Freigang, Gerhardt, Luckhardt, Maas, Thiel (1981). Investigation of Semantic Relation Labels. Eurotra-Report ET-7-D. Commission of the European Community. Luxembourg

Gerhardt, T. C. (1983). SUSY-Handbuch für semantische Disambiguierung. Dokumentation A2/3. Saarbrücken: Universität des Saarlandes: SFB 100/A2. (in preparation)

Helbig, G., Schenkel, W. (1978). Wörterbuch zur Valenz und Distribution deutscher Verben. Leipzig

Krebs, P., and H.-D. Luckhardt (1983). Das Saarbrücker Lexikonsystem. Dokumentation A2/7. Saarbrücken: Universität des Saarlandes: SFB 100/A2. (in preparation)

Luckhardt, H.-D. (1982a). SUSY - Capabilities and Range of Application. Multilingua 1-4, 213-219.

- (1982b). SATAN - Test. Beschreibung der Vorgehensweise und der Ergebnisse von Tests der deutschen Komponente des Saarbrücker automatischen Textanalysesystems SATAN. Linguistische Arbeiten des SFB 100 Neue Folge, Heft 6. Saarbrücken: Universität des Saarlandes: SFB 100.

- (1983). Erste Überlegungen zur Verwendung des Sublanguage-Konzepts in SUSY. Saarbrücken: Universität des Saarlandes: SFB 100/A2, erscheint in: Multilingua

- (1984). Eine MÜ-bezogene Valenztheorie. Saarbrücken: Universität des Saarlandes: SFB 100/A2

- (1985). SEGMENT - die praktische Anwendung einer PS-Grammatik in einem MÜ-System und ihre Relation zu GPSG und LFG. To appear in: U. Klenk (ed., 1985). Kontextfreie Syntaxen und verwandte Systeme. Linguistische Arbeiten, Tübingen: Niemeyer

- (1985a). Blackboardmodelle in der Computerlinguistik - vorgeführt am Beispiel der Analyse von Relativsätzen. Internal paper, Saarbrücken: Universität des Saarlandes: SFB 100

Luckhardt, H.-D., and H.-D. Maas (1983). SUSY - Handbuch für Transfer und Synthese. Die Erzeugung deutscher, englischer oder französischer Sätze aus SATAN - Analyseergebnissen. Linguistische Arbeiten des SFB 100 Neue Folge, Heft 7. Saarbrücken: Universität des Saarlandes: SFB 100.

Maas, H.-D. (1981). SUSY und SUSY II. Verschiedene Analysestrategien in der Maschinellen Übersetzung. Sprache und Datenverarbeitung 1-2/1981, 9-15. Saarbrücken.

Ruus, H., Spang-Hanssen, E. (1982). Argument Relations and Predicate Types for Eurotra. Eurotra-Report ET-10-DK. Commission of the European Communities. Luxembourg

Samlowski, W. (1976). Case Grammar. In: Charniak/Wilks (eds., 1976), 55-72.

Seyfert, G. (1981). Eine Wiederbelebung der Kasusgrammatik?. In: J. Pleines (1981). Beiträge zum Stand der Kasustheorie. Tübingen

SFB 100 (ed., 1980). SALEM - ein Verfahren zur automatischen Lemmatisierung. Tübingen: Niemeyer

Slocum, J. (1983). METAL - the LRC Machine Translation System. University of Texas: Linguistic Research Center

Somers, H. (1983). An Investigation into the Application of the Linguistic Theories of Valency and Case to the Automated Processing of Natural Language (with Special Reference to Machine Translation). Ph. D. thesis, University of Manchester: Centre for Computational Linguistics

Tennant, H. (1980). Syntactic Analysis in JETS. Working Paper - 26, Coord. Sc. Lab., University of Illinois, Urbana, Illinois 61801

Wahlster, W. (1982). Natürlichsprachliche Systeme. Eine Einführung in die sprachorientierte KI-Forschung. In: W. Bibel, J.H. Siekmann (ed., 1982). Künstliche Intelligenz. Frühjahrsschule Teisendorf, 203-284

Generating Japanese Text from

Conceptual Representation

Shun Ishizaki

1. INTRODUCTION

Most methods for machine generation of Japanese sentences work from intermediary representations in syntactic structures, or tree structures, especially in machine translation systems. As the first Japanese text generation program to work directly from conceptual representations,our system represents a major departure from the approach. These conceptual representations include no explicit syntactic information. Rather, the representation contains scenes that correspond to events, including input on actors, objects, time, location and relations to other events. The generator builds complete Japanese sentence structure from the representation, and then refines it.

The conceptual representations here are based on Conceptual Dependency(CD) theory [Schank 75] and Memory Organization Packets, or MOPs [Schank 80]. The event concepts we employed are not, however, limited to the so called 11 primitive actions in CD theory. MOPs are especially fruitful since one processing structure condense knowledge common to many different situations , and brings it to bear on the whole gamut.

Though CD theory and MOPs were formulated in English, MOPs are deemed particularly useful in a Japanese generator because they are independent of language. Indeed successful application of these theories to Japanese sentences would tend to corroborate their linguistic autonomy, since Japanese is radically different from English and other European languages.

This generator has several major features. First, it employs causal chains and MOPs to infer the temporal order of events in the conceptual representations. This approach is necessary in generating Japanese sentences because most clauses and sentences in Japanese newspaper articles are ordered according to time. Second, causal relations are drawn on to connect events with appropriate conjunctions. Third, the generator omits subjects in certain situations, substituting one of two case markers so that the sentences are natural. Another important aspect is that the program can generate embedded structures common in Japanese texts. This paper describes three constraints on creating embedded structures: temporal relations between events, preserving intelligibility and gaps. The process of producing common embedded structures is also described.

The conceptual representations used in this paper are based on Spanish language newspaper articles. All the stories concern to terrorism and each consists of only a few sentences. The conceptual parser[Lytinen and Schank 82] uses appropriate MOPs and causal relations among events to analyze the stories. Approximately 15 stories are parsed into conceptual representations and rendered in Japanese.

2. THE STRUCTURE OF JAPANESE LANGUAGE

2.1 WORD ORDER RULES

Basic word order in Japanese is characterised by Subject-Obect-Verb (SOV), standing in sharp contrast to the Subject-Verb-Object (SVO) of English. Some of the most prominent traits of Japanese word order are

(1) The verb is the last element in a clause.

(2) Negation is expressed by endings attached to the verb.

(3) Noun groups are usually followed by case markers which indicate subject (wa, ga), object (o, ni), place (de, ni, kara,...) and so on.

(4) Modifiers precede the words they refer to. This is true for modifying clause as well as adjectives and adverbs which modify nouns, verbs and other words.

(5) Words containing information of particular importance are often placed close to the verb.

(6) The subject usually comes at the beginning of the sentence, but may be placed anywhere before the verb.

Since it determines the structure of the sentence, the verb is the most important syntactic element as in English, though Japanese placement is at the end. The role of the verb is one reason CD theory is especially effective for Japanese.

Rule (5) indicates a great deal of flexibility regarding the position of the subject. For example, the following examples show two options:

(2-a) kyou watashi wa tokyo de eiga wo mita.
     TODAY I   TOKYO IN MOVIE   WATCHED

(2-b) kyou tokyou de eiga wo watashi wa mita.
     TODAY TOKYO IN MOVIE   I   WATCHED

The subject in (2-b) is emphasized more strongly than in (2-a). The other terms may be scrambled as well within the constraints of the features noted above.

(7) When word A modifies word B and word C modifies word D, the two modifying relations must not cross each other.

For example, word order A C B D violates rule (7), since A-B crosses C-D. A B C D and A C D B, on the other hand, are grammatical. The following noun phrase is normal:

(2-c) kareno hidoku kowareta kamera,
     HIS   BADLY BROKEN   CAMERA

with "kareno" modifying "kamera" and "hidoku" modifying "kowareta."
The word order in this phrase satisfies rule (7).

     The most important difference between Japanese and English
lies in the order of clauses, phrases, and sentences. In English,
modifiers usually follow the clauses they modify; Japanese modifiers,
however, never follow their clauses. For example,

(2-d) GUERRILLAS WEARING OLIVE-COLORED SUIT

is translated as:

(2-e) oribu-iro   no fuku wo kita   geriratachi.
     OLIVE-COLORED   SUIT   WEARING GUERRILLAS

     Subordinate clauses are never placed after their main clauses.
Clauses and sentences are generally ordered temporally in Japanese,
with goal clauses one of the few exceptions. There are, of course,
many deviations in literary expression, but this generator does not
attempt to deal with them.

2.2 CONJUNCTIVE RELATION AMONG EVENTS AND TEMPORAL ORDER

     Conjunctive relations among events in Japanese are divided
into the following two parts,

     (1) Temporal relation,
     (2) Logical relation.

     The temporal relation determines which event should come
first. Most conjunctions in Japanese newspaper stories belong to this
category, including "after," "before," "during," "lead to," "result,"
"then," and "and." In a Japanese text, this relation defines a
unvarying order for describing events to the generator.

     The logical relation describes the logical connections among
events, including "reason," "goal," and "condition." The "reason"
relation , corresponding to the conjunction BECAUSE, does not
determine the temporal order between events. For example,

(2-f) kare wa raigetsu   america e iku node,   konshu   wa isogashii.
     HE   NEXT MONTH USA   TO GO BECAUSE THIS WEEK   BUSY

     Here the time of the second event precedes the first one. But
see the next example.

(2-g) kare wa kinou   kega wo shita node,   kyou no dansu pati
     HE   YESTERDAY INJURED   BECAUSE TODAY   DANCE PARTY

     niwa denai.
     JOIN NOT

The temporal relation in (2-g) is the opposite of the one in (2-f). The logical relation for "precondition" also enters into these two examples. In these relations, the events which express reason or condition are generated first, but their temporal order cannot be determined by the logical relations.

On the other hand, the goal relation between two events dictates an unequivocal temporal ordering; that is, the goal event is generated first but the other event precedes it in the temporal order.

```
M-MO =
  CONCEPT M-MOCK-TRIAL
  ACTOR    HUM11 =
                CONCEPT TERRORIST
                ORG     OBJ3 =
                             CONCEPT TERRORIST-ORG
                             MEMBERS HUM11
                GENDER  MALE
                TYPE    GUERRILLA
                WEARING OBJO =
                             CONCEPT CLOTHING
                             TYPE    SUIT
                             COLOR   OLIVE-COLORED
  OBJECT   HUM6 =
                CONCEPT   PERSON
                NUMBER    AT-LEAST 60
                TYPE      PEASANT
  SCENE2   ACC1 =
                CONCEPT ACCUSE
                OBJECT  HUM6
                BAD-ACT UND1
                ACTOR   HUM11
                IR-FROM UND1
  SCENE4   EXEO =
                CONCEPT EXECUTE
                ACTOR   HUM11
                PLACE   LOCO =
                             CONCEPT CITY
                             NAME    SAN PEDRO PERULAPAN
                OBJECT  HUM6
                IR-FROM UND1
  SCENE1   UND1 =
                CONCEPT UNDESIRABLE-ASSISTANCE
                JUDGER  HUM11
                OBJECT  OBJ5 =
                             CONCEPT GOVERNMENT
                ACTOR   HUM6
  SCENE3   TRYO =
                CONCEPT TRY
                OBJECT  HUM6
                ACTOR   HUM11
```

Fig.1 Conceptual Representation for Story 1.

3. CONCEPTUAL REPRESENTATION

The Japanese generator starts from the conceptual representations that the parser extracts from Spanish newspaper stories. For example, Fig.1 shows a conceptual representation for story 1, while the input is shown in Fig.2, a translation from the Spanish. The parsing system is based on the IPP[Lebowitz 80], which extracts only the most salient information; the detailed data included in Fig.2 are, therefore, abbreviated in the extracted representation in Fig.1. Fig.3 shows Japanese sentences derived from the representation by the generator along with their English equivalents.

At least 60 peasants were executed by a firing squad of men wearing olive-colored uniforms in San Pedro Perulapan about 25 kilometers east of San Salvador, authorities there said. According to the same sources, the victims were tried and then executed in the town plaza by guerrillas who accused them of collaborating with the government.

Fig.2 Input Sentences for Story 1.

sukunakutomo 60 nin no noumintachi ga seifu ni   kyoryokushita
AT-LEAST   60   PEASANTS   GOVERNMENT COLLABORATED

node,   terososhiki   ni zokusu oribuiro no   fuku wo kita
BECAUSE TERRORIST-ORG   BELONG OLIVE-COLORED SUIT   WEARING

geriratachi   wa   sono   noumintachi   wo   kokuhatsushite,
GUERRILLAS   THE   PEASANTS   ACCUSED

saiban-ni-kaketa.   sorekara,   sono geriratachi   wa
TRIED   THEN   THE   GUERRILLAS

san-pedoro-perurapan   toiu   machi de sono noumintachi o
SAN PEDRO PERULAPAN   CITY   THE PEASANTS

shokeishita.
EXECUTED.

Fig.3 Generated Japaneses Text and Its
      English Equivalent.

少なくとも６０人の農民たちが
政府に協力したので，テロ組織に
属すオリーブ色の服を着た
ゲリラたちはその農民たちを
告発して，裁判にかけた．
それから，そのゲリラたちは
サン　ペドロ　ペルラパン
という町でその農民たちを
処刑した．

Fig.4 Generated Japanese in Japanese Orthography.

The information in Fig.1 is processed as follows. The parser identifies the MOP concept as MOCK-TRIAL in its concept dictionary. The MOP actor is labeled HUM11 under the concept TERRORIST. The MOP object is labeled HUM6 who number at least 60, and its type peasant. Four scenes follow the object, UND1, ACC1, TRY0 and EXE0, each with a concept, actor, object and other properties. These concepts represent events usually expressed with verbs. The IR-FROM(Initiate Reasoning FROM) in SCENE4 is a causal relation indicating UND1 let to the event EXE0.

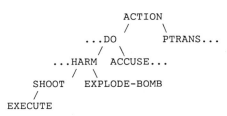

```
                        ACTION
                       /      \
               ...DO         PTRANS...
                  /   \
        ...HARM   ACCUSE...
            /   \
      SHOOT   EXPLODE-BOMB
        /
  EXECUTE
```

Fig.5 Event Concept Structure.

There are three kinds of concepts: event,noun,and slot name. We will treat event concepts first in this triad. As shown in Fig.5, these concepts have a tree structure.

The events used here are not restricted to the primitives in CD theory nor translated into these categories. Rather this system is a part of a machine translation system that seeks to dissect texts into concepts expressed in conceptual representations, then translate them into the target language. The parsing program in the MT system uses the main verbs of the input in their infinitive forms as concepts in its conceptual representations.

When a concept in the conceptual representations has no corresponding verb in the target language (Japanese), the concept is broken down into more primitive forms. Almost all concepts can be reduced to primitives in CD theory, which can be expressed in the target language. This system does not,however, perform such dissection at this stage because the input concepts used here have Japanese equivalents.

The generator checks a concept obtained from the representation to ascertain whether its antecedents include an "action" by ascending the tree structure.

The second in our triad, noun concepts have the following tree structure. The generator can trace the structure easily to find information indicating that a terrorist is a kind of PERSON and has the same properties as those of PERSON.

Our last kind of concept covers slot names in the conceptual representation, including ACTOR, OBJECT, IR-FROM, and so on.

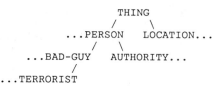

```
                    THING
                   /     \
          ...PERSON     LOCATION...
             /   \
    ...BAD-GUY   AUTHORITY...
          /
    ...TERRORIST
```

Fig.6 Noun Concept Structure.

The generator also has a Japanese dictionary with entries for
verbs, nouns and other parts of speech that correspond to those in the
conceptual structures shown in Figs. 5 and 6. For example,


```
(noumin          NOUN
    PRINT-FORM   ^NG@L1^O
    DEF          PEASANT).
```

The values for PRINT-FORM show JIS-CODE of Chinese characters. A term
in the conceptual representation is specified as a value for DEF.

The expression for a verb is, for example,


```
(yukaisuru       VERB
    PRINT-FORM   (^NM62}^O suru)
    *INFL        SAHEN
    DEF          KIDNAP),
```

where the value for PRINT-FORM means that "yukai" is expressed in
Chinese characters and "suru" in hiragana, an ending that shows the
inflection of the verb. The value for the slot "*INFL" is either 5
dan, shimo 1 dan, kami 1 dan, sahen or kahen.

Modifiers for verbs are followed by case markers. Though each
modifier has a case marker such as (TIME ni), (OBJECT o), certain
verbs indicate special case markers for modifiers. For example, the
case marker "de" usually accompanies PLACE, but the verb "sumu,"
corresponding to "live" in English, carries the expression "ni." Such
information is added as a slot, and its value is included in the entry
for "sumu".

In Japanese, proper names for foreign places and people are
expressed in the katakana syllabary. Different from hiragana and
Chinese characters, this system serves as a kind of roman alphabet for
common expressions and foreign loan words.

4. GENERATION OF JAPANESE SENTENCES

One of the main goals of this generator is to use MOPs and
causal chains to infer the temporal order of events. The temporal
order is important because most clauses and sentences are ordered
temporally in Japanese. An event is defined so that it corresponds to

a clause or a sentence containing one verb. The parser assigns a
conceptual representation and its main node to the generator. The
generator first extracts all the events related to the main node.
Then, the events are sorted temporally and appropriate conjunctions
are inserted between them. For example, in Story 1,

(UND1 node, ACC1, TRY0. sorekara EXE0.)

is the whole structure to be generated since all the events are
ordered temporally and two Japanese conjunctions are inserted there.
The IR-FROM in SCENE2 in Fig.1 corresponds to the way that UND1 causes
ACC1. This information is mapped into the Japanese structure mentioned
above, "UND1 node ACC1". The "node" refers to the "reason" relation
here, while the relation between ACC1 and TRY0 hinges on the temporal
order of the two events. This is a default relation in the MOP
representation. In Japanese expression, a conjunction is never used
twice in succession. Such cases substitute another conjunction with
almost the same meaning and a period is placed before the second
conjunction, as shown above.

The generator starts to translate the event on the left and
continues to the next one on the right. A process ends only when the
list is NIL. For each event, it generates a subject, an object(s), and
a modifier(s) for the event and its verb. During this operation, any
node corresponding to a noun phrase generates a modifier(s) for the
noun and the noun itself. These algorithms move from depth first. The
details are spelled out below.

4.1 TEMPORAL ORDERING OF EVENTS USING MOPS

4.1.1 ORDERING WITH SCENES IN MOPS

All events are interrelated by causal chains and scene
relations in MOPs. The causal chain, indicated by such connections as
LEAD-TO, REASON, GOAL, and PRECONDITIONS , specifies the temporal
order between two events, while the scene relation defines the
temporal order vis-a-vis other scenes in the MOP. Thus the scene
relation in Fig.1 aligns SCENE1, SCENE2, SCENE3, etc. in a temporal
order. Derived from general principles(i.e., M-MOCK-TRIAL) , this
order is repeated in the indexes of the scenes. When certain events
are not included in the scenes, they are linked to the scenes with
causal relations. When two events occurred simultaneously or in
succession and one of them corresponds to a scene, such relations as
simultaneity and succession are employed in the same way as causal
ones.

```
M-POLICE-CAPTURE

        ACTOR    AUTHORITY
        OBJECT   BAD-GUY
        SCENE1   (CRIME ((ACTOR . OBJECT) (IR . SCENE2)))
        SCENE2   (POLICE-SEARCH ((ACTOR . ACTOR) (OBJECT . OBJECT)
                                (LEAD-TO . SCENE3)))
        SCENE3   (ARREST ((ACTOR . ACTOR) (OBJECT . OBJECT)))
        GEN-MOP  (M-PUNISH)
```

Fig.7 MOP Representation for M-Police-Capture.

In the following MOP, M-POLICE-CAPTURE, SCENE1 is a

description of a crime, leading to SCENE2, POLICE-SEARCH. As a result of this scene, AUTHORITY will arrest BAD-GUY in SCENE3. The events will be ordered temporally using these scene numbers if the ACTORs and OBJECTs satisfy the conditions for each scene: the actor in SCENE1 must be the OBJECT(a bad-guy), and the actor in SCENE2 must be the ACTOR(an authority).

4.1.2 ORDERING WITH CAUSAL RELATIONS AND MOPS

The parser extracts causal relations among events in stories when some of the events cannot be expressed as scenes in MOPs. The causal relations include the temporal relations as well as the logical connections described in 2.2. Both the relations determine the order for generating events according to the structure of the generator. Causal relations such as LEAD-TO, RESULT, REASON, GOAL, DURING, and CONDITION , specify the generating order of the two events in ordinary Japanese sentences. While Japanese has, of course, ways to describe causal relations in other sequences, in this order the focus of the sentence is on the causal relation, as shown below in a corresponding English sentence. Temporal relations are also obtained separately from these causal links, except REASON and CONDITION.

"The reason he became rich is that he worked so hard."

There are certain cases where the temporal order cannot be determined from the parser's analysis. For example, in Story 3, the following three events are contained in STORY3, shown in Fig.8.

KIL2 : A POLICEMAN KILLED A CRIMINAL.
TRA0 : A POLICEMAN TRANSPORTED A CRIMINAL.
ESC1 : A CRIMINAL TRIED TO ESCAPE.

The input story shown in Fig.8 has a structure such as,

KIL2 during TRA0. KIL2 when ESC1.

A convict, Roger Fidel Morales Gonzales was killed by the patrolman who was driving him here from Tierra Azul. The convict tried to escape by jumping from the vehicle, but when he did the patrolman shot him fatally according to a responsible police source.

Fig.8 Story 3 Input in English.

The parser gives the following temporal orders in its conceptual representation,

TRA0-->KIL2 and ESC1-->KIL2.

The temporal relation between TRA0 and ESC1 is not clear here since the generator has to infer their connection by using MOPs and information in the conceptual representation to construct Japanese sentences. If the parser received precise information --- that the escape was from "the vehicle" and "the vehicle" was an instrument for the transporting criminal--- then TRA0 --> ESC1 would appear in the conceptual representation. In this sense, necessary functions which should be included in the generation depend on the completeness of the parser.

Information on locations is used as a clue for inference when either of the events has a concept of PTRANS (position transition). If the location where ESC1 occurred is confirmed as the destination or as a transition point after TRA0, then the generator can infer that ESC1 occurred during or after TRA0. For example, if the input said that ESC1 took place "here," the conclusion would be that ESC1 occurred after TRA0. There is, however, no such information in the conceptual representation of Story 3, and, consequently, the search fails.

The generator next considers the CONTROL and DISABLE-CONTROL relations, because CONTROL is the precondition for transport-criminal. The concept of TRA0, TRANSPORT-CRIMINAL has the following template described in the dictionary of concepts which both the parser and generator employ:

```
TEMPLATE    ACTOR         AUTHORITY
            OBJECT        BAD-GUY
            PRECONDITION (CONTROL ACTOR OBJECT).
```

This template indicates that authorities keep bad-guys under control during transportation. On the other hand, ESCAPE is the ESC1 concept, one step below DISABLE-CONT described in the event concept structure. ESCAPE satisfies, therefore, the properties of DISABLE-CONT since a concept must conform to the properties of higher concepts. At this stage, ESC1 can follow TRA0 in the concept domain. The generator has to check the correspondence between ACTOR of TRA0 and OBJECT of ESC1 as well as OBJECT of TRA0 and ACTOR of ESC1. If these checks are successful, the generator concludes that the temporal order of the events should be

TRA0 --> ESC1.

The Japanese sentence structure for Story 3 thus becomes

(TRA0 toki, ESC1 node, KIL2).

The output Japanese sentences are shown in Fig.9.

keikan ga tiera-azuru toiu machi kara hanzaisha no roja-fideru-
POLICEMAN TIERRA AZUL   CITY   CRIMINAL   ROGER FIDEL

moraresu-gonzaresu wo gosoushita toki, sono hanzaisha ga
MORALES GONZALES   TRANSPORTED WHEN, THE CRIMINAL

nigeyoutoshita node,   keikan wa sono hanzaisha wo koroshita.
TRIED TO ESCAPE BECAUSE POLICEMAN THE CRIMINAL   KILLED.

Fig.9 Story 3 Output in Japanese with its English
        Equivalent.

警官がティエラ　アズル
という町から車で犯罪者の
ロジャ　フィデル
マラレス　ゴンザレスを
護送したとき，その犯罪者がその
車から逃げようとしたので，
その警官はその犯罪者を殺した．

Fig.10 Story 3 Output in Japanese Orthography.

4.2 EVENT GENERATION

An event is generated by the following functions:

(GEN-SUBJECT)
(GEN-VERB-MODIFIERS)
(GEN-VERB).

(GEN-SUBJECT) picks an ACTOR slot from the event. The function chooses an OBJECT slot, expressing the event in a passive form when the ACTOR slot is not filled. This sequence of these functions is usually employed for Japanese. As shown in section 2.1, the subject may be placed anywhere before the verb, but the position of the subject usually depends on discourse factors such as focus or context. Since the generator does not treat such discourse problems at this stage, the standard sequence is generally employed.

While the case marker "wa" usually follows the subject in Japanese, the "ga" marker is also frequently used. The difference between them is so subtle and semantic that it is not easy to treat the distinction precisely. In general, however, we can say that "ga" is used for subjects in subordinate clauses which express time, reason, or goal while "wa" is typically used in main clauses. This approximation is incorporated in this generator. For example, in Story 1, UND1 is a subordinate clause and its main clause is TRY0. The subject case marker in UND1 is specified as "ga," shown in Fig.3.

(GEN-VERB-MODIFIERS) generates OBJECT and other modifiers for the verb. It has the following standard pairs of properties and case markers:

((TIME ni) (PLACE de) (FROM kara) (TO e) (INST de) (OBJECT o))

The object slot is omitted when a global parameter for voice information shows that the sentence should be expressed in the passive voice, information that comes from (GEN-SUBJECT). The verb modifiers are generated in this order with a case marker specified according to the verb's entry in the Japanese dictionary when a property calls for other types of case markers, as shown in section 3.

(GEN-VERB) generates a verb that is inflected according to the tense and the mode of the event. The tense inflections of the verbs are assigned in line with their endings. Moreover, verbs with homonyms are distinguished by their slot values for DEF and for *INFL. These homonyms can be distinguished in speech by their stress and inflection in Japanese.

4.3 NOUN PHRASE GENERATION

A noun phrase is generated by the following functions when the noun is processed for the first time,

        (GEN-NOUN-MODIFIERS)
        (GEN-NOUN),

Note: modifiers always precede the modified word or clause in Japanese (rule (4) above). The second time a noun is needed, it is generated by

        (GEN-ANAPHORA).

For example, in

        (HUMO   TYPE   CRIMINAL
                 NAME   FIDEL-GONZALES
                 CONCEPT   BAD-GUY),

the order of the translated noun phrase is

        hanzaisha no fideru-gonzaresu,
        CRIMINAL   FIDEL GONZALES

where the case marker "no" follows TYPE slot fillers and plays a simple modification rule. When HUMO is processed the next time, (GEN-ANAPHORA) is used, and the function generates THE CRIMINAL instead of CRIMINAL FIDEL GONZALES as shown in Fig.8. In English, the pronoun "he" would usually be generated, but in Japanese, especially in newspapers, personal pronouns are rarely used since there is a tendency to refer to the person specifically or indirectly by contrast.

The order of modifier generation for a noun is specified so that the generated Japanese noun phrases are natural. A practical example of the order is MONTH DAY RESIDENCE POSSESSION ... TYPE NUMBER AGE NAME STATUS. Modifiers not specified here are generated according to the order in the node representation and precede the modifiers above.

In noun phrase generation, concepts involved in the phrases below are usually generated last when they are not omitted. For example, the generator processes:

        (HUM17   NUMBER   7
                 PLURAL   T
                 CONCEPT PERSON)

to (7 nin no hitotachi), where "nin" is a unit for person and "hitotachi" corresponds to the PERSON concept. Most Japanese count nouns have particular units. In Story 1,

        (LOCO   NAME   (SAN PEDRO PERULAPAN)
                 CONCEPT   CITY)

is translated as

```
(san-pedoro-perurapan toiu machi).
SAN PEDRO   PERULAPAN      CITY
```

These concepts finish noun phrase generation. In the case of famous cities like Paris, however, the concept city is not generated since it would be redundant.

4.4 ELLIPSIS

Subjects in main clauses are usually omitted in Japanese when their subordinate clauses have the same subjects. For example, the whole structure of Story 1 is defined by the generator as

(UND1 node, ACC1, TRY0. sorekara EXE0)

Since the actor of the main clause (TRY0) and subordinate clause (ACC1) are both HUM11, the subject in TRY0 should be deleted in Japanese.

In Story 1, the object in event ACC1 is also the same as that in TRY0, so the subject and object are omitted in TRY0 (see Fig.3). If the two events have no common subject, an object is not omitted.

With ellipsis quite common in Japanese texts, a corresponding procedure is essential in the generator. The major consideration is that all actors, objects, and so on have to be specified--- i.e., anaphors must be resolved--- in order to carry out such ellipsis.

4.5 Example of the Generation Process

The generation algorithm is described in this section by using Story 1 as an example. We will start the generation from Fig.1. There are a top node M-M0 and four scenes, ACC1, EXE0, UND1 and TRY0, which have actors, objects and other slots. In Fig.11(a), the generator extracts all the scenes and the top node from the conceptual representation (Fig.1) obtained by the parser.

NODEs in Fig.11(a) refer to node names and GPs indicate that the NODEs are event types. JTs show Japanese words corresponding to the concepts of the nodes. ACs and OBs are actors and objects of the nodes, respectively.

In the next stage, Fig.11(b), a simple temporal relation is represented by "THEN," which means that the first event, for example ACC1, occurred, "THEN" the second event, TRY0. The number attached to the scenes usually indicates their temporal order. When there is no semantic relations between two scenes, the succeeding scenes are connected with "THEN". There are two "THEN" relations in Story 1, as shown in Fig.11(b).

In Fig.11(c), all the semantic relations are standardized, with dual relations such as R(Reason) and IR-FROM consolidated into a single relation indicating that the first event preceded the second, as in Fig.11(c).

Fig.11(d) shows redundant relations removed from list (c) if they exist. For example, (UND1 EXE0 R) signifies that UND1 is the reason for EXE0, but is divided into the three relations shown above in (c). Since relation R is also included in one of the other connections, (UND1 EXE0 R) is deleted from (c).

(a) *All the events in this story are listed*
        NODE=ACC1 GP=(GEN-EVENT) JT=告発する AC=HUM11 OB=HUM6
        NODE=TRY0 GP=(GEN-EVENT) JT=裁判にかける AC=HUM11 OB=HUM6
        NODE=EXE0 GP=(GEN-EVENT) JT=処刑する AC=HUM11 OB=HUM6
        NODE=UND1 GP=(GEN-EVENT) JT=協力する AC=HUM6 OB=OBJ5
        NODE=M-M0 GP=(GEN-EVENT) JT=NIL AC=HUM11 OB=HUM6

(b) *New relations are created with MOPs*
        ((ACC1 TRY0 THEN) (TRY0 EXE0 THEN))

(c) *All the relations are standardized by rules*
        (UND1 ACC1 R)
        (ACC1 TRY0 THEN)
        (TRY0 EXE0 THEN)
        (UND1 EXE0 R)

(d) *The relation (UND1 EXE0 R) is removed because a more precise
    relation exists*

(e) *The relations are sorted as follows*
        (UND1 ACC1 R)
        (ACC1 TRY0 THEN)
        (TRY0 EXE0 THEN)

(f) *Relations of the following pairs are inferred*   NIL

(g) *Events are connected with relational words*
        UND1 (node ",")   ACC1 R
        ACC1 (",")   TRY0 THEN
        TRY0 ("." sorekara ",") EXE0 THEN

(h) *Subject case marker 'ga' is specified*
        (UND1 ga)

(i) *The verb is inflected as follows*
        (ACC1 *RENYOU te)

(j) *The following subject is eliminated*
        (TRY0 OMIT)

(k) *The following object is eliminated*
        (TRY0 OMIT)

(i) *The whole structure is determined as follows*
        (UND1 node "," ACC1 "," TRY0 "." sorekara "," EXE0 ".")

    Fig.11 The Generation Process:Deriving the Japanese Text
           Structure from Conceptual Representation.

    In Fig.11(e), we have the relation obtained until (d) is sorted to arrange them temporally. If the generator finds any relations which it cannot sort (e), they are ordered temporally according to the methods described in section 4. (Story 3 in section 4.1.2 is an example) In this story, however, there is no such relation and the generator's response is NIL, as in Fig.11(f).

In Fig.11(g), each relation is rendered in appropriate Japanese conjunctions. There is no conjunction in the second relation in (g) because the next link has the same semantic relation, "THEN." It is convenient to omit the conjunction for the first "THEN," ending the event's verb with a special inflection, as shown in (i).

The generator uses case markers "wa" or "ga" for ACTOR slots, drawing on the rule in section 4.2 which dictates that the ACTOR slot in UND1 should be followed by "ga" in this example, as in Fig.11(h).

Fig.11(i) shows the special verb inflection in ACC1. In Japanese, such a conjunction is often used for conjunctions with simple meanings between two events.

Ellipsis in this example is demonstrated in Fig.11(j) and (k), described in section 4.4. The resulting Japanese sentence structure is obtained from the list in Fig.11(i).

We will now turn to the generation process. Japanese sentence generation from the text structure obtained in Fig.11 is shown in Fig.12. The generator has two stacks to store the necessary information. The first stack registers the list that will be generated in Japanese, labelled Phrase Stream in Fig.12. The other stack registers the context. The current context is the element farthest to the left in the stack; when the system finds "pop" in the Phrase Stream, this element is removed from Context and succeeded by the next one.

First, the list in Fig.11(i) is stored in the Phrase Stream, while and the current context is unoccupied. The furthest to the left element in the Phrase Stream is UND1, an event concept. UND1 is then stacked in the Context and "(GEN-EVENT) pop", defining an event node and replacing UND1 in the Phrase Stream.

GEN-EVENT has three functions as shown in section 4.2 and listed in Fig.12(b). GEN-SUBJECT, the first element in the Phrase Stream, works under the context UND1, indicating that the function GEN-SUBJECT should pick a subject from UND1. The function also extracts a case marker based on the rule described in section 4.2, "ga" in this example. The final output of this function is, then, "HUM6 ga," as shown in Fig.12(c).

With the thing node HUM6 on the left in the Phrase Stream, ("GEN-THING" pop) replaces HUM6 in the Phrase Stream and HUM6 is stacked as the current context. GEN-THING is then replaced by the two functions described in section 4.3, as in Fig.12(e).

In Fig.12(f), "AT-LEAST" is the element furthest to the left in the Phrase Stream and is translated directly as "sukunakutomo." In this case, "directly" means that the concept "AT-LEAST" equal to the Japanese word. When there is no such one-to-one correspondence, the generator searches out any concept with a corresponding Japanese word included in higher concepts in the event concept structure, as shown in Fig.5. For example, the concept "UNDESIRABLE-ASSISTANCE" in Fig.1 has no Japanese equivalent but comes under the higher concept "ASSISTANCE," or "kyoryokusuru" in Japanese. This example may be misleading, however, since resorting to a higher concept generally sacrifices some information in the original concept. To avoid these cases, the concept-to-Japanese dictionary needs to be enriched.

Fig.12(g) is obtained using coded information to move from the Roman alphabet to the Japanese orthography in the Japanese dictionary. The Japanese writing system is registered in the stack *SENTENCE* in Fig.12(h). With the whole Japanese lexicon stacked here, it is the source of completed sentence at the end of generation. Fig.4 is, then, obtained after these processes described above in *SENTENCE* are completed.

This generation process is based on the Rod McGuire's structure for generating English syntax. [McGuire]

(a) Phrase Stream: ((GEN-EVENT) POP node "," ACC1 "," TRY0 "."
                 sorekara "," EXE0 ".")
    Context: (UND1)

(b) Phrase Stream: (((GEN-SUBJECT) (GEN-VERB-MODIFIERS) (GEN-VERB)
                 POP node "," ACC1 "," TRY0 "." sorekara ","
                 EXE0 ".")
    Context: (UND1)

(c) Phrase Stream: ((HUM6 ga) (GEN-VERB-MODIFIERS) (GEN-VERB) POP
                 node "," ACC1 "," TRY0 "." sorekara "," EXE0
                 ".")
    Context: (UND1)

(d) Phrase Stream: (((GEN-THING) POP (ga) (GEN-VERB-MODIFIERS)
                 (GEN-VERB) POP node "," ACC1 "," TRY0 "."
                 sorekara "," EXE0 ".")
    Context: (HUM6 UND1)

(e) Phrase Stream: ((GEN-NOUN-MODIFIERS) (GEN-NOUN)) (ga)
                 (GEN-VERB-MODIFIERS) (GEN-VERB) POP node ","
                 ACC1 "," TRY0 "." sorekara "," EXE0 ".")
    Context: (HUM6 UND1)

(f) Phrase Stream: ((AT-LEAST 60 (nin no)) (GEN-NOUN)) (ga)
                 (GEN-VERB-MODIFIERS) (GEN-VERB) POP node ","
                 ACC1 "," TRY0 "." sorekara "," EXE0 ".")
    Context: (HUM6 UND1)

                 DIR-TR ORIGINAL-WORD AT-LEAST
                        JAPANESE WORD=sukunakutomo

(g) ** GEN ** 少なくとも

(h) ** SENTENCE **=

        少なくとも

Fig.12 The Generation Process: From the Japanese Text
        Structure to Japanese Sentences.

5. GENERATION OF EMBEDDED JAPANESE TEXTS

In English, embedded texts refer here to those sentences that include relative clauses with relative pronouns or relative adverbs. In Japanese, this same type of sentences is also typical though relative pronouns or adverbs are always omitted. The subordinate clauses, connected to the main clauses with conjunctions, differ from their embedded counterparts, which are linked to the principal clauses with relative pronouns or adverbs in English.

Embedded texts in the generation serve to clarify the focus of the text and to simplify the sentence structure. When Japanese texts consist of several events, they generally focus on the event in the final position. Generation of the most important events follows production of events describing preconditions or explanations.

In Japanese, the clause order is determined under certain constraints so even with an embedded structure, the primary event remains in the same place, a tract that tends to strengthen the emphasis.

Another effect of the embedded structure is to reduce the volume of the text and eliminate redundancy. Ideally, at least, the embedded sentences are simpler and easier to understand than the original texts.

5.1 TEMPORAL RELATION AMONG EVENTS IN EMBEDDED SENTENCES

Subordinate clauses are always placed before the main clause in Japanese. As noted in section 2.2, there are two types of subordinate clauses in Japanese. Since the temporal relation predominates in newspaper articles, the subordinate clause is in the past tense relative to the main clause.

For example, if the following sentence is embedded,

(5-a)   hanzaisha ga nigeyou to shita node   , keikan   wa sono
        CONVICT   ESCAPE TRIED TO BECAUSE POLICEMAN   THE

        hanzaisha wo koroshita,
        CONVICT   KILLED

their tenses are arranged in temporal order. With the focus on KILL in this sentence, (5-a) produces the following type of embedded sentence:

(5-b)   keikan wa   nigeyou to shita hanzaisha wo koroshita.
        THE POLICEMAN ESCAPE TRIED TO CONVICT   KILLED

With the temporal order of the two events, ESCAPE and KILL, the same as in (5-a), the focus of this sentence is also on KILL. If this ordering principle is neglected, an irregular structure arises:

(5-c)* keikan ga   koroshita hanzaisha wa nigeyou to shita.
        THE POLICEMAN KILLED   CONVICT   ESCAPE TRIED TO

To correct this defective sentence, the tense of TRY must be in the past progressive, as follows:

(5-d)   keikan ga   koroshita hanzaisha wa nigeyou to shiteita.
        THE POLICEMAN KILLED   CONVICT   ESCAPE WAS TRYING TO

Here the focus is on ESCAPE, but this sentence seems strange when it
is generated in isolation. This kind of tense modification should,
therefore, be avoided when the focus is not specified explicitly in
the conceptual representations. That is, (5-b) is preferred to (5-d)
in such cases. This kind of focus analysis problem is one which
parsers should resolve and integrate into their analysis systems in
the near future.

5.2 PRESERVING INTELLIGIBILITY OF RELATIONS BETWEEN CLAUSES

The embedding procedure has the side effect of eliminating
conjunctions, e.g., "because," "as," "if," "though," and "so that."
Without such conjunctions, the semantic relations between clauses are
not stated explicitly.   It is necessary, therefore, to confirm that
embedding procedure maintains a clear semantic relation between
clauses. The criterion is whether the links can be inferred easily
from description of each event. If the relation becomes ambiguous, the
clauses should not be embedded.   While it is difficult to draw up
complete rules for the criterion, the following examples are
suggestive.

(5-e) The police are searching for a man who kidnapped and killed a
      girl.

(5-f) The police are searching for a man because he kidnapped and
      killed a girl.

Two events are connected with the conjunction "because" in (5-f), but
in (5-e) the "because" relation must be inferred since there is no
explicit link. In this case, "because" means that the second event,
KIDNAPPING and KILLING , has led to the first event, SEARCHING. We
easily infer that committing a crime can justify a police search, so
the conjunction in such a context can be eliminated without confusion.

5.3 GAP CONSTRAINTS

A word is called a gap if it connects the main and embedded
subordinate clauses. For example, "girl" in the following sentence is
a gap.

(5-h) John saw a girl who had a red book.

A few criteria defining a concept as a gap are proposed.
These are a part of the conditions for building a sentence structure
from the conceptual representation.

(5-i) The guerrillas executed the peasants who collaborated with the
      government which had arrested some of them.

(5-i') geriratachi   wa, karera no uchi no nanninka wo taihoshita
       THE GUERRILLAS   THEM   OF   SOME   ARRESTED

```
seifu          ni   kyouryokushita noumintachi wo  shokeishita.
THE GOVERNMENT WITH COLLABORATED   THE PEASANT    EXECUTED
```

The last word in (5-i), "them", refers to the guerrillas. In (5-i) and (5-i'), these two sentences correspond in their meaning. Both have a type of double embedded structure; that is one sentence includes two relative clauses with one embedded in the other. Such a structure is too complicated in Japanese and should be avoided in generation. The first constraint is, then,

> (1) a clause should not be embedded into an embedded clause.

Events have standard components such as

(5-j) EVENT --> ACTOR TIME PLACE OBJECT VERB,

with the components ordered for Japanese. TIME, PLACE and OBJECT are optional. OBJECT is necessary for transitive verbs but not for intransitive.

Though each component can have modifiers, the sentence becomes too complicated if a gap occurs in the modifiers and an embedded clause modifies the word, as shown below. The next constraint is, then,

> (2) a gap should be one of the concepts that correspond to the words included on the right side of (5-j) or a concept that modifies the verb directly.

This rule proves particularly useful when the generator produces sentences from a node including considerable information. When it is not obvious whether such a node should generate one sentence or more the number of the sentences can be determined with this rule.

(5-k) The convict killed a patrolman this morning wearing a pair of glasses which he bought yesterday.

(5-k') sono hanzaisha wa kinou   katta   megane   wo kakete
       THE CONVICT   YESTERDAY BOUGHT A PAIR OF GLASSES   WEARING

       keikan wo korosita.
       PATROLMAN KILLED

In this example, the rule dictates that the event, "the patrolman bought a pair of glasses yesterday," would be generated as an independent sentence.

The subject of a main clause is usually eliminated when it is also the subject of the subordinate clause. Such deletion makes the sentence style sufficiently simple that embedding the subordinate clause is not necessary.

> (3) If the principal and the subordinate clauses have the same subject, then the subject should not be a gap.

5.4 PROCEDURE FOR EMBEDDED SENTENCE GENERATION

5.4.1 THE PROCEDURE

      We will use an example to explain the procedure. Four events are included in STORY1, as shown in Fig.1;

      UND1 : UNDESIRABLE-ASSISTANCE
      ACC1 : ACCUSE
      TRY0 : TRY
      EXE0 : EXECUTE.

These events are connected with the following three semantic relations;

      (UND1 ACC1 REASON)
      (ACC1 TRY0 THEN)
      (TRY0 EXE0 THEN),

with UND1 the reason for ACC1 and ACC1, TRY0, and EXE0 occurring in succession.

      UND1 satisfies the temporal constraint; i.e., ACC1 happened after UND1, with REASON defining the temporal order of (UND1 ACC1). The intelligibility constraint on UND1 and ACC1 is also satisfied, since the guerrillas' accusation can be inferred from the peasants' collaboration with the government. With the guerrillas and the government opposed, the former will accuse the peasants who collaborated with the government. Rules for such an inference are stored in the concept dictionary.

      HUM6, the peasants, are the actors in UND1 and the objects of ACC1. The three constraints in 5.3 are checked as follows: (1)ACC1 is not an embedded clause; (2)HUM6 fills the ACC1 object slot that appears in (5.j); and (3)HUM6 is not the subject of ACC1. Therefore, HUM6 satisfies the gap constraints.

      The generator decides to embed UND1 in ACC1 with HUM6 as a gap after it finishes process (e) in Fig.11. Then

      (EMBEDDED (ACC1 UND1))

is added to the property list of HUM6.

      This property is used to determine when to activate embedding. The generation process checks the current generating event, which is farthest to the left in the Context in Fig.12, to see if it is equivalent to the event obtained in operations,

      (CAR (GET HUM6 'EMBEDDED)).

Here the current generating context of the process has a property headed by EMBEDDED. (UND1 HUM6) then replaces HUM6 in the current context.

      HUM6 in UND1 is not generated when UND1 is generated by the process. After generating UND1, the current context becomes HUM6. HUM6 is generated next so that it follows UND1 directly, a configuration that satisfies the embedded clause structure in Japanese.

The embedded text structure for STORY 1 becomes,

(ACC1, TRY0. sorekara, EXE0),

with "sorekara" a Japanese conjunction corresponding to "after that." UND1 is embedded in ACC1 so it does not appear here, in contrast to the non-embedded structure;

(UND1 node, ACC1, TRY0. sorekara EXE0).

terososhiki ni zokusu oribuiro no   fuku wo kita   geriratachi wa
TERRORIST-ORG BELONG OLIVE-COLORED SUIT   WEARING GUERRILLAS

seifu ni   kyoryokushita sukunakutomo 60 nin no noumintachi wo"
GOVERNMENT COLLABORATED   AT-LEAST   60   PEASANTS

kokuhatsushite, saiban-ni-kaketa. sorekara, sono geriratachi wa
ACCUSED   TRIED   THEN   THE GUERRILLAS

san-pedoro-perurapan toiu machi de sono noumintachi wo shokeishita.
SAN PEDRO PERULAPAN   CITY   THE PEASANTS   EXECUTED

Fig.13 Embedded Japanese Text and its English
       Equivalent (see Fig.1).

テロ組織に属すオリーブ色の服を
着たゲリラたちは政府に
協力した少なくとも６０人の
農民たちを告発して，
裁判にかけた．それから，その
ゲリラたちはサン　ペドロ
ペルラパンという町でその
農民たちを処刑した．

Fig.14 Embedded Japanese Text of Story 1 Expressed in
       Japanese Orthography.

5.4.2 CHANGING WORD ORDER FOR EMBEDDING

The embedding process may cause some confusion of relations among modifiers and their referents. In Japanese, the TIME, PLACE, and OBJECT in (5-j) modify the verb. Such relations could be violated by embedding a clause into, for example, OBJECT; i.e., TIME and PLACE seem to modify the embedded clause without any clear clue to their relation to the verb. In this case, the word order in (5-j) must be

(5-j)' EVENT --> ACTOR OBJECT TIME PLACE VERB.

The rule for this word order change is

> (1) If the embedded clause separates a modifier and its modifying word, the modifier must be replaced near the modified word.

(5-1) Kare wa kinou   Tokyo de hon wo katta.
      HE   YESTERDAY TOKYO IN BOOK   BOUGHT

(5-m) sono hon wa yoku ureteiru.
      THE BOOK   WELL SELLING

At the word/sentence level, these two sentences are consolidated into one with an embedding structure. But without the change in word order, the following example could be obtained.

(5-n) Kare wa kinou   Tokyo de yoku ureteiru hon wo katta.
      HE   YESTERDAY TOKYO IN WELL SELLING BOOK   BOUGHT

The modifiers, kinou and Tokyo de, refer to "katta" in (5-1). Since it is unclear whether they modify "katta" or "ureteiru" in (5-n), the following sentence with the change in word order, described in rule (1), would be preferable to (5-n),

(5-o) Kare wa yoku ureteiru hon wo kinou   Tokyo de katta.
      HE   WELL SELLING BOOK   YESTERDAY TOKYO IN BOUGHT

6. CONCLUSIONS

This generator works well in translating conceptual representations to Japanese texts for the 15 terrorism stories processed so far. The conceptual representation is expected to be language independent when the culture and customs sustaining the language approximate those of the representation. In these stories, the MOPs were not changed at all for generation.

It is generally very difficult to obtain appropriate conjunctions to connect clauses in stories. This system determines appropriate conjunctions according to the causal relations inferred through MOPs and conceptual representations. It is, however, still difficult to determine connections in cases with a long causal chain.

There are many words for which translation is context-dependent. For example, HEADQUARTERS has numerous Japanese translations. When the OWNER-ORG of the HEADQUARTERS is specified with CONGRESS, however, correct translation is unambiguous. This type of word selection procedure becomes complex as the number of stories input increases. Incompleteness of the conceptual representation is one aspect of this problem.

When conceptual representations include information obtained from parsing more than one paragraph, it is difficult for the generator to translate the information appropriately into separate paragraphs; A rule for such separation is necessary. Generating natural expressions from conceptual representations for noun phrases with many modifiers (slots) is also problematic since such modifiers must be translated in separate phrases.

7. ACKNOWLEDGEMENTS

The author first wishes to thank Professor Roger C. Schank for his guidance and encouragement in this research.

Thanks are also due to Steve L. Lytinen; who developed many of the functions this generator employs. David Littleboy and Monica M. Strauss helped to prepare the English manuscript. Lawrence Birnbaum and MT Project members at Yale offered important suggestions and cooperation. Prof. David D. McDonald made a great number of suggestions on revising this manuscript.

The author also thanks Dr. Hozumi Tanaka and Dr. Takayuki Nakajima, who have supported this work at ETL.

8. REFERENCES

[Lytinen and Schank 82]
        Lytinen, Steve L. and Schank, Roger C.
        Representation and Translation.
                Research Report #234, Dept. of Computer Science,
                Yale Univ., 1982.

[Schank 75]
        Schank, Roger C.
        Conceptual Information Processing.
                North-Holland Publishing Company, 1975.

[Schank 80]
        Schank, Roger C.
        Language and Memory.
                Cognitive Science, Vol.4 No.3, 1980.

[Tanaka, et al. 81]
        Tanaka, Hozumi et al.
        Natural Language Processing and Linguistics.
                Circulars of the Electrotechnical Lab. No.205, 1981.

[Lebowitz 80]
        Lebowitz, Michael
        Generalization and Memory in an Integrated Understanding System.
                Research Report #186, Dept. of Computer Science,
                Yale Univ., 1980.

[McGuire]
        McGuire, Rod

Programs for Generation on DEC 20.
         Dept. of Computer Science, Yale Univ.

[McDonald 83]
         McDonald, David D.
         Natural Language Generation Problem: An Introduction
         to Computational Models of Discourse.
         M. Brady and R. C. Berwick ed.,
         MIT Press.

[Ishizaki 83]
         Ishizaki, Shun and Isahara, Hitoshi
         On Japanese Text Generation from Conceptual Representation
         by Using Embedded Structure.
                  Natural Language Processing Technology Symposium
                  Information Processing Society, June 1983.

[Ishizaki 83]
         Ishizaki, Shun
         Generation of Japanese Sentences from Conceptual Represen-
         tation.
                  IJCAI'83, August 1983.

Fluency in Natural Language Reports

Karen Kukich

Abstract

Pinpointing the factors that are responsible for fluency in written text is a traditionally difficult problem. This paper argues that the source of that difficulty is the knowledge-intensive nature of language generation. Not only are a variety of types of knowledge required, such as semantic, lexical, syntactic, grammar and discourse knowledge, but those various forms of knowledge are used in a highly integrated fashion during the generation of text. In this paper, the technique of knowledge-based report generation is described, and samples of text produced by a knowledge-based report generator are presented. A variety of fluency skills and defects found in the samples are identified and categorized. It is argued that the fluency skills exhibited are the result of the effective identification and integration of some specific knowledge processes, and that the fluency defects exhibited are the result of incomplete or poorly integrated knowledge processes.

1. The Nature of Fluency

Evaluating writing is an age old problem. Although most people can distinguish between poorly written prose and great, or even good, writing, no precise tools for measuring the overall quality of writing exist. Even readability scores, which are intended only to measure the grade level of written prose, are controversial [8] [7] [6] [21]. This is due at least in part to the fact that writing is an extremely complicated, knowledge-intensive activity during which an author draws upon and integrates a wide variety of accumulated semantic and linguistic knowledge. For example, semantic knowledge is required to generate and organize meaningful messages, and linguistic knowledge is required to select and shape phrases to express messages, while at the same time making use of anaphora, maintaining focus, performing effective clause-combining, and introducing lexical and syntactic variety. Given the difficulties of first identifying the processes that underly these various functions and second understanding the complex interactions of those processes, it is not surprising that the task of measuring the quality of written text remains so elusive. Yet if we are ever to succeed in building computer models capable of generating high quality text many of these same knowledge processes and interactions must be identified and implemented.

Most research in natural language text generation has concentrated on the first of these two tasks, that of identifying and scrutinizing individual processes that underly text production. Some of the research projects that have made significant contributions toward this goal include Appelt's analysis of the processes involved in planning utterances [2]; McKeown's study of the processes involved in determining relevant answers to questions [25]; Mann and Moore's study of the processes involved in filtering unnecessary facts and combining necessary ones into utterances [22]; Hobb's analysis of the processes involved in discourse organization [13]; McDonald's analysis of the processes involved in subsequent reference [24]; and Sidner's and Grosz's studies of the processes involved in focus [32] [12]. In contrast to these studies which tend to focus on a small set of processes in great detail, the work in knowledge-based report generation done by myself [20] focuses on a larger set of processes in less detail. This makes it possible to address the second task, that of understanding the interactions among knowledge processes that give rise to fluent text. That topic is the subject of this paper.

In lay terminology the concept of fluency is sufficiently nebulous to resist any more precise a definition than "having facility in the use of a language" or "flowing smoothly and effortlessly" [26]. Within the paradigm of knowledge-based report generation, fluency is the result of the effective integration and control of some subset of knowledge processing skills, including semantic skills, lexical skills, syntactic skills, grammar skills, and discourse skills (where discourse knowledge includes all those processes involved in managing a body of text longer than a single sentence or clause). A sufficient subset of these various knowledge processing skills must be successfully identified, implemented and integrated in order for fluent text to be generated. Some of the behaviors that characterize fluent text are identified and categorized in Table 1-1. When the subset of necessary knowledge processing skills is incomplete or poorly integrated, defects in textual fluency may appear. Some manifestations of the lack of fluency in text are summarized in Table 1-2.

All of the phenomena itemized in Tables 1-1 and 1-2 were culled from samples of machine-generated text. The author was a knowledge-based report generation system named Ana. In section four of this paper the actual samples of Ana's output that motivated these summary tables will be analyzed. Sections two and three provide background for the analysis. Section two contains a brief description of the architecture and output of the system, and section three discusses the design principles of knowledge-based report generation.

2. The Ana Stock Report Generation System

2.1. System Architecture

Ana is a natural language stock report generation system. Input to the Ana stock report generator is a set of half-hourly stock quotes from the Dow Jones News and Information Retrieval System. Output from the Ana system is a summary report of the day's activity on Wall Street, similar in content and format to the human-generated reports found on the financial pages of daily newspapers.

The Ana system consists of four modules: 1) a fact generator, 2) a message generator, 3) a discourse

Table 1-1: Classification of Fluency Skills

- Discourse Skills

    - appropriate use of pronouns
    - appropriate use of ellipsis
    - appropriate use of hyponyms
    - sentence length variety
    - consistent verb tense use

- Grammar Skills

    - effective clause combining
    - appropriate use of conjunctions

- Syntactic Skills

    - appropriate syntactic choice

- Lexical Skills

    - lexical variety
    - metaphorical usage

- Semantic Skills

    - interesting message choice
    - appropriate message combination
    - appropriate detail filtering

organizer, and 4) a surface generator. The first module, the fact generator, is a relatively straight-forward program written in the C programming language [14]; the remaining modules are written in the OPS5 production system language [11]. The modules operate in a linear, sequential fashion for the sake of computational manageability at the expense of psychological validity.

Data from the database serves as input to module one, the fact generator, whose function is to perform arithmetic computations and to transform the data into OPS5 format. A stream of facts is produced as output from module one.

Facts serve as input to module two, the message generator, whose function is to infer interesting messages from the facts. A stream of messages is produced as output from module two. This module consists of 142 OPS5 productions.

Messages serve as input to module three, the discourse organizer. Module three performs the function of grouping messages according to topic, and combining and eliminating messages where appropriate. A stream of ordered messages is produced as output from module three. There are 24 productions in module

Table 1-2: Classification of Fluency Defects

- Discourse Defects

  - sentences too long
  - missing ellipsis
  - overuse of pronouns
  - lack of hyponymy
  - lack of parallelism

- Grammar Defects

  - repetition of locative
  - repetition of temporal

- Syntactic Defects

  - overuse of syntactic form

- Lexical Defects

  - repetition of terms

- Semantic Defects

  - poor message choice
  - missing message class
  - redundancy due to lack of temporal recognition
  - redundancy due to lack of causal knowledge

three.

Module four, the surface generator, takes the ordered messages as input and produces the final report as output. It does this by mapping messages into phrases in its phrasal lexicon, building clauses from the phrases, and combining clauses into complex sentences according to its clause-combining grammar. Module four includes 110 grammar productions and just under 600 phrasal dictionary entries.

The fundamental knowledge constructs of the system are of two types: 1) static knowledge constructs, or memory elements, and 2) dynamic knowledge constructs, or productions. There are five types of static knowledge constructs: a) facts, b) messages, c) phrasal lexicon entries, d) clauses, and e) various processing control elements, such as counters, flags, etc. There are three main categories of dynamic knowledge constructs: a) semantic inferencing productions, b) discourse organizing productions, and c) grammar productions, which include discourse mechanics productions, message selection productions, predicate selection productions, variable instantiation productions, syntax selection productions, conjunction selection productions, clause building productions, subject selection productions, verb morphology productions, adverb selection productions, punctuation selection productions, clause writing productions, and various control productions. The first module, the fact generator, deals only with data and facts; the second module, the message generator, infers messages from facts via semantic inferencing productions; module three, the discourse organizer, works only with messages and discourse organizing productions; the fourth module, the surface generator, makes use of the remainder of the knowledge constructs, including messages, phrasal lexicon entries, clauses, and grammar productions.

2.2. Sample Output

The text in Figure 2-1 is a sample stock report generated by Ana for the date 24 June 1982. (Ana was never imbued with knowledge about capitalizing the first word of a sentence, as is evident in the unretouched text of Figure 2-1.)

Figure 2-1: Ana's Report

Thursday June 24 , 1982

wall street's securities markets meandered upward through most of the morning , before being pushed downhill late in the day yesterday . the stock market closed out the day with a small loss and turned in a mixed showing in moderate trading .

the Dow Jones average of 30 industrials declined slightly , finishing the day at 810.41 , off 2.76 points . the transportation and utility indicators edged higher .

volume on the big board was 55860000 shares compared with 62710000 shares on Wednesday advances were ahead by about 8 to 7 at the final bell .

Ana's report may be compared to a truncated version of the report which appeared in the Wall Street Journal for the same day. The truncated Wall Street Journal report, which was written by Victor J. Hillery, is reprinted in Figure 2-2 The complete text of the Wall Street Journal report is attached as an appendix.

Fluency is just one of a number of characteristics that are critical to the success of an automatic report generator. Some other important characteristics are accuracy, completeness, extendibility, tailorability, and cost-effectiveness. Reports produced by the Ana system have been analyzed with respect to each of these characteristics, and the results are reported elsewhere [20] [19]. In general, Ana's reports were found to be highly accurate and very extendible and tailorable. They did not fare quite so well in terms of cost-effectiveness; while storage and processing costs were very attractive- (due to macro-level knowledge constructs and processing), implementation costs were high (due to the need for the time and services of skilled knowledge engineers). The completeness issue is not so clear cut, so it is briefly reviewed here.

Ana's reports were significantly shorter than the corresponding reports that appeared in the Wall Street Journal. The machine-generated reports were incomplete in two ways: first, they did not cover all of the

Figure 2-2: Wall Street Journal's Report

24 June 1982

The stock market finished with mixed results after the attempt to push its rebound into a fourth session faltered in continued active trading.

Technology issues, Wednesday's star performers, were among yesterday's biggest losers. Some of the drug, oil and steel issues also were casualties.

The Dow Jones Industrial Average, which bounced back 24.55 points in the prior three sessions after plunging more than 80 points since early May, was up 5.04 points at 1:30 p.m. EDT yesterday. However, the index posted a 2.67 point loss an hour later and then closed at 810.41, down 2.76 points. The transportation and utility averages both moved higher.

New York Stock Exchange gainers led by better than two to one early in the day but at the final bell were ahead by about seven to six.

Big Board volume slowed to 55,860,000 shares from 62,710,000 Wednesday.

events that might be inferred from the data in the database, and second, they did not cover any of the events relating to the world external to the stock market. The first form of incompleteness is easily overcome; the second form is far more intractable.

The first form of incompleteness is manifested in the fact that the Ana system could not single out individual stocks to discuss, nor could it compare the current day's market performance to recent trends or to historical highs and lows. This was not due to lack of data in the database, nor was it due to a fundamental weakness of the system; rather, it was simply due the unfinished state of the system. Ana's knowledge processes were initially designed to focus on the behavior of a few composite indexes for a single day. But the same knowledge processes that detect the ups and downs of the composite indexes could be used to detect the ups and downs of individual stocks or groups of stocks, and the additional knowledge processes required to compare the current day's data to historical data or trends could be implemented using the same techniques.

The fact that Ana could not report on events in the world outside the stock market is a manifestation of the second, more severe form of incompleteness. About one quarter of the sentences that appear in typical Wall Street Journal stock reports focus on events external to the stock market. Frequently, these "extra-market sentences" as they are labelled by Kittredge [15], are couched within a quotation from a noted authority. For example, Hillery's report for 24 June 1984 contains the following sentence:

Mr. Hays also observed that "The market seemed to be telling us that some investors liked the budget resolution passed by the Senate and House this week."

Unlike the "core market sentences" which are directly inferrable from the data in the database, extra market sentences require an understanding of world events that is currently beyond the scope of a knowledge-based report generator. Some earlier research in natural language understanding that focussed on understanding UPI news wire stories might eventually help to bridge this gap between "core-domain" knowledge and "extra-domain" knowledge [5] [9] [16].

3. Knowledge-Based Report Generation Principles

The fluency of the text produced by a knowledge-based report generation system is a function of three fundamental design principles which also determine system architecture. These principles are: 1) a knowledge-engineering principle, 2) a macro-level knowledge-processing principle, and 3) a situation-dependent integrated knowledge grammar principle. Each will be discussed briefly.

3.1. The Knowledge-Engineering Principle

Natural language processing is a knowledge-intensive activity. The knowledge-engineering principle embodies the intuitive assumption that neither a person nor a machine could compose an intelligent, fluent report without having specific semantic and linguistic knowledge of the domain of discourse. It further suggests a mechanism for representing and processing the knowledge needed for text generation, namely, a production system mechanism. Finally, it specifies a methodology for implementing that knowledge, namely, a target-driven methodology, where the target is a body of naturally occurring text.

The value of the knowledge-engineering approach has been demonstrated in a number of successful expert systems. Among them are DENDRAL [10], Internist [28], MYCIN [31], EL [33], Prospector [4], R1 [23], ACE [34], and DAA [17]. These systems are successful because they are able to capture in productions precisely the domain-specific knowledge required to perform their target tasks. Productions have the pragmatic benefit of allowing knowledge to be encoded in individual packets which are easy to create and modify. They also have the theoretic benefit of allowing knowledge to be represented and processed in a way that some researchers believe to be very close to the way that people actually do it [1] [27] [29].

3.1.1. Domain-specific semantic knowledge

The need for domain specific semantic knowledge in a report generator is hardly debatable. At a minimum, the system must be able to recognize the objects of the domain of discourse, recognize relations among objects, and recognize changes of relations and changes of states of those objects. But the goal of fluency presses semantic knowledge requirements even further. Merely recognizing and reporting all possible objects, relations, and changes of state will not result in satisfactory reports. Irrelevent detail must be filtered out, and some semantic decisions concerning the importance and connectedness of facts must be made. For example, while it may be accurate to report, as Ana once did, that "after meandering upward through most of the morning, the stock market lifted briefly late in the day yesterday", the two facts reported seem strangely juxtaposed, especially when one discovers that the brief uplift at the end of the day followed a distinct downhill slide, which was far more worthy of mention.

3.1.2. Domain-specific linguistic knowledge

The need for domain specific linguistic knowledge parallels the need for domain specific semantic knowledge. Not only do specialized fields make use of unique technical terms and phrases, such as "over-the-counter stocks", "selling short", or "odd lot orders" in the domain of stock market language, but they also make use of ordinary terms and phrases in domain specific ways, as in the market "turned in a mixed showing". The former phrase was found to have at least the following two meanings in the context of stock market reports: 1) the Dow Jones average of 30 industrials was up while the number of declining stocks for the day exceeded the number of advancing stocks, and 2) the Dow Jones average of 30 industrials was down while the number of advancing stocks for the day exceeded the number of declining stocks.

In addition to specific lexical knowledge requirements, there exist specific syntactic and discourse knowledge requirements. As Sager has articulated and as studies in sublanguages have verified, "The written material in a specialized technical area displays linguistic regularities over and above those that can be stated for the language as a whole." [30] For example, Kittredge and his colleagues have found the various sublanguage grammars of weather reports, stock reports, aviation hydraulics manuals, recipes, pharmacology reports, and economics texts to differ from each other and from standard English on the following characteristics: tense dominance, use of restrictive relative clauses, use of non-restrictive relative clauses, use of embedded complements, use of subordinating clauses with conjunctions, use of passives, use of proper nouns, etc. [15]

3.1.3. Production systems for knowledge representation

Given that natural language processing is both semantically and linguistically knowledge-intensive, and given that production system languages have a proven record of success in the design of knowledge-based systems, production system languages seem naturally suited to the task of building text generators. Not only is it easy to represent domain-dependent semantic knowledge in production rules, but it is also easy to design situation-dependent, integrated knowledge grammars in production languages. One such grammar will be discussed shortly.

3.1.4. Implementation methodology

The knowledge-engineering principle dictates the methodology for implementing a report generation system. The first and most important task is to analyze a sample of naturally occurring, human-generated texts in order to discover the semantic and linguistic knowledge requirements of the domain. Semantic knowledge constructs are the messages conveyed in the text; semantic knowledge processes are the inference rules that are used to create and instantiate semantic messages from the facts in the database, and the discourse organization rules that are used to combine and order messages. Important linguistic knowledge constructs include lexical phrases used to convey messages and syntactic forms used to shape phrases into clauses; important linguistic knowledge processes are the grammar rules. A variety of linguistic knowledge processes are integrated in the grammar rules. Grammar rules are used to select phrases for expressing messages, to select syntactic forms for shaping phrases into clauses, and to combine clauses into complex sentences in accordance with discourse guidelines, such as variation in sentence length, invariance of verb tense, and use of parallelism, synonyms, hyponyms, pronouns, and ellipsis.

A preliminary analysis of a sample of twenty-four manually-generated stock reports that appeared in the Wall Street Journal and the Pittsburgh Post-Gazette revealed a set of approximately forty message classes, such as market fluctuation messages, volume of trading messages, indicator status messages, etc., It also revealed a set of approximately twelve syntactic forms used to express those messages. These included simple sentences, coordinate sentences, subordinate sentences, participial clauses, prepositional phrases, etc. In addition, many discourse organization characteristics were observed, such as the typical ordering of messages, variation in length of sentences, placement of temporal and locative phrases, etc.

Once the essential knowledge requirements have been identified, one can begin to work out the details of their implementation. One might ask, for example, what inference processes would be required to instantiate a "mixed-market" message from the facts in the database. It should be clear from the previous discussion that the inference knowledge required to infer a mixed-market message from the facts in the database can easily be represented in two production rules. Similarly, one might arrive at production rules for organizing messages once they have been created by inference rules, for selecting appropriate phrases to express messages, for selecting appropriate syntactic forms for phrases, and for combining clauses into complex sentences in accordance with discourse constraints. The mixed-market message is one of the simplest knowledge packets in the Ana system. Other knowledge processes, in particular the integrated knowledge grammar rules, are more complicated. A macro-level approach to both knowledge constructs and knowledge processes helps to minimize the complexity of the system.

3.1.5. Effect on fluency

The effect of the knowledge-engineering principle on the design of a text generator is to clearly define the scope of the semantic and linguistic knowledge required by the system. Both the set of objects, relations and states about which the system must reason, and the set of valid processes for operating on objects, relations and states are empirically set to be just those which occur naturally in the domain. Similary, the lexicon and grammar of the system is defined to be that which occurs naturally in the domain. These empirically grounded constraints help to delimit the infinite variety achievable in natural language to a subset that is consistant with the goal of fluency.

3.2. The Macro-level Knowledge Processing Principle

The macro-level principle states that macro-level knowledge structures and processes provide an effective level for representing and processing the knowledge needed for natural language report generation. By macro-level knowledge structures and processes is meant the use of semantic units consisting of whole messages, lexical items consisting of whole phrases, syntactic categories at the clause level, and a clause-combining as opposed to sentence-generating grammar. The use of macro-level constructs is motivated by both practical and theoretical considerations. Practically, the problem of dealing with the complexity of natural language is made much more tractable by working in macro-level knowledge constructs. Theoretically, the role of macro-level processing in models of human language understanding and generation warrants investigation.

3.2.1. Pragmatics of macro-level knowledge-processing

Rather than dealing with semantic primitives, the approach taken here is to work with whole semantic messages. In the case of the stock market reports these include closing market status messages, volume of trading messages, advance-decline ratio messages, Dow Jones averages messages, individual stock average messages, etc. Corresponding macro-level lexical units include whole phrases, such as "Wall Street's securities markets", "were swept into a broad and steep decline", "in heavy trading", "by a ratio of $\langle x1 \rangle$ to $\langle x2 \rangle$", etc. While the terminal syntactic categories of ordinary grammars include mostly word-level categories, such as noun, verb, adjective, preposition, etc., the terminal syntactic categories of a macro-level grammar consist mainly of clause-level categories, such as simple sentences, coordinate sentences, subordinate sentences, participial clauses, infinitive clauses, relative clauses, prepositional phrases, adverbs, punctuation, etc. Retrieval of whole phrases that can be shaped to fit a clausal terminal category with little or no processing eliminates the need for the detailed processing that is required to construct clauses from the word level. Finally, clauses can be combined to form compound-complex sentences by a macro-level clause-combing grammar that can take into consideration various discourse constraints, such as the need for variety in sentence length, the need for variety in syntactic form, the appropriate use of pronouns, ellipsis, and hyponyms, etc. This integrated knowledge grammar is briefly described in the next section.

Some semantic and linguistic flexibility is lost by operating at a macro-level. But despite the fact that there is no mechanism for generating novel semantic messages or linguistic phrases, the loss of flexibility is far less troublesome than might be imagined. Although both the semantic and linguistic boundaries of the system are set by the sublanguage constraints of the domain of discourse, the variety that exists within those boundaries is great enough allow a significant number of reports to be generated before they begin sounding repetitious to the human ear. (The exact cutoff point is a subject for experimental investigation and constitutes an instance of a Turing test.) Furthermore, due to the modularity of its production based architecture, the system can be extended indefinitely by the incremental addition of semantic knowledge packets for inferring additional messages and by the incremental addition of linguistic knowledge packets for expressing those messages. (The system that produced the examples included here contained semantic and linguistic knowledge for only ten of the forty message classes identified in the preliminary analysis of sample stock reports.)

3.2.2. Theoretics of macro-level knowledge-processing

Some support for the notion of macro-level units in human linguistic processing was suggested as early as 1975 by Joseph Becker. Becker focused on the problem of language understanding, but his comments apply equally well to language generation. In his paper, Becker states:

> I suggest that utterances are formed by the repetition, modification, and concatenation or previously-known phrases consisting of more than one word. I suspect that we speak mostly by stitching together swatches of text that we have heard before; productive processes have the secondary role of adapting old phrases to the new situation. (p. 70) [3]

He goes on to introduce the notion of a phrasal lexicon, using examples from his own text, such as: "this is not to say that", "to sweep under the rug", "as something should make apparent", "(verb) the un(verb)able", etc. He also succinctly states the philosophy of phrase-oriented language production which is implemented in the knowledge-based report generator.

> We start with the information we wish to convey and the attitudes toward that information that we wish to express or evoke, and we haul out of our phrasal lexicon some patterns that can provide the major elements of this expression. Then the problem is to stitch these phrases together into something roughly grammatical, to fill in the blanks with the particulars of the case at hand, to modify the phrases if need be, and if all else fails to generate phrases from scratch to smooth over transitions or fill in any remaining conceptual holes. (p. 70) [3]

At least one other language processing system, PHRAN, (for PHRasal ANalyzer) designed by Wilensky and Arens, recognizes the role of macro-level linguistic units [35]. PHRAN accepts English text as input and produces conceptual-dependency knowledge structures which represent the meaning of the text as output. Instead of building the meaning structures from individual words, PHRAN looks for phrases in the input text that match lexical entries at various levels of specificity, from canned literal phrases to general verb-oriented patterns. Wilensky and Arens point out that:

> Much of a language user's knowledge about the meaning of utterances is knowledge about much larger units of speech... in general, the meaning of such an utterance is not computable from the meaning of its subparts, (p. 16) [35]

and that providing the system with knowledge about whole phrases enables PHRAN to handle idioms like "kick the bucket" and "throw the book at" that other systems cannot handle.

Macro-level knowledge processing may be viewed as the top level of a theory of multi-leveled language processing. In multi-leveled language processing, a system may shift between macro-level processing, intermediate-level processing, and low-level processing as the situation requires. In a previous paper [18]an analogy was drawn between the mechanics of driving a car and multi-leveled language processing. Just as driving in third gear makes most efficient use of an automobile's resources, so also does generating language in third gear make most efficient use of human information processing resources. That is, retrieving whole phrases and applying a clause-combining grammar is cognitively economical. But when only a near match for a message can be found in a speaker's phrasal dictionary, the speaker must downshift into second gear, and either perform some additional processing on the phrase to transform it into the desired form to match the message, or perform some processing on the message to transform it into one that matches the phrase. And if not even a near match for a message can be found, the speaker must downshift into first gear and either construct a phrase from elementary lexical items, including words, prefixes, and suffixes, or reconstruct the message.

As currently configured, the Ana system operates only in third gear. Because the units of processing are linguistically mature whole phrases, the report generation system can produce fluent text without having the detailed knowledge-needed to construct mature phrases from their elementary components. But. there is nothing except the time and insight of a system implementor to prevent this detailed knowledge from being added to the system. By experimenting with additional knowledge, a system could gradually be extended to shift into lower gears, to exhibit greater interaction between semantic and linguistic components, and to do more flexible, if not creative, generation of semantic messages and linguistic phrases. Thus, a knowledge-based report generator may be viewed as a starting tool for modeling a multi-leveled theory of natural language processing.

This multi-leveled approach to natural language processing differs from the traditional stratified approaches to language processing as described in Winograd [36]. In the traditional approaches, processing is stratified according to function. Typically, there exist separate strata for semantic, syntactic, lexical, and phonological processing. In contrast, the multi-level approach advocated in the technique of knowledge-based report generation advocates the integration of semantic, syntactic, discourse, and, ultimately, phonological knowledge across strata. Strata are demarcated not by function, but by the size of the knowledge units operated on and by the level of detailed processing performed on the units.

3.3. The Integrated-Knowledge Situation-Dependent Grammar Principle

The technique of knowledge-based report generation holds that the grammatical knowledge required to produce fluent natural language reports is extremely situation-dependent. That is, at any decision point in the generation of text, the choice of a valid and appropriate grammatical item, such as a word, a phrase, or a syntactic form, is a function of a well-integrated set of rules embodying a variety of types of semantic and linguistic knowledge, including knowledge of the lexicon, syntax, discourse structure, rhetoric principles, and semantics, as well as other types of knowledge.

For example, the decision to express the message that the volume of trading on the market was high in the form of a prepositional phrase such as "in heavy trading", might be motivated by the knowledge that a prepositional phrase is a succinct way to incorporate a complete message into a fluent sentence. Such knowledge may be called a rhetoric condition. But that knowledge must be considered in conjunction with the syntax knowledge that determines whether a prepositional phrase is a valid syntactic form given the sentence structure so far. And the lexical items, such as the noun form of the message "trading", must be available.

Production systems provide an ideal mechanism for representing an integrated-knowledge situation-dependent grammar. They allow situation-dependent knowledge to be encoded in the form of situation-action rules which compete with each other to fire. Only those rules whose situation conditions are satisfied may fire, and if more than one rule is satisfied, principles such as specificity and recency of conditions are called upon to resolve the conflict over which rule will fire.

3.3.1. The clause-combining grammar

As mentioned in the previous section, most processing is done at the macro-level. This means that the typical grammatical decisions the system makes are "what phrase should I use to express the predicate of this message", "what clausal syntactic form, eg. simple sentence, participial clause, prepositional phrase, etc., should I use for the phrase", "should the subject of this clause be a phrase, a pronoun, or should it be ellided completely". A clause-combining grammar is used to select phrases and shape clauses into valid complex sentences, taking into consideration the semantic, lexical, syntactic, and discourse constraints of the situation. A context-free abstraction of the grammar's syntax rules would include the following:

Figure 3-1: Clause-Combining Grammar Rules

S --> sentence period
S --> sentence adverb
S --> sentence prepositional-phrase
S --> sentence coordinate-sentence
S --> sentence subordinate-sentence
S --> subordinate-sentence sentence
S --> sentence subordinate-participial-clause
S --> subordinate-participial-clause sentence
S --> sentence infinitive-clause
etc

However, there is no semblence of a context-free grammar incorporated in the system. The rules that select an appropriate syntactic form. such as prepositional phrase or simple sentence, in which to render a phrase, take into consideration a variety of situation-dependent knowledge, including rhetoric principles, semantic requirements. and lexical appropriateness, as well as syntactic validity.

The system's clause-combining grammar is right-branching. Its essential operations include: focus on a message, select a lexical phrase that matches the semantic attributes of the message, select a syntactic form that fits the context, process the phrase to fit the syntactic form, write the clause, and repeat the cycle. The grammar rules are constructed so that at any point in the generation of text the system has the option to lay down a period and end the current sentence. However, it is possible for things to go awry leaving a line of text hanging in mid-air. This might happen, for example, if the system opts to express its current message as a subordinate participial clause (eg. "after creeping upward all morning") contingent upon the knowledge that the next message (which it peeks at) contains a similar predicate which could be expressed as a simple sentence. But if for some reason, say, the system's lexicon were incomplete, it could not find the words to express the next message, the current sentence would be left hanging. This particular phenomenon is actually a frequent occurrence in spoken language. It is referred to as "anacoluthia". Though it happens infrequently, the Ana system is capable of this behavior, and so it received its name.

3.3.2. Knowledge integration and Situation Dependency

Each of the 110 rules in the situation-dependent, integrated-knowledge grammar of the system may specify a variety of semantic and linguistic knowledge constraints. This integration of knowledge is evident in the grammar rule shown in Figure 3-2, which may fire to select the syntactic form of subordinate participial clause. All of the OPS5 rules depicted here have been rephrased in English.

This rule integrates semantic knowledge, such as message topic and time, syntactic knowledge, such as whether the sentence requirement has been satisfied, and discourse knowledge, such as the preference to avoid using subordinate clauses as the opening form of two consecutive sentences.

3.3.3. Linguistic tailoring

One of the advantages of implementing a text generator as a production system is the ability to incorporate linguistic tailoring facilities. One such tailoring facility is a parameter for adjusting the maximum length of sentences in reports. Another is a parameter for adjusting the maximum number of messages that the text generator will attempt to combine in one sentence. Syntactic preferences are also adjustable parameters; if a reader prefers reports that are light in their use of subordinate participial clauses, for example, the syntactic form parameter for subordinate participial clauses can be turned down to, say, thirty percent. This will permit those productions which could select the syntactic form subordinate participial clause to fire on only thirty percent of the occasions on which they are otherwise appropriate. Some examples will clarify this mechanism.

When the text generator is started, one of the first productions to fire is one that sets some general linguistic parameters. That production is depicted in Figure 3-3.

Figure 3-2: Sample Grammar Rule

IF

1) there is an active goal to select a syntactic form, and
2) the sentence requirement has not been satisfied, and
3) the message currently in focus has topic <t>,
      subject class <sc>, and some non-nil time, and
4) the next sequential message has the same topic,
      subject class, and some non-nil time, and
5) the subordinate-participial-clause parameter
      is set at value <set>, and
6) the current random number is less than <set>, and
7) the last syntactic form used was either a
      prepositional phrase or a sentence initializer, and
8) the opening syntactic form of the last sentence
      was not a subordinate sentence or a
      subordinate participial clause, and
9) the time attribute of the message in focus
      does not have value 'close'

THEN

10) remove the goal of selecting a syntactic form, and
11) make the current syntactic form a subordinate
      participial clause, and
12) modify the next sequential message to put it
      in peripheral focus, and
13) set a goal to select a subordinating conjunction.

Figure 3-3: Tailorable Parameter Bank

IF

there is an active goal to set linguistic parameters,
THEN
remove that goal, and
make a parameter for number of messages with value 3, and
make a parameter for syllable length with value 30, and
make syntactic form parameters with values:

      sentence 11
      coor-sentence 11
      prep-phrase 11
      subor-sentence-pre 5
      subor-participial-pre 7
      subor-sentence-post 3
      subor-participial-post 11
      subor-participial-sentence-post 5.

When this rule fires, certain linguistic parameters are set for the report. Various text generation productions make use of those parameters. For example, one of the discourse mechanics rules that fires every time a new sentence is begun takes care of initializing a length constraint element, length-constraint, and a message constraint element, message-constraint, to the values specified in the linguistic parameter settings. That production is shown in Figure 3-4.

Figure 3-4: Sentence Initialization Rule

IF
there is an active goal to initialize the sentence, and
there is a message parameter whose value is <mess>, and
there is a message constraint element, and
there is a syllable parameter whose value is <syl>, and
there is a length constraint element, and
there is a conjunction requirement element, and
there is a sentence requirement element,
THEN
remove the current goal, and
set the value of the message constraint element at <mess>, and
set the value of the length constraint element at <syl>, and
set the value of the conjunction requirement element to nil,
and set the value of the sentence requirement element to nil.

Thus, the sentence length constraint is initialized at thirty syllables every time a new sentence is begun. Then, during the course of generating a complete sentence, it is decremented by the number of syllables in the clause after each new clause is added to the sentence. As demonstrated in the processing example of the previous section, a production whose task is to monitor the length constraint may fire when the length constraint gets low. That production is depicted in the Figure 3-5.

Figure 3-5: Sentence Length Monitor Rule

IF
there is an active goal to generate text, and
the sentence requirement is satisfied, and
the value of the length constraint element
     has fallen below 7 syllables, and
the last syntactic form generated was not a period,
THEN
remove the current goal, and
create a goal to generate a period.

The effects of adjusting the sentence length parameter are demonstrated in the text samples in Figure 3-6. The first sample text in Figure 3-6 was generated with the sentence length parameter set at thirty syllables; the second sample text in the same Figure was generated from the same input messages, but this time the sentence length parameter was set at fifteen syllables.

Adjusting the syntactic form parameters can have equally noticeable effects on the text generated by the system. For example, the grammar rule depicted earlier in Figure 3-2 selects the syntactic form subordinate participial clause in the pre-sentential position. Condition elements 5 and 6 in this rule control syntactic tailoring. Because this rule will only fire when all of its conditions are satisfied, and because condition

Figure 3-6: Sentence Length Variation Samples

Length constraint = 30 syllables

after creeping upward early in the session yesterday,
the stock market slid downhill late in the day and posted a
small loss. stock prices finished with mixed results in
moderate trading.

Length constraint = 15 syllables

after creeping upward early in the session yesterday ,
stock indexes were pushed downhill late in the day . the
stock market posted a small loss and turned in a mixed showing . trading was moderate .

element 6 specifies that the current random number must be less than the value of the syntactic form parameter of condition element 5, and because the current random number will be a random value between 1 and 10, it follows that if the the syntactic form parameter value is set low, at say a value of 3, then this production will fire on only thirty percent of the occasions on which it could. The two text samples in Figure 3-7 demonstrate the effects of adjusting the value of the syntactic form parameter for subordinate participial clauses in the pre-sentential position. The first sample was generated with the parameter set at a value of 11. Since a value of 11 will always be higher than the random number generated, it places no constraint on the firing of the production. For the second sample, the value of the parameter was lowered to 5. Under this condition, the random number will be less than the parameter value only forty percent of the time, and the firing of the production will be suppressed proportionally.

Figure 3-7: Use of Subordinate Clause Variation Samples

Subordinate-Participial-Pre = 11

after creeping upward early in the session yesterday,
the stock market slid downhill late in the day and posted a
small loss.

Subordinate-Participial-Pre = 5

wall street's securities markets meandered upward
through most of the morning, before being pushed downhill
late in the day yesterday.

The effects of the tailorable linguistic parameters are independent. For example, the syllable length constraint is not the only factor that influences sentence length. The message constraint and the syntactic form preferences also effect sentence length. Thus, even if the syllable length constraint were set a a very high value, say fifty syllables per sentence, the text generator might still exhibit a preference for shorter sentences if the message constraint were set to allow no more than two messages per sentence. One of the theoretically useful aspects of parameter driven text generation models such as Ana is their ability to allow the user to experiment with different settings for the various linguistic parameters to determine what mix might result in reports that are optimally satisfactory from the rhetoric standpoint. No such experimentation has yet been carried out, but the possibility is inviting.

4. Analysis of Fluency Skills and Defects

In Section 1 of this paper two tables were presented which identified and categorized the fluency skills and defects that appeared in the reports generated by Ana. The five categories include discourse, grammar, syntactic, lexical, and semantic skills and defects. In this section some of the actual text samples that motivated the tables are presented.

4.1. Skills

Those writing skills exhibited in Ana's reports that fall into the category of rhetoric skills include the use of pronouns, ellipsis, and hyponymy, variety in sentence length, and consistency in verb tense usage. The following excerpt demonstrates both Ana's ability to use pronouns appropriately, and the system's ability to elide a subject entirely when discourse structure warrants it. The first clause, a subordinate sentence, calls for a subject from the subject class MKT, and Ana selects the phrase "the stock market". Ana recognizes that the second clause, a simple sentence, also requires a subject from the same class, and opts to use the pronoun "it", which agrees with the subject it replaces in number. On recognizing that the third clause requires yet another subject from the same class, Ana elides the subject completely.

> *Anaphora and Ellipsis Usage:*
> after the stock market crept upward early in the ses-
> sion yesterday , it slid downhill late in the day and posted
> a small loss . stock prices turned in a mixed showing in
> moderate trading .

Typical stock market reports make frequent use of hyponyms, which are nouns that name the same referent but with varying degrees of specificity. The first time a referent is named, discourse postulates dictate that the name chosen be explicit enough to uniquely identify the referent. Subsequent references need not and should not be as explicit. For these reasons, hyponym levels, indicating the level of specificity of a name, are included as attributes of phrasal lexicon entries in the dictionary, and the text generator takes note of hyponym levels as it is selecting names for subjects. So for example, on the first occasion of reference to the stock market within a paragraph, the text generator might select a name with hyponym level 1, such as "Wall Street's securities markets". On the occasion of a second reference to the same subject within a paragraph, the text generator would be forced to choose a name with a hyponym level attribute greater than 1, such as "the stock market" or "stock prices". A third occasion of identical reference would result in the selection of a subject with an even higher hyponym level attribute, perhaps "the market". Similar reasoning applies to the use of names for the class of Dow Jones averages. In the following excerpt, the first reference to the class makes use of the most explicit name, "the Dow Jones average of 30 industrials". Subsequent references use the abbreviated names, "the transportation measure" and "the utilities index".

Hyponym Usage:
the Dow Jones average of 30 industrials gained 19.13
points in the afternoon and finished with a 16.28 point gain
at 1092.35 . the transportation measure tacked on sizable
gains , as the utility index edged higher .

Ana's discourse mechanics productions, that is, those productions that govern decisions about when to begin a new sentence, ensure sentence length variety. Those productions monitor sentence length with the explicit goal of producing two longer sentences followed by one shorter sentence. Frequently other discourse constraints, such as the need to begin a new paragraph, contribute to variety in sentence length. Such is the case in the following example.

Sentence Length Variety:
the stock market was catapulted sharply and broadly
higher yesterday , as stock prices posted gains for most of
the day . trading was active .

One of the principles of good writing style suggested by in Strunk and White's classic is the dictum: "In summaries, keep to one tense." As currently configured, it would be impossible for Ana to violate this principle because her lexicon contains only past tense verbs. This results in reports that are consistent in their use of verb tense, such as the following:

Consistent Verb Tense Usage:
Thursday April 21 , 1983

the stock market posted losses for most of the day ,
before finishing on the minus side in active trading .

the Dow Jones average of 30 industrials dropped 3.2 to
1188.27 , with the transportation and utility indicators
both edging downward .

at the final bell , volume on the big board amounted to
about 106170000 shares , down from the 110240000 shares
traded the previous day . declining stocks held a slim lead ,
with 841 stocks down and 811 stocks up .

Ana's grammatical skills, her ability to effectively combine clauses into varied compound and complex sentences, and her ability to use conjunctions appropriately, is evident in all her reports, as the following two excerpts explicitly demonstrate. In the first, three messages are combined in a complex sentence consisting of a subordinate participial clause followed by a simple sentence, followed by a subordinate participial clause. After that, two messages are combined in a simple sentence that includes a prepositional phrase. The second excerpt expresses the same five messages. However, this time, the first three are combined into a compound sentence consisting of one simple sentence followed by two coordinate sentences.

Effective Clause Combining and Appropriate Conjunction Usage:
(a)
    after meandering upward through most of the morning
yesterday , the stock market slid downhill late in the day ,
before posting a small loss . stock prices turned in a
mixed showing in moderate trading .

(b)
    the stock market meandered upward through most of the
morning but was pushed downhill late in the day and posted a
small loss yesterday . stock prices turned in a mixed showing in moderate trading .

The same excerpts also demonstrate Ana's skills in conjunction usage. Excerpt (a) makes use of two subordinating conjunctions, "after" and "before". In both instances Ana intelligently uses the temporal attributes of the messages to select the appropriate conjunction. Excerpt (b) contains two coordinating conjunctions, "but" and "and". In these instances Ana makes use of the contrast between the direction attributes of the first two messages to select the conjunction "but", and she recognizes the lack of contrast between the direction attributes of the second and third messages and selects the conjunction "and".

Ana's choice of syntax for expressing messages is highly typical of the syntax of manually written stock reports. For example, approximately fifty percent of the instances of the volume of trading messages found in a sample of stock reports taken from the Wall Street Journal and the Pittsburgh Post-Gazette are expressed in prepositional phrases. Ana follows suit. Ana's grammar also includes a syntactic construction which is somewhat atypical in everyday language but rather frequently found in stock reports. It is referred to as a "subordinate participial sentence" because it is a complete sentence containing a subject and a verb in participial form and it is introduced by a term that serves the function of a subordinating conjunction. The following excerpt illustrates the use of a prepositional phrase for the volume of trading message, and the use of the subordinate participial sentence for the mixed market message.

Conventional Syntactic Choice:
    after climbing steadily through most of the morning ,
the stock market was pushed downhill late in the day .
stock prices posted a small loss , with the indexes turning
in a mixed showing yesterday in brisk trading .

Lexical variety is apparent in Ana's writing both within individual reports and across reports. For example, to express the message that stocks were up during the morning, Ana has on various occasions used each of the following four phrases:

Lexical Variety:
(a) after climbing steadily through most of the morning
(b) the stock market rose steadily through most of the morning
(c) wall street's securities markets meandered upward
   through most of the morning
(d) after creeping upward early in the session

The terms "meander" and "creep" can be construed as the use of metaphor. Ana's phrasal lexicon is actually rich in metaphor. Just three of the many metaphorical phrases found in Ana's reports are illustrated in the following example.

Metaphorical Usage:
the stock market failed to make much headway , with
stock prices posting a small loss yesterday in relatively
light trading .

the stock market displayed a hesitant mood for most of
the day , before posting a small loss in relatively slow
trading yesterday .

the stock market crept upward early in the session yesterday , but stumbled shortly before trading ended .

The abilities to formulate relevant and interesting semantic messages and to decide when to combine or eliminate messages are essential writing skills which are evident in Ana's reports. Ana's semantic inference productions are specifically coded to recognize patterns in the numeric data that are of general or special interest, such as the patterns that signify a mixed market, or patterns that indicate high points and low points in market fluctuations. Occasionally, the phrasing selected to express these messages suggests some deep insight on Ana's part, as in the following excerpt.

Interesting Semantic Message Choice:
the Dow Jones average of 30 industrials surrendered a
16.28 gain at 4:00pm and declined slightly , finishing the
day at 1083.61 , off 0.18 points .

But no deep insight has really occurred. This message is generated by a simple pattern that recognizes that the Dow was up a great deal at some point during the day, but lost it all later.

Ana is programmed for some semblence of succinctness. Her discourse organizing productions recognize when two related messages are very similar and combine them, as in the following example.

Effective Message Combination
the Dow Jones average of 30 industrials slipped 3.2 to
1188.27 , as the transportation and utility measures both
shed a fraction .

4.2. Defects

Table 1-2 in Section 1 contains a classification of the defects that turned up in Ana's reports while Ana was being developed. Some of the defects were corrected simply by adjusting syntactic tailoring parameters; others required more solid corrections; still others have not been corrected, as indicated in the following analysis.

One of the easiest defects to correct was the generation of overly long sentences, as illustrated in the following excerpt.

Sentence Too Long:
at the final bell , volume on the big board amounted to
about 106170000 shares , down from the 110240000 shares
traded the previous day , as declining stocks held a slim
lead , with 841 stocks down and 811 stocks up .

The correction for this problem was a simple adjustment of the parameter for sentence length in the linguistic tailoring production discussed in Section 4.4.4.

Another relatively simple correction was required for the problem of missing ellipsis.

Ellipsis:
the Dow Jones average of 30 industrials showed a day-long
loss and THE DOW declined slightly , to finish the day at
830.57 , off 1.43 points .

This defect was eliminated when the production for eliding subjects was generalized to include the DOW subject class.

At one point during Ana's development an adjustment made her pronoun selection productions too general, and the result was the following defect.

Overuse of Pronouns:
after the stock market crept upward early in the session IT faltered late in the day yesterday with IT being
mixed . IT posted a small loss in moderate trading .

Prior to the time Ana was given hyponym knowledge, her reports exhibited hyponym defects. The following is one such report.

Hyponymy:
the DOW JONES average of 30 industrials erased a 16.28 point
gain and declined slightly , finishing the day at 1083.61 ,
off 0.18 points . the DOW JONES transportation average rose ,
as the DOW JONES utility average was up slightly .

This problem was corrected by assigning a hyponym attribute to each subject entry in the phrasal dictionary, and by adding a hyponym level condition to Ana's subject selection productions.

A final discourse defect has not been corrected. The problem of the lack of parallelism between the noun phrases "the winners" and "losers" in the following excerpt has no simple solution.

Lack of Parallelism:
as THE winners were ahead of losers by a moderate
margin of 8 to 7 .

Because the smallest linguistic unit over which Ana has control is a whole phrase, Ana cannot recognize the lack of parallelism at the level of the determiner. To correct this problem, Ana would have to have to ability to shift down into lower gear and make adjustments to subelements of phrases, i.e., words. Instilling this ability into Ana would increase her linguistic processing flexibility by at least an order of magnitude, but it would also increase her computational complexity by the same amount. To do just that is an attractive future research project.

The placement of adverbial clauses is an unresolved problem for Ana's grammar. Before a "quick fix" was applied, Ana generated the following misguided prose.

Unconventional ordering of Temporal Adverbial Clauses:

volume on the New York Stock Exchange plunged
to 77030000 shares from 109850000 ON WEDNESDAY
AT THE FINAL BELL , as declining issues
were ahead of gainers by nearly 9 to 7 .

Repetition of Locative Adverbial Clauses:

as losers AMONG NEW YORK STOCK EXCHANGE issues
were ahead of gainers by nearly 9 to 7 ON THE
NEW YORK STOCK EXCHANGE .

In the first excerpt, the ordering of the temporal adverbial clauses "on Wednesday" and "at the final bell" seems awkward; the reverse ordering "at the final bell on Wednesday" seems far more natural. In the second excerpt, repetition of the locative clauses "among New York Stock Exchange issues" and "on the New York Stock Exchange" is unquestionably bad. Both problems arose because the first adverbial phrases were included in the subject or predicate entries of the dictionary, so they were retrieved as part of the subject or predicate, and then the second adverbial phrases were generated by the adverbial clause productions in the clause-combining grammar. The "quick fix" solution to this problem was to edit the phrasal dictionary to remove the adverbial clauses. The more general solution would be the same solution described above, that is, to alter Ana's grammar to allow it to shift into lower gear and recognize adverbial clauses in its phrasal lexicon and avoid adverbial redundancy. Again, this is an inviting research project.

As discussed in the previous section, Ana's syntax selection productions use a variety of types of knowledge to arrive at a choice of syntax. However, one piece of knowledge that is not yet well integrated into Ana's syntax selection productions is the knowledge to avoid the overuse of a single syntactic form. The result of this lack of knowledge is illustrated in the following two excerpts. The first suffers from overuse of subordinate sentences, and the second suffers from overuse of subordinate participial sentences.

Overuse of Subordinate Sentence:
the Dow Jones average of 30 industrials erased a 16.28
point gain and declined slightly , finishing the day at
1083.61, off 0.18 points. the transportation index climbed
4.13 points to 475.14, AS the utility average rose a fraction.

volume on the New York Stock Exchange was 109850000
shares compared with 98250000 shares on Tuesday, AS winners
overwhelmed the losers 1057 to 545.

Overuse of Subordinate Participial Sentence:
the stock market posted losses for most of the day ,
WITH stock prices posting a small loss in relatively slow
trading .

the Dow Jones average of 30 industrials showed a day-
long loss and declined slightly , finishing the day at
830.57 , off 1.43 points . the utility measure shed a fraction , WITH the transportation measure rising a fraction .

volume on the big board was 47280000 shares compared
with 53870000 shares on Thursday , WITH declining issues
being ahead of gainers by nearly 8 to 7 .

Adjusting the syntactic parameters for these two syntactic forms corrected the problem of their overuse. However, a more useful solution would be to incorporate aditional syntax monitoring productions into the system to monitor and constrain redundancy in syntax.

Just as redundancy is a problem for grammar and syntax, so also is it a problem for lexical processing, and it is even more difficult to resolve at the lexical level, again due to the lack of word-level recognition. The following excerpt illustrates the fact that Ana did not recognize her redundant use of the word "slight".

Repetition of Lexical Terms:
after climbing steadily through most of the morning ,
the stock market was pushed downhill late in the day yesterday . stock prices closed out the day with a SLIGHT loss ,
with the indexes turning in a mixed showing in brisk trading.

the Dow Jones average of 30 industrials surrendered a
16.28 gain at 4:00pm and declined SLIGHTly , finishing the
day at 1083.61 , off 0.18 points . the transportation indicator climbed 4.13 points to 475.14 , as the Dow Jones utility average was up SLIGHTly .

Correcting semantic problems in a knowledge-based report generator is usually a more difficult problem, at least at the beginning of the calibration period. But some semantic problems have quick fixes, such as the problem of poor message choice illustrated in the following excerpt.

Poor Message Selection:
after meandering upward through most of the morning,
the stock market lifted briefly late in the day.

For this particular afternoon, the market did indeed lift briefly late in the day, but only after it slid downhill all afternoon. The downhill slide was in fact a far more salient event than the brief upturn, and should have been the preferred message if only one message was to be expressed. It was in fact very easy to correct Ana's semantic inference productions to give preference to the downhill slide message on just those occasions when both the downhill slide message and the brief upturn message compete for expression. However, the question remains as to whether the semantic inference module should be allowed to generate both messages, leaving the decision as to whether one or both should be expressed up to the discourse organizer.

Occasionally Ana generates a report that seems to be missing a relevant message. The following is an illustration:

Missing Message:
The Dow Jones average of 30 industrials posted a
19.13 point gain at 3:30pm and spurted 16.28 points
to 1092.35.

On reading this excerpt, one is left with the feeling that an important fact must have been omitted. If the Dow was up by more than 19 points at 3:30, and by more than 16 points at its close, then it must have dropped backed slightly in the interim, and that fact should have been reported. This problem has not been corrected, because it is just the case which requires the message generator to be modified to generate more than one afternoon message, and the discourse organizer to be modified to decide the order of expression for more than one message.

One of the most difficult semantic problems to correct arises from the system's lack of causal knowledge. This lack caused Ana to generate the following blunders:

Apparent Redundancy due to lack of temporal or causal knowledge:

after posting losses for most of the day ,
the stock market posted   a modest loss

the Dow Jones average of 30 industrials posted
a 16.93 point gain at 4:00pm
and spurted   16.93 points to 1191.47

This problem was partially corrected by incorporating temporal knowledge into the discourse organizer. Now, when the discourse organizer recognizes that an interesting Dow fluctuation message is generated for the time 4pm, that time is identical to the time of the Dow closing status message and it adds that attribute to the closing status message so that the phrase selected actually expresses it. The result is the following:

Corrected Redundancy
the Dow Jones average of 30 industrials gained 19.13
points in the afternoon and finished with a 16.28 point gain
at 1092.35 .

However, this solution is less than satisfactory because it avoids incorporating the causal knowledge which is needed for other reasoning.

5. Conclusion

The technique of knowledge-based report generation is useful in helping to identify many of the specific knowledge processes, and the interactions among those processes, that appear to be responsible for fluency skills and defects in natural language text. While the broad brush approach to implementation described here sucessfully demonstrates the effects of an integrated-knowledge grammar, much work remains to be done in refining the details of such a grammar.

Acknowledgements I am deeply appreciative of the many helpful suggestions made by David McDonald for improving the content of this paper. And I am greatly indebted to the guidance and support of Michael Lesk throughout the course and development of this project.

1. Appendix

Sample Wall Street Journal Stock Report

by Victor J. Hillery

24 June 1982

The stock market finished with mixed results after the attempt to push its rebound into a fourth session faltered in continued active trading.

Technology issues, Wednesday's star performers, were among yesterday's biggest losers. Some of the drug, oil and steel issues also were casualties.

The Dow Jones Industrial Average, which bounced back 24.55 points in the prior three sessions after plunging more than 80 points since early May, was up 5.04 points at 1:30 p.m. EDT yesterday. However, the index posted a 2.67 point loss an hour later and then closed at 810.41, down 2.76 points. The transportation and utility averages both moved higher.

New York Stock Exchange gainers led by better than two to one early in the day but at the final bell were ahead by about seven to six.

"It looked as though the market was consolidating after its rally earlier this week," commented L. Crandall Hays, vice president of Robert W. Baird & Co., Milwaukee.

Mr. Hays also observed that "The market seemed to be telling us that some investors liked the budget resolution passed by the Senate and House this week." However, an informal coalition of Wall Street leaders was formed this week to push for major changes in the federal government's budgets.

"The rebound this week has been met with a great deal of skepticism and described as technical, but perhaps it will surprise many people," said Larry Wachtel, first vice president at Bache Halsey Stuart Shields Inc.

Fred Dietrich, vice president of Dickinson Co., Chicago, expects the advance to continue. He said "The tax cut coming next month will be just the medicine the economy needs to start up, and as it improves, corporations will become more liquid, enabling interest rates to go down."

Eldon A. Grimm, senior vice president at Birr Wilson & Co., noted that "Institutions were kicking out a lot of poor performers as they dressed up their portfolios for the end-of-quarter reports."

Recently, the eight strongest stocks in the Dow Jones Industrial Average of 30 issues have been Alcoa,

American Can, General Motors, General Foods, Goodyear, Procter & Gamble, Sears and Westinghouse," said James Finucane, \ analyst with Illinois Co., Chicago. "Demand for many of these stems from imputed economic benefit to the consumer from the tax cut July 1 and increased Social Security payments," he added. "When these stocks begin to underperform the industrial average, perhaps at mid-July, we may be closer to the end" of the retreat.

Big Board volume slowed to 55,860,000 shares from 62,710,000 Wednesday. Somewhat lower institutional activity was indicated by the decline in trades of 10,000 shares or more to 905 from 1,053 in the prior session.

NLT Big Gainer

NLT Corp. was a standout performer, topping the actives on turnover of more than 1.5 million shares and jumping 5 1/4 to 34 1/4. American General began a tender offer through a unit for up to 15 million NLT common at $38 each. American General rose 3/4 to 39 1/4.

Rol Corp., which was weak recently, rebounded 1 7/8 to 24 1/8. The company attributed the recent weakness to apparent institutional selling.

Flightsafety was a prominent loser, skidding 5 7/8 to 18 7/8; the stock was removed by Morgan Stanley & Co. from its recommended list of emerging growth companies.

Other losers included Gulf Resources & Chemical, which fell 1 1/4 to 14. Zopress Commercial S. A. said it holds 15.4% of Gulf Resources and after expiration of a legal waiting period will be able to acquire up to 25%.

Technology Issues Fall

In the technology area, Digital Equipment, an active issue, fell 1 to 70 1/4. Teledyne slid 2 1/8 to 98 7/8; Texas Instruments, 2 1/8 to 85 1/2; NCR, 1 1/2 to 53 7/8; Motorola, 3 3/8 to 60 3/8, and National Semiconductor, 2 1/4 to 19 7/8.

Tandy dropped 1 1/8 to 27 7/8 in active trading; its recent weakness has been ascribed to concern about the many personal computers introduced during recent weeks.

Hitachi slipped 1 1/4 to 24 1/8; officials of Hitachi and Matsushita have been charged with conspiring to steal International Business Machines' secrets.

First Interstate Bancorp rose 1/2 to 25; a 750,000-share block jointly handled by Goldman Sachs and First Boston traded at 24 1/2.

American Bakeries eased 1/8 to 10 3/8; a 360,500-share block handled by Bear Stearns traded at 10.

The American Stock Exchange index fell 1.31 to 253.82, as gainers held a slim lead over the losers. Turnover slowed to 3,720,000 from 4,440,000 Wednesday.

Amex losers included Page Petroleum, down 3/4 to 6 1/8; the company said that cost overruns temporarily impaired its ability to retire all of its obligations.

Among gainers, Visual Graphics advanced 1/2 to 5 3/8; it reported net for the fourth quarter ended March 31, of 45 cents a share, up from 31 cents in the year-earlier period. Guilford Mills rose 3/4 to 21 1/2; a group of investors agreed to acquire the company.

In over-the-counter trading, the Nasdaq composite index rose 0.26 to 171.12. Winners outpaced losers 611 to 386. turnover slowed to 26,903,400 shares from 30,959,700 Wednesday.

References

1. John R. Anderson. *Language, Memory, and Thought.* Lawrence Erlbaum Associates, Publishers, Hillsdale, NJ, 1976.

2. Douglas E.Appelt. TELEGRAM: A Grammar Formalism for Language Planning. Proceedings of the 21st Annual Meeting of the Association for Computational Linguistics, ACL, MIT, Cambridge, MA, 15-17 June 1983, pp. 74-78.

3. Joseph Becker. The Phrasal Lexicon. Theoretical Issues in Natural Language Processing, ACL, Cambridge, Massachusetts, 10-13 June 1975, pp. 70-73.

4. A. N. Campbell and V. F. Hollister and R. O. Duda and P. E. Hart. "Recognition of a Hidden Mineral Deposit by an Artificial Intelligence Program". *Science 217,* 4563 (3 September 1982), 927-929.

5. Jaime Carbonell. Politics. In Roger C. Schank and Christopher K. Riesbeck, Ed., *Inside Computer Understanding*, Lawrence Erlbaum Associates, Hillsdale, New Jersey, 1981, pp. 259-317.

6. L. L. Cherry and W. Vesterman. Writing Tools- The STYLE and DICTION Programs. Bell Laboratories, Murray Hill, NJ, January 16, 1980.

7. Esther Coke. Readability Scores and their Interpretation. Bell Laboratories, Murray Hill, NJ, 1980.

8. Charles R. Cooper and Lee Odell (Ed.). *Evaluating Writing: Describing, Measuring, Judging.* National Council of Teachers of English, 1977. NCTE Stock Number 16221.

9. Gerald DeJong. An Overview of the FRUMP System. In W. G. Lehnert and M. H. Ringle, Ed., *Strategies for Natural Language Processing*, Lawrence Erlbaum Associates, New Jersey, 1982, pp. 149-176.

10. Edward Feigenbaum and B. G. Buchanan and J. Lederberg. "On Generality and Problem-Solving: A Case Study Using the DENDRAL Program". *Machine Intelligence x* (1971), 165-190.

11. C. L. Forgy. OPS-5 User's Manual. CMU-CS-81-135, Dept of Computer Science, Carnegie-Mellon University, Pittsburgh, PA 15213, July 1981.

12. Barbara J. Grosz. Focusing in Dialog. Proceedings of TINLAP-2, ACL, 1976?, pp. 96-103.

13. Jerry R. Hobbs. Towards an Understanding of Coherence in Discourse. In W. G. Lehnert and M. H. Ringle, Ed., *Strategies for Natural Language Processing*, Lawrence Erlbaum Associates, New Jersey, 1982, pp. 223-243.

14. Brian W. Kernighan, Dennis M. Ritchie. *The C Programming Language.* Prentice-Hall, Inc., Englewood Cliffs, NJ 17632, 1978.

15. Richard Kittredge, John Lehrberger. *Sublanguages: Studies of Language in Restricted Semantic Domains.* Walter DeGruyter, New York, 1983.

16. Janet Kolodner. *Retrieval and Organizational Strategies in Conceptual Memory: A computer model.* Ph.D. Th., Yale University, November 1980.

17. T. J. Kowalski, D. E. Thomas. The VLSI Design Automation Assistant: A Prototype System. Proceedings of the Twentieth Design Automation Conference, IEEE, Miami, FL, June 27, 1983, pp. 479-483.

18. Karen Kukich. Design and Implementation of a Knowledge-Based Report Generator. Proceedings of the 21st Annual Meeting of the Association for Computational Linguistics, ACL, MIT, Cambridge, Massachusetts, 15-17 June 1983, pp. 145-150.

19. Karen Kukich. The Feasibility of Automatic Natural Language Report Generation. Proceedings of the Eighteenth Hawaii International Conference on System Sciences, Volume 1, ACM, IEEE, University of Hawaii, University of Southwestern Louisiana, Honalulu, Hawaii, 2-4 January 1985, pp. 546-556.

20. Karen Kukich. *Knowledge-Based Report Generation: A Knowledge Engineering Approach to Natural Language Report Generation.* Ph.D. Th., Information Science Department, University of Pittsburgh, 1983.

21. Nina MacDonald and Stacey A. Keenan and Patricia S. Gingrich and Mary I. Fox and Lawrence T. Frase and James L. Colleymore. Writer's Workbench: Computer Aids for Writers. Bell Laboratories, Murray Hill, NJ, April 1 1981.

22. William C. Mann and James A. Moore. "Computer Generation of Multiparagraph English Text". *American Journal of Computational Linguistics 7*, 17 (1981), 17-29.

23. John J. McDermott. "Domain knowledge and the design process". *Design Studies 3*, 1 (January 1982), 31-36.

24. David D. McDonald. Subsequent Reference: Syntactic and Rhetorical Constraints. Proceedings of TINLAP-2, ACM, 1978, pp. 64-72.

25. Kathleen Rose McKeown. *Generating Natural Language Text in Response to Questions about Database Structure.* Ph.D. Th., University of Pennsylvania Computer and Information Science Department, 1982.

26. William Morris (Ed.). *The American Heritage Dictionary of the English Language.* American Heritage Publishing Co., Inc and Houghton Mifflin Company, Boston/New York, 1969.

27. Allen Newell. Production Systems: Models of Control Structures. In William Chase, Ed., *Visual Information Processing*, Academic Press, New York, 1973, pp. 463-526.

28. Harry Pople. DIALOG:A Model of Diagnostic Logic for Internal Medicine. Proceedings of the Fourth IJCAI, IJCAI, September 1975, pp. 848-855.

29. M. D. Rychener. *Production systems as a programming language for artificial intelligence applications.* Ph.D. Th., Carnegie-Mellon University, 1976. University Microfilms International order no. 77-13,843.

30. Naomi Sager. Information Structures in Texts of a Sublanguage. The Information Community: Alliance for Progress - Proceedings of the 44th ASIS Annual Meeting, Volume 18, White Plains, N.Y., October 1981.

31. E. H. Shortliffe. *Computer Based Medical Consultations: Mycin.* American Elsevier, New York, 1976.

32. Candace L. Sidner. *Towards a Computational Theory of Definite Anaphora Comprehension in nglish Discourse.* Ph.D. Th., MIT, 1979.

33. R. M Stallman and G. J. Sussman. "Forward Reasoning and Dependency-directed Bactracking in a System for Computer-Aided Circuit Analysis". *Artificail Intelligence 9* (1977), 135-196.

34. Gregg T. Vesonder and Salvatore J. Stolfo and John E. Zielinski and Frederick D. Miller and David H. Copp. ACE: An Expert System for Telephone Cable Maintenance. Proceedings of the Eighth IJCAI, IJCAI, 1983.

35. Robert Wilensky and Yigel Arens. PHRAN -- A Knowledge-Based Natural Language Understander. Proceedings of the 18th Annual Meeting of the Association for Computational Linguistics, ACL, University of Pennsylvania, Philadelphia, Pennsylvania, June 19-22, 1980, pp. 117-121.

36. Terry Winograd. *Language as a Cognitive Process, Volume 1: Syntax.* Addison Wesley Publishing Co, Reading, MA, 1983.

PHRED: A Generator for Natural Language Interfaces[*]

Paul S. Jacobs†

ABSTRACT

PHRED (PHRasal English Diction) is a natural language generator designed for use in a variety of domains. It was constructed to share a knowledge base with PHRAN (PHRasal ANalyzer) as part of a real-time user-friendly interface. The knowledge base consists of **pattern-concept pairs,** i.e., associations between linguistic structures and conceptual templates. Using this knowledge base, PHRED produces appropriate and grammatical natural language output from a conceptual representation.

PHRED and PHRAN are currently used as central components of the user interface to the UNIX Consultant System (UC). This system answers questions and solves problems related to the UNIX operating system. UC passes the conceptual form of its responses, usually either questions or answers to questions, to the PHRED generator, which expresses them in the user's language. Currently the consultant can answer questions and produce its responses in either English or Spanish.

There are a number of practical advantages to PHRED as the generation component of a natural language system. Having a knowledge base shared between analyzer and generator eliminates the redundancy of having separate grammars and lexicons for input and output. It avoids possibly awkward inconsistencies caused by such a separation, and allows for interchangeable interfaces, such as the English and Spanish versions of the UC interface.

The phrasal approach to language processing realized in PHRED has proven helpful in generation as in analysis. PHRED commands the use of idioms, grammatical constructions, and canned phrases without a specialized mechanism or data structure. This is accomplished without restricting the ability of the generator to utilize more general linguistic knowledge.

As the generation component of a natural language interface, PHRED affords extensibility, simplicity, and processing speed. Its design incorporates a cognitive motivation as well. It diverges from the traditional computational approach by focusing on the use of specialized phrasal knowledge. This phrasal approach minimizes the autonomy of the individual word, the bane of some earlier approaches to language processing. The two-stage process used by PHRED to select appropriate linguistic structures also fits well with cognitive theories of language and memory.

---

[*] This research was sponsored in part by the Office of Naval Research under contract N00014-80-C-0732, the National Science Foundation under grants IST-8007045 and IST-8208602, and the Defense Advanced Research Projects Agency (DOD), ARPA Order No. 3041, Monitored by the Naval Electronic Systems Command under contract N00039-82-C-0235. I am grateful to Robert Wilensky for his guidance and for his important comments on numerous drafts of this paper, and to Lisa Rau for many helpful suggestions.

† Author's current address: Artificial Intelligence Branch, GE Corporate R & D, Schenectady NY 12301.

1. Introduction

The PHRED (PHRasal English Diction) system is a language generation module for natural language interfaces. The generator operates from a declarative knowledge base of linguistic knowledge, common to that used by PHRAN (PHRasal ANalyzer) (Wilensky and Arens, 1980). PHRED and PHRAN together form an interface for analyzing natural language and producing natural language responses. This interface serves as the linguistic component to the UNIX Consultant system (UC) (Wilensky, Arens, and Chin, 1984), a program for responding to inquiries about the UNIX operating system. As the entire UC system operates in several seconds of CPU time, it is an important feature of PHRED that it requires no more than two or three seconds to produce a complete sentence.

The principal knowledge structure used by PHRAN and PHRED is the **pattern-concept pair**, which links a phrasal pattern to a conceptual template. This structure has proven particularly effective in the encoding of specialized linguistic knowledge, *i.e.* knowledge about particular phrases and their specialized meanings. Part of the theoretical basis of PHRED is the notion that such specialized constructs are an essential component of language use. This idea has among its advocates Chafe (1968), Harris (1968), and Kittredge and Lehrberger (1983), and is behind other generation systems such as Kukich's Ana (1983).

The shared linguistic knowledge base is an unusual feature of PHRED and PHRAN. Computer programs that can effectively communicate in natural language must be capable both of analyzing a range of utterances to derive their meaning or intent, and of producing appropriate and intelligible responses. Historically these two tasks have been treated independently, principally because some of the hard problems in language production differ from those of language analysis. In the MARGIE system, for example, the BABEL generator (Goldman, 1975) employed a discrimination net as its principal data structure to facilitate the selection of an appropriate verb and an ATN grammar to apply syntactic constraints, while the ELI analyzer (Riesbeck, 1975) in the same system attached routines to individual words to control the interpretations considered during the parsing process.

Throughout the short history of natural language generation systems, programs that produce language have treated generation as a process of *decision making* (McDonald, 1980), *choice* (Mann and Matthiessen, 1983), or *planning* (Appelt, 1982). These systems have employed knowledge structures specifically geared, to varying degrees, to the task of constraining the selection of lexical and grammatical elements. The design of analyzers, on the other hand, focuses on the problem of ambiguity in natural language and makes use of knowledge structures designed to constrain the consideration of alternative interpretations. While the *tasks* of analysis and generation are thus inescapably different, much of the same *knowledge* can be used in performing both tasks.

Even in systems with both analysis and generation components, the knowledge used to derive meaning from language is not used to produce language from meaning. Such systems may be able to use a word or grammatical structure without being able to recognize the same structure, or *vice versa,* and must duplicate a great deal of information if the generator uses language similar to that understood by the analyzer. Intuitively, it seems that the knowledge used to constrain the interpretation of language can be used to constrain the choice of language. A natural language system with a parsimonious knowledge representation could encompass an interface capable of both analysis and production without excessive duplication, with knowledge *about* language as well as mechanisms for its analysis and generation.

PHRED was conceived as the generation component of such an interface. PHRED, along with its companion analysis program PHRAN, embodies an approach to natural language processing founded on the principle that knowledge about language is in essence declarative, consisting of associations between linguistic and conceptual structures of varying degrees of specificity (Wilensky, 1981). Such declarative knowledge should be used for both analysis and generation, and the form of the knowledge should be independent of the particular language. From its initial conception the "English" part of PHRED's acronym was anomalous, as both the analyzer and generator were envisioned as being able to utilize knowledge bases of multiple languages.

The UNIX Consultant, designed to aid novice users of the UNIX operating system by conversing in natural language, is one application of the PHRED generator. The PHRAN analyzer receives the user's input and passes a conceptual interpretation to UC, which then passes its response in conceptual form to PHRED to be converted into natural language output. Below are some examples of questions to UC, with the responses generated by PHRED:

User: How do I delete a file?

UC: **Typing 'rm filename' causes the file filename to be removed from the current directory.**

User: Cómo se borra un archivo?

UC: **Para borrar el archivo de nombre filename del espacio de trabajo, se escribe 'rm filename'.**

User: How do I delete all the files from a directory?

UC: **Typing 'rm *' will remove all files within the current directory from the current directory.**

Typing 'rm -r directoryname' will cause all files and directories recursively inside of directoryname to be deleted from directoryname and removes the directory directoryname from the working directory.

The Spanish example above, a rough paraphrase of the first English question, illustrates the ability of UC to answer questions posed in either language, using the same knowledge about UNIX. The PHRAN/PHRED knowledge base includes the information that "borrar" and "escribe" used with certain objects refer to specific concepts in the UNIX world, the same concepts as "deleting" and "typing", respectively. Also in the phrasal knowledge base is knowledge that "espacio de trabajo" and "working directory" have a specialized denotation in the UNIX world. Such specialized linguistic knowledge is common in this domain.

While PHRAN and PHRED were originally tested using an English vocabulary used for various stories and news articles, it was a relatively easy task to accommodate linguistic knowledge bases for English and Spanish in order for the same programs to operate in the UC domain. Adding a new vocabulary or language capability to the UC system has required no modification to the program, although the system has not had extensive testing with many languages.

PHRED is implemented in Franz LISP and runs compiled on a VAX 11/780. The English linguistic knowledge base of UC contains about 150 patterns, in addition to knowledge of the morphological characteristics of 30 verbs and 50 nouns commonly used in communicating UNIX information. The compiled program occupies about 100K bytes of memory, of which about 20K is code used also by PHRAN. Output from PHRED in the UC system requires 1-3 seconds of CPU time, roughly a third of the total time used by the system. For sentences of the length typically produced by the generator, the amount of time used is roughly proportional to the length of output. Experiments with larger knowledge bases have suggested that the time used by the generator is not heavily dependent on the size of the knowledge base.

The next section describes the PHRED knowledge base and outlines its role in the generation process. Section 3 covers this process in more detail, and Section 4 traces a complete example of generation using PHRED. Section 5 compares the PHRED approach with other research. Section 6 discusses some current and future research directions.

2. The PHRED Knowledge Base

The knowledge base shared by the phrasal analyzer (PHRAN) and phrasal generator (PHRED) consists of pattern-concept pairs, where the pattern contains a linguistic structure and the concept its internal representation. While this representation may be classified as within the systemic/functional tradition (cf. Halliday, 1968; Kay, 1979), the implementation of the PHRED knowledge base differs in certain important details. The use of the PC pair in PHRED may be distinguished from some other language production mechanisms (McDonald, 1980; Mann and Matthiessen, 1983; McKeown, 1982) in which grammatical information and conceptual information are separated: The "pattern" component of each PC pair may include conceptual information, and the properties associated with each PC pair may combine linguistic and conceptual attributes. Like the systems described above, however, PHRED uses these properties for indexing and applying each pattern, particularly using information about agreement among constituents of the pattern and relationships between properties of constituents and properties of the entire pattern.

The following is a simple example of a pattern-concept pair, representing some of the knowledge about the use of the verb "remove":

Pattern: <agent> <root = remove> <physob>
        <<word = from> <container>>

Concept: (state-change (object ?rem-object)
             (state-name location)
             (from (inside-of (object ?cont)))
             (to (not (concept (inside-of (object ?cont))))))

Properties:
    tense = (value 2 tense)
    rem-object = (value 3)
    cont = (value 5)
    forms = (active-s passive-s)

Specifications of components of the pattern in angle brackets (◇) include linguistic information (root = remove) or conceptual categories (agent, container) or a combination of linguistic and conceptual specifications. Additional information associated with each PC pair determines the correspondences between elements of the conceptual structure and constituents of the linguistic structure: The special "value" indicator designates the association of a property of the PC pair with a property of one of its constituents, specified by number. Thus "tense = (value 2 tense)" implies that the tense of the pattern is the tense of the second constituent, the verb. "cont = (value 5)" indicates that the token unified with the variable "?cont" in the conceptual template corresponds to the fifth constituent, the object of "from". The above PC pair can be used by PHRED, depending on the concept being expressed, to produce the sentence "You should remove the files from your directory" or the infinitive phrase "to remove a file from the top level directory". The final output is determined by the combination of this PC pair with the input attributes and one or more **ordering patterns**, which embody general linguistic constraints and constraints on surface order.

In addition to the linguistic patterns and associated conceptual representation, PC pairs contain a set of properties, or attributes, and other information that guides their use. Some of this information, such as "tense = (value 2 tense)" above, is used to determine correspondences between a pattern and its constituents. Other properties are used for indexing purposes. There is also a facility for "escapes", or the ability to call a special procedure from within the declarative knowledge representation. While this facility was often exploited in early versions of PHRAN, it is problematic for knowledge bases shared with PHRED. Procedures called during analysis are seldom useful to the generator or *vice versa*. Therefore such procedure calls have seldom been used in PHRED, and an attempt has been made to encode all knowledge in a declarative form that can be used by both the generator and the analyzer.

The "pattern" part of the PC pairs is a list of constituents, where each constituent in a pattern is generally described either as a pattern of speech (p-o-s) or as a member of a descriptive category (e.g. person, physical object). Patterns may also be formed by conjunction and disjunction of other patterns and may contain specifications of constraints. For example, the constituent

    <and   root = remove   voice = active   form = infinitive>

is a single-constituent pattern which would generate the infinitive verb "to remove", while

<and   p-o-s = noun-phrase <or person physob>>

represents a noun-phrase which refers to a person or physical object.

Patterns are used to represent lexical entries, determiners and particles that refer to nothing, as well as very specific phrases that refer to particular objects. The pattern

<word = the> <word = big> <word = apple>

represents the phrase "the big apple" used to refer to New York City. This phrase can also be produced by the general pattern

<p-o-s = article> <p-o-s = np2>

when used to refer to an apple.

Specialized linguistic constructs are often partially frozen patterns that behave as a particular grammatical unit. The phrase "kick the bucket" behaves as a verb which conjugates but does not passivize. It corresponds to the pattern

<and   p-o-s = verb   root = kick> <word = the> <word = bucket>

which functions as an intransitive verb.

Part of the knowledge associated with a pattern-concept pair is the correspondence between the properties of the pattern's constituents and the properties of the entire pattern. Associated with the "kick the bucket" pattern above is the knowledge that the person, number and tense of the pattern correspond to the person, number and tense of the first constituent, the form of the verb "kick". In generation, this results in the recursive application of constraints from a pattern to its components: To generate a past-tense verb meaning "died", the system will operate recursively on the pattern above to generate a past-tense form of "kick".

Patterns do not necessarily represent a fixed word order. For example, in

<person> <root = tell> <person>
<word = to> <word = get> <word = lost>

the pattern retains its meaning when used in a passive form or infinitive phrase. Such patterns are used in combination with **ordering patterns,** which control the various ways in which a pattern may be linguistically realized. An example of an ordering pattern that could be used in conjunction with the "get lost" pattern above is the passive infinitive ordering, used to produce, for example, "the man to be told to get lost" or "the file to be removed from the current directory":

Pattern:
```
<and  #3  p-o-s = noun-phrase   case = objective>
<and  #2  p-o-s = verb   form = infinitive   voice = passive>
<<word = by>
  <and  #1  p-o-s = noun-phrase   case = objective>>
<<#rest>>
```

Properties:
```
p-o-s = inf-phrase
voice = passive
forms = (passive-s)
```

The "#2" and "#3" within the ordering pattern indicate that the constraints on the second and third constituents of the coordinated pattern are conjoined with the first and second constituents of the ordering pattern, respectively. The "#rest" indicates where additional constituents are generally inserted. This information guides the combination of the ordering pattern with other PC pairs. An extra set of angle brackets is used to mark a constituent that is optional to the pattern, such as the "by" phrase. The "p-o-s = inf-phrase" property specifies that the pattern produces an infinitive phrase, and the "forms = (passive-s)" property restricts the use of this ordering to patterns that have "passive-s" among their forms.

Patterns that have an unspecified word order do not have a "p-o-s" attribute, and thus do not produce a particular pattern of speech independently. These are combined by PHRED with ordering patterns to allow for idioms or expressions that may appear in various forms, such as "bury the hatchet" in "The hatchet was buried at Appomattox." The same effect could be accomplished without ordering rules by increasing the number of fixed-word-order patterns combinatorially. The use of the ordering patterns, however, has a certain elegance as well as a practical value: it allows the specification of certain specialized constructs as relations among particular constituents, regardless of where the constituents appear in the actual output. In this case, the specialized meaning of "telling someone to get lost" is effectively represented by the relationship between the verb "tell" and its complement "to get lost". This meaning may be realized in a variety of forms; for example, the combination of the "get lost" pattern with a passive ordering may produce the sentence "John was told by Bill to get lost."

While there are similarities between the ordering rules used by PHRED and transformational grammar rules, there are some important differences: PHRED assumes no syntactic derivation; rather, the final ordering of a pattern of speech is produced by combining a set of linguistic patterns. Furthermore, there is no strict sequence in which the patterns must be applied: A given ordering pattern may be chosen either before or after a pattern with which it is to be combined. The combination of ordering patterns is constrained by the interactions among the properties of the patterns, instead of by controlling the order in which they are used. In this way PHRED is more flexible than other systems that handle word order as a final phase of the generation process (*cf.* Goldman, 1975).

The pattern-concept pair representation falls into a class of linguistic representations known as **feature systems**, including lexical functional grammar (Kaplan and Bresnan, 1983), functional grammar (Kay, 1979) and functional unification grammar

(Kay, 1984). These systems, which developed in parallel, may be described using a common notation, and vary mostly in the way in which they are typically applied. Pattern-concept pairs have been applied primarily to the problem of representing the specialized linguistic knowledge that seems necessary to use language as a communicative tool. This emphasis causes minor variations to seem important. For example, most unification grammar implementations require that a syntactic category be among the features, or attributes, of every linguistic pattern. The omission of this requirement for pattern-concept pairs facilitates the representation of patterns that have a specialized meaning but do not have rigid surface structures. This is illustrated by the "get lost" pattern and by the specialized knowledge about "borrar" and "escribe" in the UNIX domain.

The next section describes how the knowledge base described here is utilized as part of a real-time generation system.

3. The Generation Process

The production of an utterance in PHRED is a recursive process that can be divided into three phases: **Fetching** is the retrieval of pattern-concept pairs from the knowledge base. **Restriction** consists of validating a potential pattern-concept pair to confirm that it fulfills a given set of constraints and adding new constraints to the pattern. **Interpretation** is the generation of lexical items that match the constraints of the restricted pattern.

The generation algorithm implemented in PHRED is similar to those used in other unification-based systems (*cf.* McKeown, 1982; Appelt, 1983). Because of the expectation that PHRED would serve as part of a real-time interface, however, the system was designed to avoid the expensive unification process. Thus the *fetching* phase of PHRED accomplishes much of the task of checking the constraints of a pattern against the constraints to be satisfied, a function that could be performed by unification. The more time-consuming unification process is applied only after the fetching phase has produced a candidate pattern.

A second important aspect of the PHRED algorithm, also addressed to the problem of avoiding unnecessary computation, is the overall strategy for handling alternative patterns. Once the fetching mechanism has retrieved a pattern, PHRED uses this pattern unless it is found to violate a constraint. This is similar to the strategy implemented in MUMBLE (McDonald, 1980), which also avoids comparisons of linguistic structures of comparable validity. Unlike MUMBLE, PHRED does limited backtracking under some circumstances. The backtracking mechanism, however, relies on the fact that the fetching mechanism generally produces *some* useful patterns and that most constraint violations are due to incorrect selections among ordering patterns.

Each of these phases and its role in the generation process will now be discussed in further detail.

3.1. Fetching

While PHRAN and PHRED use the same knowledge structures, the way in which these structures are accessed for the purpose of generation naturally differs from their access by the analyzer. PHRAN must recognize a set of lexemes as possibly corresponding to a pattern and thereby retrieve an appropriate pattern-concept pair from the knowledge base. PHRED, on the other hand, accesses the knowledge base by fetching pattern-concept pairs whose template fits the concept and constraints to be expressed.

Because fetching can be a time-consuming part of the generation process, it is important for the fetching mechanism to operate efficiently, but also to produce only those PC pairs that are likely to be useful. For this purpose, PHRED uses a hashing scheme designed to produce an ordering, or stream, of candidate patterns with a minimum of computation. Specifically, it performs some quick computation to select a sequence of PC pairs that might be of help in constructing a particular utterance. These pairs are then considered as PHRED continues its work. As the generator uses the first available appropriate utterance rather than evaluate all potential candidates, the ordering of this stream influences the choice process as well as the number of patterns ultimately considered.

The implementation of PHRED permits conceptual attributes to influence the search of linguistic alternatives, but separates this process from other aspects of language planning. High-level text goals are not included in the knowledge structures that influence the fetching process. In this regard, the system within which PHRED operates does not promote the desirable interaction among text planning and structural choices, as suggested by Appelt (1982) and Danlos (1984). Higher-level planning in the Unix Consultant, for modularity, is performed by a separable planning component.

The role of fetching in PHRED is to provide access to the pattern-concept pairs in the knowledge base. The input to the fetching mechanism is a set of constraints and conceptual attributes. Using this input as a guide, the fetching mechanism chooses PC pairs that serve as building blocks for the language produced. The pattern components of these PC pairs may include general patterns and ordering patterns as well as specialized phrases and lexical choices.

In producing the phrase "the file filename to be removed from the current directory", the fetching stage is given the following input:

```
p-o-s = inf-phrase
voice = passive
concept =
    (state-change (object file1)
            (state-name location)
            (from (inside-of (object current-directory)))
            (to (not (concept (inside-of (object current-directory))))))
```

From this input, the fetching mechanism must retrieve the "remove" pattern shown earlier as well as the ordering patterns necessary to produce a passive infinitive phrase.

The design of the hashing scheme that accomplishes this retrieval is based on the following reasoning: The input to the fetching mechanism may be described at least in part by a set of conceptual and linguistic properties, as may the pattern-concept pairs in the data base. The process of restriction, described in the next section, relies heavily on matching these two sets of properties. This process may therefore be expedited by computing an address in memory that "points" to PC pairs that have a particular set of attributes. Since there are combinatorially many such sets, there must be (1) a large number of addresses, or "buckets", and (2) an effective means of selecting which sets of "important" properties to use in computing each address.

The selection of "important" properties is determined as follows: All conceptual attributes, including those that are included within the concept part of the input, are considered important, and the linguistic attributes that are used for each p-o-s type are specified in the knowledge base. The fetching mechanism first searches buckets found through large sets of attributes, then buckets that correspond to smaller sets of attributes. The idea of this process is to consider first the PC pairs that most closely fit the input to the fetching mechanism. Since a hash into an empty bucket takes very little time, there is no great loss of time efficiency in using a fairly large number of hashes. Although the access to a PC pair through multiple buckets requires some additional space, this space is negligible compared to the size of the knowledge structures themselves.

The fetching component of PHRED, like the other parts of the system, is geared towards simplicity and uniformity. In spite of some of the differences among, for example, the selection of a verb, the choice of a referring expression and the selection of an article that agrees with its head noun, the same method is used for fetching in all three cases. The same hashing scheme is employed also to retrieve ordering patterns from the knowledge base. Such orderings can be effectively retrieved from their attributes in the same manner that any other PC pair is fetched. Thus, while the nature of the knowledge contained in the attributes of a lexical structure is arguably different from the knowledge within an ordering PC pair, these different types of knowledge may be accessed through the same mechanism. The principle behind this uniformity is that the level of specificity of the knowledge required to realize particular concepts and constraint cannot be predetermined; thus general and specific knowledge should be accessed in the same fashion.

The main loop of PHRED passes to the fetching component the set of constraints that a PC pair must satisfy. Typically, if there is a specific phrase, structural formula or other pattern that directly satisfies these constraints, it will appear in the stream before more general patterns. A pattern of unfixed word order will generally appear in the stream before an ordering pattern, because the ordering patterns tend to have few or no conceptual attributes. Most often, the unfixed pattern is chosen based on the concept that has been passed to the fetching mechanism, while the ordering pattern is chosen to select an ordering that produces the appropriate pattern-of-speech. The manner in which these patterns are combined is discussed in the next section. The fetching mechanism is repeatedly called to return patterns from the stream until all possible constraints are satisfied. For example, to produce the phrase "... not to remove the file", a negative ordering, infinitive, and "remove" pattern must all be fetched before the phrase can be restricted.

The construction of hash keys based on successively smaller sets of attributes assures that the PC pairs whose concept most closely matches the input concept will be considered first. The fetching mechanism produces a stream of pattern-concept pairs that are returned one at a time as they are requested by the generator. The rest of the program is insulated from the retrieval process. This way, some of the hashing computation can be postponed until it is required.

In the case of the "remove" example given above, the PC pair is indexed according to a combination of the semantic attributes "state-change", "location", "inside-of", and "not-inside-of". This combination is used at the time the PC pair is read in to determine which buckets should include the PC pair. The indexing mechanism ignores variables (e.g. "?actor"). During generation, a bucket indicating this PC pair will be found, based on the same semantic attributes. Some empty buckets, based on different combinations of attributes, will be searched also. A bucket including the passive infinitive ordering pattern is found by using the p-o-s and voice attributes.

Buckets that correspond to more complete sets of attributes are searched first. For example, if the "delete" pattern were constrained to be used only for the deletion of files, it would be retrieved before the "remove" PC pair because the bucket identified by the conjunction of the "file" attribute of file1 with the other semantic attributes of the concept is searched first.

A simple pattern, such as the word "the", does not really have a concept associated with it, and thus is indexed according to sets of its linguistic attributes only: A search for a definite article would find a bucket based on the properties "p-o-s = article" and "ref = def" and would thereby yield the pattern for "the".

The fetching component of PHRED constitutes about 10K bytes of object code, one tenth of the total program. A profile of PHRED shows that more than half of the CPU time consumed by the generator is spent in the fetching process. Earlier versions of the program, which did no ordering of candidate patterns in the fetching phases, spent less time fetching but more time overall.

When the fetching mechanism retrieves a pattern that has the appropriate "p-o-s" attribute, control is passed to the restriction phase. This phase is considered below.

3.2. Restriction

Each time a candidate pattern is returned from the stream by the fetching mechanism, it is passed to the restriction phase, along with any other unfixed-order patterns that have been retrieved. The restriction mechanism creates an instance of the pattern, adding new constraints to the pattern constituents while verifying that the PC pair meets the constraints given. There are three main aspects of this process:

unification of the variables within the PC pair's conceptual template and its associated properties with the target concept and properties, **elaboration** of the pattern constituents to include properties from corresponding properties in the pattern indicated by the "value" marker, and **combination** of the properties of constituents among the pattern and ordering patterns.

The following is an example of an instance of the "remove" PC pair given earlier, after restriction:

```
Pattern:
        <and  object   concept = file1   p-o-s = noun-phrase   case = objective>
        <and   root = remove    form = infinitive   voice = passive>
        <<word = by>
          <and   agent   concept = user1   case = objective>>
        <<word = from>
          <and   container   concept = directory1   case = objective>>


Concept: (state-change (object file1)
                       (state-name location)
                       (from (inside-of (object directory1)))
                       (to (not (concept (inside-of (object directory1))))))

Properties:
        p-o-s = inf-phrase
        tense = (value 2 tense)
        rem-object = file1
        cont = directory1
        forms = (passive-s)
```

This PC pair is the product of applying the restriction process twice in succession, once to the passive infinitive ordering and once to the "remove" pattern. Unification has occurred to bind the variables "?cont" and "?rem-object". Elaboration has added the tokens bound to these variables to the individual constituents. Combination of the "remove" pattern with the passive infinitive ordering has produced a pattern whose constituents are specified by the conglomeration of constraints of the PC pairs used.

Any of these three aspects of the restriction phase may result in failure. In the above example, unification would fail in an attempt to bind the multiple occurrences of "?cont" to different tokens, or if some variable binding violated an input constraint. Elaboration results in failure if a property to be added to a constituent does not fit the other properties. For example, if "directory1" in the example is not a container, the pattern would be judged inappropriate. Combination could likewise result in failure if the constraints from the ordering rule were incompatible with those from the "remove" pattern, for example if it had no passive form.

Properties marked by "value" in the PC pair are treated as variables and unified along with the other properties. If these variables remain unbound throughout the restriction process, however, the pattern retains the property with its "value" marker. This is necessary for future stages of the production process to obtain the property on demand. For example, a noun-phrase pattern in Spanish, where there is gender agreement between the subject of a passive infinitive phrase and the past participle, maintains the "gender = (value 2)" property to reflect that the gender of the NP is the gender of its NP2. This property is not determined until the head noun is chosen, after which it can be retrieved through the NP if necessary.

Restriction uses about 60% of the code of the generator and most of the CPU time not consumed by fetching. The bulk of this time is spent doing repeated unification when a large number of patterns are required. Because the nature of the knowledge structures in the system seems to require such unification, the fetching mechanism, as described in the previous section, is designed to prevent the consideration of patterns that might lead to failure during unification.

The next step in the generation process, after restriction, is to go through each constituent of the restricted pattern and invoke the generation process on the individual constituents, if necessary. This phase is described in the next section.

3.3. Interpretation

The third major phase in PHRED is interpretation, the application of constraints to a restricted pattern to produce a surface structure suitable for output.

The process of interpreting a given constituent may have three possible results: (1) the successful completion of an element of surface structure, (2) the recursive application of the fetch-restrict-interpret sequence on the given constituent, or (3) failure, if the generator is unable to produce a specified pattern of speech.

The first result occurs when the pattern provides a complete specification of a word or words for output, such as "the big apple", which is specified by the pattern

<word = the> <word = big> <word = apple>

The second case occurs if a constituent contains a more general set of constraints, for example,

<and p-o-s = verb root = remove tense = past>

which requires another recurrence of the fetch-restrict-interpret sequence.

In the third result, where no output produces the desired pattern of speech subject to the constraints given by the uninterpreted pattern, the system must back up to select an alternate pattern. To be efficient, the system must utilize as much as possible the patterns that have already been selected. If the constituent that fails in the interpretation phase is optional to the pattern to which it belongs, it is deleted. Otherwise, failure results in backing up to the level where the failed pattern was fetched, getting another pattern from the stream, and attempting restriction of the new pattern. Most often this new pattern will be an ordering rule, and most of the failed pattern will be used in the restriction of the ordering pattern. A simple case of this is where the generator fails to produce a pattern of speech for the subject of a sentence and instead generates a passive sentence. In this case the restricted version of the PC pair as it was before the combination with the active ordering pattern is backed up on a stack so that the passive ordering can be tried.

Failure during interpretation is rare, and generally results from an insufficiency of the knowledge base in producing a reference. While a better model of the generation process might allow for the anticipation of such failures, such anticipation would in general require decisions considerably more complex than those made by PHRED. This complexity would be underutilized in light of the infrequency with which back-up is necessary. Although the back-up algorithm employed in these failures is time-consuming, it increases the likelihood that some successful utterance will be produced.

The agreement of constituents within a pattern is assured during the interpretation phase. A constituent that must agree with another has a form such as the following:

<and   p-o-s = verb   root = remove   tense = past
number = (matches 1)   person = (matches 1)>

This specifies a past tense form of "remove" that matches its subject in person and number. Interpretation results in the substitution of properties from the matched constituent to produce, for example,

<and   p-o-s = verb   root = remove   tense = past
number = singular   person = third>

In English there are only limited forms of agreement. There are few examples where it passes from right to left, such as in subject-aux inversion where the verb agrees with a subject that follows it. In other languages agreement within a pattern may be much more complex. In the Spanish example, *"Juan les habló a sus amigos"* ("John spoke to his friends") the indirect pronoun *les*, which precedes the verb, agrees with the indirect object, which follows the verb.

In all cases PHRED can ensure proper agreement if some order of interpreting the constituents allows the correct application of constraints. The surface order of the constituents is the default order for their interpretation, but interpretation of a constituent where necessary is done only after that of constituents with which it must agree. In English, nouns within noun phrases are interpreted before their attached determiners, because the determiner must sometime agree in number with the head noun. In more inflected languages verbs must generally be produced last.

Anaphora are handled specially during interpretation. In the case of constituents for which PHRED has already produced references, the generator applies a set of heuristics that will remove the constituent entirely if it is not necessary to the utterance, pronominalize, or regenerate the entire constituent. The principal heuristics are (1) If the anaphoric constituent is optional, remove it from the current pattern, and (2) pronominalize other anaphoric constituents wherever possible. There are of course many cases in which an alternative reference would be preferable, but the method used by PHRED is generally effective in producing coherent references. The heuristics lead, for example, to the production of "Mary was told by John that he wanted the book to be given to him" rather than "Mary was told by John that John wanted the book to be given to John by Mary". It is apparent that these heuristics would break down in the generation of longer texts, a task for which neither PHRED nor the PHRAN/PHRED knowledge base was designed.

The interpretation mechanism occupies about 20% of the code of the generator, and requires a small amount of time relative to the rest of the program.

This discussion has described the overall design of PHRED and presented some details of its implementation. The next section traces an example of the generation process and discusses the role of each of the three phases considered here.

4. A Detailed Example

Below is an annotated trace of PHRED while generating the sentence, "Typing 'rm filename' causes the file filename to be removed from the current directory." This is a fairly simple example, but demonstrates well the process used by PHRED to produce an output. At each step in the trace, the generator prints out which phase it is going through, and what the input to that phase is. Ellipses (...) are used to indicate information that has been omitted because it reduplicates other material. As earlier in the text, symbols preceded by a question mark indicate variables, such as "?actor". Symbols surrounded by asterisks, e. g. "*user*" are tokens that have special processing implications in the UNIX Consultant. Other special tokens are indicated by atoms followed by numerals, such as "file1".

The input to the generator is the concept that the UNIX consultant has chosen to express, in response to a question about removing files in UNIX. The concept represents UC's knowledge that using the 'rm' command is an established plan (here "planfor") for deleting a file (here "file1"):

```
-------------------------------------------------
***Fetching***
```

```
concept =
  (planfor
    (result
      (state-change (object file1)
                    (state-name location)
                    (from (inside-of (object current-directory)))
                    (to (not (concept (inside-of (object current-directory)))))))
    (method
      (mtrans (actor *user*)
              (object
                (command (name rm)
                         (args (filename))))
              (from *user*)
              (to *UNIX*))))
```

There are a number of patterns that could potentially be used to express the concept that an action is a plan for something. Two of the possible constructs in the PHRED knowledge base are an imperative, e.g. "Use 'rm' to delete a file", and a future or present tense declarative, e.g. "'Rm' will delete a file". In this case, PHRED selects another pattern with the verb "cause". The stream of candidate patterns includes first the constructs found in a bucket reached through the "planfor" concept, followed by other sentence-level PC pairs. In examples such as this one, where PHRED's fetching mechanism reaches several constructs through the same bucket, the generator selects a random order in the stream for the alternatives. For this example, therefore, a random selection ultimately determines the form of the output. After the selection is made, the restriction process is applied to the first pattern.

Restricting

Pattern: <p-o-s = act-phrase>
            <and p-o-s = verb   root = cause>
            <and p-o-s = inf-phrase   voice = passive>

Concept: (planfor (result ?result) (method ?method))

Properties:
            method = (value 1)
            result = (value 3)
            p-o-s = sentence
            form = (declarative active)
            tense = (value 2)

The restriction process here results in the addition of the appropriate conceptual components to the constituents of the restricted pattern. The conceptual content of the first and third constituents, which will produce a gerund phrase and passive infinitive phrase, respectively, have been added. This results from the *unification* of the variables "method" and "result" in the list of properties above and the *elaboration* of the constituents specified by the terms "(value 1)" and "(value 3)" attached to these variables. *Combination* with an active sentence pattern adds the subject-verb agreement, and the restricted pattern enters the interpretation phase:

Interpreting

Pattern:

```
<and p-o-s = act-phrase
     concept =
         (mtrans (actor *user*)
                 (object
                     (command (name rm) (args (filename))))
                 (from *user*)
                 (to *UNIX*))>

<and   p-o-s = verb   root = cause
       person = (matches 1)   number = (matches 1)>

<and  p-o-s = inf-phrase
      voice = passive
           concept =
                    (state-change (object file1)
                        (state-name location)
                        (from (inside-of (object current-directory)))
                        (to (not (concept (inside-of (object current-directory)))))))>
```

Properties:

```
tense = value 2
form = (declarative active)
p-o-s = sentence
result = value 3
method = value 1
concept = ...
method = ...
result = ...
```

At this point the generator has successfully applied the input concept to restrict the surface structure chosen, and recursively interprets this structure, starting with the gerund phrase:

Interpreting

Pattern:

```
<and  p-o-s = act-phrase
      concept =
          (mtrans (actor *user*)
                  (object
                      (command (name rm) (args (filename))))
                  (from *user*)
                  (to *UNIX*))>
```

Interpreting a simple constituent results in a reinvocation of the fetch-restrict-interpret sequence on that constituent:

```
--------------------------------------------------
***Fetching***

concept =
            (mtrans (actor *user*)
                (object
                    (command (name rm) (args (filename))))
                (from *user*)
                (to *UNIX*)))
p-o-s = act-phrase
```

Since there is no pattern that directly generates a gerund phrase (here "p-o-s = act-phrase") with the given concept, the fetch above yields an ordering pattern that can be used for combination with other patterns to produce the final phrase. Thus another fetch is performed before any restriction is done, this time without the "p-o-s" attribute.

```
--------------------------------------------------
***Fetching***

concept = (mtrans ... )
```

PHRED searches for a way of expressing the "mtrans", or communicative transfer, of the 'rm' command to the operating system. The hashing mechanism gives preference to the terms for technical transmission of commands, because the concepts associated with these terms match the input concept more closely, but a problematic pattern still results:

```
--------------------------------------------------
***Restricting***

Pattern: <person> <root do> <command>


Concept:  (mtrans (actor ?actor)
                (object ?command)
                (from ?actor)
                (to *UNIX*))

Properties:
            command = (command (name ?name) (args nil))
            name = (value 3 command-name)
```

This pattern fails during unification because it requires that the command not have arguments, something that the fetching mechanism failed to detect because the bucket that includes the pattern is found by considering less specific attributes. This failure is illustrative of a class of examples where PHRED's hashing mechanism, in short-cutting the complexity of unification, picks the wrong pattern. With the gerund ordering pattern still being saved, the fetching mechanism is called again for another candidate. The pattern returned here by the fetching mechanism is the next one in the stream after the failed "do" pattern. This new pattern, with the verb "type", is then passed through restriction:

Restricting

Pattern: \<person\> \<root = type\> \<command-spec\>

Concept: (mtrans (actor ?actor)
                 (object ?command)
                 (from ?actor)
                 (to *UNIX*))

Properties:
        command = (value 3)

Unification of the variables in the above PC-pair with those in the input concept is followed by elaboration of the constituents and combination with the gerund ordering pattern. This yields the following result:

Restricting

Pattern:
                \<and   root = type   form = progressive\>
                \<and   command-spec
                        concept = (command (name rm) (args (filename)))\>

Properties:
        p-o-s = act-phrase

The combination of the "type" pattern with the gerund ordering satisfies the necessary constraints, producing a two-constituent pattern which then proceeds to the interpretation phase:

Interpreting

Pattern:
                \<and   p-o-s = verb   root = type   form = progressive\>
                \<and   command-spec
                        concept = (command (name rm) (args (filename)))\>

PHRED recursively invokes the interpretation procedure on each of the two constituents, starting with the progressive verb:

Interpreting

Pattern:
        \<and   p-o-s = verb   root = type   form = progressive\>

Fetching

p-o-s = verb   form = progressive   root = type

This fetch uses a hash on the root and form of the verb given to retrieve the progressive form "typing", whose properties unify trivially with the given constraints:

Restricting

Pattern:
    \<word = typing>

Properties:
    form = progressive   p-o-s = verb   root = type

Interpreting

Pattern:
       \<word = typing>

Properties:
    root = type   p-o-s = verb   form = progressive

The word "typing" and its properties are now completely specified, so no further restriction is needed. The next constituent in the gerund phrase, the noun phrase that describes the command 'rm', is thus passed to the interpretation mechanism:

Interpreting

Pattern:
    \<p-o-s = noun-phrase command-spec
        concept = (command (name rm) (args (filename)))>

As usual, interpretation first results in a fetch:

Fetching

concept = (command (name rm) (args (filename)))
p-o-s = noun-phrase

The pattern selected for the command is a specific formula for expressing commands to UNIX, the command name following by its arguments, in quotes:

Restricting

Pattern:
    \<word = |'|> \<command> \<p-o-s = args> \<word = |'|>

Properties:
    p-o-s = noun-phrase
    concept = (command (name ?command) (args ?args))
    args = (value 3 name)
    command = (value 2 command-name))

The formula for producing 'rm filename' is straightforward, and results in very little additional work by the generator:

```
-------------------------------------------------
```
Interpreting

Pattern:

        <word = I'I>
        <and command command-name = rm>
        <and p-o-s = args name = filename>
        <word = I'I>

Properties:

        p-o-s = noun-phrase
        ...

```
-------------------------------------------------
```
Interpreting

Pattern: <word = I'I>

```
-------------------------------------------------
```
Interpreting

Pattern: <command command-name = rm>

```
-------------------------------------------------
```
Fetching

command-name = rm

```
-------------------------------------------------
```
Restricting

Pattern: <word = rm>

```
-------------------------------------------------
```
Interpreting

Pattern: <word = rm>

```
-------------------------------------------------
```
Interpreting

Pattern: <and p-o-s = args name = (filename)>

```
-------------------------------------------------
```
Interpreting

Pattern: <word = I'I>

Having completed the clause "Typing 'rm filename' ", the generator now returns to the highest level of the surface structure to finish the sentence. The next constituent in this surface structure is the conjugated form of the verb "cause":

```
-------------------------------------------------
```
Interpreting

Pattern: <p-o-s = verb root = cause person = (matches 1) number = (matches 1)>

The interpretation mechanism finds the person and number of the first constituent of the surface structure. Since this is a singular gerund phrase, it has the third person and singular properties. These are then used in fetching the appropriate verb form:

```
---------------------------------------------------
***Fetching***

p-o-s = verb   root = cause   form = basic   person = third   number = singular
```

As with "typing", hashing results in the retrieval of the correct verb, and restriction is a simple process:

```
---------------------------------------------------
***Restricting***

Pattern: <word = causes>

Properties:
         tense = present   root = cause   person = third   number = singular   form = basic

---------------------------------------------------
***Interpreting***

Pattern: <word = causes>

Properties: ...
```

Having completed the specification of the verb "causes", PHRED continues its depth-first interpretation with the third and final top-level constituent, the infinitive phrase:

```
---------------------------------------------------
***Interpreting***

Pattern:
         <and   p-o-s = inf-phrase   voice = passive
            concept =
                (state-change (object file1)
                              (state-name location)
                              (from (inside-of (object current-directory)))
                              (to (not (concept (inside-of (object current-directory)))))))>


---------------------------------------------------
***Fetching***

concept = (state-change ... )
p-o-s = inf-phrase
voice = passive

---------------------------------------------------
***Fetching***

     ...
```

The first fetch in this case again brings the ordering pattern, the second the "remove" pattern. The restriction process is applied first to the "remove" pattern:

```
------------------------------------------------------
***Restricting***
```

Pattern: <person> <root = remove> <physob> <<word = from> <container>>

Concept:

        (state-change (object ?rem-object))
                (state-name location)
                (from (inside-of (object ?container)))
                (to (not (concept (inside-of (object ?container))))))

Properties:

        rem-object = (value 3)
        ...

At this point, the generator is producing an expression for the passive infinitive phrase following the verb "causes". After unification and elaboration of the pattern above, the pattern is then combined with the ordering pattern for the passive infinitive phrase, a somewhat more specialized pattern than is necessary for the construction of such phrases. The restriction process results in the determination of the final ordering of the constituents, and another round of restriction:

```
------------------------------------------------------
***Restricting***
```

Pattern:
        <and physob   concept = file1>
        <and   p-o-s = verb   root = be   form = infinitive>
        <and   p-o-s = verb   root = remove   form = perfective>
        <<word = from>
          <and container   concept = current-directory>>

Properties:
                subject = ?inf-phrase-subject
                voice = passive
                object = ?inf-phrase-object
                p-o-s = inf-phrase
                form = (passive)

Having completed the restriction of the infinitive, PHRED passes control to the interpretation mechanism, which then proceeds to generate each part of the infinitive phrase pattern:

```
------------------------------------------------------
***Interpreting***
```

Pattern:
                <and   physob   concept = file1>
                <and   p-o-s = verb   root = be   form = infinitive>
                <and   p-o-s = verb   root = remove   form = perfective>
                <<word = from>
                  <and container   concept = current-directory>>

Properties:
                p-o-s = inf-phrase
                concept = ...
                ...

As the interpretation starts with the first constituent of the infinitive phrase, PHRED now must produce a referent for the specified file. To do this, it expands the token "file1" to get the necessary information from its attributes.

```
-----------------------------------------------------
***Interpreting***

Pattern:
        <and  physob  concept = (file (name (filename)))

Properties:
        concept =  ...
        p-o-s = noun-phrase

-----------------------------------------------------
***Fetching***

p-o-s = noun-phrase
concept =  ...
```

PHRED uses a structural formula, directly associated by a PC pair with the concept of a file, to refer to the hypothetical file:

```
-----------------------------------------------------
***Restricting***

Pattern: <word = the> <word = file> <name>

Concept:   (file (name (filename)))

Properties:
                ref = def
                p-o-s = noun-phrase
                person = third
                number = singular
                name = (value 3 name)
```

This pattern is the default reference for files, which is superceded when more information about a given file must be conveyed. The noun phrase now reaches the interpretation phase, resulting in the simple verification that its constituents are complete:

```
-----------------------------------------------------
***Interpreting***

Pattern:    <word = the> <word = file> <and   p-o-s = args   name = (filename)>

Properties:
                concept  =  ...  p-o-s = noun-phrase   ref = def
        ...
```

Having completed the reference, the system now continues with the infinitive phrase. The second constituent of the infinitive phrase is the infinitive of the verb "be":

```
-----------------------------------------------------
***Interpreting***
```

Pattern: <and   p-o-s = verb   root = be   form = infinitive>

As with the other verbs, fetching yields the appropriate form:

```
-----------------------------------------------------
***Fetching***
```

p-o-s = verb   root = be   form = infinitive

```
-----------------------------------------------------
***Restricting***
```

Pattern: <word = to> <word = be>

Properties:
     p-o-s = verb   root = be   form = infinitive   voice = active

```
-----------------------------------------------------
***Interpreting***
```

Pattern: <word = to> <word = be>

Properties: ...

The third constituent of the passive infinitive phrase is the past participle of the verb "remove", which is interpreted next. This process similarly results in the completed verb form:

```
-----------------------------------------------------
***Interpreting***
```

Pattern: <p-o-s = verb root = remove form = perfective>

```
-----------------------------------------------------
***Fetching***
```

p-o-s = verb
root = remove
form = perfective

   ...
```
-----------------------------------------------------
***Interpreting***
```

Pattern: <removed>

Properties: ...

The final constituent of the infinitive phrase and of the sentence is the optional prepositional phrase specifying from where the file is being deleted. The extra angle brackets in the pattern below indicate to the interpretation mechanism that if it fails to produce a reference or if the reference in the prepositional phrase is anaphoric, the entire constituent may be omitted:

```
-----------------------------------------------------
***Interpreting***
```

Pattern: <<word = from> <and container concept = current-directory>>

The first constituent of the prepositional phrase, the word "from", is already complete:

```
-----------------------------------------------------
***Interpreting***
```

Pattern: <word = from>

The second constituent, the referent for the "current-directory", is interpreted next:

```
-----------------------------------------------------
***Interpreting***
```

Pattern: <and   p-o-s = noun-phrase container concept = current-directory>

```
-----------------------------------------------------
***Fetching***
```

p-o-s = noun-phrase   concept = current-directory   ref = def

Unlike the previous noun phrase, there is no specific structural formula for referring to the current directory. PHRED thus uses a general noun phrase pattern:

```
-----------------------------------------------------
***Restricting***
```

Pattern:

    <and p-o-s = article   consonance = (matches 2)   number = (matches 2)>
    <and p-o-s = noun   number = singular>

Properties:

    p-o-s = noun-phrase
    person = third
    number = singular
    ...
    concept = (value 2)
    number = (value 2 number)
    person = (value 2 person)
    ...

"Consonance" here is the property used to handle the distinction between "a" and "an", which depends on the choice of noun. "Hard" consonance is used for nouns or adjectives beginning with a consonant sound, and "soft" for those beginning with a vowel sound. For definite articles, the property is not used.

Elaboration of the pattern above results in a two-constituent pattern to be interpreted, the second constituent of which must refer to the "current-directory" concept.

```
-------------------------------------------------
***Interpreting***
```

Pattern:
```
        <and   p-o-s = article   consonance = (matches 2)
              number = (matches 2)   ref = def>
        <and   p-o-s = noun   concept = current-directory
              number = singular>
```

Properties: ...

While there is no special noun phrase for referring to the "current-directory" concept, there are special noun constructs. PHRED selects randomly between two ways of referring to this concept, "current directory" and "working directory".

```
-------------------------------------------------
***Interpreting***
```

Pattern: <and p-o-s = noun concept = current-directory   number = singular>

```
-------------------------------------------------
***Fetching***
```

p-o-s = noun   number = singular   person = third   concept = current-directory

The reference selected for the directory is the compound noun "current directory". This is interpreted before the article within the noun phrase, since articles are produced after head nouns to ensure agreement:

```
-------------------------------------------------
***Restricting***
```

Pattern: <word = current> <word = directory>

Properties:
        concept = ... consonance = hard   person = third   number = singular   p-o-s = noun

```
-------------------------------------------------
***Interpreting***
```

Pattern: <word = current> <word = directory>

Properties: ...

The interpretation mechanism judges the noun compound to be completed, and the final determiner is then interpreted:

```
-------------------------------------------------
***Interpreting***
```

Pattern: <and   p-o-s = article   ref = def   number = singular   consonance = hard>

```
   ...
-----------------------------------------------------
***Interpreting***

Pattern: <word = the>

Properties: ...

-----------------------------------------------------
```

After the final part of the surface structure is complete, a walk through the surface structure tree is used to produce the final output:

> Typing 'rm filename' causes the file filename to be removed
> from the current directory.

5. Comparison with Other Research

PHRED differs in design from most other natural language generation systems because of its conception as a generator to accompany PHRAN as part of a language interface. The application of specialized phrasal knowledge seems to be an effective means of satisfying the demands on a generator in a domain such as that of the UNIX Consultant. The use of a declarative knowledge base shared between analyzer and generator has helped to make the system practical and easily extensible. PHRED's simplicity and the speed with which it applies this knowledge have made it well-suited for use in real-time natural language interfaces.

Primarily for historical reasons, most research in computational linguistics has focused on rules governing syntax. In language analysis, it is often practical to design systems whose principal function is to apply and test such rules by determining the grammaticality of the input. Such systems generally use compositional rules, if any, for determining the semantic content of the input. The task of language generation, however, is inextricably tied to the *appropriateness* of the linguistic output as well as to its grammaticality. Because of this, work in generation focuses not on the representation of core syntactic rules but on the means by which a *choice* is made among syntactic and lexical constructs. Compositional rules generally fail to constrain this choice adequately. For this reason systems that are designed for language generation have often employed either special choice systems of the type found in systemic grammar (Halliday, 1968), or have had pattern-based grammars of the type found in PHRAN/PHRED and in unification grammar (Kay, 1984), which require a sophisticated mechanism for dealing with the interaction of the patterns. Thus PHRAN/PHRED is the first interface in a natural language-based artificial intelligence system to use an entirely common representation and knowledge base for linguistic knowledge employed in both analysis and production.

The declarative pattern-concept pair representation, its theory, and its role in PHRED, are considered in the discussion that follows.

5.1. The PC Pair

The pattern-concept pair representation differs on the surface from traditional grammars because the grammar is embedded implicitly in the knowledge structures. These knowledge structures often require the combination of a number of patterns to produce an utterance. In this way the representation is comparable to unification grammar, which contains patterns associated with functional descriptions. The restriction process described in this paper is similar to the unification procedure in TELEGRAM (Appelt, 1983), which employs a unification grammar.

One difference between PHRED's knowledge structures and those in unification grammar is that conceptual attributes of the PC pairs, as well as functional attributes, or properties, are used to constrain a pattern. Unification grammar, like most feature systems, generally fosters the separation of conceptual and functional components. Another distinction is that, in unification grammar, the syntactic category is given special status; in pattern-concept pairs it is treated as an attribute, and does not necessarily have to be specified for every pattern. This is important for patterns that can be used in conjunction with many different orderings to produce a variety of syntactic structures.

A general difference between the PC pair and other representations lies in the level of specificity of the patterns. The PC pair makes it easy to encode specialized phrases and constructs to be used by the generator. It allows the generator to apply the same mechanisms to both general and specific constructions, and to choose PC pairs based on their conceptual attributes. This is, naturally, a distinction based on how the pattern-concept pairs are used rather than on their basic structure. The same result might well be achieved within the basic framework of lexical functional grammar or unification grammar.

Semantic grammar (Burton, 1976) is another representation scheme that, like that of PHRED, facilitates the use of semantic attributes in language processing. There are versions of such grammars that allow for varying degrees of interaction between syntax, semantics, and pragmatics. PHRED differs from true semantic grammars primarily in that it facilitates the interaction of the more general patterns with the more specialized. Semantic grammars are often too constrained to be adapted to a new domain. Many of the knowledge structures in PHRED, by comparison, are general enough so that much of the linguistic knowledge used within the UNIX domain existed in the PHRAN/PHRED knowledge base before UC was even conceived.

The pattern-concept pair representation has developed in parallel with research on idiomatic and specialized use of language, done primarily by cognitive linguists. Similar ideas may be found in a variety of grammatical theories emphasizing the study of levels of linguistic and conceptual knowledge and the relations between them (cf. Lockwood, 1972; Makkai, 1972). The concept of units of meaning linked to lexical units is described, for example, by Pike (1962) and Lamb (1973).

Much of the work on specialized language questions the cognitive validity of traditional generative theories of grammar. Chafe (1968) identifies certain idioms, such as "by and large" and "all of a sudden" which would be ungrammatical were they not given special status as idiomatic constructions. Other expressions, such as "kick the bucket", are grammatical, but have a meaning that is not determined by any compositional relationship among their components. Chafe argues that these idiomatic constructs sufficiently pervade everyday language to warrant an approach to language that handles these constructs not as special cases or exceptions but as an integral part of a language.

Becker (1975) presents the idea of the phrasal lexicon as a means of handling canned and idiomatic phrases. Becker identifies in particular a range of phrases that are grammatical and even comprehensible via compositional rules, yet which suggest specialized contextual knowledge. The expression "It only hurts when I laugh" can theoretically be handled using traditional theories of grammar, but treating it as such would be ignoring an important component of the expression's meaning. The existence of such expressions, which involve either partially or entirely specialized knowledge, has generally been treated as of minor importance in computational theories of language. However, a cognitively realistic representation must take into account the role of both general syntactic knowledge and specialized knowledge about particular phrases.

While these arguments are directed at developing cognitively valid theories of linguistic representation, the handling of idiomatic constructs and of specialized phrasal knowledge has a substantial influence on the robustness and efficiency of a system. If specialized linguistic knowledge is indeed as pervasive as Chafe argues, a system that deals only with "core" grammatical and productive constructs will handle but a small portion of a language. A generator working within such a system would be severely limited in the range of utterances that it could produce and in its ability to produce an output appropriate to a given context. On the other hand, failing to take advantage of linguistic generalizations can introduce redundancy and possibly inefficiency into the knowledge base. Robust and efficient language processing therefore demands a representation that takes advantage of both specialized idiomatic and general syntactic knowledge. Experience with the UNIX Consultant has suggested that the interaction of specialized and general linguistic knowledge is important for a natural language interface. This interaction is accomplished in PHRED by allowing the generator to combine ordering patterns with patterns used to relate linguistic constructs to their particular meanings.

Fillmore (1979) gives arguments for the idea of the **structural formula,** a phrase or construction that cannot be described strictly as the composition of its components but may still have a certain degree of structural freedom. Fillmore presents "<Time unit> in and <Time unit> out" as an example of such a formula, manifest in expressions such as "day in and day out" and "week in and week out". More recently, Fillmore and others extend this idea to a theory of **grammatical constructions** (*cf.* Fillmore, Kay, and O' Connor, 1984; Lakoff, 1984), focusing on expressions that exhibit certain regularities and obey some grammatical constraints but whose behavior cannot be determined by "core" grammar. Examples of such expressions are "let alone" as in "He didn't make first lieutenant, let alone general", and the deictic "there", as in "There goes Harry, shooting his mouth off again". Fillmore, Kay, and O' Connor point out the difference between attempting to develop a minimal base of knowledge from which a linguistic competence can be *computed,* and attempting to develop a knowledge base that represents how human linguistic knowledge is in fact *stored.*

As an example of this distinction, consider the division drawn by Fillmore, Kay, and O' Connor between idioms of **decoding,** such as "kick the bucket", and "spill the beans", and idioms of **encoding** only, such as "answer the door", and "wide awake." All of these are grammatical idioms; that is, they have a syntactic structure and word order compatible with core grammatical constructs. The idioms of decoding, however, require specialized knowledge both for the comprehension of their meaning and their appropriate use. The idioms of encoding could possibly be comprehended using knowledge about their components only, but specialized knowledge is required to predict their use. Whether this specialized knowledge is to be stored in a given representational model therefore depends on what problem the model is addressing: competence, comprehension, or production.

We have thus distinguished three potential classes of linguistic knowledge: (1) The knowledge that is required to determine the *membership* of a given phrase or sentence in a language, (2) that which is necessary to determine the *meaning* of a phrase, and (3) that which determines appropriate *use* of the phrase. Computational linguistics has emphasized the first class, and thus many systems have attempted to define the second and third knowledge classes by adding auxiliary knowledge to a grammar for a linguistic competence. The PHRAN/PHRED pattern-concept pair representation, on the other hand, attempts to *subsume* the three classes into a single framework. Since the goal of PHRAN and PHRED is proficient analysis and use of language, the distinction between grammatical and extragrammatical idioms becomes of minor importance. It seems counterintuitive to treat phrases such as "all of a sudden" as of a different nature from "kick the bucket" simply because the former is extragrammatical. Further, the emphasis on the ability to compute a linguistic competence using a small set of rules is diminished. If specialized knowledge about a given phrase is required for its appropriate use, there is no reason why this knowledge cannot also be used for its syntactic analysis, even if in a system that performs analysis alone such knowledge would be redundant.

Consider the phrase "answer the door". A pure syntactic analyzer would require no special knowledge to recognize the construct as a valid verb phrase. It is possible as well that the meaning of the phrase could be determined based on the structure of the verb phrase and its constituents. However, in order for PHRED to give the phrase its deserved distinction from "respond to the door" or other less appropriate utterances, special knowledge, that "answer the door" means to open a door in response to a knock or doorbell, is required. Since this knowledge is encoded into the common knowledge base, it may also be used by PHRAN to determine the meaning of the phrase.

The development of a knowledge base for the purposes of both language analysis and language production therefore changes the nature of the linguistic knowledge base and its use. Information that is redundant when considered from a formal linguistic standpoint may be important for a particular aspect of language processing. Such specialized knowledge may then be used by other components of the system. Thus the emphasis in the PHRAN/PHRED representation is on the *storage* of such redundant information rather than on its *computation*. Specialized knowledge about phrases and constructions is an integral part of the knowledge base and is used preferentially to general knowledge that requires more computation, both for analysis and production.

Of course, fundamental differences between analysis and generation still exist in PHRAN and PHRED. While the two programs have a shared knowledge base, they have entirely independent methods of accessing and applying their linguistic knowledge. PHRAN accesses patterns by recognizing sequences of constituents; PHRED must select a pattern based on the concept it is to express and the constraints that the pattern must satisfy. The PHRED approach to language generation is committed to the representation of linguistic knowledge in a declarative form that can be shared by the analyzer. The knowledge structures used by the generator are the same as those used by the analyzer, but the *process* that makes use of this knowledge to produce an utterance still reflects the basic choice problem.

The appropriateness of natural language output seems enhanced by the pattern-concept pair representation. Much of the knowledge used to produce language, particularly in specialized domains, is specialized knowledge. A natural language program that treats grammatical constructions and canned or idiomatic phrases independently of "core" grammar requires special rules and procedures to make use of such phrases. In PHRED specialized constructs are selected and produced using the same mechanism as the more productive constructs, facilitating the interaction of linguistic knowledge of varying levels of generality. In this way a wider range of appropriate utterances may be produced from a given conceptual form.

This discussion has focussed on the general representational aspects of PHRED. The next section concentrates on the details that relate specifically to other generation systems.

5.2. PHRED and other Generation Systems

PHRED differs from other generation systems primarily in the way it applies its knowledge to the generation task. Many language generation systems used in conjunction with large programs separate the linguistic knowledge base and lexicon from the conceptual knowledge base of the system (McDonald, 1980; Mann and Matthiessen, 1983; McKeown, 1982). This has a variety of advantages, particularly the ability to develop and modify one module without affecting another. It also has the disadvantage of inhibiting the use of conceptual information by the generator, or of requiring redundant representation of such information, unless the modules are specifically designed to utilize common knowledge. In PHRED linguistic knowledge, e. g. pattern concept pairs, is maintained separately from world knowledge, e. g. knowledge about the UNIX domain, to permit such advantages as the interchangeability of English and Spanish knowledge bases in UC. However, the generator may access the conceptual knowledge base of the system and such knowledge may interact with the syntactic knowledge. For example, the verbs "remove" and "delete" are synonymous when used to refer to actions on files, but "delete" may not generally be used with physical objects. PHRED restricts the use of "delete" during elaboration by examining the semantic nature of its object. If the object is not a file, the use of "delete" to refer to the action of removing it is prohibited.

Certain other complete natural language systems, like PHRAN/PHRED, exploit knowledge shared between analyzer and generator. The HAM-ANS question-answerer (Wahlster *et. al.*, 1983; Busemann, 1984) makes use of a shared lexicon. The VIE-LANG system (Steinacker and Buchberger, 1983) shares a "syntactico-semantic" lexicon, but the generator accesses this lexicon using a discrimination net with specialized choice knowledge.

A notable difference in implementation between PHRED and other generators is in the fetching mechanism. The division of the choice problem into an initial biasing and an evaluation component allows PHRED to bias its construction of utterances using a specialized hashing scheme. This has proven a boon for both simplicity and efficiency, as some of the rules that govern choice are carried out by a simple hashing process and thus fewer patterns reach the restriction phase. The basic choice mechanism as implemented in PHRED therefore encompasses two different phenomena, which may be viewed as **predisposition** and **selection.** Predisposition is the process by which access to a knowledge base is influenced by various factors -- such as the context, the concept to be expressed, or specific constraints on the desired output -- to influence the order or priority in which elements of the knowledge base are considered. Selection is the evaluation of an element from the knowledge base. Intuitively, predisposition is the underlying access process that influences the likelihood of considering a particular word or phrase; selection is the judgement process that determines whether the word or phrase is appropriate. This resembles the notion of "register" in the systemic tradition (*cf.* Halliday, 1978), but the biasing is not limited to situational influences.

There are three motivations for a design that provides for both a predisposition and a selection phase of the choice process. First, a system that employs as its principal choice mechanism, for example, a discrimination net such as Goldman's (Goldman, 1975) or a unification scheme such as McKeown's (McKeown, 1982) may apply its choice algorithm to many unlikely candidates, sometimes causing inefficiency. For example, the system might consider the verbs "smoke" and "inhale" every time it chooses the verb "breathe". A fast indexing mechanism that quickly selects candidates trims the time spent evaluating inappropriate choices.

The second motivating force lies in the distinction between utterances that are technically correct in expressing a given concept and those that are generally appropriate to a given context. "John inhaled air" is technically correct but generally inappropriate in place of "John breathed". This type of distinction can be embedded in a choice mechanism by attempting to axiomatize the rules that determine appropriateness, or it can be embedded in a predisposition mechanism that happens to order the choices according to the context. Predisposition thus provides a means for biasing choice without blurring the distinction between correctness and appropriateness.

The third motivation is cognitive validity. The predisposition-selection distinction fits the intuition that people have when they hear an unusual sentence: "It's okay but I wouldn't say it." In the example of "breathe" and "inhale air" both utterances may fit the input conceptualization, but fluent speakers tend to choose the former. Fluent speakers also bias their predisposition mechanisms according to the nature and formality of the context. Pawley and Syder (1980) find that one of the differences between native and non-native speakers of a language is that non-native speakers take a long time to develop the predisposition component necessary for fluency. Chafe has pointed out some of the influential factors in the variations between spoken and written, or informal and formal, language (Chafe, 1984). While some of this work is still in its early stages, the evidence strongly suggests a contextual biasing component distinct from the selection or evaluation phase of production.

The goal behind the PHRED indexing scheme is to incorporate as much of the choice problem as possible into the fetching, or predisposition, phase. Some language generators (Goldman, 1975; McDonald, 1980) use indexing tools that model choice as a multistage evaluation or decision-making process. The division of this process in

PHRED into an "automatic" biasing component and a judgement component has some practical advantages. The hashing algorithm that drives the fetching mechanism orders the stream of patterns retrieved before any of them is actually evaluated, and thus the more time-consuming restriction process is spared having to apply heuristics to make certain choices. For example, a general heuristic used by a number of language generators can be expressed as "Choose the most specific pattern that matches the input constraints". In PHRED, this heuristic is realized by the hashing mechanism, which orders candidate patterns in terms of the number of buckets that yield them. In this way the sentence "John asked Bill to leave" is generally produced without considering the alternative "John informed Bill that he wanted him to leave".

Appelt (1982) has presented language generation as the multi-level process of planning utterances to satisfy multiple goals. A division in this multi-stage process can be made between the task domain and the linguistic domain, i. e.., between the system level and the interface level. PHRED operates at the interface level. User input to the UNIX consultant system is first analyzed by PHRAN, producing a conceptual knowledge structure that motivates the system's response (Wilensky, Arens, and Chin, 1984). The planning component of the system exists entirely within the task domain of UC. Independent of the language being used, the UC planner makes the choice of illocutionary act, speech act, and the message to be conveyed. PHRED expresses the message in natural language.

While the ability to handle complex problems in language planning, such as the generation of references requiring knowledge about the hearer's knowledge, might be desirable even at the PHRED level, it is difficult to perform such planning within a real-time system. It is both counter-intuitive and inefficient to treat language production as primarily a reasoning process involving complex inference mechanisms. In fact, the need for such reasoning in language production seems rare. Thus the UC system draws a convenient, if arbitrary, division between the choices of responses and speech acts made by the UC planner and the lexical and structural choices made by PHRED.

Other systems, such as Penman (Mann, 1983), and TEXT (McKeown, 1982) attack the problem of generating coherent multisentential text. This involves the influence of linguistic rules governing reference and focus on the process of deciding what to say. PHRED is not well equipped for this problem. While PHRED produces multisentential text when UC passes it successive concepts to express, it has no knowledge of coherence. Nor is there substantial communication between the PHRED level of production and the higher levels of language planning. Such communication, as described by Appelt (1982), would allow the generator to subsume multiple UC goals. In PHRED and UC much of the process of producing utterances is not considered as planning *per se* but as the application of prestored knowledge about how language is used. The distinction between this prestored knowledge and general planning is analogous to the difference between compiled and interpreted code in programs. More research is required on how knowledge is compiled and on how the use of prestored knowledge about patterns of speech can be used in conjunction with general knowledge about planning.

This discussion has described some of the advantages of the PHRED approach to language generation, as well as some of the areas not really addressed in PHRED. The next section considers some of the promising ways in which the research described here can be extended.

6. Future Directions

PHRED is a successful implementation of a real-time generation system covering a range of linguistic phenomena, and has served also to open up new ground for further work. This work involves aspects of language processing not directly involved in PHRED as well as problems with the PHRED approach and implementation.

6.1. Structured Associations

Much of the work on specialized language discussed earlier, as well as research on metaphor by Lakoff and others (Lakoff, 1977; Lakoff and Johnson, 1980) has suggested that there exist a range of underlying **motivations*** for many idioms and grammatical constructions, knowledge of which can help govern the use of language. For example, PHRED in its current form has the knowledge that the phrase "kick the bucket" does not passivize but "bury the hatchet" does, without any attempt to represent the motivation for the latter phrase. Knowing that "bury the hatchet" is motivated, i.e., that "bury" refers to terminating and "hatchet" to war, helps to explain the grammatical properties of the phrase. Ross (1981) has suggested that in many cases the variety of forms in which idioms of this type can appear depends on the ability of the noun component of the idiom to function independently as a noun. Passivization, however, seems subject to a more specific constraint; that is, the ability of the noun component of the idiom to *refer*. To take advantage of this knowledge, a representation of the "bury the hatchet" idiom must encode the information not only that the expression refers to making peace, but that the "hatchet" part of the idiom refers to war or to the tools of war.

As another example where motivation might be useful, PHRED now generates "John took a punch from Mary" and "Mary gave John a punch" without representing the common metaphorical derivation of the two sentences. For example, PHRED might have a pattern

<person> <root = give> <person> <striking-action>

to produce the sentence "Ali gave Frazier a punch". This is thus specialized knowledge about "giving" and a potential object. There might also be a pattern

---

* The term **motivation** as employed here is due to Charles Fillmore and George Lakoff, personal communication.

<person> <root = take> <striking-action> <<word = from> <person>>

used to produce "Frazier took a punch from Ali". Similar patterns might exist for "getting a punch" and "receiving a punch". Treating these patterns independently seems cognitively unrealistic, because motivated phrases are in general easier to use and remember, and inefficient, since a more general representation of the "striking as transfer" metaphor might eliminate the need for some of the specialized knowledge about each of the patterns. While knowing the motivation does not obviate entirely the need for specialized knowledge, it can lead to a more parsimonious encoding of the specialized knowledge.

A potential improvement to the PHRAN/PHRED representation is the treatment of knowledge used to associate language and meaning as **structured associations.**† The structured association is an explicit relation between two knowledge structures that also associates their corresponding "components". These components may be **aspectuals,** or attributes, of the two structures or other arbitrarily related structures. A structured association may be used to relate the concept of a striking action to the concept of a transfer, with the patient of the action corresponding to the recipient of the transfer and the actor of the striking action corresponding to the source of the transfer. A structured association might also relate linguistic structures to associated concepts. The "bury the hatchet" expression may be related to a concept by a structured association, with the "hatchet" part corresponding to the "war" part of the concept and "bury" corresponding to the action of terminating the war. Metaphors and pattern-concept pairs alike may thus be represented as types of structured associations (*cf.* Jacobs, 1985).

The structured association derives from the idea of a "view" (*cf.* Moore and Newell, 1973; Bobrow and Winograd, 1977; Wilensky, 1984; Jacobs and Rau, 1984), but is more general. The term "view" is used principally to describe relationships used to understand analogous concepts, while the structured association relates arbitrary knowledge structures. Also, the structured association is not a primitive relation, as structured associations themselves are a conceptual hierarchy.

Gentner's **structure-mapping** theory (Gentner, 1983) addresses problems in understanding analogy that are comparable to some of the metaphorical issues discussed above. Gentner focuses on the process by which structure-mappings are synthesized rather than on the explicit representation of associations that may be used for such mappings.

Incorporating structured associations into a hierarchical knowledge base could further facilitate the interaction of general and specialized linguistic knowledge. Thus PHRED, and PHRAN as well, could gain efficiency in representation from the generalizations which apply without losing the advantages of having specialized patterns.

---

† The term **structured association** and the use of structured associations in language processing were suggested by Robert Wilensky, personal communication.

6.2. Context and Memory Models

Another major area for future work is in the development of models of memory that help account for the role of context in language processing. A kind of spreading activation model (Arens, 1982) was used in UC to help resolve references and to activate particular goals, plans and speech acts. The idea behind an activation-based model is that subtle changes in context can influence language processing without requiring the addition of large amounts of conceptual information to all of the linguistic knowledge structures.

A spreading-activation model has the potential of being especially useful in the predisposition, or fetching phase, of generation. Information about objects and events that have been explicitly referred to or activated in the current context, as well as about the topic of conversation and the participants in the conversation, can influence the language considered. There are, however, three major practical difficulties with using spreading activation as a means of controlling the effect of context on language production. First, the spreading activation model is a parallel one that tends to produce slow, awkward simulations. Second, the encoding of knowledge into a network suitable for such a memory model must involve either a complex method of acquiring the knowledge from data or a contrived set of associative strengths based on introspection. Finally, while spreading activation is often effective in describing subconscious effects such as associative priming, it is difficult to account for the interaction of such effects with conscious or planned behavior. Most likely, a memory model will prove useful as a means of modeling the predisposition process and will simplify, but not replace, language planning and language selection.

7. Conclusion

PHRED is a practical language generator for use in natural language interfaces. The phrasal approach to language processing allows the generator to serve as an effective communicative tool within specialized domains without sacrificing the ability to adapt the system to new functions. The simple and efficient design of the program, particularly the process by which PHRED avoids expensive unification, allows it to serve as part of a real-time user interface. The use of a knowledge base shared with the PHRAN analyzer makes it easy to adapt the interface to a variety of domains in which understanding and production of fairly robust language is required.

In addition to its value as a useful language processing mechanism, PHRED has paved for the way for better models of language generation and linguistic representation. The PHRED approach supports a view of generation as a knowledge-intensive process in which the knowledge structures that relate language to meaning play a key role. The way in which these knowledge structures are accessed and applied emerges as the central issue in this model. The construction of robust, efficient and extensible natural language interfaces demands continued work at refining the means by which this "knowledge about language" is captured.

References

Appelt, D. 1982. Planning Natural Language Utterances to Satisfy Multiple Goals. SRI International AI Center Technical Note 259.

Appelt, D. 1983. Telegram: A grammar formalism for language planning. In *Proceedings of the 21st Annual Meeting of the Association for Computational Linguistics*, Cambridge, Massachusetts.

Arens, Y. 1982. The context model: language and understanding in context. In *Proceedings of the Fourth Annual Conference of the Cognitive Science Society*, Ann Arbor, Michigan.

Becker, J. D. 1975. The Phrasal Lexicon. In R. Schank and B. L. Webber (eds.), *Theoretical Issues in Natural Language Processing*. Cambridge, Mass.

Bobrow, D. and Winograd, T. 1977. An Overview of KRL, a Knowledge Representation Language. *Cognitive Science 1* (1).

Burton, R. 1976. Semantic Grammar: an Engineering Technique For Constructing Natural Language Understanding Systems. Bolt Beranek and Newman Report No. 3453.

Busemann, S. 1984. Topicalization and pronominalization. Extending a natural language generation system. In *Proceedings of the Sixth European Conference on Artificial Intelligence*, Pisa, Italy.

Chafe, W. L. 1968. Idiomaticity as an Anomaly in the Chomskyan Paradigm. *Foundations of Language 6 (1)*.

Chafe, W. L. 1984. Integration and Involvement in Speaking, Writing, and Oral Literature. In D. Tannen (ed), *Oral and written language*. Ablex, Norwood, N.J.

Danlos, L. 1984. Conceptual and linguistic decisions in generation. In *Proceedings of the Tenth International Conference on Computational Linguistics*. Stanford, California.

Fillmore, C. J. 1968. The Case for Case. In E. Bach and R. Harms (eds.), *Universals in Linguistic Theory*. Holt, Rinehart and Winston, New York.

Fillmore, C. J. 1979. Innocence: a second idealization for linguistics. In *Proceedings of the Fifth Berkeley Linguistics Symposium*, Berkeley, California.

Fillmore, C. J.; Kay, P.; and O' Connor, M. C. 1984. Regularity and Idiomaticity in Grammar: The Case of Let Alone. University of California, Cognitive Science Working Paper.

Gentner, D., 1983. Structure-Mapping: A Theoretical Framework for Analogy, *Cognitive Science 7*, pp. 155-170.

Goldman, N. 1975. Conceptual Generation. In R. C. Schank (ed.), *Conceptual Information Processing*. American Elsevier Publishing Company, Inc., New York.

Halliday, M. A. K. 1968. Notes on Transitivity and Theme in English. *Journal of Linguistics 4*.

Halliday, M. A. K. 1978. *Language as Social Semiotic*. University Park Press, Baltimore.

Harris, Z. 1968. *Mathematical Structures of Language*. John Wiley and Sons, New York.

Hudson, R. 1976. *Arguments for a Non-Transformational Grammar*. University of Chicago Press, Chicago.

Jacobs, P. 1983. Generation in a natural language interface. In *Proceedings of the Eighth International Joint Conference on Artificial Intelligence*, Karlsruhe, Germany.

Jacobs, P. and Rau, L. 1984. Ace: associating language with meaning. In *Proceedings of the Sixth European Conference on Artificial Intelligence*, Pisa, Italy.

Jacobs, P. 1985. A Knowledge-Based Approach to Language Production. University of California at Berkeley, Computer Science Division Report #UCB/CSD 86/254.

Kaplan, R. M. and Bresnan, J. (eds.) 1983. *The Mental Representation of Grammatical Relations*. MIT Press, Cambridge.

Kay, M. 1979. Functional grammar. In *Proceedings of the Fifth Annual Meeting of the Berkeley Linguistic Society.*

Kay, M. 1984. Functional unification grammar: a formalism for machine translation. in *Proceedings of the Tenth International Conference on Computational Linguistics,* Stanford, California.

Kempen, G. and Hoenkamp, E. 1982. An Incremental Procedural Grammar for Sentence Formulation. University of Nijmegen (the Netherlands) Department of Psychology, Internal Report 82-FU-14.

Kittredge, R. and Lehrberger, J. 1983. *Sublanguages: Studies of Language in Restricted Domains.* Walter DeGruyter, New York.

Lakoff, G. 1977. Linguistic gestalts. In *Proceedings of the Thirteenth Regional Meeting of the Chicago Linguistics Society,*

Lakoff, G. and Johnson, D. 1980. *Metaphors we Live By.* University of Chicago Press, Chicago.

Lakoff, G. 1984. There-constructions: a case study in grammatical construction theory. University of California, Linguistics Working Paper.

Lamb, S. The Crooked Path of Progress in Cognitive Linguistics. In A. Makkai and D. Lockwood (eds.), *Readings in Stratificational Linguistics.* University of Alabama Press, University, Alabama.

Lockwood, D. 1972. *Introduction to Stratificational Linguistics.* Harcourt Brace and Jovanovich, New York.

Makkai, A. 1972. *Idiom Structure in English.* Mouton, The Hague.

Makkai, A. (ed.) 1975. *A Dictionary of American Idioms.* Barron's Educational Series, New York.

Mann, W. 1983. An overview of the Penman text generation system. In *Proceedings of the National Conference on Artificial Intelligence,* Washington, D. C.

Mann, W., and Matthiessen, C. 1983. Nigel: A systemic grammar for text generation, University of Southern California, ISI Technical Report #ISI/RR-83-105.

McDonald, D. D. 1980. Language Production as a Process of Decision-making Under Constraints. Ph. D. dissertation, MIT.

McKeown, K. 1982. Generating Natural Language Text in Response to Questions about Database Structure. Ph. D. thesis, University of Pennsylvania.

Moore, J. and Newell, A., 1974. How can MERLIN Understand? In L. Gregg (ed.), *Knowledge and Cognition.* Erlbaum Associates, Inc.

Pawley, A. and Syder, F. H., 1980. Two Puzzles for Linguistic Theory: Nativelike Selection and Nativelike Fluency. Unpublished manuscript.

Pike, K. 1962. Dimensions of Grammatical Constructions. In R. Brand (ed.), *Kenneth L. Pike: Selected Writings.* Mouton, The Hague.

Riesbeck, C. 1975. Conceptual Analysis. In R. C. Schank (ed.), *Conceptual Information Processing.* American Elsevier Publishing Company, Inc., New York.

Rosch, E. 1977. Human categorization. In N. Warren (ed.), *Studies in Cross-Cultural Psychology (Vol. I).* London, Academic Press.

Ross, John Robert. 1973. Nouniness. In Osamu Fujimura (ed.), *Three Dimensions of Linguistic Theory.* Tokyo, TEC Corporation.

Ross, John Robert. 1981. Nominal Decay. Unpublished manuscript.

Schank, R. C. (ed.) 1975. *Conceptual Information Processing.* American Elsevier Publishing Company, Inc., New York.

Steinacker, I. and Buchberger, E. 1983. Relating syntax and semantics: The syntactico-semantic lexicon of the system VIE-LANG. In *Proceedings of the First European Meeting of the ACL,* Pisa, Italy.

Wahlster, W.; Marburger, H.; Jameson, A.; and Busemann, S. 1983. Overanswering yes-no questions: Extended responses in a natural language interface to a vision system. In *Proceedings of the Eighth International Joint Conference on Artificial*

Intelligence, Karlsruhe, W. Germany.

Wilensky, R. and Arens, Y. 1980. PHRAN--A Knowledge-Based Approach to Natural Language Analysis. University of California at Berkeley, Electronics Research Laboratory Memorandum #UCB/ERL M80/34.

Wilensky, R. 1981. A knowledge-based approach to natural language processing: A progress report. In *Proceedings of the Seventh International Joint Conference on Artificial Intelligence,* Vancouver, British Columbia.

Wilensky, R. 1984. KODIAK - A knowledge representation language. In *Proceedings of the Sixth Annual Conference of the Cognitive Science Society,* Boulder, Colorado.

Wilensky, R.; Arens, Y.; and Chin, D. 1984. Talking to UNIX in English: An Overview of UC. *Communications of the Association for Computing Machinery 27 (6).*

GENERATING LANGUAGE
WITH A PHRASAL LEXICON

Eduard H. Hovy

Abstract

In this paper, we ask: How should language be represented in a generator program? In particular, how do the concepts the generator must express, the grammar it is to use, and the words and phrases with which it must express them, relate? The answer presented here is that all linguistic knowledge — all language — should be contained in the lexicon. The argument is the following: A generator performs three types of task to produce text (deciding what material to include; ordering the parts within paragraphs and sentences; and expressing the parts as appropriate phrases and parts of speech). It gets the information it requires to do these tasks from three sources: from the grammar, from partially frozen phrases (including multi-predicate phrasal patterns), and from certain words. In a functionally organized system, there is no reason why an a priori distinction should be made between the contents of the lexicon and the contents of the grammar. From the generator's perspective, the difference between these sources is not important. Rules of grammar, multi-predicate phrases, and phrasal and verb predicate patterns can all be viewed as phrases, frozen to a greater or lesser degree, and should all be part of the lexicon. Some such "phrases" can be quite complex, prescribing a series of actions and tests to perform the three tasks: these can be thought of as specialist procedures. Others can be very simple: templates. This paper also describes the elements that constitute the lexicon of a phrasal generator program and the way the elements are used.

This paper was written while the author was at Yale University Computer Science Department, 2158 Yale Station, New Haven, CT 06520-2158, U.S.A.

This work was supported in part by the Advanced Research Projects Agency monitored by the Office of Naval Research under contract N00014-82-K-0149. It was also supported by AFOSR contract F49620-87-C-0005.

1   The Three Tasks of a Generator

In this paper, we assume that the generator's input is a list of structures built using a representation scheme that is not based on the syntax of any language[1]. We assume these structures have been assembled by some encapsulating system (or text planner) that plays a further role in the realization process only to guide decisions, as stated below. If an element of the list of input structures can be said directly, in one word or frozen phrase, the generator's task is easy; otherwise, the generator has to break up the element into parts and concentrate on each part, recursively. We assume also that the order in which it examines the parts will be reflected in the order of the words of the text; hence, the generator must use the ordering conventions of the language to guide its traversal of the input.

During its traversal, the generator must consider progressively "smaller" pieces of the input element, or it must consider pieces from a progressively "narrower" point of view, so that it will eventually produce text and not just blindly continue traversing the whole network in which the elements are defined. That is to say, if the generator starts out with the goal of making a sentence about some input X, then its next goal could be to make a sentence subject of some part X1 of X, and its next goal to make a noun phrase of some part X2 of X1, and so forth. This sequence of goals must eventually end in the "narrowest" goal, namely the goal to output one or more words from the lexicon without spawning any further goals. Though this sequence need not monotonically decrease in scope (since, for example, whole sentences can be relativized and subordinated to other sentences), it must always terminate. (Of course, the pieces of the input do not really become "smaller", however size is measured; it is simply convenient to think of them doing so, in the sense that the agent of an event is somehow contained within the event and that the agent's age (or some other characteristic) is in turn contained within the agent, which means that more words of the sentence describe the event than the agent, and in turn more words the agent than the age.)

Therefore, from the piece of the input under consideration, the generator must

---

[1] One example of such a scheme is Conceptual Dependency Theory, [Schank 72, 75], extended in [Schank & Abelson 77] and [Schank 82]; a similar scheme is developed in [Jackendoff 85]. Assume also that the representation structures are defined within a property inheritance network such as those in common use (as described, for example, in [Stefik & Bobrow 85], [Charniak, Riesbeck, & McDermott 80], or [Bobrow & Winograd 77]).

select the following: which section(s) it is going to work on next; in what order it is going to do so; and what work it is going to do on each section; — in such a fashion that it is guaranteed eventual termination. Thus the generator must perform three tasks:

- **inclusion:** select which portions of the input to consider further (which portions will eventually appear in the text. Not all the input need appear; the criteria for determining this resides in the text planner)

- **ordering:** select the order in which to consider them (in which order they will appear in the text)

- **casting:** select a syntactic class or type for each portion — that is, the form of its textual realization (how they will eventually appear in the text)

Consider the following example, using a representation similar to Conceptual Dependency notation ([Schank 72, 75]), where MTRANS means "transfer of information":

```
#{ACTION  =  MTRANS-6
    [ACT :  MTRANS]
    [ACTOR :  JIM]
    [OBJECT :  #{STATE-CHANGE  =  DEATH-10
                   [TYPE :  HEALTH]
                   [ACTOR :  JANET]
                   [FROM :  ALIVE]
                   [TO :  DEAD]
                   [TIME :  PAST]}]
    [FROM :  JIM]
    [TO :  SUE]
    [MANNER :  QUIET]
    [TIME :  PAST]}]
```

From this representation, a generator should be able to produce at least the following sentences:

1. Jim told Sue that Janet died

2. Jim told Sue of Janet's death

3. He told her of Janet's dying

4. Jim told Sue

5. He whispered to her that Janet died

6. Jim quietly told Sue of it

7. Quietly, Jim let Sue know that Janet died

8. Jim whispered

9. Sue was told by Jim that Janet died

10. Sue heard of Janet's death

11. She heard of Janet's dying from him

12. Sue was quietly informed of Janet's death

13. Janet's death was what Jim quietly informed Sue of

14. That was what Sue heard from Jim

These sentences are produced in the following way: Initially, of course, the generator simply has the goal to make a sentence from MTRANS-6. Its first decision is: which aspects should be included? JIM and SUE and DEATH-10? Only JIM and SUE? Only DEATH-10? Then, if more than one are selected, it has to choose a sentence subject (in sentences (1) through (8), JIM is the subject, and in (9) through (12), SUE is). It also has to decide whether to include the adverb QUIET and how to order it with respect to the rest of the sentence (compare (5), (6), and (7)). When it starts building the subject, the generator must make a casting decision — actions and state-changes can be cast as nominals or pronominalized (DEATH-10 in (13) and (14)); objects can be named, described or pronominalized ((1) and (3)). Later, when it builds the predicate, inclusion decisions pertain to adverbs ((5) and (6)) and to other parts of the topic ((10) and (11)); casting decisions include verb choice ((1), (5), (10)) and predicate form (see (1), (2), and

(3)). These decisions are made by the text planner, which we assume has access to the speaker's goals with respect to the hearer and to some characterization of the conversational situation and of the hearer. For a description of how such aspects may be modelled and used in language generation, see [Hovy 87a, 87b].

The form of each generated sentence is determined by the sequence of inclusion, ordering, and casting decisions made in the realization process. At any point in the process, the generator needs information on which linguistic options exist — which decision tasks it must/may perform on the current input. The question of interest in this chapter is *how and where in the generator should this information reside?*

2 Formative Information

Most work on the representation of the structure of language makes a distinction between the *grammar* and the *lexicon*. The former is a body of the rules that govern how words can be put together; the latter is the collection of words and their idiosyncratic features. See, for example, [Chomsky 65, p 84] (his italics):

> "The grammar will contain no rules...that introduce the formatives belonging to lexical categories. Instead, the base of the grammar will contain a *lexicon*, which is simply an unordered list of all lexical formatives"

In this spirit, the simplest generator programs contain as distinct entities: a set of grammar rules, a lexicon, and a mechanism that produces text (by accepting an input representation, building a syntactic tree structure on applying the rules of grammar to the input, inserting into the tree lexical entries that are accessed from the input representation, and finally saying the words).

2.1 Rules of Grammar

In this section, the following argument is presented: Clearly, some rules of grammar have formative properties. Also, some individual words have formative properties. If, now, one organizes a generator on functional principles, then the formative information should not be divided between grammatical rules and lexical entries, but should be represented homogeneously and be accessed in the same way.

The rules of English grammar are concerned with phrasal constituents or *syntactic environments*[2] (such as noun phrase and adjective). Based on their function, these rules can be divided into two groups. Rules from one group specify the *order of environments* within encompassing environments — for example, within the environment NOUN GROUP, the order

[ARTICLE ADJECTIVES HEAD-NOUN POST-NOMINAL-MODIFIERS]

or, within a PREDICATE environment, the order of various noun groups:

[NG (subject) VERB NG (object) { NG (location) NG (direction) ...}]

Rules from the other group specify *how different environments and their relationships are signalled* — for example, the case information provided by " 's" in "John's book" or by the preposition in "to the store"; or the number agreement between subject and verb.

Some attempts at writing rules of the first kind — the ordering or *formative* rules — don't take any actual words into account at all. Words are simply inserted during the generation process (see, for example, [Simmons & Slocum 72], who used a semantic net with carefully preselected words). But divorcing the formative rules from the lexical entities can cause problems. For example, generators built along these lines run the risk of building a syntax tree into which they cannot grammatically insert words, as in (b):

    (a) John beat Pete in the race

    (b) * Pete lost John in the race (*i.e.:* Pete lost the race to John)

To ensure that this doesn't happen, you must either (a) make the formative rules of grammar smart enough to distinguish between such cases as subjects that win and subjects that lose, or you must (b) associate the various sentence structures with the words that control them (such as "beat" and "lose"), and make the rules examine the words in order to build appropriate trees. Obviously, alternative (a)

---

[2]In this paper, we will refer to phrasal constituents as syntactic environments, because we will discuss a more general type of environment of which phrasal constituents are one subtype.

amounts to building rules that depend on words in any case, so most systems opt for (b) by associating with certain words in the lexicon information about how they can combine with other words and syntactic environments. However, this information does not completely specify formation (ordering). For example, in the lexicon in [Stockwell, Schachter & Partee 72], the word "let" includes the features

"let":
+ V
− ADJ
+ TO-DEL
+ [___ +NEUT +DAT −LOC −INS +AGT]
+ DAT → OBJ

(that is, "let" is a verb but not an adjective (which some linguists consider a type of verb); "to" is deleted (otherwise, "John let Pete to win the race"); the predicate may not contain the cases INSTRUMENTIVE or LOCATIVE .) Still, these constraints are not sufficient to prohibit sentences such as "John let win the race Pete" or "win the race let John Pete"; additional rules are required in the grammar.

Associating this grammatical information with individual words subsumes part of the function of formative grammar rules into the lexicon. The subsumption takes place to varying degrees. In the transformational approach (see, say, [Chomsky 57, 65] or [Stockwell, Schachter & Partee 72, p 719]), the generator accesses the lexicon twice: once (after applying the phrase structure rules that build the basic sentence pattern, but before the transformation rules that reorganize it) for the words, such as verbs, with information used by the formative grammar rules, and once again (at the end, just before realization into speech or writing) for the words without this information, such as prepositions and pronouns.

In the deep case approach ([Fillmore 68]), the syntactic environments of sentences are determined by functional primitives called *cases*. These cases are attached to certain lexical entries, which also contain features that determine their behaviour in syntactic environments. In [Fillmore 71], Fillmore states that the lexicon of a generative grammar

"must make available to its users, for each lexical item,

1. the nature of the deep-structure syntactic environments into which the item may be inserted;

2. the properties of the item to which the rules of grammar are sensitive;

3. the presuppositions or 'happiness conditions' for the use of the item, the conditions which must be satisfied in order for the item to be used 'aptly';

4. its meaning; and

5. the phonological or orthographic shapes which the item assumes under given grammatical conditions."

In order to subsume the formative aspects of words into the lexicon, we would add to these requirements the following:

6. the order of the syntactic environments required by the item

In other approaches, the subsumption is stronger: the definitions of words also include ordering information explicitly. This is the case in the systemic/functional tradition, as embodied by systemic grammar [Halliday 76] and [Mann 82], functional grammar [Kay 79], unification grammar [Kay 84], lexical functional grammar [Kaplan & Bresnan 83], and the grammar developed by [Gross 84] and [Danlos 85]. In any of these systems, for example, the verb "beat" would contain the formative pattern:

"beat":
[VERB [OBJECT loser (mandatory)] [PREPGROUP instance *in*]
  [DIFFERENCE *by*]]
"She [beat] [him] [in the election] [by 3 votes]"

Here *loser* and *instance* indicate which aspects of the input element to say in the environments. In comparison, the verb "win" would contain:

"win":
[VERB [OBJECT instance] [DIFFERENCE *by*]]
"She [won] [the election] [by 3 votes]"

and "lose" would contain:

"lose":
[VERB [OBJECT instance] [PREPGRP winner *to*] [DIFFERENCE *by*]]
"He [lost] [the election] [to her] [by 3 votes]"

This method works well for cases where words — typically, verbs and nouns — require idiosyncratic combinations of words and phrasal constituents. Whenever the generator encounters a word with formative information, it uses that information to help build its sentence. But what of the general formative rules that are not tied to specific words? For example, in Kay's unification grammar, the functional description for NOUN PHRASE is

$$
\begin{aligned}
\text{CAT} \;&=\; \text{NP} \\
\text{PATTERN} \;&=\; (\;\ldots\;\text{N}\;\ldots\;)
\end{aligned}
$$

either: [ADJ = NONE]
or: [PATTERN = (ADJ ...)]
    [ADJ = [CAT = ADJ]]
    [[LEX = ANY]]

either: [PP = NONE]
or: [PATTERN = (... PP)]
    [PP = [PATTERN = (PREP NP)]]
    [[CAT = PP]]
    [[PREP = [CAT = PREP]]]
    [[[LEX = ANY]]]
    [[NP = [CAT = NP]]]

Reading from the top, this means: a NOUN PHRASE must have a NOUN. It need not have adjectives, but if it does, they are ANY words of CATegory ADJ and precede the noun. The noun phrase need not have any preposition phrases either, but if it does, they are of CATegory PP and follow the noun. Here, PPs consist of a PREP, where the preposition is ANY word of CATegory PREP, and an NP. This grammar is used in the generators of McKeown [McKeown 82] and Jacobs [Jacobs 85], and the latter mentions some implementational difficulties and proposes solutions to them.

Rules such as these have but one function: to provide the types and the order of the constituents of syntactic environments. But this is exactly the function of the formative patterns associated with verbs and nouns, as described above! From a functional perspective, there is no reason why general formative rules of grammar should be viewed as being different from the formative patterns contained in the lexicon. They serve the same purpose. Therefore, they should be defined and used in the same way as the verb patterns are. In other words, *all* the formative information should either be contained in rules of the grammar or be associated with words in the lexicon. This paper describes a computer implementation of the latter option. Here, though not associated with specific verbs and nouns, all the standard phrasal constituents (S, VP, etc.) are incorporated into the lexicon and accessed in a unified manner.

2.2   Becker's Phrasal Lexicon

There is a lot more to language than grammar and words. Though not discussed as much by linguists, frozen and partially frozen phrases must also appear in the lexicon; generators must be able to use them to create sentences in the same way it uses grammar rules and words. This view is engagingly described by Becker in [Becker 75] (from the abstract):

> "... [U]tterances are composed by the recitation, modification, concatenation, and interdigitation of previously-known phrases consisting of more than one word. I suspect that we speak mostly by stitching together swatches of text that we have heard before...
>
> ... A high proportion of utterances are produced in stereotyped social situations, where the phatic and ritualistic functions of language demand not novelty, but rather an appropriate combination of formulas, clichés, allusions, slogans, and so forth."

Becker estimates that we know about as many stock phrases as we know single words (about 25,000), and about as many lexical similes (such as "pleased as punch" or "white as a sheet") as there are strong verbs in English (some 100). Thus any study of language that limits itself only to words and ignores phrases is hopelessly incomplete.

Becker's categorization of the types of phrases (p 6) ranges from multi-sentence paragraphs (such as the Pledge of Allegiance), through "sentence builders" (such as *X gave Y a song and dance about Z; sell X short*), to polywords (such as *for good; two bits; the facts of life*). But not all phrases are so colourful, Becker says (p 32):

> "...most of the lexical phrases that we actually use are too humble and uninteresting that they would never appear on a list devoted to picturesque expressions like *Davey Jones's Locker*. Yet these humble expressions do most of the work of language production for us."

Clearly, phrases such as these provide a lot of formative information — the same kind of information provided by formative grammar rules and by certain words. With respect to formative function, no principled difference exists between general patterns such as [SUBJECT VERB OBJECT] and specific ones such as [*the facts of life*], since intermediate patterns exist along the whole range of generality — patterns such as [[VERB *bury*] *the hatchet*] (giving "buried the hatchet" and "will bury the hatchet", but not "bury the hatchets" or "bury the red hatchet"). Thus multi-predicate phrases such as the enhancer phrase

[*not only* [SENTENCE (verb relocated, with "*do*")] , *but* [SENTENCE]]

(described in [Hovy 86]) exist in the lexicon side by side with the verbs "beat", "win", and "lose", discussed earlier. (The use of such phrases in language analysis is described in [Wilensky 81] and [Riesbeck & Martin 85], and some research on how they may be learned is reported in [Zernik & Dyer 85].)

Taking this view seriously, I believe that all formative aspects of language should be treated as phrasal. Multi-predicate phrases, formative rules of grammar, and words with idiosyncratic formative requirements — all entities that deal with the ordering of words and syntactic environments — should be contained in the lexicon as frozen, semi-frozen, and very general phrases. The lexicon should be the sole repository of the patterns that make up language — some very specific, some very general.

Just as for verbs and nouns, phrases in the lexicon are associated with the concepts in memory that they describe. If an idiosyncratic phrase exists for the expression of a memory concept, the generator must have the option of using it instead of general all-purpose sentence-formation rules. Though there is no reason to associate the rule [SUBJECT VERB OBJECT], or even the verbs "huff" and "puff", specifically with the story of the three pigs, the fixed phrase "he huffed and he puffed" belongs just there. Similarly, "kick the bucket" is tied to the state change DIE; "the big apple" is tied to New York City. And *nothing prohibits specific phrases from contradicting general rules.* ("You pays your money and you takes your chances" and "I ain't done nothing" are not ungrammatical; they're just rather special.) This fact makes it impossible in principle to capture all the forms of language in a few general rules; thus, the endeavor of trying to create a formal, complete, consistent set of rules to describe all of language tries to describe structure where there is none, and is therefore destined to fail.

Thus, in summary, verbs, nouns, and other words in the lexicon are associated with the representation elements they describe. When idiosyncratic forms of expression exist, the forms are associated with the lexical entries. Similarly, fixed and semi-fixed phrases are associated with representation elements and have similar patterns. Formative patterns consist of other formative patterns and of lexicon entries. Although the general formative rules of grammar are not associated with any specific representational element, their formative patterns are defined similarly. This homogeniety enables the generator builder to add new forms of expression — words, phrases, or rules of grammar — with ease.

3 Syntax Specialists

3.1 PAULINE

PAULINE (Planning And Uttering Language In Natural Environments) is a generator program that produces various texts from a single input representation under various settings that model pragmatic aspects of conversations. Different aspects of the program are described in [Hovy 87a, 87b, 86, 85]. Its linguistic knowledge is based on the ideas discussed here.

Many generators rely on some single central process to examine the input representation, to check its features, and to perform the inclusion, ordering, and casting of its aspects. This approach is most practical when the three decision types are relatively straightforward. This is the case in most functional/systemic generators to date: typically, the inclusion decisions simply are of the form "does aspect X appear in the formative pattern?"; ordering is given by the pattern; and casting is given by the pattern and by the feature constraints of the parts of the input. However, generators that are able to realize the same input in various ways (say, by taking into account pragmatic issues, as PAULINE does) have to make more complex decisions, and hence requires a more complex control structure. In addition to syntactic constraints, their inclusion decisions depend on the pragmatic import of the pieces of the input; their ordering decisions, where alternatives exist, may carry pragmatic weight; and pragmatic issues can affect how pieces are cast as well. And, just as it makes sense to associate information about idiosyncratic syntactic phenomena with the words that control them, it makes sense to associate the pragmatic decisions with words (and other lexicon elements) as well. *It is possible to encode all the relevant decisions as functional descriptors of the lexicon entries themselves; that is, to spread the functionality of the central process into the lexicon.*

In PAULINE, the extended functional descriptors are called *syntax specialists* — each syntactic goal is achieved by a procedure, the specialist, that accepts a piece of input, performs the three tasks, and produces an ordered list of words and/or other syntactic goals, each associating another specialist with a piece of the input. Thus syntax specialists are the repositories of information about the linguistic options. They control the operation of the three types of decision. Sometimes the specialists are very simple — so simple that they contain no procedural information — and then they are implemented as patterns. Alternatively they may be quite complex — directing much processing and altering the state of the generator — and then they are implemented as procedures.

The specialists correspond to the *clause templates* of [Danlos 85, 86], or to the *realization classes* of McDonald's generator MUMBLE (for example, [McDonald & Pustejovsky 85]); they can be viewed as implementations of the *systems* in the systemic grammar of [Halliday 76] (for a clear exposition, see [Patten & Ritchie 86]), and so resemble the systems in Nigel, the systemic grammar implemented by [Mann 82, 83a, 83b]. However, PAULINE's specialist functions differ from systems in a number of ways: most importantly, they are not activated as soon as their input conditions are fulfilled, but rather are activated in a sequence determined by their predecessors (described at the end of this paper). This is a simplification of the systemic scheme. PAULINE's specialists differ from Nigel's systems in particular in that they can index phrases as well as words in the lexicon; they can index to more than one word via discrimination nets, as is described below; and their decisions refer to pragmatic criteria as well as to grammatical criteria.

Each syntax specialist must achieve the goal to create its syntactic environment with the input it receives. Thus the generator's NOUN GROUP and RELATIVE CLAUSE specialists make different decisions when given the same input element. Starting with the representation of "John shot Mary with a gun", when the generator's goal is to make a SENTENCE, it can say that sentence; if its goal is to make a noun group, the NOUN GROUP specialist can return "John's shooting of Mary with a gun"; and the RELATIVE CLAUSE specialist may produce "that John used to shoot Mary" or "who shot Mary with a gun". Each specialist must know of the different ways its goal can be achieved, and must be able to select an appropriate alternative. For example, an alternative noun group formulation for the above example is "John's use of a gun to shoot Mary"; and an alternative relative clause is "who was shot with a gun by John". The criteria by which these decisions are made can be grouped into three classes: syntactic, semantic, and pragmatic. *Syntactic criteria* are binding; if they are ignored, ungrammatical sentences result. (For example, when saying a verb, choices concern singular or plural endings, appropriate tenses, and aspect.) *Semantic criteria* depend on the nature of the input and its relations to other concepts and the constraints of use of words. (For example, for the representation element INGEST, the verb must match features of the OBJECT: a liquid gives "drink", a solid "eat", and a gas "breathe". This idea was first described in [Goldman 75].) Clearly, some input representations may be handled by a number of such syntax specialists. Picking one can be a problem. In this regard, pragmatic criteria can help make the decision[3]. *Pragmatic criteria* relate to the affective values of words and their interactions with the speaker's

---

[3]In [McCawley 78], McCawley notes that additional information is conversationally implicated, under the Gricean cooperative principle, when the speaker chooses a less direct way of saying something than the most straightforward one, if such exists. For instance, he uses Householder's

goals, and are determined by strategies such as those described in [Hovy 87a]. The responsibility for accessing the relevant syntactic, semantic, and pragmatic information resides within each specialist.

3.2 Specialists and Phrase Structure Symbols

It is quite natural to identify certain syntax specialists with their equivalent phrase structure entities. This identification can help answer some linguistic questions. For example, at issue for a number of years has been the question whether certain SVO languages are configurational (i.e., whether they have a verb phrase or not). Rather than follow the traditional lines of argument by constructing test sentences for each language, one can build (or, perhaps, carefully imagine building) a generator and note whether a number of decisions have to be made before the verb can be uttered, once the subject has been said. Certainly, for example, this is the case in English: both the sentences "she seeks the ball" and "she searches for the ball" derive from the same semantic source, yet "search" requires a preposition for the object. If a VP specialist exists, it will do the work of accessing the verb, finding the required preposition, and associating the preposition with the goal to create the object environment; after that, the verb specialist can proceed with conjugation, etc. On the other hand, if no verb phrase specialist exists, then the verb specialist will have to post the object's preposition so that, after its completion, the object specialist can find it.

Now from a linguistic point of view, there is nothing wrong with such a transferral of information across specialists; however, programming experience with large systems with many interacting modules has taught that it is to be avoided[4]. This

---

example ([Householder 75], p 75) that "pale red" is not "pink", whereas "pale blue", "pale yellow", "pale green", etc., all correspond to [colour + white] in the colour wheel. Similarly, in contrast to "let me in", "let me come in" implies that the speaker doesn't want to partake in the activities inside. This point indicates that the generator's casting decisions must take into account the conversational implicature that each specialist would have, if used. This idea of implicature is useful to the phrasal lexicon builder: it provides him with a criterion of organization — the pseudo-syntactic class (i.e., the syntax specialist) that expresses the input *without* implicature must be the one most closely associated with it in the network.

[4] "If a variable is not local it is said to be a *free variable* or a *special variable*. It is bad style to use special variables because it is difficult to understand a program if variables appear in it whose values and 'meaning' are given elsewhere." [Charniak & McDermott 85, p 74, their italics]

principle of encapsulation of information is very useful to the generator builder, since it helps delimit the extent of syntax specialists. By it, for example, English has a verb phrase. Whether or not other languages should have one is a purely practical matter: certainly this will depend on the types of decisions required to produce predicates. Thus, with respect to configurationality, *the notion that there exists a distinct entity called verb phrase, an entity that is the same in all languages with verb phrases, is certainly false.* It is quite conceivable that two languages each have some decisions that must be made across the whole predicate, but that the decisions are not at all similar; in this case, though they would both have "verb phrases", the contents of these specialists would be completely dissimilar.

However, not all rules of grammar deal with information that can be neatly encapsulated in parts of sentences. Some rules necessarily operate across specialists. These are the non-formative rules mentioned earlier — the rules that deal with tense, number agreement, declension, etc., anything relating to the scoping and interrelations of syntactic environments. For example, number agreement (in, say, English) is scoped within sentences, and adjectival declension (in, say, German) is scoped within preposition/noun groups. That is, information about head-noun number that is determined by the subject specialist is used for conjugation by the verb specialist in English and German, and, in German, gender information that is determined by the head-noun specialist is used with article information determined by the noun group specialist to determine the appropriate endings for adjectives. This information is scoped over (has to be kept available for the duration of) the governing syntactic environment. These rules do not require separate syntax specialists. Rather, they are implicitly contained within the specialists. Thus they can apply anywhere the general and the specific formative phrases are used.

Thus, where functionally justified, syntax specialists exist, and may correspond to the traditional phrase structure entities, where each specialist creates a specific syntactic environment and, in doing so, may spawn goals to create other environments. But PAULINE's syntax specialists are not limited to the standard phrase structure symbols. As described earlier, some multi-predicate phrases and some words contain formative information just as phrase-structure symbols do. Accordingly, specialists exist to create the requisite phrasal and word-bound environments. This approach to organizing language recognizes many more entities than standard linguistic systems do: in fact, *any* grouping of the information and decisions that are applicable to more than a single instance may be considered a specialist. For example, English has a number of highly idiomatic ways of referring to money. This knowledge must appear somewhere in a generator's lexicon, and it seems sensible to group the indices to the relevant patterns as well as the criteria for deciding among them together in a specialist. Though not a phrase structure entity, a phrase, or a word, this specialist exists in the lexicon and performs its function similarly. Similarly, PAULINE has, in its phrasal lexicon, a specialist that knows how to say (i.e., that creates an environment appropriate for expressing) the time; another specialist for saying colours; another for measurements, ages, etc. These specialists are described in more detail at the end of this paper.

3.3 Relations among Elements of the Lexicon

What is the relationship between verb-based formative patterns, general formative rules of grammar, special-purpose entities suchas the colour specialist, and phrases such as Becker describes? If they exist side by side in the lexicon, which ones are accessed by the generator under which circumstances? How do specific patterns differ from more general ones of the same form?

In the main, some generalities hold across the formative patterns. Very general rules, such as [SUBJECT VERB OBJECT], seem to apply at all times, even to very specific ones that express specific concepts. Sometimes, however, patterns can be ungrammatical, as were some examples given before: [*you pays your money and you takes your chances*] or [SUBJECT *ain't done nothing*]. This is consistent with the general theory of memory organization described in [Schank 82], in which special cases, exceptions, and idiosyncracies remain associated with specific episodes in memory while less specific cases are generalized to the point of maximum applicability.

Other patterns appear to be instances of general rules without in fact being so. For example, to announce Pete's demise, you can say "Pete kicked the bucket" or "Pete died", where the former uses the idiosyncratic phrase accessed directly from the state change DIE:

    1. [SUBJECT [VERB *kick*] *the bucket*]

and the latter uses the general phrase

    2. [SUBJECT PREDICATE]

Phrase 1 is, of course, a partially frozen expression with only one meaning. In a phrasally organized lexicon, this phrase will be indexed only under the concept DIE and nowhere else; in contrast, phrase 2 is part of the general sentence-building knowledge, able to produce many more different sentences than phrase 1. But that does not imply that the two phrases are different *in nature*. Both consist of an ordered list of elements, where some elements are words and others determine the syntactic environments into which words will eventually be placed. How, now, are phrases 1 and 2 related? After replacing PREDICATE in phrase 2 by its definition,

2a. [SUBJECT   VERB   OBJECT   PREPOSITION-PHRASES]

phrase 1 seems to be a specialization of phrase 2. This is not, however, the case; *the bucket* in phrase 1 is not part of an OBJECT environment, since this phrase cannot become "the red bucket" or "the buckets". It is consistent instead to view *the bucket* as part of the VERB environment, making "kick" an intransitive verb here. This explains the unacceptability of (b):

(a)   He tied the noose around his neck, kicked the chair from under himself, and kicked the bucket

(b)   * He tied the noose around his neck, kicked the chair from under himself, and the bucket

Therefore no explicit relationship exists between phrase patterns 1 and 2.

In general, when syntactic generalities do exist between phrases and words, these generalities should be exploited (say, by the creation of a specialist). This idea was noted by Jacobs, who says ([Jacobs 85], p 42):

"... a system which deals only with "core" grammatical and productive constructs will handle but a small portion of the language... On the other hand, failing to take advantage of linguistic generalizations can introduce redundancy and possibly inefficiency into the knowledge base. Robust and efficient language processing therefore demands a balance between specialized and generalized knowledge."

As mentioned above, this approach results in the creation of a large number of pseudo-syntactic classes to capture the generalities. For example, Jacobs describes a concept called *transfer-event*, of which one *view* (see [Wilensky 84]) uses "take" and another uses "give". This transfer-event is not a semantic concept (that is, it is not part of his concept representation network); in PAULINE, it would be implemented as a syntax specialist. It produces the sentences

(a) "Frazier gave Ali a punch"

(b) "Ali took a punch from Frazier"

(c) "John gave Mary the book"

(d) "Mary took the book from John"

It should be clear that formative grammar rules, phrasal patterns, and syntax specialists are but slightly different incarnations of the same type of information: inclusion, casting, and ordering requirements. The differences are caused by ease of use in a system; what is a specialist function in one system with one notation may easily be a pattern in a more powerful system.

Why does one care about the relationship between the rules of grammar and the lexicon? One cares because, if all the formative grammar rules can be incorporated into the lexicon, and if the elements of the lexicon are inextricably tied to the system's network of concept representations, then the right way to build a set of representations is to pay a lot of attention to the ways in which the representation elements are expressed in language — not only the words existing for entities, but also the phrases and sentences. If the elements under consideration do not easily support such words and phrases they are suspect. Hence, generating from a representation is an excellent way of discovering its shortcomings (which is a paraphrase of McGuire's maxim: *when the generating gets tough, check that representation*).

4 A Phrasal Grammar

4.1 PAULINE's Specialists

In this section, most of the specialists that constitute PAULINE's grammar are briefly described. (Compare this with the somewhat similar grammar given in [Clippinger 74].)

The specialists can be arranged in a rough hierarchy depending on how much effect they have on the final text. At the level of largest effect, the specialists control the formation of multi-predicate sentences, such as enhancer and mitigator phrases and relations between topics. At the next level, the specialists determine sentence content and organization to form various types of sentences (questions, imperatives). At lower levels, the content and organization of predicates, adverbial clauses, and noun groups are determined. Finally, words are chosen. The hierarchy does not reflect the order in which specialists actually do their work during the generation of sentences: halfway though the generation of a sentence, words will already have been chosen for some pieces of the input while other pieces are still completely uninterpreted. Furthermore, the hierarchy is not strict: for example, the choice of verb has an effect on the sentence wider than simply one word, for it often determines the presence and order of preposition groups.

- PAULINE's phrasal lexicon contains a large number of multi-predicate patterns. When appropriate, depending on the relationships between the sentence topics, the program casts the topics into these patterns. Multi-predicate patterns are used to express the following:

  - **Slanting phrases** such as "Not only X, but Y" and "X, however, Y"

  - **Reminding phrases** such as "X, which reminds me of Y" and "X. In a similar case, Y"

  - **Goal phrases** such as " X in order to Y" and "X so that Y"

  - **Result phrases** such as "X. As a result, Y" and "Y because X"

- SAY-SENT-TOP — This specialist determines which type of sentence to make and establishes the appropriate syntax goal. The decision is based on the input: objects and states are described by SAY-ATTRIB-SENT, relations between concepts by SAY-RELATION-SENT, and events and state changes by SAY-EVENT-SENT. If implemented, SAY-IMPERATIVE and SAY-QUESTION would be included here.

- SAY-RELATION-SENT — Builds a sentence to express the relation between two concepts. The input is the concept representing the relation, which contains a primary (earlier/antecedent/closer) part and a secondary part. This specialist builds one of the sentence patterns
  - [SAY-PRE-SENT SAY-COMPL SAY-LINK SAY-PRE-SENT SAY-COMPL]
  - [SAY-LINK SAY-COMPL , SAY-COMPL]
  (as in "[that night,] [Pete brushed his teeth] [because] [earlier] [he had eaten cake]" and "[because] [Pete had eaten cake] , [he brushed his teeth]"), where

each COMPL specialist is associated with one part of the relation. From the relation concept, the SAY-LINK specialist can find a suitable relation word. PAULINE contains the following relations between entities:

- **Causal** such as result, precondition
- **Temporal** such as before, after, during
- **Spatial** such as in front of, behind, between
- **Comparative** such as less than, more than, older
- **Intergoal** such as subgoal to, opposing

- SAY-ATTRIB-SENT — This specialist expands into the list of specialists
  - [PRE-SENT SAY-SUBJECT SAY-VERB SAY-ADVERB SAY-ATTRIB
    SAY-POST-SENT]

  after selecting from the input and the rhetorical goals which aspect of the input to describe. If the input is an object, the attribute is an adjective; if an action, an adverb; if a state, a degree; if a state-change, an adverb or a degree. The attribute can be said in various ways:

  - "the bag is red"
  - "the colour is red"
  - "the bag's colour is red"
  - "the colour of the bag is red"
  - "red is the colour of the bag"
  - "the bag has a colour"
  - "the bag has a red colour"

- SAY-EVENT-SENT — This specialist expands into the sequence
  - [SAY-PRE-SENT SAY-SUBJECT SAY-PREDICATE]

  after finding which aspect of the input to make the sentence subject.

- SAY-COMPL — Builds a sentence without the SAY-PRE-SENT specialist; i.e., expands into
  - [SAY-SUBJECT SAY-PREDICATE]

- SAY-REL-CLAUSE — Builds a relative clause. The input marks which aspect is shared by the surrounding syntactic environment; this aspect is associated with the SAY-REL-PRONOUN specialist, and the rest is treated like a sentence

- SAY-PREDICATE — This specialist builds a sentence predicate from its input. It also selects a verb, unless rhetorical planning has already chosen a verb and has included it in the syntax goal. To get a predicate pattern, it checks the verb; if no idiosyncratic pattern is found, the standard pattern is used:
  − [SAY-VERB   SAY-OBJECT   SAY-ADVERB   SAY-POST-SENT]

  In the lexicon, the formative pattern associated with a verb is a list of units. Each unit gives the position in the sentence predicate of its corresponding aspect of the input representation entity. The absence of an aspect in the pattern means that the aspect cannot be said; a required aspect is so marked. This information is used for the *inclusion* decisions. The *ordering* is given in the pattern; when various orders are possible, the pattern itself is written as a specialist function that queries the rhetorical strategies for assistance (for example, the typical adverbial clauses of time, instrument, and location are handled by SAY-POST-SENT). The *casting* function is done by associating specialists and aspects of the input, as prescribed by each unit in the pattern. For example, to express the Conceptual Dependency representation primitive MTRANS, PAULINE has more than 20 words. (MTRANS stands for transfer of information; the aspect OBJECT contains the message and the aspect TO the hearer; see [Schank 72, 75]). Some of these words are "tell" (two versions) and "say":

  − "tell":
    [SAY-VERB [SAY-OBJECT (aspect TO)] SAY-ADVERB
    SAY-POST-SENT *that* [SAY-COMPL (aspect OBJECT)]]
    "He told her quietly yesterday that [she should see the film]"

  − "tell-1":
    [SAY-VERB [SAY-OBJECT (aspect TO)] SAY-ADVERB
    SAY-POST-SENT [SAY-PRED (aspect OBJECT) infinitive]]
    "He told her quietly yesterday [to see the film]"

  − "say":
    [SAY-VERB [SAY-OBJECT (aspect TO) *to*] SAY-POST-SENT
    that [SAY-COMPL (aspect OBJECT)]]
    "He said to her yesterday that [she should see the film]"

- SAY-LINK-WORD — This specialist controls the use of words said at the beginning of a sentence to link it to the previous sentence, for example "and", "but", "as a result", "so". The question of when to include SAY-LINK-WORD in the expansion stream illustrates the general problem of where to plan how much of the text.

- SAY-PRE-SENT — Returns the specialists of all the pre-subject clauses. Check pragmatic strategies to see how many aspects to include, and how many to include before the subject.

- SAY-PREPGROUP — Returns [preposition SAY-NOUN-GROUP]

- SAY-SUBJECT, SAY-OBJECT, SAY-POSSESSIVE — Set the case of the syntax goal to *nominative*, *accusative*, and *genitive*, respectively, and return
  – SAY-NOUN-GROUP

- SAY-ACT-AS-OBJECT — Builds a noun group of an event or state change (for example, "Sam's shot" if the input has been said before; "John's being shot by Sam", passive for pro-victim affects; "Sam's shooting John" otherwise)

- SAY-NOUN-GROUP — Decides whether to pronominalize or not; if not, selects a head noun and returns
  – [SAY-ART SAY-PRE-NOUN-MODS SAY-HEAD-NOUN
      SAY-POST-NOUN-MODS]
  Sets up the context for the noun group: number, case, gender (the latter are used in languages with case and gender declension), etc.

- The following build parts of noun groups: SAY-ART, SAY-HEAD-NOUN, SAY-PRE-NOUN-MODS, SAY-POST-NOUN-MODS, SAY-PRONOUN, SAY-REL-PRONOUN. Pre- and post-nominal modifiers are selected by the rhetorical strategies from the aspects of the input, and ordered by their affective preference. If none exists, a default order is used. Some modifiers can only appear before or after the head noun; of the rest, PAULINE places equally many in each position, unless required to do otherwise by its pragmatic strategies.

- SAY-VERB — Selects the appropriate tense form and auxiliary verbs and conjugates the (already selected) verb

- SAY-PRE-VERB-MODS — Modify the verb with either [INTENT ALSO], as in "Mike also hit Jim"; if the action has been represented as intentional, say so; otherwise, STRESS can be said

- SAY-ADVERB — Modify the verb by saying any or all of
  - [PREP-MODIFYING-VERB STRESS ADVERB REPEATER BACK/AGAIN]
  as in "Jim knocked Mike down very hard again"; for example:

    - INTENT: "purposely", "intentionally", "wilfully", "on purpose", / "accidentally", "unintentionally", "by accident"
    - ALSO: "also"
    - STRESS: "really", "easily", "badly" / "only", "just", "narrowly"
    - PREPOSITION: any preposition associated with the verb
    - REPEATER: "repeatedly" / "once"
    - BACK/AGAIN: "back" / "again"
    - ADVERB: any adverb

Most of the specialists listed above correspond to traditional phrase structure symbols such as NOUN GROUP and PREDICATE. But, just as specialists may be used to build multi-predicate sentences, they may be used for other purposes. For example, people talk about money in various highly idiomatic ways. All PAULINE's phrasal knowledge relating to money is grouped together in a single specialist. The phrasal lexicon contains the following specialists:

- SAY-MONEY — Realize the phrases "the measly *$15*" (as head noun); "the *35c* book" (as pre-nominal modifier); and "a green truck *worth 300 bucks*" (as post-nominal modifier). As with all the other variations, options are selected by referring to the relevant pragmatic criteria: for example, "bucks" is not selected when pragmatics call for being very formal.

- The specialists SAY-AMOUNT and SAY-DIFFERENCE express other numerical amounts. The former builds the patterns
  - "a [size] number/amount (of [unit])"
  - "[amount] [unit]"
  - "the most/fewest/X number of [unit]"
  the latter expresses the numerical difference between two amounts.

- The following are adverbial clause specialists: SAY-SOURCE, SAY-RECIPIENT, SAY-TO, SAY-FROM, SAY-TIME, SAY-LOC, SAY-INSTRUMENT,

SAY-PRE-INSTR, SAY-MEASURE. Each specialist is able to produce various English forms. For example, depending on the nature of the input it receives, SAY-TIME can produce: "now / today / tomorrow / yesterday"; "at 5 o'clock"; "in the future / past"; "15 hours from now"

- The following specialists are all used to build noun groups: SAY-NAME, SAY-AGE, SAY-GENDER, SAY-NUMBER, SAY-TITLE, SAY-NATION, SAY-RESID, SAY-WEARING, SAY-OCCUP, SAY-DESCRIP, SAY-SIZE, SAY-COLOR, SAY-OWNER, SAY-OPINION, SAY-ROLE, SAY-MONEY. Each specialist must be able to produce various forms, depending on its position. For example, SAY-AGE can produce the following forms:
  - *predicate:* "...*is 23 years old*"
  - *head-noun:* "the fat but pretty *23-year-old* from Irkutsk"
  - *pre-head-noun:* "the *23-year-old* fat woman, Marta"
  - *post-head-noun:* "Marta, *a 23-year-old, ...*"

  and SAY-GENDER the following:
  - *predicate:* "...*is male*"
  - *head-noun:* "the green *man* from Mars"
  - *pre-head-noun:* "the large *male* dinosaur"
  - *post-head-noun:* "the student *who is male...*"

4.2 The Expansion Cycle

Using the information contained in its specialists as well as the formative information obtained from phrases and words in the lexicon, PAULINE generates sentences expressing input topics. The generation process applies specialist procedures to progressively "smaller" pieces of the input, as described at the beginning of this paper, and eventually arrives at words, which it outputs. In doing so, it implicitly creates, in depth-first fashion, the syntax tree of the sentence. Each node in the tree corresponds to a point at which a specialist was applied.

Syntax goals are used to pass information to subsequent specialists (that is, "down" the tree). A syntax goal is the goal to produce in the text a syntactic, phrasal, or word-bound environment, as described above. Each specialist can spawn zero or more syntax goals, which it fills with the information appropriate to each goal. The principal components of a syntax goal are its specialist function (which, of course, determines the type of goal) and its topic (that is, the subpart of the representation upon which the specialist is to operate). Depending on the type of goal, additional components for noun groups are such items as case, gender, and head noun; for predicates such items as tense, number, and mood; and for general use such items as desired slant and stress. Thus inclusion decisions are reflected in the choice of topic; casting decisions in the choice of specialist; and ordering decisions in the order of syntax goals.

The central generator data structure is a stream — a list of units. Of it, the first unit (the stream head) is always evaluated. Each unit is either a word or a syntax goal (the goal to create some syntactic environment). If it is a word, the unit is output and removed from the stream. Otherwise it is a syntax goal. Initial syntax goals are spawned by the planner; after that, each syntax goal produces a list of other syntax goals and/or words (this process was described as a "cascade" in [McDonald 81]), until all the words have been said. Generation proceeds by applying the specialist to the topic and replacing whatever the say-function produces back on the front of the stream. This is a straightforward way to implement the left-to-right generation of language. The central stream expansion function simply loops until the stream is empty. The generator (that is, its realization component; the text planning component is described in, say, [Hovy 87a]) starts with the syntax goal to produce sentence(s) from the input topic.

5 Conclusion

In order to produce language from representations, a generator must perform a series of actions that involve decisions of three types: inclusion, ordering, and casting. The decisions determine the form and content of the text. Which decisions are available at any point in the process — that is, which linguistic options exist — is information provided by the grammar of the language, by the fixed and semi-fixed phrases of the language, and by idiosyncratic constraints associated with certain words in the language. Since, to a generator, no sharp line of demarcation exists, there is no compelling reason why some of this information should be contained in a body of rules called the grammar and the rest of it in a collection of words (and even of phrases) called the lexicon. Thus it makes sense to collect all the information pertaining to the decisions in the lexicon. Groupings of information can be thought of, and implemented, as specialist functions (when certain types of generator action are required) or as phrasal templates (otherwise). In a phrasal lexicon, groupings exist for all regularities in human language: multi-predicate phrases, the standard grammatical phrase structure entities, predicate patterns associated with verbs, the patterns used to express notions such as age, measure, money, etc.

6 Bibliography

1. Becker, J.D.,
   The Phrasal Lexicon, Bolt, Beranek and Newman Technical Report no 3081, 1975.

2. Bobrow, D.G. & Winograd, T.,
   An Overview of KRL, a Knowledge-Representation Language, in *Cognitive Science*, Vol 1, No 1, 1977.

3. Charniak, E. & McDermott, D.V.,
   Introduction to Artificial Intelligence, Addison Wesley, 1985.

4. Charniak, E., Riesbeck, C.K. & McDermott, D.V.,
   Artificial Intelligence Programming, Lawrence Erlbaum Associates, 1980.

5. Chomsky, N.,
   Syntactic Structures, Mouton, 1957.

6. Chomsky, N.,
   Aspects of the Theory of Syntax, MIT Press, 1965.

7. Clippinger, J.H.,
   A Discourse Speaking Program as a Preliminary Theory of Discourse Behavior and a Limited Theory of Psychoanalytic Discourse, Ph.D. dissertation, University of Pennsylvania, 1974.

8. Danlos, L.,
   Génération Automatique de Texts en Langues Naturelles, Ph.D. dissertation, University of Paris, Masson, 1985.

9. Danlos, L.,
   A Robust Syntactic Component in Generation, Proceedings of the Third International Workshop on Language Generation, Nijmegen, the Netherlands, 1986.

10. Fillmore, C.J.,
    The Case for Case, in **Universals in Linguistic Theory**, Bach E. & Harms R. (eds), New York, Holt, Reinhart & Winston, 1968.

11. Fillmore, C.J.,
    Types of Lexical Information, in **Semantics: an Interdisciplinary Reader in Philosophy, Linguistics, and Psychology**, Steinberg D.D. & Jacobovits L.A. (eds), 1971.

12. Goldman, N.M.,
    Conceptual Generation, in **Conceptual Information Processing**, Schank R.C. (ed), North-Holland Publishing Company, 1975.

13. Gross, M.,
    Lexicon-Grammar and the Syntactic Analysis of French, Proceedings of the Computational Linguistics Society Conference Coling 84, 1984.

14. Halliday, M.A.K.,
    Halliday: System and Function in Language, (selected papers, edited by G.R. Kress), Oxford University Press, 1976.

15. Householder, F.W.,
    Linguistic Speculations, Cambridge University Press, 1971.

16. Hovy, E.H.,
    Integrating Text Planning and Production in Generation, IJCAI Conference Proceedings, 1985.

17. Hovy, E.H.,
    Putting Affect into Text, Proceedings of the Cognitive Science Society Conference, 1986.

18. Hovy, E.H., 1987a,
    Generating Natural Language under Pragmatic Constraints, in *Journal of Pragmatics*, vol XI no 6, 1987, forthcoming.

19. Hovy, E.H., 1987b,
    Interpretation in Generation, to appear in Proceedings of the AAAI, 1987.

20. Jackendoff, R.,
    Semantics and Cognition, MIT Press, 1985.

21. Jacobs, P.S.,
    A Knowledge-Based Approach to Language Production, Ph.D. dissertation, University of California (Berkeley), 1985.

22. Kaplan, R.M. & Bresnan, J.,

    The Mental Representation of Grammatical Relations, MIT Press, 1983.

23. Kay, M.,

    Functional Grammar, in *Proceedings of the Fifth Annual Meeting of the Berkely Linguistics Society*, 1979.

24. Kay, M.,

    Functional Unification Grammar: a Formalism for Machine Translation, in *Proceedings of the Tenth International Conference on Computational Linguistics*, Stanford, 1984.

25. Mann, W.C.,

    The Anatomy of a Systemic Choice, Information Sciences Institute Technical Report no RR-82-104, 1982.

26. Mann, W.C., 1983a,

    An Overview of the Nigel Text Generation Grammar, Information Sciences Institute Technical Report no RR-83-113, 1983.

27. Mann, W.C., 1983b,

    An Overview of the Penman Text Generation System, Information Sciences Institute Technical Report no RR-83-114, 1983.

28. McCawley, J.D.,

    Conversational Implicature and the Lexicon, in **Syntax and Semantics**, volume 9, Academic Press, 1978.

29. McDonald, D.D.,

    Natural Language Generation as a Computational Problem: an Introduction, University of Massachusetts (Amherst) Technical Report no 81-33, 1981.

30. McDonald, D.D. & Pustejovsky, J.D.,

    Description-Directed Natural Language Generation, IJCAI Conference Proceedings, 1985.

31. McKeown, K.R.,

    Generating Natural Language Text in Response to Questions about Database Queries, Ph.D. dissertation, University Of Pennsylvania, 1982.

32. Patten, T. & Ritchie, G.
    A Formal Model of Systemic Grammar, Proceedings of the Third International Workshop on Language Generation, Nijmegen, the Netherlands, 1986.

33. Riesbeck, C.K. & Martin, C.E.,
    Direct Memory Access Parsing, Yale University Technical Report no 354, 1985.

34. Schank, R.C.,
    'Semantics' in Conceptual Analysis, in *Lingua* vol 30 no 2, 1972, North-Holland Publishing Company.

35. Schank, R.C.,
    Conceptual Information Processing, North-Holland Publishing Company, 1975.

36. Schank, R.C. & Abelson, R.P.,
    Scripts, Plans, Goals and Understanding, Lawrence Erlbaum Associates, 1977.

37. Schank, R.C.,
    Dynamic Memory: A Theory of Reminding and Learning in Computers and People, Cambridge University Press, 1982.

38. Simmons, R.F. & Slocum, J.,
    Generating English Discourse from Semantic Networks, in *Communications of the ACM* vol 15 no 10, 1972.

39. Stefik, M. & Bobrow, D.G.,
    it Object-Oriented Programming: Themes and Variations, in *AI Magazine* vol 6 no 4, 1986.

40. Stockwell, R.P., Schachter, P. & Partee, B.P.,
    The Major Syntactic Structures of English, Holt, Reinhart and Winston, 1972.

41. Wilensky, R.,
    A Knowledge-Based Approach to Natural Language Processing: A Progress Report, IJCAI Conference Proceedings, 1981.

42. Wilensky, R.,
   KODIAK — A Knowledge Representation Language Cognitive Science Conference Proceedings, 1984.

43. Zernik, U. & Dyer, M.G.,
   Failure-Driven Acquisition of Figurative Phrases by Second-Language Speakers, Proceedings of the Cognitive Science Society Conference, 1985.

Index

Contributors

Douglas E. Appelt Artificial Intelligence Center, SRI International, Menlo Park, California 94024, USA

Ernst Buchberger Institut fuer Medizinische Kybernetik und Artificial Intelligence, Universitaet Wien, A-1010 Vienna, Austria

Stephan Busemann Technical University of Berlin, Computer Science Department, D-1000 Berlin 10, Federal Republic of Germany

Richard P. Gabriel Lucid, Inc., Menlo Park, California 94025, USA

Helmut Horacek Forschungsstelle fuer Informationswissenschaft und Kuenstliche Intelligenz, D-2000 Hamburg 13, Federal Republic of Germany

Eduard H. Hovy Information Sciences Institute, University of Southern California, Marina del Rey, California 90292-6695, USA

Shun Ishizaki Electrotechnical Laboratory, Sakura-mura, Nihari-gun, Ibaraki, 305, Japan

Paul S. Jacobs General Electric, Corporate Research and Development, Schenectady, New York 12301, USA

Karen Kukich Bell Communications Research, 435 South Street, Morristown, New Jersey 07960, USA

Heinz-Dirk Luckhardt Petrusstrasse 12, D-6602 Dudweiler, Federal Republic of Germany

William C. Mann Information Sciences Institute, Marina del Rey, California 90292-6695, USA

David D. McDonald Brattle Research, Cambridge, Massachusetts, 02138, USA